L

D0849635

THE LOEB CLASSICAL LIBRARY

FOUNDED BY JAMES LOEB 1911

EDITED BY

JEFFREY HENDERSON

PLOTINUS
I

LCL 440

PLOTINUS

PORPHYRY ON PLOTINUS
ENNEAD I

WITH AN ENGLISH TRANSLATION BY
A. H. ARMSTRONG

HARVARD UNIVERSITY PRESS
CAMBRIDGE, MASSACHUSETTS
LONDON, ENGLAND

ISBN 978-0-674-99484-3

Printed on acid-free paper and bound by
Edwards Brothers, Ann Arbor, Michigan

CONTENTS

NOTE ON REVISION

THE text and translation of this revision (1987) are now in accordance with the latest published changes and corrections in the Henry-Schwyzer text as recorded in the *Addenda et Corrigenda ad Textum* in the third volume of the Oxford Classical Text (*Plotini Opera* III, Oxford 1982, pp. 304–7).

Section III of the Preface has been completely revised.

PREFACE

I. THE ENNEADS

PLOTINUS, as Porphyry tells us in his *Life* (ch. 4), did not begin to write till the first year of the reign of Gallienus (253/4), when he was forty-nine years old and had been settled at Rome and teaching philosophy for ten years. He continued to write till his death in 270 in his sixty-sixth year. His writings thus all belong to the last sixteen years of his life and represent his mature and fully developed thought. We should not expect to find in them, and, in the opinion at least of the great majority of Plotinian scholars, we do not in fact find in them, any major development. The earliest of them are the fruit of over twenty years' study and teaching of philosophy. (He came to Alexandria to study philosophy at the age of twenty-seven, in 232.) There is a good deal of variation, and it is even perhaps sometimes possible to trace a genuine development, in his repeated handling of particular problems. Plotinus had an intensely active and critical mind, and was not easily satisfied with his own or other people's formulations. But in all essentials his philosophy was fully mature before he began to write; and we have very little evidence indeed upon which to base speculation about the stages of its growth.

Plotinus's writings grew naturally out of his teaching. He never set out to write down a sys-

tematic exposition of his philosophy, but as important
and interesting questions came up for discussion in
his school he wrote treatises on the particular problems involved (Porphyry, *Life*, 4. 11, 5. 60). Thus
it seems likely that the treatise V. 5, *That the Intelligibles are not outside the Intellect; and on the Good*
was the result of the discussion which Porphyry
records in chapter 18 of the *Life*; and III. 4, *On Our
Allotted Guardian Spirit*, was, Porphyry says (*Life*,
10. 31), provoked by the conjuration of Plotinus's
guardian spirit in the temple of Isis. The treatises
were not intended for publication, but for circulation among carefully selected members of the school
(*Life*, 4. 14–16). They give us, therefore, an extremely unsystematic presentation of a systematic
philosophy. No reader of the *Enneads* can long remain unaware that Plotinus has a fully and carefully
worked-out philosophical system. But neither his
writings nor Porphyry's description of his teaching
(*Life*, 13 and 18) have any suggestion of the dry,
tidy, systematic, authoritarian presentation of the
scholastic text-book. His teaching was informal
and left plenty of room for the freest discussion, and
in his writings we find his philosophy presented, not
step by step in an orderly exposition, but by a perpetual handling and rehandling of the great central
questions, always from slightly different points of
view and with reference to different types of objections and queries.

Plotinus appointed Porphyry to take charge of
the revision[1] and arrangement of his writings (*Life*,

---

[1] διόρθωσις, the word used by Porphyry, need imply no
more than the correction of the spelling and supplying of
punctuation which he says that he undertook (*Life*, 26. 37).

7. 51, 24. 2), and the *Enneads* as we have them are
the result of his editorial activity. He did not,
however, publish his edition till more than thirty
years after the death of Plotinus (i.e., somewhere
between 301 and 305), and in the interval another
edition of the treatises was published by Eustochius,
also a pupil of Plotinus and the doctor who attended
him in his last illness; of this only a few traces
remain.[1] Porphyry has given us a good deal of
information about his editorial methods in the *Life*;
the full title of the work is *On the Life of Plotinus
and the Order of his Books*, and it looks as if one of
his main purposes in writing it was to explain, and
perhaps to justify against actual or possible criticism, the principles which governed his edition. He
adopted the same principle of arrangement, he tells
us (*Life*, ch. 24) as that used by Apollodorus of
Athens in his edition of Epicharmus and Andronicus
the Peripatetic in his edition of Aristotle and Theophrastus; that is, he arranged the treatises according to subject-matter and not in chronological
order.[2] In fact, a division of Plotinus's works

There is no reason to believe that he made any important
modifications of the text of Plotinus's treatises as he received
them.

[1] For a discussion of the evidence that the edition of Eustochius existed, and that Eusebius in several places in the
Praep. ev. cites Plotinus according to it and not to Porphyry's
edition see P. Henry, *Recherches sur la Préparation Évangélique
d'Eusèbe*, pp. 73–80, and *États du Texte de Plotin*, 77 ff.
(where the Eusebius texts are printed), and H-R. Schwyzer's
article *Plotin* in *Pauly's Realencyclopädie* B. XXI. col. 488–
490.

[2] He gives us, however, the chronological order of the
treatises in chs. 4–6 of the *Life*.

according to subject-matter is bound to have a great deal that is arbitrary in it because Plotinus does not, as has already been remarked, write systematically; there is no tidy separation of ethics, metaphysics, cosmology, and psychology in his treatises. Porphyry's arrangement therefore is by no means altogether satisfactory and should not be taken as a safe guide to the content of the treatises; the student of Plotinus's ethics must be familiar with the Sixth (and all the other) Enneads as well as the First, and anyone interested in his metaphysics will be very ill advised to neglect the so-called "ethical" and "psychological" treatises. It is however interesting, if not very useful, to the student of Plotinus to understand how Porphyry made his division. He arranged the whole body of treatises into six Enneads, or sets of nine, forming three volumes (*Life*, chs. 24–26). The treatises on the Categories and those of which the principal subject is the One form one volume (the Sixth Ennead), those dealing chiefly with Soul and Intellect another (the Fourth and Fifth Enneads), and all the other treatises go into the first volume (the First, Second, and Third Enneads); the First Ennead has an ethical emphasis, the Second is predominantly cosmological, the Third has a greater variety of subject-matter than any of the others. It is clear from what Porphyry says in ch. 24 of the *Life* that his reason for adopting the six–nine division was nothing better than the pleasure in the symmetry of sacred number characteristic of his age. To achieve it he had to do some vigorous cutting-up of the treatises as he received them. He subdivided a number of the longer treatises (III. 2–3, IV. 3–5, VI. 1–3, VI.

4–5): more curiously, he not only cut up one treatise but also put the pieces into different Enneads (III. 8, V. 8, V. 5, and II. 9 were written by Plotinus as a single treatise[1]); and it is possible, though not certain, that it was he who, to make up his number, collected the short notes on various subjects which constitute III. 9 into a single treatise.

II. The Thought of Plotinus

A

Plotinus is, like other philosophers of the Hellenistic and Roman periods, a practical religious and moral teacher and also a professional philosopher, engaged in the critical interpretation of a long and complicated school-tradition which we are beginning to know and understand a good deal better than formerly,[2] and working in an intellectual *milieu* which included not only those esoteric pietists the Gnostics and Hermetists, with whom he is sometimes rather misleadingly coupled, but a considerable number of other professional philosophers (about whom we know next to nothing) of very varying schools and points of view.[3] His philosophy is both an account of an ordered structure of living reality, which proceeds eternally from its transcendent First

[1] On the problems raised by the appearance of these subdivisions as separate treatises in Porphyry's chronological list see Schwyzer, art. cit., col. 487.

[2] Some important modern books dealing with this tradition are listed at the end of this *Introduction*.

[3] Cp. Porphyry, *Life*, ch. 20 (the preface to Longinus's book).

Principle, the One or Good, and descends in an unbroken succession of stages from the Divine Intellect and the Forms therein through Soul with its various levels of experience and activity to the last and lowest realities, the bodies perceived by our senses: and it is also a showing of the way by which the human self, which can experience and be active on every level of being, is able, if it will, to ascend by a progressive purification and simplification to that union with the Good which alone can satisfy it. There are two movements in Plotinus's universe, one of outgoing from unity to an ever-increasing multiplicity, and the other of return to unity and unification: and closely connected with these two movements is what is perhaps the deepest tension in his thought. This results from two opposed valuations of the movement from unity to multiplicity and two correspondingly different ways of regarding the First Principle. When Plotinus's attention is concentrated on the great process of spontaneous production by which the whole of derived reality streams out from the First Principle, he sees that First Principle as the superabundant spring of creativity, the Good which is source of all goodness, the One from whose rich unity all multiplicity unfolds: and to emphasise the goodness of the splendid multiplicity of derived being is all the more to exalt the goodness of its source. The One as creative source of all being is properly described in the language of positive transcendence, as better than all good existing and conceivable. But when his mind is bent on the ascent to the Good by the stripping off of our lower and the transcending even of our higher self, when the First Principle appears no longer as superabundant source but as the goal of pure unity which we attain by a radical simplification, by putting away all the varied multiplicity of being: then in comparison with that One and Good so passionately desired everything else seems so hopelessly inferior that he can think of its very existence as due to a fault, and represent the timeless coming forth of the Divine Intellect[1] and of Soul[2] as acts of illegitimate self-assertion. Plato, when he fixed his mind on God, had a very poor opinion of the human race:[3] and Plotinus, when he fixes his mind on God, sometimes seems to have a very poor opinion of the whole of existence. But in neither philosopher was this way of looking at things a settled conviction, governing the whole of their philosophy. Plato's whole life and work show that he did, after all, usually think the human race worth taking seriously: and the positive view of derived reality, as good from the Good, greatly predominates over the negative in the Enneads. The tension between the two attitudes of mind is most apparent when Plotinus is considering the lowest level of reality, the material world. There is a very noticeable fluctuation in his thought about the precise degree of goodness or badness to be attributed to the body and the rightness or wrongness of the soul's descent into it. Plotinus is rightly conscious at this point of a similar tension in the thought of Plato, and in his effort to present Plato's thought as perfectly reasonable and consistent he tries hard, if not altogether successfully, to resolve it.[4] The same basic tension probably accounts for a certain in-

[1] III. 8. 8.   [2] III. 7. 11.   [3] *Laws* 804B.
[4] E.g., in IV. 8. 5.

consistency in his description of the matter of the sense-world. He speaks several times[1] of this matter as derived from the principles immediately preceding it (i.e., Soul), and so ultimately from the Good; which would imply (as the later Neo-Platonists saw) that it was itself good in its own kind, even if that kind was the lowest possible. But for Plotinus the matter of the sense-world is the principle of evil, and in I. 8 in particular he speaks of it as absolute evil in a way which suggests an ultimate dualism and is hardly compatible with its derivation from the Good.[2] It is possible to produce a philosophical reconciliation of these contrasting emphases, and even of Plotinus's divergent accounts of the matter of the sense-world. But I am not sure that they are ever fully reconciled in Plotinus himself. There are, too, perhaps other fluctuations and tensions besides this major one. There are elements in his experience which do not fit into his system, elements in the tradition he inherited which are not fully assimilated, and lines of thought suggested which if they had been followed up might have led to a radical revision of his philosophy—the same, after all, might be said of almost any great philosopher. But his thought cannot be resolved into a mere jumble of conflicting elements. Tension is not the same thing as in-

[1] II. 3. 17; III. 4. 1; IV. 8. 6.

[2] And a yet further inconsistency is introduced into his thought at this point by his attitude to celestial matter, the matter of the bodies of the "visible gods," the sun, moon and stars, which he regards, in accordance with the beliefs of the astral or cosmic piety of his time, as not a principle of evil because it is not a principle of resistance to form but perfectly docile and subdued to it, so that it in no way troubles the life of the celestial intelligences. Cp. II. 1. 4; II. 9. 8.

coherence, as anyone can see who turns from reading the *Enneads* to read the *Hermetica*.

B

It is impossible to read any treatise in the *Enneads* intelligently without some at least elementary understanding of Plotinus's system as a whole, because they are, as has been said already, an unsystematic presentation of a systematic philosophy. I shall therefore try to give here a summary account of how Plotinus conceives his First Principle, the One or Good, and of the stages in the descent or expansion of reality from that Principle, and also to say something about the way of return to the Good, to follow and show which was Plotinus's main object in living, writing, and teaching.

Plotinus insists repeatedly that the One or Good is beyond the reach of human thought or language, and, though he does in fact say a good deal about It, this insistence is to be taken seriously. Language can only point the mind along the way to the Good, not describe, encompass, or present It. As Plotinus himself says (VI. 9. 3), "strictly speaking, we ought not to apply any terms at all to It; but we should, so to speak, run round the outside of It trying to interpret our own feelings about It, sometimes drawing near and sometimes falling away in our perplexities about It." There is, however, a certain amount which ought to be said about the language Plotinus uses about the One if we are not to misunderstand completely the direction in which he is pointing. The One is not, as has sometimes been suggested, conceived as a mere negation, an ultimate void, a great blank behind the universe in attaining to which the human personality disintegrates into unconscious nothingness, but as a positive reality of infinite power and content and superabundant excellence. The extreme negativity—partly inherited from the school-tradition—of the language which Plotinus uses about Him[1] is designed either to stress the inadequacy of all our ways of thinking and speaking about Him or to make clear the implications of saying that He is absolutely One and Infinite and the source of all defined and limited realities. Building on Plato's remark in Book VI of the *Republic*, Plotinus insists that the Good is "beyond being," that He cannot properly be even said to exist—surely the extreme of negation. But it is perfectly clear from all that Plotinus says about Him, in the very passages where His existence is denied, that He is existent in some sense, and the supreme Existence. What Plotinus is saying is that the unity of the Good is so absolute that no predicates at all can be applied to Him, not even that of existence; and that as the Source of being to all things He is not a thing Himself. Again, Plotinus insists that the One does not think, because thought for him always implies a certain duality of thinking and its object, and it is this that he is concerned to exclude in speaking of the One. But he is anxious to make clear that this does not mean that the life of the One is mere unconsciousness, to show

---

[1] Though the terms for One and Good are both neuter in Greek, Plotinus when speaking about his First Principle, even in passages where these neuter terms are used, passes over quite naturally from neuter to masculine pronouns and adjectives. I have followed him in this as closely as possible in my translation.

that He is more, not less, than Mind at the highest level at which we can conceive it, and so in some passages he attributes to the One a "super-intellection," a simple self-intuition, an immediate self-consciousness higher than the thought of the Divine Intellect.[1] And when he calls the One "formless" he does so because He is infinite, without limits, and because, precisely as One (here Plotinus follows the school-tradition very closely), He is the principle of form, number, measure, order, and limit; and a source or principle for Plotinus is always other and more than that which it produces.

Plotinus, by his use of negative language, stresses the transcendence of the One to an extreme degree. But he is very careful to exclude all ideas of a quasi-spatial sort about this transcendence. The One is not a God "outside" the world. Nor is He remote from us, but intimately present in the centre of our souls; or rather we are in Him, for Plotinus prefers to speak of the lower as in the higher, rather than the other way round; body is in soul, and soul in Intellect, and Intellect in the One (he is quite aware that whichever way we put it we are using an inadequate spatial metaphor). The hierarchical order of levels of being does not imply the remoteness of the One, because they are not spatially separate or cut off from each other; they are really distinct, but all are present together everywhere. And just because the One is not any particular thing He is present to all things according to their capacity to receive Him.

From the One proceeds the first great derived reality, Intellect, the Divine Mind which is also the

[1] Cp. V. 4. 2; VI. 7. 38–9; VI. 8. 16.

PREFACE

World of Forms or Ideas, and so the totality of true being in the Platonic sense. I have chosen Intellect as the best available translation of Plotinus's word for this second reality, Νοῦς: it should be understood in a sense like that of the Scholastic term *intellectus* as opposed to *ratio*—a distinction which derives from and corresponds exactly to the Greek distinction between νόησις (the proper activity of νοῦς) and διάνοια. So understood, Intellect means the activity of direct mental sight or immediate grasp of the object of thought, or a mind which grasps its object in this direct way and not as the conclusion of a process of discursive reasoning (*ratio* or διάνοια). I shall say more shortly about the relation of the Plotinian Intellect to its objects.

The procession of Intellect from the One is necessary and eternal, as are also the procession of Soul from Intellect and the forming and ordering of the material universe by Soul. The way in which Intellect proceeds from the One and Soul in its turn from Intellect is rather loosely and inadequately described as "emanation." The background of Plotinus's thought at this point is certainly a late Stoic doctrine of the emanation of intellect from a divinity conceived as material light or fire, and his favourite metaphor to describe the process is that of the radiation of light or heat from sun or fire (he also uses others of the same sort, the diffusion of cold from snow or perfume from something scented). But he is not content merely to use these traditional analogies and leave it at that, to allow the generation of spiritual beings to be thought of in terms of a materialistically conceived automatism. Intellect proceeds from the One (and Soul from Intellect) without in any way affecting its source. There is no activity on the part of the One, still less any willing or planning or choice (planning and choice are excluded by Plotinus even on a much lower level when he comes to consider the forming and ruling of the material universe by Soul). There is simply a giving-out which leaves the source unchanged and undiminished. But though this giving-out is necessary, in the sense that it cannot be conceived as not happening or as happening otherwise, it is also entirely spontaneous: there is no room for any sort of binding or constraint, internal or external, in Plotinus's thought about the One. The reason for the procession of all things from the One is, Plotinus says, simply that everything which is perfect produces something else. Perfection is necessarily productive and creative. Here we touch an element in Plotinus's thought which is of great importance, the emphasis on life, on the dynamic, vital character of spiritual being. Perfection for him is not merely static. It is a fullness of living and productive power. The One for him is Life and Power, an infinite spring of power, an unbounded life, and therefore necessarily productive. And as it is one of the axioms which Plotinus assumes without discussion that the product is always less than, inferior to, the producer, what the One produces must be that which is next to Him in excellence, namely Intellect: when Plotinus concentrates his mind on the inferiority of even this derived reality to its source, of any sort of multiplicity to the pure unity to which he aspires, then he comes to think of its production as unfortunate even though necessary, and of the will to separate existence of Intellect and

Soul as a sort of illegitimate self-assertion. But this does not mean that he ever thinks that the One might not produce, that there is any possibility of the derived realities not existing, of all things relapsing back into the original partless unity. Plotinus, when he gives a more precise account of how Intellect proceeds from the One, introduces a psychological element into the process which goes beyond his light-metaphor. He distinguishes two "moments" in this timeless generation; the first in which Intellect is radiated as an unformed potentiality, and the second in which it turns back to the One in contemplation and so is informed and filled with content and becomes the totality of real existence. Here we meet another of the great principles of the philosophy of Plotinus: that all derived beings depend for their existence, their activity, and their power to produce in their turn, on their contemplation of their source. Contemplation always precedes and generates activity and production.

Intellect is for Plotinus also the Platonic World of Forms, the totality of real beings: it is both thought and the object of its thought. This unity of thought and Forms in a single reality obviously derives from the Middle Platonist teaching that the Forms were the "thoughts of God." But it is clear from the opposition which Plotinus's teaching on this point aroused from Porphyry on his entrance into the school and from Longinus [1] that it was by no means universally accepted by contemporary Platonists. And Plotinus's doctrine of the absolute co-equality and unity-in-diversity of thought, life, and being

[1] *Life*, ch. 18 and 20.

goes a good deal beyond anything that we know any of his predecessors to have taught. Plotinus's World of Forms is an organic living community of interpenetrating beings which are at once Forms and intelligences, all " awake and alive," in which every part thinks and therefore in a real sense is the whole; so that the relationship of whole and part in this spiritual world is quite different from that in the material world, and involves no sort of separation or exclusion. This unity-in-diversity is the most perfect possible image of the absolute unity of the One, whom Intellect in its ordinary contemplation cannot apprehend as He is in His absolute simplicity. It represents His infinity as best it can in the plurality of Forms. Intellect is itself infinite in power and immeasurable, because it has no extension and there is no external standard by which it could be measured, but finite because it is a complete whole composed of an actually existing number (all that can possibly exist) of Forms, which are themselves definite, limited realities.

Looked at from the point of view of our own human nature and experience, Intellect, as has already been suggested, is the level of intuitive thought which grasps its object immediately and is always perfectly united to it, and does not have to seek it outside itself by discursive reasoning: and we at our highest are Intellect, or Soul perfectly formed to the likeness of Intellect (this is a point on which there is some variation in Plotinus's thought). Plotinus in some passages at least admits the existence of Forms of individuals, and this enables him to give our particular personalities their place in the world of Intellect, with the eternal value and status which this implies. And this means that in that world, where the laws of space and time do not apply and the part is the whole, we are Being and the All.   This is the explanation of a number of passages in Plotinus which at first reading have a pantheistic sound.[1]   In order to understand them correctly we must remember: (i) that they refer to Intellect (Being or the All), not to the One; (ii) that to become Intellect does not involve the destruction or absorption of the particular personality but its return to its perfect archetypal reality, distinguished in unity from all other archetypal realities, individual and universal.

Soul in Plotinus is very much what it is in Plato, the great intermediary between the worlds of intellect and sense and the representative of the former in the latter.   It proceeds from Intellect and returns upon it and is formed by it in contemplation as Intellect proceeds from and returns upon the One; but the relationship of Soul to Intellect is a much more intimate one.   Soul at its highest belongs to the world of Intellect.   Universal Soul has two levels, the higher where it acts as a transcendent principle of form, order, and intelligent direction (without deliberate choice or previous planning), and the lower where it operates as an immanent principle of life and growth.   This latter is in fact (though Plotinus is reluctant to admit it) a fourth distinct hypostasis, and has its own name, Nature. It is related to the higher soul as the higher soul is to Intellect and, like it, acts or produces as a necessary result of contemplation; but because its contemplation is the last and lowest sort of contemplation, a

[1] Notably VI. 5. 12.

sort of dream,[1] it is too weak to produce anything which is itself productive. So what it produces is the immanent forms in body, the ultimate level of spiritual being, which are non-contemplative and so sterile, and below which lies only the darkness of matter.

The characteristic of the life of Soul is movement from one thing to another; unlike Intellect, it does not possess being as a whole, but only one part at a time, and must always be moving from one to the other; it is on the level of discursive thought, which does not hold its object in immediate possession but has to seek it by a process of reasoning; and its continual movement from one thing to another produces time, which is "the life of the soul in movement";[2] this movement of soul is the cause of all physical movement in space and time.

Our individual souls are "Plotinian parts" of Universal Soul, parts, that is, which in the manner proper to spiritual being have the whole in a certain sense present in them and can if they wish expand themselves by contemplation into universality and be the whole because they completely share Universal Soul's detachment from the body it rules. The individual soul's descent into body is for Plotinus both a fall and a necessary compliance with the law of the universe and the plan of Universal Soul.[3] The spiritual state of the soul in body depends on its attitude. If it devotes itself selfishly to the interests of the particular body to which it is attached it becomes entrapped in the atomistic particularity of the material world and isolated from the whole. The root sin of the soul is self-isolation, by which it is

[1] III. 8. 4.   [2] III. 7. 11.   [3] IV. 8. 5.

imprisoned in the body and cut off from its high destiny. But the mere fact of being in body does not necessarily imply imprisonment in body. That comes only if the soul surrenders to the body; it is the inward attitude which makes the difference. It is always possible for a man in the body to rise beyond the particularism and narrowness of the cares of earthly life to the universality of transcendent Soul and to the world of Intellect. Universal Soul is in no way hampered by the body of the universe which it contains and administers; and the celestial bodies of the star-gods in no way interfere with their spiritual life.[1] It is not embodiment as such but embodiment in an earthly, animal body which the Platonist regards as an evil and a handicap.

The material universe for Plotinus is a living, organic whole, the best possible image of the living unity-in-diversity of the World of Forms in Intellect. It is held together in every part by a universal sympathy and harmony, in which external evil and suffering take their place as necessary elements in the great pattern, the great dance of the universe. As the work of Soul, that is as a living structure of forms, it is wholly good and everlasting as a whole, though the parts are perishable (the universe of Intellect is of course eternal as a whole and in every part). All in it that is life and form is good; but the matter which is its substratum is evil and the principle of evil, though, paradoxically, it is also the last and lowest stage of procession from the Good. Matter according to Plotinus never really unites with form; it remains a formless darkness upon which form is merely superimposed. It is non-

[1] II. 9. 8.

being in the sense not of a "zero" but a "minus," a force or principle of negation (in criticising the Aristotelian account of matter Plotinus identifies ὕλη and στέρησις). The pessimistic way of looking at procession from the One which I mentioned before is very much in evidence here. If all procession, because it is necessarily not only a going-out but a falling below the highest, is more or less an evil, then, Plotinus would seem to think, the last and lowest degree of procession will be an absolute falling below any trace of good, a complete negativity which will be the ultimate evil and source of all other evil. (In Plotinus's thought there is no such thing as purely spiritual evil: evil is confined to the material universe.) Matter then is responsible for the evil and imperfection of the material world; but that world is good and necessary, the best possible image of the world of spirit on the material level, where it is necessary that it should express itself for the completion of the whole. It has not the goodness of its archetype, but it has the goodness of the best possible image.

C

The primary object of all Plotinus's philosophical activity is to bring his own soul and the souls of others by way of Intellect to union with the One. His last words [1] "Try to bring back the god in you to the divine in the All" are a summing up of his

[1] According to the text now adopted by P. Henry (see his essay *La Dernière Parole de Plotin; Studi Classici e Orientali* II, pp. 113–30, Pisa, 1953) and which I translate: see note on *Life*, ch. 2. 26–7.

whole life and work. They are also a summing up of his religion—the two are the same, for I think this work of return can properly be called a religious work. Plotinus, like his contemporaries, believed in a great hierarchy of gods and spirits inside and outside the visible universe. But he does not appear to attach much religious importance to the beings in the lower ranks of this hierarchy (though he insists, as against the Gnostics, on proper respect being paid to the high gods of the visible universe, the sun, moon, and stars); nor does he consider that external religious rites are any help to the ascent of the soul. He takes a sacramental view of the visible universe, in that he regards it as a sign, or sacrament in the large sense, of the invisible; but there is no room for sacramentalism in his religion. The process of return is one of turning away from the external world, of concentrating one's powers inwardly instead of dissipating them outwardly, of rediscovering one's true self by the most vigorous intellectual and moral discipline, and then waiting so prepared for the One to manifest His presence. The rediscovery of one's true self is a return to Intellect; for, as we have seen, Plotinus teaches that our selves at their highest belong to the sphere of Intellect. This does not however mean that Plotinus simply reduces spiritual life to intellectual life. Intellect to him means something more than, and something different from, what we usually understand by the term; and in the ascent of the soul the moral life counts for at least as much as the intellectual life. The following passage[1] shows how misleading it would be to describe Plotinus as a

[1] VI. 7. 36, 6–10.

one-sided intellectualist (and his life here confirms his teaching): "We learn about the Good by comparisons and negations and knowledge of the things which proceed from It and intellectual progress by ascending degrees; but we advance towards it by purifications and virtues and adornings of the soul and by gaining a foothold in the world of Intellect and settling ourselves firmly there and feasting on its contents." Here moral and true intellectual life form an indissoluble unity.

The fact that we can only attain to the One when we are firmly established in Intellect has some important consequences, which are not always fully appreciated, for Plotinus's account of the final union. The first is that there is for him no short cut, no mysticism which does not demand moral and intellectual perfection. Union with the One transcends our moral and intellectual life, because in it we ascend to the source of intellect and goodness which is more than they are, but it is only possible because our intellectual and moral life has reached its perfection. We are "carried out by the very surge of the wave of Intellect."[1] It is the completion and confirmation, not the negation and destruction, of all that has been done to bring ourselves to perfection, to the fullest consciousness and activity. And again, because it is as Intellect that we attain to union, it would seem that it is not Plotinus's thought that our individual personalities are finally absorbed and disappear. It is true that in the union we rise above Intellect to a state in which there is no consciousness of difference from the One, in which there is no longer seer and seen,

[1] VI. 7. 36.

but only unity. But universal Intellect, of which we are then a part, exists continually in that state of union without prejudice to its proper life of intuitive thought and unity-in-diversity. There is never any suggestion in Plotinus that all things except the One are illusions or fleeting appearances.

III. Text, Editions, Translations

For full information about the history of the text of Plotinus, reference should be made to the Preface of the great critical edition of P. Henry and H–R. Schwyzer (Vols. I & II Paris & Brussels, Desclée de Brouwer; Vol. III Paris–Brussels–Leiden, Desclée de Brouwer and Brill 1951–73; *editio minor*, extensively revised, *Plotini Opera* I–III Oxford, Clarendon Press 1964–82), whose text is printed and translated in these volumes, and to the massive prolegomena to this edition published by P. Henry under the general title of *Études Plotiniennes* (Vol. I. *Les États du Texte de Plotin* 1938, Vol. II. *Les Manuscrits des Ennéades* 1941 and 1948; both Desclée de Brouwer). Briefly, their conclusions are: (i) The archetype of our present MSS represented the text of Porphyry's edition with remarkable fidelity. This archetype was certainly written after the beginning of the sixth century, and probably between the ninth and twelfth centuries. (ii) The extant MSS cannot safely be divided into *boni* and *deteriores*; in reconstituting the text of the archetype the primary MSS of four of the five families into which the MSS can be grouped (WXYZ) [1] must be used, and no one MS or family can

[1] The fifth family (D) consists of 1 MS (Marcianus Graecus

be given predominant authority. (iii) As the text of the archetype is believed on good grounds to represent faithfully the text of Porphyry's edition, there is little room for conjectural emendation.

The text presented by the editors is therefore both extremely conservative and eclectic, in the sense that it does not rely exclusively on any one MS or family of MSS. Its conservatism has been criticised, perhaps in some particular cases justifiably. But in the case of Plotinus there are special reasons for ultra-conservatism. We have always to remember Porphyry's words in ch. 8 of the *Life* about his master's method of work " when Plotinus had written anything he could never bear to go over it twice : even to read it through once was too much for him, as his eyesight was not strong enough. In writing he did not form the letters with any regard to appearance or divide his syllables correctly, and he paid no attention to spelling." [1] And anyone who reads the *Enneads* will soon discover that Plotinus writes a Greek very much of his own, which is certainly not bad or barbarous, but is highly unconventional and irregular : it is therefore extremely dangerous to emend him according to any preconceived ideas of Greek, or even late Greek philosophical, usage, and very difficult to establish any reliable internal criteria derived from the *Enneads* themselves which will enable us to state with any confidence what oddities of language were impossible for Plotinus. As a translator, with no pretensions to competence as a textual critic, I can

209) which, though the oldest, is too fragmentary and faulty to be of use in constituting the text.

[1] Cp. also Longinus's experience recorded in *Life*, ch. 19–20.

only say that in most difficult and disputed passages I have found that the Henry-Schwyzer text is easier to understand and gives a better sense than the versions of their predecessors. And since the publication of the first volume in 1951, the editors have been engaged in a continual process of critical (often self-critical) revision of the text, in the freest discussion with other Plotinian scholars, by which it has been greatly improved. Particularly notable contributions to this revision were made by the late Professor Jesus Igal of Bilbao; and it has gone on in continual and fruitful interaction with the Harder-Beutler-Theiler edition of Plotinus (see below). Full account of this revision, at the stage which it has so far reached (H–R. Schwyzer is still continuing it), has been taken in the last four volumes of the Loeb Plotinus (IV–VII, containing *Enneads* IV–VI); on the text of this revision of Vol. I see the Note on page vi; Vols. II and III represent the stage reached when Vol. I of the *editio minor* (= OCT) was published in 1964, with a few later revisions.

A full, severe, and sometimes entertaining account of the previous editions will be found in Henry and Schwyzer's Preface. They are as follows:

  P. Perna. Basel 1580.
  F. Creuzer and G. H. Moser. Oxford 1835.
  A. Kirchhoff. Leipzig 1856.
  H. F. Mueller. Berlin 1878–80.
  R. Volkmann. Leipzig 1883–4.
  E. Bréhier. Paris 1924–38.

Before his death Richard Harder had begun to prepare a Greek text of Plotinus to accompany a revision of his admirable German translation (first published

PREFACE

1930–37). The first volume of his text (containing the treatises 1–21 in the chronological order given in Porphyry's *Life*, which he preferred to Porphyry's later arrangement of them in Enneads) was published in 1956. After his death in 1957 the work was continued by R. Beutler and W. Theiler and completed in 1971. (*Plotins Schriften* V–VI Hamburg, Meiner 1956–71); in spite of Harder's too modest remarks in his preface to the first volume, this ranks as a major critical edition of great value; its relation to the Henry-Schwyzer text is one of friendly independence. After these two great editions, the principal help to students of Plotinus which has appeared in recent years is the *Lexicon Plotinianum*, compiled by J. H. Sleeman and G. Pollet (Leiden, Brill; Leuven, University Press 1980), which accords with the Henry-Schwyzer text.

There are several good commentaries on individual works of Plotinus. I have found the following particularly helpful; all have Greek texts.

W. Beirwaltes *Plotin. Über Ewigheit und Zeit* (III 7) Frankfurt, Klostermann 1967; 3rd edition 1981.

V. Cilento *Paideia antignostica* (III 8, V 8, V 5, II 9, now generally recognised as parts of a single long work) Florence, Le Monnier 1971.

J. Bertier, L. Brisson and others *Plotin, Traité sur les nombres* (VI 6) Paris, Vrin 1980.

M. Atkinson *Plotinus: Ennead V 1* Oxford, Clarendon Press 1983.

Since Marsilius Ficinus re-introduced Plotinus to Western Europe with his great Latin translation in 1492, translations of the *Enneads* have played an important part in Plotinian studies, and their number is rapidly increasing. Harder's German translation has already been referred to. V. Cilento's Italian version with critical commentary (*Plotino: Enneadi* Bari, Laterza 1947–9) is of great scholarly value. J. Igal, whose contributions to the revision of the Henry-Schwyzer text were so great (see above), was engaged on a Spanish translation at the time of his death: two volumes, with a long and excellent introduction, have been published (*Porfirio, Vida de Plotino*; *Plotino, Eneadas I–II* and *Plotino, Eneadas III–IV* Madrid, Gredos 1982 and 1985), and the third is in active preparation. There is a good Dutch translation by R. Ferwerda (Amsterdam, Ambo Athenaeum—Polak and Van Gennep 1984), and translations into Polish and Hebrew. A Japanese translation is now appearing (*Plotinos Zenshū*, tr. Michitaro Tanaka, Muneaki Mizuchi and Yasuhiko Tanogashira, 5 vols., Tokyo, Chūō-Kōron Sha 1986–7). P. Hadot has published the first volume of an important new French translation, to be completed by various hands under his direction, with extensive introductions and commentaries (*Plotin, Traité 38* (VI7), Paris, Editions du Cerf, 1988). The English translation by Stephen MacKenna and B. S. Page (4th edition London, Faber 1969—the third of the one-volume editions revised by Page) is of much scholarly value and will always hold the affection of some readers because of its noble esoteric-majestic style. My debt to it is considerable, but I have had a better critical text at my disposal and have tried to give a plainer version and one closer to the Greek.

Since the appearance of the first volume of the Henry-Schwyzer text in 1951 there has been a great increase in interest in Plotinus and later Platonism;

PREFACE

this is part of the general growth of interest in late antiquity, the period of transition from the ancient to the mediaeval world. The number of scholarly writings on Plotinus and his predecessors and successors is now very large and continues to grow rapidly. Good introductions to these studies are provided by *The Cambridge History of Later Greek and Early Mediaeval Philosophy* (Cambridge University Press 1970, edited by A. H. Armstrong, who also wrote Part III, "Plotinus") and two excellent books in Duckworth's *Classical Life and Letters* series: John Dillon *The Middle Platonists* and R. T. Wallis *Neoplatonism* (London 1977 and 1972). A complete survey of everything published on Plotinus up to 1949 will be found in B. Marien's *Bibliografica critica degli studi Plotiniani* (Bari, Laterza 1949, published with the last volume of Cilento's translation). Two full bibliographical surveys of later publications have been published in *Aufstieg und Niedergang der römischen Welt* (ed. H. Temporini and W. Haase, Berlin–New York, De Gruyter) II.36.1. (1987): the first, by H. J. Blumenthal, covering the period 1951–71, pp. 528–70 and the second, by K. Corrigan and P. O'Cleirigh, covering 1971–86, pp. 571–623.

SIGLA

A = Laurentianus 87, 3.
A′ = Codicis A primus corrector.
E = Parisinus Gr. 1976.
B = Laurentianus 85, 15.
R = Vaticanus Reginensis Gr. 97.
J = Parisinus Gr. 2082.
U = Vaticanus Urbinas Gr. 62.
S = Berolinensis Gr. 375.
N = Monacensis Gr. 215.
M = Marcianus Gr. 240.
C = Monacensis Gr. 449.
V = Vindobonensis philosophicus Gr. 226.
Q = Marcianus Gr. 242.
L = Ambrosianus Gr. 667.
D = Marcianus Gr. 209.

W = AE.
X = BRJ.
Y = USM.
Z = QL.

mg = in margine.
ac = ante correctionem.
pc = post correctionem.
γρ = γράφεται.

ORDO ENNEADVM COMPARATVR
CVM ORDINE CHRONOLOGICO

Enn.	chron.	Enn.	chron.	Enn.	chron.
I 1	53	II 1	40	III 1	3
I 2	19	II 2	14	III 2	47
I 3	20	II 3	52	III 3	48
I 4	46	II 4	12	III 4	15
I 5	36	II 5	25	III 5	50
I 6	1	II 6	17	III 6	26
I 7	54	II 7	37	III 7	45
I 8	51	II 8	35	III 8	30
I 9	16	II 9	33	III 9	13

Enn.	chron.	Enn.	chron.	Enn.	chron.
IV 1	21	V 1	10	VI 1	42
IV 2	4	V 2	11	VI 2	43
IV 3	27	V 3	49	VI 3	44
IV 4	28	V 4	7	VI 4	22
IV 5	29	V 5	32	VI 5	23
IV 6	41	V 6	24	VI 6	34
IV 7	2	V 7	18	VI 7	38
IV 8	6	V 8	31	VI 8	39
IV 9	8	V 9	5	VI 9	9

ORDO CHRONOLOGICVS COMPARATVR
CVM ORDINE ENNEADVM

chron.	Enn.	chron.	Enn.	chron.	Enn.
1	I 6	19	I 2	37	II 7
2	IV 7	20	I 3	38	VI 7
3	III 1	21	IV 1	39	VI 8
4	IV 2	22	VI 4	40	II 1
5	V 9	23	VI 5	41	IV 6
6	IV 8	24	V 6	42	VI 1
7	V 4	25	II 5	43	VI 2
8	IV 9	26	III 6	44	VI 3
9	VI 9	27	IV 3	45	III 7
10	V 1	28	IV 4	46	I 4
11	V 2	29	IV 5	47	III 2
12	II 4	30	III 8	48	III 3
13	III 9	31	V 8	49	V 3
14	II 2	32	V 5	50	III 5
15	III 4	33	II 9	51	I 8
16	I 9	34	VI 6	52	II 3
17	II 6	35	II 8	53	I 1
18	V 7	36	I 5	54	I 7

PORPHYRY

ON THE LIFE OF PLOTINUS AND
THE ORDER OF HIS BOOKS

ΠΟΡΦΥΡΙΟΥ

ΠΕΡΙ ΤΟΥ ΠΛΩΤΙΝΟΥ ΒΙΟΥ ΚΑΙ ΤΗΣ ΤΑΞΕΩΣ ΤΩΝ ΒΙΒΛΙΩΝ ΑΥΤΟΥ

1. Πλωτῖνος ὁ καθ' ἡμᾶς γεγονὼς φιλόσοφος ἐῴκει μὲν αἰσχυνομένῳ ὅτι ἐν σώματι εἴη. ᾿Απὸ δὲ τῆς τοιαύτης διαθέσεως οὔτε περὶ τοῦ γένους αὐτοῦ διηγεῖσθαι ἠνείχετο οὔτε περὶ τῶν γονέων
5 οὔτε περὶ τῆς πατρίδος. Ζωγράφου δὲ ἀνασχέσθαι ἢ πλάστου τοσοῦτον ἀπηξίου ὥστε καὶ λέγειν πρὸς ᾿Αμέλιον δεόμενον εἰκόνα αὐτοῦ γενέσθαι ἐπιτρέψαι· οὐ γὰρ ἀρκεῖ φέρειν ὃ ἡ φύσις εἴδωλον ἡμῖν περι- τέθεικεν, ἀλλὰ καὶ εἰδώλου εἴδωλον συγχωρεῖν αὐτὸν ἀξιοῦν πολυχρονιώτερον καταλιπεῖν ὡς δή
10 τι τῶν ἀξιοθεάτων ἔργων; Ὅθεν ἀπαγορεύοντος καὶ καθεδεῖσθαι ἕνεκα τούτου ἀρνουμένου ἔχων φίλον ὁ ᾿Αμέλιος Καρτέριον τὸν ἄριστον τῶν τότε γεγονότων ζωγράφων εἰσιέναι καὶ ἀπαντᾶν εἰς τὰς συνουσίας ποιήσας—ἐξῆν γὰρ τῷ βουλομένῳ φοιτᾶν εἰς τὰς συνουσίας—τὰς ἐκ τοῦ ὁρᾶν φαντασίας

---

[1] Eunapius (p. 6. Boissonade) says Plotinus came from Egypt and that his birthplace was Lyco. David, in his preface to his commentary on Porphyry's *Eisagoge* (4. pp. 91. 23–92. 1), gives the name of Plotinus's birthplace as Lycopolis, probably the town of that name in Upper Egypt (though the town of the same name in the Delta may be meant). But the reliability of this information must remain somewhat suspect. It is

2

PORPHYRY

ON THE LIFE OF PLOTINUS AND
THE ORDER OF HIS BOOKS

1. PLOTINUS, the philosopher of our times, seemed ashamed of being in the body. As a result of this state of mind he could never bear to talk about his race or his parents or his native country.[1] And he objected so strongly to sitting to a painter or sculptor that he said to Amelius,[2] who was urging him to allow a portrait of himself to be made, "Why really, is it not enough to have to carry the image in which nature has encased us, without your requesting me to agree to leave behind me a longer-lasting image of the image, as if it was something genuinely worth looking at?" In view of his denial and refusal for this reason to sit, Amelius, who had a friend, Carterius, the best painter of the time, brought him in to attend the meetings of the school—they were open to anyone who wished to come, and accustomed him by pro-

difficult to see what good source of information could have been open to Eunapius which was not available to Porphyry.

[2] For Amelius Gentilianus from Etruria cp. *Life*, ch. 3, 7, 10, 17 (his epistle dedicatory to Porphyry), 18, and 20. He was, as the *Life* makes clear, the leading member of the school in which he seems to have acted as Plotinus's chief assistant (cp. especially ch. 18). He was extremely pious (ch. 10) and a diffuse and voluminous writer. Nothing survives of the hundred volumes of the notes which he made at the meetings of the school.

3

15 πληκτικωτέρας λαμβάνειν διὰ τῆς ἐπὶ πλέον προσ-
οχῆς συνείθισεν. Ἔπειτα γράφοντος ἐκ τοῦ τῇ
μνήμῃ ἐναποκειμένου ἰνδάλματος τὸ εἴκασμα καὶ
συνδιορθοῦντος εἰς ὁμοιότητα τὸ ἴχνος τοῦ Ἀμελίου εἰκόνα αὐτοῦ γενέσθαι ἡ εὐφυΐα τοῦ Καρτερίου
παρέσχεν ἀγνοοῦντος τοῦ Πλωτίνου ὁμοιοτάτην.

2. Κωλικῇ δὲ νόσῳ πολλάκις καταπονούμενος
οὔτε κλυστῆρος ἠνέσχετο, οὐκ εἶναι πρὸς τοῦ
πρεσβύτου λέγων ὑπομένειν τὰς τοιαύτας θεραπείας,
οὔτε τὰς θηριακὰς ἀντιδότους λαβεῖν ὑπέμεινε,
5 μηδὲ τῶν ἡμέρων ζῴων τὰς ἐκ τοῦ σώματος
τροφὰς προσίεσθαι λέγων. Λουτροῦ δὲ ἀπεχόμενος
καὶ τρίψεσι καθ’ ἑκάστην ἡμέραν χρώμενος ἐπὶ
τῆς οἰκίας, ἐπειδὴ τοῦ λοιμοῦ ἐπιβρίσαντος συνέβη
τοὺς τρίβοντας αὐτὸν ἀποθανεῖν, ἀμελήσας τῆς
τοιαύτης θεραπείας κατ’ ὀλίγον τὴν τοῦ κυνάγχου
10 ἀγριότητα κατασκευαζομένην ἔσχε. Κἀμοῦ μὲν
παρόντος οὐδέν πω τοιοῦτον ὑπεφαίνετο· ἀποπλεύ-
σαντος δὲ εἰς τοσοῦτον ἠγριώθη τὸ πάθος, ὡς
ἔλεγεν ἐπανελθόντι Εὐστόχιος ὁ ἑταῖρος ὁ καὶ
παραμείνας αὐτῷ ἄχρι θανάτου, ὡς καὶ τῆς φωνῆς
περιαιρεθῆναι τὸ τορὸν καὶ εὔηχον βραγχῶντος
15 αὐτοῦ καὶ τὴν ὄψιν συγχυθῆναι καὶ τὰς χεῖρας καὶ
τοὺς πόδας ἑλκωθῆναι· ὅθεν ἐκτρεπομένων αὐτοῦ
τὰς συναντήσεις τῶν φίλων διὰ τὸ ἀπὸ στόματος
πάντας προσαγορεύειν ἔθος ἔχειν, τῆς μὲν πόλεως
ἀπαλλάττεται, εἰς δὲ τὴν Καμπανίαν ἐλθὼν εἰς
Ζήθου χωρίον ἑταίρου παλαιοῦ αὐτῷ γεγονότος καὶ

---

[1] A much more highly coloured account of Plotinus's last
illness appears in Firmicus Maternus, *Mathesis* I. 7. 14 ff.
H. Oppermann (*Plotins Leben*, Heidelberg 1929, ch. I) regards
this as an independent account based on a lost biography by

gressive study to derive increasingly striking mental
pictures from what he saw.   Then Carterius drew a
likeness of the impression which remained in his
memory.   Amelius helped him to improve his sketch
to a closer resemblance, and so the talent of Carterius gave us an excellent portrait of Plotinus
without his knowledge.

2. He often suffered from a disease of the bowels,
but would not submit to an enema, saying that it was
unsuitable for an elderly man to undergo this sort of
treatment.   He refused also to take medicines containing the flesh of wild beasts, giving as his reason
that he did not approve of eating the flesh even
of domestic animals.   He kept away from the bath
and had himself massaged every day at home.
When the plague broke out and his masseurs died he
gave up treatment of this kind, and soon contracted
acute diphtheria.   While I was with him no symptoms
of this kind appeared, but after I left on my voyage
his disease increased so much in violence (as our friend
Eustochius, who stayed with him till his death, told
me when I returned) that his voice lost its clearness
and sonority as his throat grew worse, and his sight
became blurred and his hands and feet ulcerated.[1]
So, since his friends avoided meeting him because he
had the habit of greeting everyone by word of mouth,
he left the city and went to Campania, to a property
belonging to Zethus, an old friend of his who was

Eustochius prefixed to his edition of Plotinus's writings (cp.
Introduction, p. ix). Henry (*Plotin et l'Occident*, Louvain,
1934, ch. I) considers it, more probably, as a rhetorical
amplification of the account given here by Porphyry.   Both
agree, however, that the disease described here of which
Plotinus died was in fact *elephantiasis Graecorum*, i.e., a form
of leprosy.

20 τεθνηκότος κατάγεται. Τὰ δ' ἀναγκαῖα αὐτῷ ἔκ
τε τῶν τοῦ Ζήθου ἐτελεῖτο καὶ ἐκ Μητουρνῶν
ἐκομίζετο ἐκ τῶν Καστρικίου· ἐν Μητούρναις γὰρ
ὁ Καστρίκιος τὰς κτήσεις εἶχε. Μέλλων δὲ τελευ-
τᾶν, ὡς ὁ Εὐστόχιος ἡμῖν διηγεῖτο, ἐπειδὴ ἐν
Ποτιόλοις κατοικῶν ὁ Εὐστόχιος βραδέως πρὸς
25 αὐτὸν ἀφίκετο, εἰπὼν ὅτι σὲ ἔτι περιμένω καὶ
φήσας πειρᾶσθε τὸν ἐν ἡμῖν θεὸν ἀνάγειν πρὸς τὸ
ἐν τῷ παντὶ θεῖον, δράκοντος ὑπὸ τὴν κλίνην
διελθόντος ἐν ᾗ κατέκειτο καὶ εἰς ὀπὴν ἐν τῷ
τοίχῳ ὑπάρχουσαν ὑποδεδυκότος ἀφῆκε τὸ πνεῦμα
30 ἔτη γεγονώς, ὡς ὁ Εὐστόχιος ἔλεγεν, ἕξ τε καὶ
ἑξήκοντα, τοῦ δευτέρου ἔτους τῆς Κλαυδίου βασιλείας πληρουμένου. Τελευτῶντι δὲ αὐτῷ ἐγὼ μὲν
ὁ Πορφύριος ἐτύγχανον ἐν Λιλυβαίῳ, διατρίβων,
Ἀμέλιος δὲ ἐν Ἀπαμείᾳ τῆς Συρίας, Καστρίκιος
δὲ ἐν τῇ Ῥώμῃ· μόνος δὲ παρῆν ὁ Εὐστόχιος.
35 Ἀναψηφίζουσι δὲ ἡμῖν ἀπὸ τοῦ δευτέρου ἔτους
τῆς Κλαυδίου βασιλείας εἰς τοὐπίσω ἔτη ἕξ τε καὶ
ἑξήκοντα ὁ χρόνος αὐτῷ τῆς γενέσεως εἰς τὸ
τρισκαιδέκατον ἔτος τῆς Σεβήρου βασιλείας πίπτει.
Οὔτε δὲ τὸν μῆνα δεδήλωκέ τινι καθ' ὃν γεγέννηται,
οὔτε τὴν γενέθλιον ἡμέραν, ἐπεὶ οὐδὲ θύειν ἢ
40 ἑστιᾶν τινα τοῖς αὑτοῦ γενεθλίοις ἠξίου, καίπερ ἐν
τοῖς Πλάτωνος καὶ Σωκράτους παραδεδομένοις
γενεθλίοις θύων τε καὶ ἑστιῶν τοὺς ἑταίρους, ὅτε
καὶ λόγον ἔδει τῶν ἑταίρων τοὺς δυνατοὺς ἐπὶ τῶν
συνελθόντων ἀναγνῶναι.

3. Ἃ μέντοι ἡμῖν αὐτὸς ἀφ' ἑαυτοῦ ἐν ταῖς ὁμι-

6

dead. His wants were provided for partly from the estate of Zethus and partly from that of Castricius at Minturnae; for Castricius had his property there. When he was on the point of death, Eustochius told us, as Eustochius had been staying at Puteoli and was late in coming to him he said, "I have been waiting a long time for you." Then he said, "Try to bring back the god in us to the divine in the All!" and, as a snake crept under the bed on which he was lying and disappeared into a hole in the wall, he breathed his last. It was the end of the second year of the reign of Claudius, and according to Eustochius he was sixty-six years old. At the time of his death I, Porphyry, was staying at Lilybaeum, Amelius was at Apamea in Syria, and Castricus was in Rome: only Eustochius was with him. If we reckon sixty-six years back from the second year of the reign of Claudius the date of his birth falls in the thirteenth year of the reign of Severus; [1] but he never told anyone the month in which he was born or the day of his birth, because he did not want any sacrifice or feast on his birthday, though he sacrificed and entertained his friends on the traditional birthdays of Plato and Socrates; on these occasions those of his friends who were capable of it had to read a discourse before the assembled company.

3. All the same, he did often in the course of conversation spontaneously tell us something about his

[1] I.e., Plotinus was born in A.D. 205 and died in 270. For a discussion of the chronology of his life see Schwyzer, art. cit. (Introduction, p. xxxii), col. 472–4.

λίαις πολλάκις διηγεῖτο, ἦν τοιαῦτα. Προσφοιτᾶν
μὲν γὰρ τῇ τροφῷ καίπερ εἰς γραμματοδιδασκάλου
ἀπιόντα ἄχρις ὀγδόου ἔτους ἀπὸ γενέσεως ὄντα
5 καὶ τοὺς μαζοὺς γυμνοῦντα θηλάζειν προθυμεῖσθαι·
ἀκούσαντα δέ ποτε ὅτι ἀτηρόν ἐστι παιδίον,
ἀποσχέσθαι αἰδεσθέντα. Εἰκοστὸν δὲ καὶ ὄγδοον
ἔτος αὐτὸν ἄγοντα ὁρμῆσαι ἐπὶ φιλοσοφίαν καὶ τοῖς
τότε κατὰ τὴν Ἀλεξάνδρειαν εὐδοκιμοῦσι συστα-
θέντα κατιέναι ἐκ τῆς ἀκροάσεως αὐτῶν κατηφῆ
10 καὶ λύπης πλήρη, ὡς καί τινι τῶν φίλων διηγεῖσθαι
ἃ πάσχοι· τὸν δὲ συνέντα αὐτοῦ τῆς ψυχῆς τὸ
βούλημα ἀπενέγκαι πρὸς Ἀμμώνιον, οὗ μηδέπω
πεπείρατο. Τὸν δὲ εἰσελθόντα καὶ ἀκούσαντα
φάναι πρὸς τὸν ἑταῖρον· τοῦτον ἐζήτουν. Καὶ ἀπ'
ἐκείνης τῆς ἡμέρας συνεχῶς τῷ Ἀμμωνίῳ παραμέ-
15 νοντα τοσαύτην ἕξιν ἐν φιλοσοφίᾳ κτήσασθαι, ὡς
καὶ τῆς παρὰ τοῖς Πέρσαις ἐπιτηδευομένης πεῖραν
λαβεῖν σπεῦσαι καὶ τῆς παρ' Ἰνδοῖς κατορθουμένης.
Γορδιανοῦ δὲ τοῦ βασιλέως ἐπὶ τοὺς Πέρσας παριέ-
ναι μέλλοντος δοὺς ἑαυτὸν τῷ στρατοπέδῳ συν-
εισῄει ἔτος ἤδη τριακοστὸν ἄγων καὶ ἔννατον.
20 Ἕνδεκα γὰρ ὅλων ἐτῶν παραμένων τῷ Ἀμμωνίῳ
συνεσχόλασε. Τοῦ δὲ Γορδιανοῦ περὶ τὴν Μεσο-
ποταμίαν ἀναιρεθέντος μόλις φεύγων εἰς τὴν
Ἀντιόχειαν διεσώθη. Καὶ Φιλίππου τὴν βασιλείαν

---

[1] Ammonius (c. 175–242) was a self-taught philosopher who
wrote nothing. We know very little about his teaching: the
scanty evidence is fully reported and discussed by Schwyzer,

early life, to the following effect. Up to the age of eight, though he was already going to school, he used to keep going to his nurse and baring her breasts and wanting to suck; but when someone once told him that he was a little pest he was ashamed and stopped. In his twenty-eighth year he felt the impulse to study philosophy and was recommended to the teachers in Alexandria who then had the highest reputation; but he came away from their lectures so depressed and full of sadness that he told his trouble to one of his friends. The friend, understanding the desire of his heart, sent him to Ammonius,[1] whom he had not so far tried. He went and heard him, and said to his friend, "This is the man I was looking for." From that day he stayed continually with Ammonius and acquired so complete a training in philosophy that he became eager to make acquaintance with the Persian philosophical discipline and that prevailing among the Indians. As the Emperor Gordian was preparing to march against the Persians, he joined the army and went on the expedition; he was already in his thirty-ninth year, for he had stayed studying with Ammonius for eleven complete years. When Gordian was killed in Mesopotamia Plotinus escaped with difficulty and came safe to Antioch. After Philip

art. cit. col. 477–81. (See also E. R. Dodds, *Numenius and Ammonius* in Entretiens Hardt V). The nickname Saccas and the story that he once earned his living as a porter appears for the first time in Theodoret. Porphyry never mentions it. Porphyry (in Eusebius H.E. 6. 19. 7) says that he was brought up a Christian, but later became a pagan. This may be true, but cannot be taken as certain, any more than Eusebius' denial (6. 19. 10). The name Ammonius was common in Egypt, and there may have been some confusion of persons.

κρατήσαντος τεσσαράκοντα γεγονὼς ἔτη εἰς τὴν
Ῥώμην ἄνεισιν. Ἐρεννίῳ δὲ καὶ Ὠριγένει καὶ
25 Πλωτίνῳ συνθηκῶν γεγονυιῶν μηδὲν ἐκκαλύπτειν
τῶν Ἀμμωνίου δογμάτων ἃ δὴ ἐν ταῖς ἀκροάσεσιν
αὐτοῖς ἀνεκεκάθαρτο, ἔμενε καὶ ὁ Πλωτῖνος συνὼν
μέν τισι τῶν προσιόντων, τηρῶν δὲ ἀνέκπυστα τὰ
παρὰ τοῦ Ἀμμωνίου δόγματα. Ἐρεννίου δὲ
30 πρώτου τὰς συνθήκας παραβάντος, Ὠριγένης μὲν
ἠκολούθει τῷ φθάσαντι Ἐρεννίῳ. Ἔγραψε δὲ
οὐδὲν πλὴν τὸ "Περὶ τῶν δαιμόνων" σύγγραμμα
καὶ ἐπὶ Γαλιήνου "Ὅτι μόνος ποιητὴς ὁ βασιλεύς".
Πλωτῖνος δὲ ἄχρι μὲν πολλοῦ γράφων οὐδὲν
35 διετέλεσεν, ἐκ δὲ τῆς Ἀμμωνίου συνουσίας ποιούμενος τὰς διατριβάς· καὶ οὕτως ὅλων ἐτῶν δέκα
διετέλεσε, συνὼν μέν τισι, γράφων δὲ οὐδέν. Ἦν
δὲ ἡ διατριβή, ὡς ἂν αὐτοῦ ζητεῖν προτρεπομένου
τοὺς συνόντας, ἀταξίας πλήρης καὶ πολλῆς φλυα-
ρίας, ὡς Ἀμέλιος ἡμῖν διηγεῖτο. Προσῆλθε δὲ
40 αὐτῷ ὁ Ἀμέλιος τρίτον ἔτος ἄγοντι ἐν τῇ Ῥώμῃ
κατὰ τὸ τρίτον ἔτος τῆς Φιλίππου βασιλείας καὶ
ἄχρι τοῦ πρώτου ἔτους τῆς Κλαυδίου βασιλείας
παραμείνας ἔτη ὅλα συγγέγονεν εἴκοσι καὶ τέσσαρα,
ἕξιν μὲν ἔχων ὅτε προσῆλθεν ἀπὸ τῆς Λυσιμάχου

---

[1] Or, possibly, "With reference to Gallienus, *That the
Emperor is the Only Poet.*" But it is very difficult to believe
that a fellow-philosopher whom Plotinus respected could
have perpetrated such a fulsome piece of court flattery as
this suggests, and the context leads one to expect a treatise
about the teaching of Ammonius. Origen the Christian writer
also attended the lectures of Ammonius (Porphyry in Eusebius
H.E. 6. 19. 6), but it seems clear to most of those who have
studied the question that the Origen mentioned here and in

had become Emperor he came to Rome, at the age of forty.   Erennius, Origen, and Plotinus had made an agreement not to disclose any of the doctrines of Ammonius which he had revealed to them in his lectures.   Plotinus kept the agreement, and, though he held conferences with people who came to him, maintained silence about the doctrines of Ammonius. Erennius was the first to break the agreement, and Origen followed his lead; but he wrote nothing except the treatise *On the Spirits* and, in the reign of Gallienus, *That the King is the Only Maker*.[1]   Plotinus for a long time continued to write nothing, but began to base his lectures on his studies with Ammonius.   So he continued for ten complete years, admitting people to study with him, but writing nothing.   Since he encouraged his students to ask questions, the course was lacking in order and there was a great deal of pointless chatter, as Amelius told us.   Amelius came to him during his third year in Rome (the third year of the reign of Philip), and stayed with him till the first year of the reign of Claudius, twenty-four years in all.   He came with a philosophical training from the school of Lysimachus,

chs. 14 and 20 of the *Life* was quite a different person. Origen was not an uncommon name at Alexandria; there are chronological difficulties against identifying the two (for which see Schwyzer, art. cit., col. 480); there is no trace of the writings mentioned here among the known works of the Christian Origen; and, most important of all, the references in the *Life* clearly imply that the Origen mentioned here was a perfectly normal Platonist, enjoying the friendship and respect of other Platonists and of Plotinus himself. In the passage quoted by Eusebius, Porphyry speaks of the Christian Origen in a very different and thoroughly hostile tone, as one would expect the greatest antiChristian writer of antiquity to speak of the great Christian apologist.

PORPHYRY

συνουσίας, φιλοπονίᾳ δὲ ὑπερβαλλόμενος τῶν καθ'
αὑτὸν πάντων διὰ τὸ καὶ σχεδὸν πάντα τὰ Νουμη-
45 νίου καὶ γράψαι καὶ συναγαγεῖν καὶ σχεδὸν τὰ
πλεῖστα ἐκμαθεῖν· σχόλια δὲ ἐκ τῶν συνουσιῶν
ποιούμενος ἑκατόν που βιβλία συνέταξε τῶν σχολίων, ἃ Οὐστιλλιανῷ Ἡσυχίῳ τῷ Ἀπαμεῖ, ὃν
υἱὸν ἔθετο, κεχάρισται.

4. Τῷ δεκάτῳ δὲ ἔτει τῆς Γαλιήνου βασιλείας
ἐγὼ Πορφύριος ἐκ τῆς Ἑλλάδος μετὰ Ἀντωνίου
τοῦ Ῥοδίου γεγονὼς καταλαμβάνω μὲν τὸν
Ἀμέλιον ὀκτωκαιδέκατον ἔτος ἔχοντα τῆς πρὸς
5 Πλωτῖνον συνουσίας, μηδὲν δέ πω γράφειν τολμή-
σαντα πλὴν τῶν σχολίων ἃ οὐδέπω εἰς ἑκατὸν τὸ
πλῆθος αὐτῷ συνῆκτο. Ἦν δὲ ὁ Πλωτῖνος τῷ
δεκάτῳ ἔτει τῆς Γαλιήνου βασιλείας ἀμφὶ τὰ
πεντήκοντα ἔτη καὶ ἐννέα. Ἐγὼ δὲ Πορφύριος τὸ
πρῶτον αὐτῷ συγγέγονα αὐτὸς ὢν τότε ἐτῶν
10 τριάκοντα. Ἀπὸ μέντοι τοῦ πρώτου ἔτους τῆς
Γαλιήνου ἀρχῆς προτραπεὶς ὁ Πλωτῖνος γράφειν
τὰς ἐμπιπτούσας ὑποθέσεις, τὸ δέκατον ἔτος τῆς
Γαλιήνου ἀρχῆς, ὅτε τὸ πρῶτον αὐτῷ ἐγὼ ὁ
Πορφύριος ἐγνωρίσθην, γράψας εὑρίσκεται εἴκοσι
καὶ ἓν βιβλίον ἃ καὶ κατείληφα ἐκδεδομένα ὀλίγοις.
15 Οὐδὲ γὰρ ἦν πω ῥᾳδία ἡ ἔκδοσις οὐδὲ εὐσυνειδήτως
ἐγίγνετο οὐδ' ἁπλῶς κἀκ τοῦ ῥᾴστου, ἀλλὰ μετὰ
πάσης κρίσεως τῶν λαμβανόντων. Ἦν δὲ καὶ τὰ
γεγραμμένα ταῦτα ἃ διὰ τὸ μὴ αὐτὸν ἐπιγράφειν
ἄλλος ἄλλο ἑκάστῳ τοὐπίγραμμα ἐτίθει. Αἱ δ'
οὖν κρατήσασαι ἐπιγραφαί εἰσιν αἵδε· θήσω δὲ
20 καὶ τὰς ἀρχὰς τῶν βιβλίων, εἰς τὸ εὐεπίγνωστον
εἶναι ἀπὸ τῶν ἀρχῶν ἕκαστον τῶν δηλουμένων
βιβλίων·

12

and was the most industrious of all Plotinus's associates; he wrote out and collected almost all the works of Numenius, and nearly knew the greater part of them by heart. He made notes of the meetings of Plotinus's school and put together about a hundred volumes of these notes, which he has presented to Hostilianus Hesychius of Apamea, his adopted son.

4. In the tenth year of the reign of Gallienus, I, Porphyry, arrived from Greece with Antonius of Rhodes, and found that Amelius, though he had been with Plotinus for eighteen years, had not yet brought himself to write anything except the notebooks, which he had not yet brought up to their total of a hundred. In the tenth year of the reign of Gallienus Plotinus was about fifty-nine years old. I, Porphyry, when I first joined him was thirty. From the first year of Gallienus Plotinus had begun to write on the subjects that came up in the meetings of the school : in the tenth year of Gallienus, when I, Porphyry, first came to know him, I found that he had written twenty-one treatises, and I also discovered that few people had received copies of them. The issuing of copies was still a difficult and anxious business, not at all simple and easy ; those who received them were most carefully scrutinised. These were the writings, to which, since he gave them no titles himself, each gave different titles for the several treatises. The following are the titles which finally prevailed. I add the first words of the treatises, to make it easy to recognise from them which treatise is indicated by each title.[1]

---

[1] As is customary in translations of the *Life*, these first words have been omitted here and the Ennead reference substituted.

α΄ Περὶ τοῦ καλοῦ· [I. 6].
οὗ ἡ ἀρχή· τὸ καλὸν ἔστι μὲν ἐν ὄψει πλεῖστον.

β΄ Περὶ ψυχῆς ἀθανασίας· [IV. 7].
25 οὗ ἡ ἀρχή· εἰ δέ ἐστιν ἀθάνατος ἕκαστος.

γ΄ Περὶ εἱμαρμένης· [III. 1].
οὗ ἡ ἀρχή· πάντα τὰ γινόμενα.

δ΄ Περὶ οὐσίας τῆς ψυχῆς· [IV. 2].
οὗ ἡ ἀρχή· τὴν τῆς ψυχῆς οὐσίαν.

30 ε΄ Περὶ νοῦ καὶ τῶν ἰδεῶν καὶ τοῦ ὄντος·
[V. 9].
οὗ ἡ ἀρχή· πάντες ἄνθρωποι ἐξ ἀρχῆς γενόμενοι.

ς΄ Περὶ τῆς εἰς τὰ σώματα καθόδου τῆς
ψυχῆς· [IV. 8].
οὗ ἡ ἀρχή· πολλάκις ἐγειρόμενος.

ζ΄ Πῶς ἀπὸ τοῦ πρώτου τὸ μετὰ τὸ πρῶτον
35 καὶ περὶ τοῦ ἑνός· [V. 4].
οὗ ἡ ἀρχή· εἴ τι ἐστὶ μετὰ τὸ πρῶτον.

η΄ Εἰ αἱ πᾶσαι ψυχαὶ μία· [IV. 9].
οὗ ἡ ἀρχή· ἆρα ὥσπερ ψυχήν.

θ΄ Περὶ τἀγαθοῦ ἢ τοῦ ἑνός· [VI. 9].
40 οὗ ἡ ἀρχή· ἅπαντα τὰ ὄντα.

ι΄ Περὶ τῶν τριῶν ἀρχικῶν ὑποστάσεων·
[V. 1].
οὗ ἡ ἀρχή· τί ποτε ἄρα ἐστὶ τὸ πεποιηκὸς τὰς ψυχάς.

ια΄ Περὶ γενέσεως καὶ τάξεως τῶν μετὰ τὸ
πρῶτον· [V. 2].
οὗ ἡ ἀρχή· τὸ ἓν πάντα.

45 ιβ΄ Περὶ τῶν δύο ὑλῶν· [II. 4].
οὗ ἡ ἀρχή· τὴν λεγομένην ὕλην.

ιγ΄ Ἐπισκέψεις διάφοροι· [III. 9].
οὗ ἡ ἀρχή· νοῦς φησιν ὁρᾷ ἐνούσας ἰδέας.

14

THE LIFE OF PLOTINUS

1. On Beauty (I. 6).

2. On the Immortality of the Soul (IV. 7).

3. On Destiny (III. 1).

4. On the Essence of the Soul (IV. 2).

5. On Intellect, the Forms, and Being (V. 9).

6. On the Descent of the Soul into Bodies (IV. 8).

7. How That which is after the First comes from the First; and about the One (V. 4).

8. If All Souls are One (IV. 9).

9. On the Good or the One (VI. 9).

10. On the Three Primary Hypostases (V. 1).

11. On the Origin and Order of the Beings which come after the First (V. 2).

12. On the Two Kinds of Matter (II. 4).

13. Various Considerations (III. 9).

ιδ´ Περὶ τῆς κυκλοφορίας· [II. 2].

50   οὗ ἡ ἀρχή· διὰ τί κύκλῳ κινεῖται.

ιε´ Περὶ τοῦ εἰληχότος ἡμᾶς δαίμονος·
   [III. 4].

   οὗ ἡ ἀρχή· τῶν μὲν αἱ ὑποστάσεις.

ις´ Περὶ εὐλόγου ἐξαγωγῆς· [I. 9].

   οὗ ἡ ἀρχή· οὐκ ἐξάξεις, ἵνα μὴ ἐξίῃ.

55 ιζ´ Περὶ ποιότητος· [II. 6].

   οὗ ἡ ἀρχή· ἆρα τὸ ὂν καὶ οὐσία.

ιη´ Εἰ καὶ τῶν καθέκαστά εἰσιν ἰδέαι· [V. 7].

   οὗ ἡ ἀρχή· εἰ καὶ τοῦ καθέκαστον.

ιθ´ Περὶ ἀρετῶν· [I. 2].

60   οὗ ἡ ἀρχή· ἐπειδὴ τὰ κακὰ ἐνταῦθα.

κ´ Περὶ διαλεκτικῆς· [I. 3].

   οὗ ἡ ἀρχή· τίς τέχνη ἢ μέθοδος.

κα´ Πῶς ἡ ψυχὴ τῆς ἀμερίστου καὶ μεριστῆς
   οὐσίας μέση εἶναι λέγεται· [IV. 1].

65   οὗ ἡ ἀρχή· ἐν τῷ κόσμῳ τῷ νοητῷ.

Ταῦτα μὲν οὖν εἴκοσι καὶ ἓν ὄντα, ὅτε αὐτῷ τὸ πρῶτον προσῆλθον ὁ Πορφύριος, εὕρηται γεγραμμένα· πεντηκοστὸν δὲ καὶ ἔννατον ἔτος ἦγε τότε ὁ Πλωτῖνος.

5. Συγγεγονὼς δὲ αὐτῷ τοῦτό τε τὸ ἔτος καὶ ἐφεξῆς ἄλλα ἔτη πέντε—ὀλίγον γὰρ ἔτι πρότερον τῆς δεκαετίας ἐγεγόνειν ὁ Πορφύριος ἐν τῇ Ῥώμῃ, τοῦ Πλωτίνου τὰς θερινὰς μὲν ἄγοντος ἀργούς, 5 συνόντος δὲ ἄλλως ἐν ταῖς ὁμιλίαις—ἐν δὴ τοῖς ἓξ ἔτεσι τούτοις πολλῶν ἐξετάσεων ἐν ταῖς συνουσίαις γιγνομένων καὶ γράφειν αὐτὸν ἀξιούντων Ἀμελίου τε καὶ ἐμοῦ, γράφει μὲν

16

14. On the Circular Motion (II. 2).

15. On our Allotted Guardian Spirit (III. 4).

16. On the Reasonable Departure (I. 9).

17. On Quality (II. 6).

18. Whether there are Ideas of Particulars (V. 7).

19. On Virtues (I. 2).

20. On Dialectic (I. 3).

21. In What Way the Soul is Said to be a Mean between Undivided and Divided Being (IV. 1).

These treatises, twenty-one in all, I, Porphyry, found already written when I first came to him. Plotinus was then in his fifty-ninth year.

5. I, Porphyry, had in fact already been in Rome a little before the tenth year of Gallienus, while Plotinus was taking his summer holiday and only engaging in general conversation with his friends. While I was with him this year and for five years afterwards, in these six years many discussions took place in the meetings of the school and Amelius and I kept urging him to write, so he wrote:

Περὶ τοῦ τί τὸ ὂν πανταχοῦ ὅλον εἶναι ἓν
καὶ ταὐτὸν βιβλία δύο· [VI. 4–5].

10   α΄ τούτων δὲ τὸ πρῶτον ἀρχὴν ἔχει· ἆρα γε ἡ ψυχὴ
      πανταχοῦ·
      β΄ τοῦ δὲ δευτέρου ἡ ἀρχή· ἓν καὶ ταὐτὸν ἀριθμῷ.

Γράφει δὲ ἐφεξῆς ἄλλα δύο, ὧν

      γ΄ τὸ μὲν Περὶ τοῦ τὸ ἐπέκεινα τοῦ ὄντος
      μὴ νοεῖν καὶ τί τὸ πρώτως νοοῦν καὶ τί
      τὸ δευτέρως· [V. 6].

15   οὗ ἡ ἀρχή· τὸ μέν ἐστι νοεῖν ἄλλο ἄλλο, τὸ δὲ αὐτὸ
      αὑτό·

      δ΄ τὸ δὲ Περὶ τοῦ δυνάμει καὶ ἐνεργείᾳ·
      [II. 5].

      οὗ ἡ ἀρχή· λέγεται τὸ μὲν δυνάμει.

      ε΄ Περὶ τῆς τῶν ἀσωμάτων ἀπαθείας·
      [III. 6].·

      οὗ ἡ ἀρχή· τὰς αἰσθήσεις οὐ πάθη λέγοντες.

20   ς΄ Περὶ ψυχῆς πρῶτον· [IV. 3].

      οὗ ἡ ἀρχή· περὶ ψυχῆς ὅσα ἀπορήσαντας δεῖ.

      ζ΄ Περὶ ψυχῆς δεύτερον· [IV. 4].

      οὗ ἡ ἀρχή· τί οὖν ἐρεῖ.

      η΄ Περὶ ψυχῆς τρίτον ἢ περὶ τοῦ πῶς
      ὁρῶμεν· [IV. 5].

25   οὗ ἡ ἀρχή· ἐπειδήπερ ὑπερεθέμεθα.

      θ΄ Περὶ θεωρίας· [III. 8].

      οὗ ἡ ἀρχή· παίζοντες τὴν πρώτην.

      ι΄ Περὶ τοῦ νοητοῦ κάλλους· [V. 8].

      οὗ ἡ ἀρχή· ἐπειδή φαμεν.

30   ια΄ Περὶ νοῦ καὶ ὅτι οὐκ ἔξω τοῦ νοῦ τὰ
      νοητὰ καὶ περὶ τἀγαθοῦ· [V. 5].

      οὗ ἡ ἀρχή· τὸν νοῦν τὸν ἀληθῆ νοῦν.

18

Next he wrote another two of which the first is the treatise

and the other

Then came

33. Against the Gnostics (II. 9).

34. On Numbers (VI. 6).

35. How Distant Objects appear Small (II. 8).

36. Whether Well-Being depends on Extension of Time (I. 5).

37. On Complete Intermingling (II. 7).

38. How the Multitude of the Forms came into being and On the Good (VI. 7).

39. On Free Will (VI. 8).

40. On the Universe (II. 1).

41. On Sense-Perception and Memory (IV. 6).

42. On the Kinds of Being I (VI. 1).

43. On the Kinds of Being II (VI. 2).

44. On the Kinds of Being III (VI. 3).

45. On Eternity and Time (III. 7).

Ταῦτα τὰ εἴκοσι καὶ τέτταρα ὄντα ὅσα ἐν τῷ
60 ἑξαέτει χρόνῳ τῆς παρουσίας ἐμοῦ Πορφυρίου
ἔγραψεν, ἐκ προσκαίρων προβλημάτων τὰς ὑποθέσεις λαβόντα, ὡς ἐκ τῶν κεφαλαίων ἑκάστου τῶν
βιβλίων ἐδηλώσαμεν, μετὰ τῶν πρὸ τῆς ἐπιδημίας
ἡμῶν εἴκοσι καὶ ἑνὸς τὰ πάντα γίνεται τεσσαρακονταπέντε.

6. Ἐν δὲ τῇ Σικελίᾳ διατρίβοντός μου—ἐκεῖ
γὰρ ἀνεχώρησα περὶ τὸ πεντεκαιδέκατον ἔτος τῆς
βασιλείας Γαλιήνου—ὁ Πλωτῖνος γράψας πέντε
βιβλία ἀποστέλλει μοι ταῦτα·

5   α΄ Περὶ εὐδαιμονίας· [I. 4].

           οὗ ἡ ἀρχή· τὸ εὖ ζῆν καὶ εὐδαιμονεῖν.

        β΄ Περὶ προνοίας πρῶτον· [III. 2].

           οὗ ἡ ἀρχή· τὸ μὲν τῷ αὐτομάτῳ·

        γ΄ Περὶ προνοίας δεύτερον· [III. 3].

10   οὗ ἡ ἀρχή· τί τοίνυν δοκεῖ περὶ τούτων.

        δ΄ Περὶ τῶν γνωριστικῶν ὑποστάσεων καὶ
           τοῦ ἐπέκεινα· [V. 3].

           οὗ ἡ ἀρχή· ἆρα τὸ νοοῦν ἑαυτὸ ποικίλον δεῖ εἶναι.

        ε΄ Περὶ ἔρωτος· [III. 5].

           οὗ ἡ ἀρχή· περὶ ἔρωτος πότερα θεός.

15 Ταῦτα μὲν οὖν τῷ πρώτῳ ἔτει τῆς Κλαυδίου
πέμπει βασιλείας· ἀρχομένου δὲ τοῦ δευτέρου,
ὅτε καὶ μετ᾽ ὀλίγον θνήσκει, πέμπει ταῦτα·

        α΄ Τίνα τὰ κακά· [I. 8].

           οὗ ἡ ἀρχή· οἱ ζητοῦντες πόθεν τὰ κακά.

20   β΄ Εἰ ποιεῖ τὰ ἄστρα· [II. 3].

           οὗ ἡ ἀρχή· ἡ τῶν ἄστρων φορά.

22

These twenty-four treatises are those which he wrote during the six-year period when I, Porphyry, was with him. He took their subjects from problems which came up from time to time in the meetings of the school, as I have shown in the summaries of the several treatises. With the twenty-one treatises written before I came to Rome the total comes to forty-five.

6. While I was living in Sicily—I went there about the fifteenth year of the reign of Gallienus—Plotinus wrote and sent me these five treatises:

46. On Well-Being (I. 4).

47. On Providence I (III. 2).

48. On Providence II (III. 3).

49. On the Knowing Hypostases and That Which is Beyond (V. 3).

50. On Love (III. 5).

He sent me these in the first year of the reign of Claudius. At the beginning of the second year, shortly before his death, he sent these:

51. On the Nature of Evils (I. 8).

52. Whether the Stars are Causes (II. 3).

γ΄ Τί τὸ ζῷον; [I. 1].

οὗ ἡ ἀρχή· ἡδοναὶ καὶ λῦπαι.

δ΄ Περὶ εὐδαιμονίας· [I. 7].

25

οὗ ἡ ἀρχή· ἆρ᾽ ἄν τις ἕτερον εἴποι.

Ταῦτα μετὰ τεσσαρακονταπέντε τῶν πρώτων
καὶ δευτέρων γραφέντων γίνεται τέτταρα καὶ
πεντήκοντα. Ὥσπερ δὲ ἐγράφη, τὰ μὲν κατὰ
πρώτην ἡλικίαν, τὰ δὲ ἀκμάζοντος, τὰ δὲ ὑπὸ
30 τοῦ σώματος καταπονουμένου, οὕτω καὶ τῆς
δυνάμεως ἔχει τὰ βιβλία. Τὰ μὲν γὰρ πρῶτα
εἴκοσι καὶ ἐν ἐλαφροτέρας ἐστὶ δυνάμεως καὶ
οὐδέπω πρὸς εὐτονίαν ἀρκοῦν μέγεθος ἐχούσης,
τὰ δὲ τῆς μέσης ἐκδόσεως τυχόντα τὸ ἀκμαῖον
τῆς δυνάμεως ἐμφαίνει καί ἐστι τὰ κ̄δ̄ πλὴν τῶν
35 βραχέων τελεώτατα, τὰ μέντοι τελευταῖα ἐννέα
ὑφειμένης ἤδη τῆς δυνάμεως γέγραπται καὶ μᾶλλόν
γε τὰ τελευταῖα τέσσαρα ἢ τὰ πρὸ τούτων πέντε.

7. Ἔσχε δὲ ἀκροατὰς μὲν πλείους, ζηλωτὰς δὲ
καὶ διὰ φιλοσοφίαν συνόντας Ἀμέλιόν τε ἀπὸ τῆς
Τουσκίας, οὗ τὸ ὄνομα ἦν Γεντιλιανὸς τὸ κύριον,
αὐτὸς δὲ διὰ τοῦ ρ̄ Ἀμέριον αὐτὸν καλεῖν ἠξίου
5 ἀπὸ τῆς ἀμερείας ἢ τῆς ἀμελείας πρέπειν αὐτῷ
καλεῖσθαι λέγων. Ἔσχε δὲ καὶ ἰατρικόν τινα
Σκυθοπολίτην Παυλῖνον ὃν ὁ Ἀμέλιος Μίκκαλον
προσηγόρευε, παρακουσμάτων πλήρη γεγονότα.
Ἀλλὰ μὴν καὶ Ἀλεξανδρέα Εὐστόχιον ἰατρικὸν
ἔσχεν ἕτερον, ὃς περὶ τὰ τελευταῖα τῆς ἡλικίας
10 γνωρισθεὶς αὐτῷ διέμενε θεραπεύων ἄχρι τοῦ
θανάτου καὶ μόνοις τοῖς Πλωτίνου σχολάζων
ἕξιν περιεβάλλετο γνησίου φιλοσόφου. Συνῆν δὲ
καὶ Ζωτικὸς κριτικός τε καὶ ποιητικός, ὃς καὶ τὰ

53. What is the Living Being? (I. 1).

54. On Well-Being (I. 7).

These, with the forty-five of the first and second sets that he wrote, amount to fifty-four. The power of the treatises varies according to the period in which he wrote them, in early life, in his prime, or in his illness. The first twenty-one show a slighter capacity, not yet attaining to the dimensions of his full vigour. Those produced in his middle period reveal his power at its height: these twenty-four, except for the short ones, are of the highest perfection. The last nine were written when his power was already failing, and this is more apparent in the last four than in the five which precede them.

7. He had many hearers, and some who were brought together by a real enthusiasm for philosophy. Among these was Amelius of Tuscany, whose family name was Gentilianus; the master preferred to substitute R for L and call him Amerius, saying that it suited him better to take his name from *amereia* (indivisibility) than *ameleia* (indifference). There was also a medical man, Paulinus of Scythopolis, whom Amelius used to call Mikkalos—he always got things wrong. There was too another medical man, Eustochius of Alexandria, who came to know Plotinus towards the end of his life and stayed with him and tended him till his death. He devoted himself entirely to the thought of Plotinus and acquired the character of a genuine philosopher.[1] Zoticus the critic and poet was also one of the com-

---

[1] For the edition which Eustochius made of the writings of Plotinus see Introduction (p. ix) and the references there given.

Ἀντιμάχου διορθωτικὰ πεποίηται καὶ τὸν
"'Ατλαντικὸν" εἰς ποίησιν μετέβαλε πάνυ ποιη-
15 τικῶς, συγχυθεὶς δὲ τὰς ὄψεις πρὸ ὀλίγου τῆς
Πλωτίνου τελευτῆς ἀπέθανεν. Ἔφθασε δὲ καὶ ὁ
Παυλῖνος προαποθανὼν τοῦ Πλωτίνου. Ἔσχε δὲ
καὶ Ζῆθον ἑταῖρον, Ἀράβιον τὸ γένος, Θεοδοσίου
τοῦ Ἀμμωνίου γενομένου ἑταίρου εἰς γάμον
λαβόντα θυγατέρα. Ἦν δὲ καὶ οὗτος ἰατρικὸς
20 καὶ σφόδρα πεφίλωτο τῷ Πλωτίνῳ· πολιτικὸν
δὲ ὄντα καὶ ῥοπὰς ἔχοντα πολιτικὰς ἀναστέλλειν
ὁ Πλωτῖνος ἐπειρᾶτο. Ἐχρῆτο δὲ αὐτῷ οἰκείως,
ὡς καὶ εἰς τοὺς ἀγροὺς πρὸς αὐτὸν ἀναχωρεῖν πρὸ
ἓξ σημείων Μητουρνῶν ὑπάρχοντας, οὓς Καστρί-
25 κιος ἐκέκτητο ὁ Φίρμος κεκλημένος, ἀνδρῶν τῶν
καθ' ἡμᾶς φιλοκαλώτατος γεγονὼς καὶ τόν τε
Πλωτῖνον σεβόμενος καὶ Ἀμελίῳ οἷα οἰκέτης
ἀγαθὸς ἐν πᾶσιν ὑπηρετούμενος καὶ Πορφυρίῳ
ἐμοὶ οἷα γνησίῳ ἀδελφῷ ἐν πᾶσι προσεσχηκώς.
Καὶ οὗτος οὖν ἐσέβετο Πλωτῖνον τὸν πολιτικὸν
ᾑρημένος βίον. Ἠκροῶντο δὲ αὐτοῦ καὶ τῶν ἀπὸ
30 τῆς συγκλήτου οὐκ ὀλίγοι ὧν ἔργον ἐν φιλοσοφίᾳ
μάλιστα ἐποίουν Μάρκελλος Ὀρρόντιος καὶ Σαβι-
νίλλος. Ἦν δὲ καὶ Ῥογατιανὸς ἐκ τῆς συγκλήτου,
ὃς εἰς τοσοῦτον ἀποστροφῆς τοῦ βίου τούτου
προκεχωρήκει ὡς πάσης μὲν κτήσεως ἀποστῆναι,
35 πάντα δὲ οἰκέτην ἀποπέμψασθαι, ἀποστῆναι δὲ
καὶ τοῦ ἀξιώματος· καὶ πραίτωρ προϊέναι μέλλων
παρόντων τῶν ὑπηρετῶν μήτε προελθεῖν μήτε
φροντίσαι τῆς λειτουργίας, ἀλλὰ μηδὲ οἰκίαν
ἑαυτοῦ ἑλέσθαι κατοικεῖν, ἀλλὰ πρός τινας τῶν
φίλων καὶ συνήθων φοιτῶντα ἐκεῖ τε δειπνεῖν
40 κἀκεῖ καθεύδειν, σιτεῖσθαι δὲ παρὰ μίαν· ἀφ' ἧς

26

panions of Plotinus; he corrected the text of Antimachus and made the "Story of Atlantis"[1] into a very good poem. He became blind and died a little before the death of Plotinus: Paulinus also predeceased him. Another of his companions was Zethus, an Arab by race, who married the daughter of Theodosius, a friend of Ammonius. He was another medical man and a close friend of Plotinus, who kept trying to divert him from the affairs of state in which he was active and influential.[2] Plotinus was on terms of great intimacy with him and used to go and stay at his place in the country, six miles from Minturnae. This had formerly belonged to Castricius, surnamed Firmus, who was the greatest lover of beauty of all of us and venerated Plotinus. He was Amelius's faithful servant and helper in every need and as devoted to me, Porphyry, as if I was his own brother. He was again an admirer of Plotinus who had chosen a public career. A good many members of the Senate also attended his lectures, of whom Marcellus Orrontius and Sabinillus worked hardest at philosophy. There was also Rogatianus, a senator, who advanced so far in renunciation of public life that he gave up all his property, dismissed all his servants, and resigned his rank. When he was on the point of appearing in public as praetor and the lictors were already there, he refused to appear or have anything to do with the office. He would not even keep his own house to live in, but went the round of his friends and acquaintances, dining at one house and sleeping at another (but he only ate every other day). As a

[1] Presumably that in Plato's *Critias*.
[2] Or, possibly, "for he was fond of them and had leanings towards a statesman's life."

δὴ ἀποστάσεως καὶ ἀφροντιστίας τοῦ βίου ποδα-
γρῶντα μὲν οὕτως, ὡς καὶ δίφρῳ βαστάζεσθαι,
ἀναρρωσθῆναι, τὰς χεῖρας δὲ ἐκτεῖναι μὴ οἷόν τε
ὄντα χρῆσθαι ταύταις πολὺ μᾶλλον εὐμαρῶς ἢ οἱ
τὰς τέχνας διὰ τῶν χειρῶν μετιόντες. Τοῦτον
45 ἀπεδέχετο ὁ Πλωτῖνος καὶ ἐν τοῖς μάλιστα
ἐπαινῶν διετέλει εἰς ἀγαθὸν παράδειγμα τοῖς
φιλοσοφοῦσι προβαλλόμενος. Συνῆν δὲ καὶ Σερα-
πίων Ἀλεξανδρεὺς ῥητορικὸς μὲν τὰ πρῶτα, μετὰ
ταῦτα δὲ καὶ ἐπὶ φιλοσόφοις συνὼν λόγοις, τοῦ
δὲ περὶ χρήματα καὶ τὸ δανείζειν μὴ δυνηθεὶς
50 ἀποστῆναι ἐλαττώματος. Ἔσχε δὲ καὶ ἐμὲ Πορφύριον Τύριον ὄντα ἐν τοῖς μάλιστα ἑταῖρον, ὃν καὶ
διορθοῦν αὐτοῦ τὰ συγγράμματα ἠξίου.

8. Γράψας γὰρ ἐκεῖνος δὶς τὸ γραφὲν μεταλαβεῖν οὐδέποτ' ἂν ἠνέσχετο, ἀλλ' οὐδὲ ἅπαξ γοῦν
ἀναγνῶναι καὶ διελθεῖν διὰ τὸ τὴν ὅρασιν μὴ
ὑπηρετεῖσθαι αὐτῷ πρὸς τὴν ἀνάγνωσιν. Ἔγραφε
5 δὲ οὔτε εἰς κάλλος ἀποτυπούμενος τὰ γράμματα
οὔτε εὐσήμως τὰς συλλαβὰς διαιρῶν οὔτε τῆς
ὀρθογραφίας φροντίζων, ἀλλὰ μόνον τοῦ νοῦ
ἐχόμενος καί, ὃ πάντες ἐθαυμάζομεν, ἐκεῖνο ποιῶν
ἄχρι τελευτῆς διετέλεσε. Συντελέσας γὰρ παρ'
ἑαυτῷ ἀπ' ἀρχῆς ἄχρι τέλους τὸ σκέμμα, ἔπειτα
10 εἰς γραφὴν παραδιδοὺς ἃ ἐσκέπτετο, συνεῖρεν
οὕτω γράφων ἃ ἐν τῇ ψυχῇ διέθηκεν, ὡς ἀπὸ
βιβλίου δοκεῖν μεταβάλλειν τὰ γραφόμενα· ἐπεὶ
καὶ διαλεγόμενος πρός τινα καὶ συνείρων τὰς
ὁμιλίας πρὸς τῷ σκέμματι ἦν, ὡς ἅμα ἀποπλη-
ροῦν τὸ ἀναγκαῖον τῆς ὁμιλίας καὶ τῶν ἐν σκέψει
15 προκειμένων ἀδιάκοπον τηρεῖν τὴν διάνοιαν·
ἀποστάντος γοῦν τοῦ προσδιαλεγομένου οὐδ'

result of this renunciation and indifference to the needs of life, though he had been so gouty that he had to be carried in a chair, he regained his health, and, though he had not been able to stretch out his hands, he became able to use them much more easily than professional handicraftsmen. Plotinus regarded him with great favour and praised him highly, and frequently held him up as an example to all who practised philosophy. Another companion was Serapion of Alexandria, who began as a rhetorician and afterwards took to the study of philosophy as well, but was unable to free himself from the degradation of finance and money-lending. I myself, Porphyry of Tyre, was one of Plotinus's closest friends, and he entrusted to me the editing of his writings.

8. When Plotinus had written anything he could never bear to go over it twice; even to read it through once was too much for him, as his eyesight did not serve him well for reading. In writing he did not form the letters with any regard to appearance or divide his syllables correctly, and he paid no attention to spelling. He was wholly concerned with thought; and, which surprised us all, he went on in this way right up to the end. He worked out his train of thought from beginning to end in his own mind, and then, when he wrote it down, since he had set it all in order in his mind, he wrote as continuously as if he was copying from a book. Even if he was talking to someone, engaged in continuous conversation, he kept to his train of thought. He could take his necessary part in the conversation to the full, and at the same time keep his mind fixed without a break on what he was considering. When the person he had been talking to was gone he did not go over

ἐπαναλαβὼν τὰ γεγραμμένα, διὰ τὸ μὴ ἐπαρκεῖν
αὐτῷ πρὸς ἀνάληψιν, ὡς εἰρήκαμεν, τὴν ὅρασιν,
τὰ ἑξῆς ἂν ἐπισυνῆψεν, ὡς μηδένα διαστήσας
χρόνον μεταξὺ ὅτε τὴν ὁμιλίαν ἐποιεῖτο. Συνῆν οὖν
20 καὶ ἑαυτῷ ἅμα καὶ τοῖς ἄλλοις, καὶ τήν γε πρὸς
ἑαυτὸν προσοχὴν οὐκ ἄν ποτε ἐχάλασεν, ἢ μόνον
ἐν τοῖς ὕπνοις, ὃν ἂν ἀπέκρουεν ἥ τε τῆς τροφῆς
ὀλιγότης—οὐδὲ γὰρ ἄρτου πολλάκις ἂν ἥψατο—καὶ
ἡ πρὸς τὸν νοῦν αὐτοῦ διαρκὴς ἐπισροφή.

9. Ἔσχε δὲ καὶ γυναῖκας σφόδρα φιλοσοφίᾳ προσ-
κειμένας, Γεμίναν τε, ἧς καὶ ἐν οἰκίᾳ κατῴκει,
καὶ τὴν ταύτης θυγατέρα Γεμίναν, ὁμοίως τῇ μητρὶ
καλουμένην, Ἀμφίκλειάν τε τὴν Ἀρίστωνος τοῦ
5 Ἰαμβλίχου υἱοῦ γεγονυῖαν γυναῖκα[, σφόδρα φιλοσοφίᾳ προσκειμένας]. Πολλοὶ δὲ καὶ ἄνδρες καὶ
γυναῖκες ἀποθνήσκειν μέλλοντες τῶν εὐγενε-
στάτων φέροντες τὰ ἑαυτῶν τέκνα, ἄρρενάς τε
ὁμοῦ καὶ θηλείας, ἐκείνῳ παρεδίδοσαν μετὰ τῆς
ἄλλης οὐσίας ὡς ἱερῷ τινι καὶ θείῳ φύλακι. Διὸ
10 καὶ ἐπεπλήρωτο αὐτῷ ἡ οἰκία παίδων καὶ παρθέ-
νων. Ἐν τούτοις δὲ ἦν καὶ Ποτάμων, οὗ τῆς
παιδεύσεως φροντίζων πολλάκις ἓν καὶ μεταποιοῦν-
τος ἠκροάσατο. Ἠνείχετο δὲ καὶ τοὺς λογισμούς,
ἀναφερόντων τῶν ἐν ἐκείνοις παραμενόντων, καὶ
τῆς ἀκριβείας ἐπεμελεῖτο λέγων, ἕως ἂν μὴ
15 φιλοσοφῶσιν, ἔχειν αὐτοὺς δεῖν τὰς κτήσεις καὶ
τὰς προσόδους ἀνεπάφους τε καὶ σῳζομένας. Καὶ
ὅμως τοσούτοις ἐπαρκῶν τὰς εἰς τὸν βίον φροντίδας
τε καὶ ἐπιμελείας τὴν πρὸς τὸν νοῦν τάσιν οὐδέποτ᾽
ἂν ἐγρηγορότως ἐχάλασεν. Ἦν δὲ καὶ πρᾶος καὶ

---

[1] Or, possibly, "repeating the multiplication table." This
meaning for πολλάκις ἕν, though it does not seem to occur else-

what he had written, because his sight, as I have said, did not suffice for revision. He went straight on with what came next, keeping the connection, just as if there had been no interval of conversation between. In this way he was present at once to himself and to others, and he never relaxed his self-turned attention except in sleep : even sleep he reduced by taking very little food, often not even a piece of bread, and by his continuous turning in contemplation to his intellect.

2. There were women, too, who were greatly devoted to philosophy : Gemina, in whose house he lived, and her daughter Gemina, who had the same name as her mother, and Amphiclea, who became the wife of Ariston, son of Iamblichus. Many men and women of the highest rank, on the approach of death, brought him their children, both boys and girls, and entrusted them to him along with all their property, considering that he would be a holy and god-like guardian. So his house was full of young lads and maidens, including Potamon, to whose education he gave serious thought, and would even listen to him revising the same lesson again and again.[1] He patiently attended to the accounts of their property when their trustees submitted them, and took care that they should be accurate ; he used to say that as long as they did not take to philosophy their properties and incomes must be kept safe and untouched for them. Yet, though he shielded so many from the worries and cares of ordinary life, he never, while awake, relaxed his intent concentration upon the intellect. He was gentle, too, and at the

where, would give a better sense than any rendering or emendation so far put forward.

πᾶσιν ἐκκείμενος τοῖς ὁπωσοῦν πρὸς αὐτὸν
20 συνήθειαν ἐσχηκόσι. Διὸ εἴκοσι καὶ ἐξ ἐτῶν
ὅλων ἐν τῇ Ῥώμῃ διατρίψας καὶ πλείστοις
διαιτήσας τὰς πρὸς ἀλλήλους ἀμφισβητήσεις
οὐδένα τῶν πολιτικῶν ἐχθρόν ποτε ἔσχε.

10. Τῶν δὲ φιλοσοφεῖν προσποιουμένων Ὀλύμπιος Ἀλεξανδρεύς, Ἀμμωνίου ἐπ᾽ ὀλίγον μαθητὴς
γενόμενος, καταφρονητικῶς πρὸς αὐτὸν ἔσχε διὰ
φιλοπρωτίαν· ὃς καὶ οὕτως αὐτῷ ἐπέθετο, ὥστε
5 καὶ ἀστροβολῆσαι αὐτὸν μαγεύσας ἐπεχείρησεν.
Ἐπεὶ δὲ εἰς ἑαυτὸν στρεφομένην ᾔσθετο τὴν
ἐπιχείρησιν, ἔλεγε πρὸς τοὺς συνήθεις μεγάλην
εἶναι τὴν τῆς ψυχῆς τοῦ Πλωτίνου δύναμιν, ὡς
ἀποκρούειν δύνασθαι τὰς εἰς ἑαυτὸν ἐπιφορὰς εἰς
τοὺς κακοῦν αὐτὸν ἐπιχειροῦντας. Πλωτῖνος μέν-
10 τοι τοῦ Ὀλυμπίου ἐγχειροῦντος ἀντελαμβάνετο
λέγων αὐτῷ τὸ σῶμα τότε ὡς τ ὰ σ ύ σ π α σ τ α
β α λ ά ν τ ι α ἕλκεσθαι τῶν μελῶν αὐτῷ πρὸς ἄλληλα
συνθλιβομένων. Κινδυνεύσας δὲ ὁ Ὀλύμπιος πολλάκις αὐτός τι παθεῖν ἢ δρᾶσαι τὸν Πλωτῖνον
ἐπαύσατο. Ἦν γὰρ καὶ κατὰ γένεσιν πλέον τι
15 ἔχων παρὰ τοὺς ἄλλους ὁ Πλωτῖνος. Αἰγύπτιος
γάρ τις ἱερεὺς ἀνελθὼν εἰς τὴν Ῥώμην καὶ διά
τινος φίλου αὐτῷ γνωρισθεὶς θέλων τε τῆς ἑαυτοῦ
σοφίας ἀπόδειξιν δοῦναι ἠξίωσε τὸν Πλωτῖνον ἐπὶ
θέαν ἀφικέσθαι τοῦ συνόντος αὐτῷ οἰκείου δαίμονος
καλουμένου. Τοῦ δὲ ἑτοίμως ὑπακούσαντος γίνεται
20 μὲν ἐν τῷ Ἰσίῳ ἡ κλῆσις· μόνον γὰρ ἐκεῖνον τὸν

_____

[1] On the details of Porphyry's account of this curious
episode see E. R. Dodds, *The Greeks and the Irrational*.
Appendix II, iii, *A Séance in the Iseum*. Since Porphyry
connects the writing of the treatise *On Our Allotted Guardian
Spirit* (III. 4) with the affair, it must have taken place before

32

disposal of all who had any sort of acquaintance with him. Though he spent twenty-six whole years in Rome and acted as arbitrator in very many people's disputes, he never made an enemy of any of the officials.

10. One of those claiming to be philosophers, Olympius of Alexandria, who had been for a short time a pupil of Ammonius, adopted a superior attitude towards Plotinus out of rivalry. This man's attacks on him went to the point of trying to bring a star-stroke upon him by magic. But when he found his attempt recoiling upon himself, he told his intimates that the soul of Plotinus had such great power as to be able to throw back attacks on him on to those who were seeking to do him harm. Plotinus was aware of the attempt and said that his limbs on that occasion were squeezed together and his body contracted "like a money-bag pulled tight." Olympius, since he was often rather in danger of suffering something himself than likely to injure Plotinus, ceased his attacks. Plotinus certainly possessed by birth something more than other men. An Egyptian priest who came to Rome and made his acquaintance through a friend wanted to give a display of his occult wisdom and asked Plotinus to come and see a visible manifestation of his own companion spirit evoked. Plotinus readily consented, and the evocation took place in the temple of Isis:[1] the Egyptian

his own arrival in Rome, when he found that treatise already written (ch. 4) and his account of it must be based on hearsay evidence. The treatise which Porphyry regards as prompted by it has in fact nothing to do with theurgic conjurations of this sort. As so often in the *Enneads*, Plotinus takes a popular religious or superstitious belief as his starting-point and transforms it into something quite different in bringing it into line with his own philosophy.

τόπον καθαρὸν φῆσαι εὑρεῖν ἐν τῇ Ῥώμῃ τὸν
Αἰγύπτιον. Κληθέντα δὲ εἰς αὐτοψίαν τὸν δαίμονα
θεὸν ἐλθεῖν καὶ μὴ τοῦ δαιμόνων εἶναι γένους·
ὅθεν τὸν Αἰγύπτιον εἰπεῖν· "μακάριος εἶ θεὸν
ἔχων τὸν δαίμονα καὶ οὐ τοῦ ὑφειμένου γένους τὸν
25 συνόντα." Μήτε δὲ ἐρέσθαι τι ἐκγενέσθαι μήτε
ἐπιπλέον ἰδεῖν παρόντα τοῦ συνθεωροῦντος φίλου
τὰς ὄρνεις, ἃς κατεῖχε φυλακῆς ἕνεκα, πνίξαντος
εἴτε διὰ φθόνον εἴτε καὶ διὰ φόβον τινά. Τῶν οὖν
θειοτέρων δαιμόνων ἔχων τὸν συνόντα καὶ αὐτὸς
30 διετέλει ἀνάγων αὐτοῦ τὸ θεῖον ὄμμα πρὸς
ἐκεῖνον. Ἔστι γοῦν αὐτῷ ἀπὸ τῆς τοιαύτης
αἰτίας καὶ βιβλίον γραφὲν "Περὶ τοῦ εἰληχότος
ἡμᾶς δαίμονος", ὅπου πειρᾶται αἰτίας φέρειν
περὶ τῆς διαφορᾶς τῶν συνόντων. Φιλοθύτου δὲ
γεγονότος τοῦ Ἀμελίου καὶ τὰ ἱερὰ κατὰ νουμη-
νίαν καὶ τὰς ἑορτὰς ἐκπεριιόντος καί ποτε ἀξιοῦντος
35 τὸν Πλωτῖνον σὺν αὐτῷ παραλαβεῖν ἔφη· "ἐκείνους δεῖ πρὸς ἐμὲ ἔρχεσθαι, οὐκ ἐμὲ πρὸς ἐκείνους."
Τοῦτο δὲ ἐκ ποίας διανοίας οὕτως ἐμεγαληγόρησεν,
οὔτ' αὐτοὶ συνεῖναι δεδυνήμεθα οὔτ' αὐτὸν ἐρέσθαι
ἐτολμήσαμεν.

---

[1] If Plotinus had anything more in mind when he said this
than a determination to stop Amelius bothering him, it may
have been something like the view of the sort of spirits who

34

said it was the only pure spot he could find in Rome. When the spirit was summoned to appear a god came and not a being of the spirit order, and the Egyptian said, "Blessed are you, who have a god for your spirit and not a companion of the subordinate order." It was not however possible to ask any questions of the god or even to see him present for longer, as the friend who was taking part in the manifestation strangled the birds which he was holding as a protection, either out of jealousy or because he was afraid of something. So the companion of Plotinus was a spirit of the more god-like kind, and he continually kept the divine eye of his soul fixed on this companion. It was a reason of this kind that led him to write the treatise "On Our Allotted Guardian Spirit," in which he sets out to explain the differences between spirit-companions. When Amelius grew ritualistic and took to going round visiting the temples at the New Moon and the feasts of the gods and once asked if he could take Plotinus along, Plotinus said, "They ought to come to me, not I to them."[1] What he meant by this exalted utterance we could not understand and did not dare to ask.

attend sacrifices which is to be found in Porphyry's *De Abstinentia* II. 37–43; i.e., that they are δαίμονες, sublunary spirits of the lowest rank, and those of them who delight in blood-sacrifices are thoroughly evil δαίμονες. This crowd of lower spirits the philosopher, who lives on the level of Intellect and has the One for his guardian spirit (III. 4. 6), naturally regards as his inferiors, so that it is their duty to attend on him, not his on them. But there are higher ranks of divinities in the Platonic universe, and there is no suggestion, here or in the *Enneads*, that Plotinus thought himself superior to *them*.

35

11. Περιῆν δὲ αὐτῷ τοσαύτη περιουσία ἠθῶν κατανοήσεως, ὡς κλοπῆς ποτε γεγονυίας πολυτελοῦς περιδεραίου Χιόνης, ἥτις αὐτῷ συνῴκει μετὰ τῶν τέκνων σεμνῶς τὴν χηρείαν διεξάγουσα, καὶ
5 ὑπ᾽ ὄψιν τοῦ Πλωτίνου τῶν οἰκετῶν συνηγμένων ἐμβλέψας ἅπασιν· οὗτος, ἔφη, ἐστὶν ὁ κεκλοφώς, δείξας ἕνα τινά. Μαστιζόμενος δὲ ἐκεῖνος καὶ ἐπὶπλεῖον ἀρνούμενος τὰ πρῶτα ὕστερον ὡμολόγησε καὶ φέρων τὸ κλαπὲν ἀπέδωκε. Προεῖπε δ᾽ ἂν καὶ τῶν συνόντων παίδων περὶ ἑκάστου οἷος
10 ἀποβήσεται· ὡς καὶ περὶ τοῦ Πολέμωνος οἷος ἔσται, ὅτι ἐρωτικὸς ἔσται καὶ ὀλιγοχρόνιος, ὅπερ καὶ ἀπέβη. Καί ποτε ἐμοῦ Πορφυρίου ᾔσθετο ἐξάγειν ἐμαυτὸν διανοουμένου τοῦ βίου· καὶ ἐξαίφνης ἐπιστάς μοι ἐν τῷ οἴκῳ διατρίβοντι καὶ εἰπὼν μὴ εἶναι ταύτην τὴν προθυμίαν ἐκ νοερᾶς
15 καταστάσεως, ἀλλ᾽ ἐκ μελαγχολικῆς τινος νόσου, ἀποδημῆσαι ἐκέλευσε. Πεισθεὶς δὲ αὐτῷ ἐγὼ εἰς τὴν Σικελίαν ἀφικόμην Πρόβον τινὰ ἀκούων ἐλλόγιμον ἄνδρα περὶ τὸ Λιλύβαιον διατρίβειν· καὶ αὐτός τε τῆς τοιαύτης προθυμίας ἀπεσχόμην τοῦ τε παρεῖναι ἄχρι θανάτου τῷ Πλωτίνῳ ἐνεποδίσθην.

12. Ἐτίμησαν δὲ τὸν Πλωτῖνον μάλιστα καὶ ἐσέφθησαν Γαλιῆνός τε ὁ αὐτοκράτωρ καὶ ἡ τούτου γυνὴ Σαλωνίνα. Ὁ δὲ τῇ φιλίᾳ τῇ τούτων καταχρώμενος φιλοσόφων τινὰ πόλιν κατὰ
5 τὴν Καμπανίαν γεγενῆσθαι λεγομένην, ἄλλως δὲ κατηριπωμένην, ἠξίου ἀνεγείρειν καὶ τὴν πέριξ χώραν χαρίσασθαι οἰκισθείσῃ τῇ πόλει, νόμοις δὲ χρῆσθαι τοὺς κατοικεῖν μέλλοντας τοῖς Πλάτωνος

11. He had a surpassing degree of penetration into character. Once a valuable necklace was stolen, belonging to Chione, who lived with her children in his house in honourable widowhood. The slaves of the house were assembled before the eyes of Plotinus, and he looked carefully at them all; then, pointing to one man he said, "This is the thief." The man was flogged, and persisted at first in denial, but finally confessed and gave back what he had stolen. He was, too, in the habit of foretelling how each of the children who lived with him would turn out; that Polemon, for instance, would be amorous and short-lived, as he actually was. He once noticed that I, Porphyry, was thinking of removing myself from this life. He came to me unexpectedly while I was staying indoors in my house and told me that this lust for death did not come from a settled rational decision but from a bilious indisposition, and urged me to go away for a holiday. I obeyed him and went to Sicily, since I had heard that a distinguished man called Probus was living near Lilybaeum. So I was brought to abandon my longing for death and prevented from staying with Plotinus to the end.

12. The Emperor Gallienus[1] and his wife Salonina greatly honoured and venerated Plotinus. He tried to make full use of their friendship: there was said to have been in Campania a city of philosophers which had fallen into ruin; this he asked them to revive, and to present the surrounding territory to the city when they had founded it. Those who settled there were to live according to

[1] Joint emperor with Valerian 253–60, sole emperor 260–68.

καὶ τὴν προσηγορίαν αὐτῇ Πλατωνόπολιν θέσθαι,
ἐκεῖ τε αὐτὸς μετὰ τῶν ἑταίρων ἀναχωρήσειν
10 ὑπισχνεῖτο. Καὶ ἐγένετ᾽ ἂν τὸ βούλημα ἐκ τοῦ
ῥᾴστου τῷ φιλοσόφῳ, εἰ μή τινες τῶν συνόντων
τῷ βασιλεῖ φθονοῦντες ἢ νεμεσῶντες ἢ δι᾽ ἄλλην
μοχθηρὰν αἰτίαν ἐνεπόδισαν.

13. Γέγονε δ᾽ ἐν ταῖς συνουσίαις φράσαι μὲν
ἱκανὸς καὶ εὑρεῖν καὶ νοῆσαι τὰ πρόσφορα δυνατώ-
τατος, ἔν δέ τισι λέξεσιν ἁμαρτάνων· οὐ γὰρ ἂν
εἶπεν “ἀναμιμνήσκεται”, ἀλλὰ “ἀναμνημίσκε-
5 ται”, καὶ ἄλλα τινὰ παράσημα ὀνόματα ἃ καὶ
ἐν τῷ γράφειν ἐτήρει. Ἦν δ᾽ ἐν τῷ λέγειν ἡ
ἔνδειξις τοῦ νοῦ ἄχρι τοῦ προσώπου αὐτοῦ τὸ
φῶς ἐπιλάμποντος· ἐράσμιος μὲν ὀφθῆναι, καλ-
λίων δὲ τότε μάλιστα ὁρώμενος· καὶ λεπτός τις
ἱδρὼς ἐπέθει καὶ ἡ πραότης διέλαμπε καὶ τὸ
10 προσηνὲς πρὸς τὰς ἐρωτήσεις ἐδείκνυτο καὶ τὸ
εὔτονον. Τριῶν γοῦν ἡμερῶν ἐμοῦ Πορφυρίου
ἐρωτήσαντος, πῶς ἡ ψυχὴ σύνεστι τῷ σώματι,
παρέτεινεν ἀποδεικνύς, ὥστε καὶ Θαυμασίου τινὸς
τοὔνομα ἐπεισελθόντος τοὺς καθόλου λόγους πράτ-
τοντος καὶ εἰς βιβλία ἀκοῦσαι αὐτοῦ λέγειν
15 θέλειν, Πορφυρίου δὲ ἀποκρινομένου καὶ ἐρωτῶντος
μὴ ἀνασχέσθαι, ὁ δὲ ἔφη· “ἀλλὰ ἂν μὴ Πορφυρίου ἐρωτῶντος λύσωμεν τὰς ἀπορίας, εἰπεῖν τι
καθάπαξ εἰς τὸ βιβλίον οὐ δυνησόμεθα.”

14. Ἐν δὲ τῷ γράφειν σύντομος γέγονε καὶ
πολύνους βραχύς τε καὶ νοήμασι πλεονάζων ἢ

---

[1] Though *laws* with a small *l* seems to be required in the
translation, there can be little doubt that the constitution of
Platonopolis was to be that of the “second-best state”

the laws of Plato,[1] and it was to be called Platonopolis; and he undertook to move there with his
companions. The philosopher would easily have
gained his wish if some of the courtiers, moved by
jealousy, spite, or some such mean motive, had not
prevented it.

13. In the meetings of the school he showed an
adequate command of language and the greatest
power of discovering and considering what was
relevant to the subject in hand, but he made mistakes
in certain words: he did not say *anamimnesketai* but
anamnemisketai and made other slips which he also
constantly committed in his writing. When he was
speaking his intellect visibly lit up his face: there was
always a charm about his appearance, but at these
times he was still more attractive to look at: he
sweated gently, and kindliness shone out from him,
and in answering questions he made clear both his
benevolence to the questioner and his intellectual
vigour. Once I, Porphyry, went on asking him for
three days about the soul's connection with the
body, and he kept on explaining to me. A man
called Thaumasius came in who was interested in
general statements and said that he wanted to
hear Plotinus speaking in the manner of a set
treatise, but could not stand Porphyry's questions
and answers. Plotinus said, "But if when Porphyry asks questions we do not solve his difficulties we shall not be able to say anything at all
to put into the treatise".

14. In writing he is concise and full of thought.
He puts things shortly and abounds more in ideas

described in Plato's *Laws*, rather than the ideal, but in Plato's
own opinion unrealisable, constitution of the *Republic*.

λέξεσι, τὰ πολλὰ ἐνθουσιῶν καὶ ἐκπαθῶς φράζων
† καὶ τὸ συμπαθείας ἢ παραδόσεως †. Ἐμμέμικται
5 δ' ἐν τοῖς συγγράμμασι καὶ τὰ Στωικὰ λανθάνοντα
δόγματα καὶ τὰ Περιπατητικά· καταπεπύκνωται
δὲ καὶ ἡ " Μετὰ τὰ φυσικὰ " τοῦ Ἀριστοτέλους
πραγματεία. Ἔλαθε δὲ αὐτὸν οὔτε γεωμετρικόν
τι λεγόμενον θεώρημα οὔτ' ἀριθμητικόν, οὐ
μηχανικόν, οὐκ ὀπτικόν, οὐ μουσικόν· αὐτὸς δὲ
10 ταῦτα ἐξεργάζεσθαι οὐ παρεσκεύαστο. Ἐν δὲ
ταῖς συνουσίαις ἀνεγινώσκετο μὲν αὐτῷ τὰ
ὑπομνήματα, εἴτε Σεβήρου εἴη, εἴτε Κρονίου ἢ
Νουμηνίου ἢ Γαΐου ἢ Ἀττικοῦ, κἀν τοῖς Περιπατη-
τικοῖς τά τε Ἀσπασίου καὶ Ἀλεξάνδρου Ἀδράστου
15 τε καὶ τῶν ἐμπεσόντων. Ἐλέγετο δὲ ἐκ τούτων
οὐδὲν καθάπαξ, ἀλλ' ἴδιος ἦν καὶ ἐξηλλαγμένος
ἐν τῇ θεωρίᾳ καὶ τὸν Ἀμμωνίου φέρων νοῦν ἐν
ταῖς ἐξετάσεσιν. Ἐπληροῦτο δὲ ταχέως καὶ δι'
ὀλίγων δοὺς νοῦν βαθέος θεωρήματος ἀνίστατο.
Ἀναγνωσθέντος δὲ αὐτῷ τοῦ τε " Περὶ ἀρχῶν "
Λογγίνου καὶ τοῦ " Φιλαρχαίου ", " φιλόλογος
20 μέν ", ἔφη, " ὁ Λογγῖνος, φιλόσοφος δὲ οὐδαμῶς ".
Ὠριγένους δὲ ἀπαντήσαντός ποτε εἰς τὴν συνουσίαν
πληρωθεὶς ἐρυθήματος ἀνίστασθαι μὲν ἐβούλετο,

---

[1] On Severus, Cronius, Numenius, Gaius and Atticus, see
John Dillon *The Middle Platonists* (Duckworth, London 1977).
Atticus was the chief representative of the anti-Aristotelian
group among the Middle Platonists. Cronius and Numenius
are usually mentioned together and classed as Pythagoreans,
though the boundary between Platonists and Pythagoreans
was ill-defined, and Porphyry here quite naturally groups
them with the Platonists. Numenius (late 2nd century) was

than in words; he generally expresses himself in a tone of rapt inspiration, and states what he himself really feels about the matter and not what has been handed down by tradition. His writings, however, are full of concealed Stoic and Peripatetic doctrines. Aristotle's *Metaphysics*, in particular, is concentrated in them. He had a complete knowledge of geometry, arithmetic, mechanics, optics and music, but was not disposed to apply himself to detailed research in these subjects. In the meetings of the school he used to have the commentaries read, perhaps of Severus, perhaps of Cronius or Numenius or Gaius or Atticus, and among the Peripatetics of Aspasius, Alexander, Adrastus, and others that were available.[1] But he did not just speak straight out of these books but took a distinctive personal line in his consideration, and brought the mind of Ammonius to bear on the investigations in hand. He quickly absorbed what was read, and would give the sense of some profound subject of study in a few words and pass on. When Longinus's[2] work *On Principles* and his *Lover of Antiquity* were read to him, he said, "Longinus is a scholar, but certainly not a philosopher." When Origen[3] once came to a meeting of the school he was filled with embarrassment and

one of the most important philosophers of the generation before Plotinus, who was sometimes accused of plagiarising his thought (see below, ch. 17). Alexander of Aphrodisias (head of the Peripatetic school at Atheus at the beginning of the 3rd century) was the greatest of the ancient commentators on Aristotle. Aspasius and Adrastus were Aristotelian commentators of the 2nd century. This passage shows clearly how scholarly and professional a philosopher Plotinus was and how he worked, though with great originality, on the basis of an extensive school tradition.

[2] For Longinus see below, ch. 19 n.1.   [3] See note on ch. 3.

λέγειν δὲ ὑπὸ Ὠριγένους ἀξιούμενος ἔφη ἀνίλ-
λεσθαι τὰς προθυμίας, ὅταν ἴδῃ ὁ λέγων, ὅτι
πρὸς εἰδότας ἐρεῖ ἃ αὐτὸς λέγειν μέλλει· καὶ
25 οὕτως ὀλίγα διαλεχθεὶς ἐξανέστη.
15. Ἐμοῦ δὲ ἐν Πλατωνείοις ποίημα ἀναγνόντος
"Τὸν ἱερὸν γάμον", καί τινος διὰ τὸ μυστικῶς
πολλὰ μετ' ἐνθουσιασμοῦ ἐπικεκρυμμένως εἰρῆσθαι
εἰπόντος μαίνεσθαι τὸν Πορφύριον, ἐκεῖνος εἰς
5 ἐπήκοον ἔφη πάντων· "ἔδειξας ὁμοῦ καὶ τὸν
ποιητὴν καὶ τὸν φιλόσοφον καὶ τὸν ἱεροφάντην."
Ὅτε δὲ ὁ ῥήτωρ Διοφάνης ἀνέγνω ὑπὲρ Ἀλκι-
βιάδου τοῦ ἐν τῷ "Συμποσίῳ" τοῦ Πλάτωνος
ἀπολογίαν δογματίζων χρῆναι ἀρετῆς ἕνεκα μαθή-
σεως εἰς συνουσίαν αὐτὸν παρέχειν ἐρῶντι ἀφρο-
10 δισίου μίξεως τῷ καθηγεμόνι, ἦιξε μὲν πολλάκις
ἀναστὰς ἀπαλλαγῆναι τῆς συνόδου, ἐπισχὼν δ'
ἑαυτὸν μετὰ τὴν διάλυσιν τοῦ ἀκουστηρίου ἐμοὶ
Πορφυρίῳ ἀντιγράψαι προσέταξε. Μὴ θέλοντος
δὲ τοῦ Διοφάνους τὸ βιβλίον δοῦναι διὰ τῆς
15 μνήμης ἀναληφθέντων τῶν ἐπιχειρημάτων ἀντιγράψας ἐγὼ καὶ ἐπὶ τῶν αὐτῶν ἀκροατῶν συνηγμένων ἀναγνοὺς τοσοῦτον τὸν Πλωτῖνον ηὔφρανα,
ὡς κἂν ταῖς συνουσίαις συνεχῶς ἐπιλέγειν·
"Βάλλ' οὕτως, αἴ κέν τι φόως ἄνδρεσσι γένηαι."[1]
Γράφοντος δὲ Εὐβούλου Ἀθήνηθεν τοῦ Πλατωνικοῦ διαδόχου καὶ πέμποντος συγγράμματα ὑπὲρ
20 τινων Πλατωνικῶν ζητημάτων ἐμοὶ Πορφυρίῳ
ταῦτα δίδοσθαι ἐποίει καὶ σκοπεῖν καὶ ἀναφέρειν
αὐτῷ τὰ γεγραμμένα ἠξίου. Προσεῖχε δὲ τοῖς
μὲν περὶ τῶν ἀστέρων κανόσιν οὐ πάνυ τι μαθημα-

---

[1] Iliad 8.282 (with ἄνδρεσσι for Δαναοῖσι).

wanted to stop lecturing, and when Origen urged him to continue he said, " It damps one's enthusiasm for speaking when one sees that one's audience knows already what one is going to say "; and after talking for a little while he brought the session to an end.

15. At Plato's feast I read a poem, " The Sacred Marriage "; and because much in it was expressed in the mysterious and veiled language of inspiration someone said, " Porphyry is mad." But Plotinus said, so as to be heard by all, " You have shown yourself at once poet, philosopher, and expounder of sacred mysteries." The rhetorician Diophanes read a defence of Alcibiades in Plato's " Banquet " in which he asserted that a pupil for the sake of advancing in the study of virtue should submit himself to carnal intercourse with his master if the master desired it. Plotinus repeatedly started up to leave the meeting, but restrained himself, and after the end of the lecture gave me, Porphyry, the task of writing a refutation. Diophanes refused to lend me his manuscript, and I depended in writing my refutation on my memory of his arguments. When I read it before the same assembled hearers I pleased Plotinus so much that he kept on quoting during the meeting, " So strike and be a light to men." [1]

Eubulus the Platonic Successor wrote to him from Athens and sent treatises on some Platonic questions. Plotinus had them given to me, Porphyry, with instructions to consider them and submit my notes on them to him.

He studied the rules of astronomy, without going very far into the mathematical side, but went more

τικῶς, τοῖς δὲ τῶν γενεθλιαλόγων ἀποτελεσμα-
τικοῖς ἀκριβέστερον. Καὶ φωράσας τῆς ἐπαγγε-
25 λίας τὸ ἀνεχέγγυον ἐλέγχειν πολλὰ τῶν ἐν τοῖς
συγγράμμασιν οὐκ ὤκνησε.

16. Γεγόνασι δὲ κατ' αὐτὸν τῶν Χριστιανῶν
πολλοὶ μὲν καὶ ἄλλοι, αἱρετικοὶ δὲ ἐκ τῆς παλαιᾶς
φιλοσοφίας ἀνηγμένοι οἱ περὶ Ἀδέλφιον καὶ
Ἀκυλῖνον οἳ τὰ Ἀλεξάνδρου τοῦ Λίβυος καὶ
Φιλοκώμου καὶ Δημοστράτου καὶ Λυδοῦ συγ-
5 γράμματα πλεῖστα κεκτημένοι ἀποκαλύψεις τε
προφέροντες Ζωροάστρου καὶ Ζωστριανοῦ καὶ
Νικοθέου καὶ Ἀλλογενοῦς καὶ Μέσσου καὶ ἄλλων
τοιούτων πολλοὺς ἐξηπάτων καὶ αὐτοὶ ἠπατημένοι,
ὡς δὴ πού Πλάτωνος εἰς τὸ βάθος τῆς νοητῆς
οὐσίας οὐ πελάσαντος. Ὅθεν αὐτὸς μὲν πολλοὺς
10 ἐλέγχους ποιούμενος ἐν ταῖς συνουσίαις, γράψας δὲ
καὶ βιβλίον ὅπερ "Πρὸς τοὺς Γνωστικοὺς"
ἐπεγράψαμεν, ἡμῖν τὰ λοιπὰ κρίνειν καταλέλοιπεν.
Ἀμέλιος δὲ ἄχρι τεσσαράκοντα βιβλίων προκε-
χώρηκε πρὸς τὸ Ζωστριανοῦ βιβλίον ἀντιγράφων.
15 Πορφύριος δὲ ἐγὼ πρὸς τὸ Ζωροάστρου συχνοὺς
πεποίημαι ἐλέγχους. Ὅλως νόθον τε καὶ νέον τὸ
βιβλίον παραδεικνὺς πεπλασμένον τε ὑπὸ τῶν τὴν
αἵρεσιν συστησαμένων εἰς δόξαν τοῦ εἶναι τοῦ
παλαιοῦ Ζωροάστρου τὰ δόγματα, ἃ αὐτοὶ εἵλοντο
πρεσβεύειν.

17. Τῶν δ' ἀπὸ τῆς Ἑλλάδος τὰ Νουμηνίου
αὐτὸν ὑποβάλλεσθαι λεγόντων καὶ τοῦτο πρὸς

---

[1] Cp. *Enn.* II. 3. *Whether the Stars are Causes.*

[2] These sectaries were Gnostics. It is very likely that we now
have some of the works to which Porphyry here refers.

carefully into the methods of the casters of horo-
scopes. When he had detected the unreliability
of their alleged results he did not hesitate to
attack many of the statements made in their
writings.[1]

16. There were in his time many Christians and
others, and sectarians who had abandoned the old
philosophy, men of the schools of Adelphius and
Aculinus, who possessed a great many treatises of
Alexander the Libyan and Philocomus and Demo-
stratus and Lydus, and produced revelations
by Zoroaster and Zostrianus and Nicotheus and
Allogenes and Messus and other people of the kind,[2]
deceived themselves and deceiving many, alleging
that Plato had not penetrated to the depths of intelligible reality. Plotinus hence often attacked
their position in his lectures, and wrote the treatise
to which we have given the title " Against the
Gnostics ";[3] he left it to us to assess what he
passed over. Amelius went to forty volumes in
writing against the book of Zostrianus. I, Porphyry,
wrote a considerable number of refutations of the
book of Zoroaster, which I showed to be entirely
spurious and modern, made up by the sectarians to
convey the impression that the doctrines which they
had chosen to hold in honour were those of the
ancient Zoroaster.

17. When the people from Greece began to say
that Plotinus was appropriating the ideas of

The collection of Gnostic books found at Nag Hammadi in
Upper Egypt in 1945 includes "Revelations" attributed to
Allogenes (the Foreigner, a Gnostic name for Seth), Zostrianus,
Messus, and possibly Zoroaster.
  [3] II. 9.

Ἀμέλιον ἀγγέλλοντος Τρύφωνος τοῦ Στωικοῦ τε
καὶ Πλατωνικοῦ γέγραφεν ὁ Ἀμέλιος βιβλίον ὃ
5 ἐπεγράψαμεν "Περὶ τῆς κατὰ τὰ δόγματα τοῦ
Πλωτίνου πρὸς τὸν Νουμήνιον διαφορᾶς", προσ-
εφώνησε δὲ αὐτὸ Βασιλεῖ ἐμοί· Βασιλεὺς δὲ
τοὔνομα τῷ Πορφυρίῳ ἐμοὶ προσῆν, κατὰ μὲν
πάτριον διάλεκτον Μάλκῳ κεκλημένῳ, ὅπερ μοι
καὶ ὁ πατὴρ ὄνομα κέκλητο, τοῦ δὲ Μάλκου
10 ἑρμηνείαν ἔχοντος βασιλεύς, εἴ τις εἰς Ἑλληνίδα
διάλεκτον μεταβάλλειν ἐθέλοι. Ὅθεν ὁ Λογγῖνος
μὲν προσφωνῶν τὰ "Περὶ ὁρμῆς" Κλεοδάμῳ
τε κἀμοὶ Πορφυρίῳ "Κλεόδαμέ τε καὶ Μάλκε"
προὔγραψεν· ὁ δ' Ἀμέλιος ἑρμηνεύσας τοὔνομα,
ὡς ὁ Νουμήνιος τὸν Μάξιμον εἰς τὸν Μεγάλον,
15 οὕτω τὸν Μάλκον οὗτος εἰς τὸν Βασιλέα, γράφει·
"'Ἀμέλιος Βασιλεῖ εὖ πράττειν. Αὐτῶν μὲν
ἕνεκα τῶν πανευφήμων ἀνδρῶν, οὓς διατεθρυλ-
ληκέναι ἐς ἑαυτὸν φῄς, τὰ τοῦ ἑταίρου ἡμῶν
δόγματα εἰς τὸν Ἀπαμέα Νουμήνιον ἀναγόντων,
20 οὐκ ἂν προηκάμην φωνήν, σαφῶς ἐπίστασο.
Δῆλον γὰρ ὅτι καὶ τοῦτο ἐκ τῆς παρ' αὐτοῖς
ἀγαλλομένης προελήλυθεν εὐστομίας τε καὶ εὐγλωτ-
τίας, νῦν μὲν ὅτι πλατὺς φλήναφος, αὖθις δὲ ὅτι
ὑποβολιμαῖος, ἐκ τρίτων δὲ ὅτι καὶ τὰ φαυλότατα
τῶν ὄντων ὑποβαλλόμενος, τῷ διασιλλαίνειν αὐτὸν

---

[1] In fact, the system of Numenius, as far as we know it
from scattered quotations and references in later authors,
shows some resemblances to that of Plotinus, notably in its
descending hierarchy of three gods, the Supreme Good or
Mind, the Second Mind, and the cosmos conceived as an
ensouled divine being. But there are also most important
differences in the way Plotinus conceives his Three Hypostases

Numenius,[1] and Trypho the Stoic and Platonist told Amelius, the latter wrote a book to which we gave the title " On the Difference between the Doctrines of Plotinus and Numenius." He dedicated it to me under the name of Basileus [King]. Basileus was in fact my name, for in my native language I was called Malcus (my father's name), and if one translates Malcus into Greek it is interpreted as Basileus. So when Longinus dedicated his work " On Impulse " to me, Porphyry, and Cleodamus, he began his preface " My dear Cleodamus and Malcus." But Amelius translated Malcus into Basileus, as Numenius did Maximus into Megalos.

This is his letter to me.

" Amelius to Basileus, greeting. You may be sure that, for their own sakes, I should never have said a word in reply to their worships who have been, you say, pestering you with their continual attempts to attribute our friend's doctrines to Numenius of Apamea. For it is obvious that it is only that glibness and readiness of speech in which they take such pride and delight which makes them say at one time that he is a big driveller, at another that he is a plagiarist, or again that his fundamental principles are the meanest of realities:[2] they are clearly attacking him in this

---

and their relation to each other, and as far as we can tell from the evidence available, Amelius and Porphyry seem to be amply justified in claiming originality for their master.

[2] Possibly this is the result of a misunderstanding (which can be paralleled among modern interpreters of Plotinus) of the extreme negativity of the language which he sometimes uses about the One or Good.

PORPHYRY

25 δηλαδὴ κατ' αὐτοῦ λεγόντων. Σοῦ δὲ τῇ προφάσει
ταύτῃ οἰομένου δεῖν ἀποχρῆσθαι πρὸς τὸ καὶ τὰ
ἡμῖν ἀρέσκοντα ἔχειν προχειρότερα εἰς ἀνάμνησιν
καὶ τὸ ἐπ' ὀνόματι ἑταίρου ἀνδρὸς οἵου τοῦ
Πλωτίνου μεγάλου εἰ καὶ πάλαι διαβεβοημένα
ὁλοσχερέστερον γνῶναι ὑπήκουσα, καὶ οὖν ἥκω
30 ἀποδιδούς σοι τὰ ἐπηγγελμένα ἐν τρισὶν ἡμέραις,
ὡς καὶ αὐτὸς οἶσθα, πεπονημένα. Χρὴ δὲ αὐτὰ
ὡς ἂν μὴ ἐκ τῆς τῶν συνταγμάτων ἐκείνων
παραθέσεως οὔτ' οὖν συντεταγμένα οὔτε ἐξειλεγ-
μένα, ἀλλ' ἀπὸ τῆς παλαιᾶς ἐντεύξεως ἀναπεπο-
λημένα καὶ ὡς πρῶτα προὔπεσεν ἕκαστα οὕτω
35 ταχθέντα ἐνταῦθα νῦν συγγνώμης δικαίας παρὰ
σοῦ τυχεῖν, ἄλλως τε καὶ τοῦ βουλήματος τοῦ
ὑπὸ τὴν πρὸς ἡμᾶς ὁμολογίαν ὑπαγομένου πρός
τινων ἀνδρὸς οὐ μάλα προχείρου ἑλεῖν ὑπάρχοντος
διὰ τὴν ἄλλοτε ἄλλως περὶ τῶν αὐτῶν ὡς ἂν
δόξειε φοράν. Ὅτι δέ, εἴ τι τῶν ἀπὸ τῆς οἰκείας
40 ἑστίας παραχαράττοιτο, διορθώσει εὐμενῶς, εὖ
οἶδα. Ἠνάγκασμαι δ' ὡς ἔοικεν, ὥς πού φησιν
ἡ τραγῳδία, ὧν φιλοπράγμων τῇ ἀπὸ τῶν τοῦ
καθηγεμόνος ἡμῶν δογμάτων διαστάσει εὐθύνειν
τε καὶ ἀποποιεῖσθαι. Τοιοῦτον ἄρα ἦν τὸ σοὶ
χαρίζεσθαι ἐξ ἅπαντος βούλεσθαι. Ἔρρωσο."

18. Ταύτην τὴν ἐπιστολὴν θεῖναι προήχθην οὐ
μόνον πίστεως χάριν τοῦ τοὺς τότε καὶ ἐπ'
αὐτοῦ γεγονότας τὰ Νουμηνίου οἴεσθαι ὑποβαλ-
λόμενον κομπάζειν, ἀλλὰ καὶ ὅτι πλατὺν αὐτὸν
5 φλήναφον εἶναι ἡγοῦντο καὶ κατεφρόνουν τῷ μὴ

---

¹ Amelius seems to be referring to his use of the word
εὐθύνειν which occurs in the tragedians (though not ex-

way just for the sake of mocking and jeering at him. But I have conformed to your idea that we should use the occasion to provide ourselves with a statement of the doctrines which we accept in a form easier to remember, and—even though they have long been famous—to make them more widely known, so as to increase the reputation of a friend as eminent as Plotinus is. So here is the work I promised you, written, as you know yourself, in three days. You must treat it with justified indulgence, as there has been no selection or arrangement corresponding to the order of the original attack; I have simply put down my recollections of our former discussions in the order in which they occurred to me; and besides, the intention of our friend, who is being put on trial for the opinions which he shares with us, is not very easy to grasp, because he treats the same subjects in different ways in different places. I am sure, however, that if I have misrepresented any of the doctrines of our spiritual home, you will have the kindness to correct me. As it says in the tragedy,[1] I must correct and reject, since I am a busy man and far from the teachings of our master. So you can see what a business it was to gratify your request as completely as you wished. Farewell."

18. I thought this letter worth inserting, to demonstrate not only that people in his own time thought that he was making a show on a basis of plagiarism from Numenius, but also that they considered he was a big driveller and despised him because they did not understand what he meant

clusively in them). It is the only trace of tragic diction in the works which follow. Amelius's style throughout this letter is excessively pompous and high-flown.

νοεῖν ἃ λέγει καὶ τῷ πάσης σοφιστικῆς αὐτὸν
σκηνῆς καθαρεύειν καὶ τύφου, ὁμιλοῦντι δὲ
ἐοικέναι ἐν ταῖς συνουσίαις καὶ μηδενὶ ταχέως
ἐπιφαίνειν τὰς συλλογιστικὰς ἀνάγκας αὐτοῦ τὰς
ἐν τῷ λόγῳ λαμβανομένας. Ἔπαθον δ' οὖν τὰ
ὅμοια ἐγὼ Πορφύριος, ὅτε πρῶτον αὐτοῦ ἠκροασά-
10 μην. Διὸ καὶ ἀντιγράψας προσήγαγον δεικνύναι
πειρώμενος ὅτι ἔξω τοῦ νοῦ ὑφέστηκε τὸ νόημα.
Ἀμέλιον δὲ ποιήσας ταῦτα ἀναγνῶναι, ἐπειδὴ
ἀνέγνω, μειδιάσας "σὸν ἂν εἴη", ἔφη, "ὦ
Ἀμέλιε, λῦσαι τὰς ἀπορίας, εἰς ἃς δι' ἄγνοιαν
τῶν ἡμῖν δοκούντων ἐμπέπτωκε". Γράψαντος
15 δὲ βιβλίον οὐ μικρὸν τοῦ Ἀμελίου πρὸς τὰς τοῦ
Πορφυρίου ἀπορίας, καὶ αὖ πάλιν πρὸς τὰ
γραφέντα ἀντιγράψαντός μου, τοῦ δὲ Ἀμελίου
καὶ πρὸς ταῦτα ἀντειπόντος, ἐκ τρίτων μόλις
συνεὶς τὰ λεγόμενα ἐγὼ ὁ Πορφύριος μετεθέμην
καὶ παλινῳδίαν γράψας ἐν τῇ διατριβῇ ἀνέγνων·
20 κἀκεῖθεν λοιπὸν τά τε βιβλία τὰ Πλωτίνου
ἐπιστεύθην, καὶ αὐτὸν τὸν διδάσκαλον εἰς φιλο-
τιμίαν προήγαγον τοῦ διαρθροῦν καὶ διὰ πλειόνων
γράφειν τὰ δοκοῦντα. Οὐ μὴν ἀλλὰ καὶ Ἀμέλιος
εἰς τὸ συγγράφειν πρόθυμον ἐποίησεν.

19. Ἣν δὲ ἔσχε καὶ Λογγῖνος περὶ τοῦ Πλωτίνου δόξαν ἐξ ὧν μάλιστα πρὸς αὐτὸν ἐγὼ γράφων
ἐσήμαινον, δηλώσει μέρος ἐπιστολῆς γραφείσης
πρός με ἐπέχον τοῦτον τὸν τρόπον. Ἀξιῶν γάρ

---

[1] Longinus (c. 213–272), scholar, rhetorician, and chief
minister of Zenobia of Palmyra till her defeat and his execu-
tion by Aurelian, had been a pupil of Ammonius, and maintained a philosophical position opposed to that of Plotinus,
especially disagreeing with him about the Platonic Forms or

and because he was so completely free from the staginess and windy rant of the professional speechifier : his lectures were like conversations, and he was not quick to make clear to anybody the compelling logical coherence of his discourse. I, Porphyry, experienced something of the sort when I first heard him. The result was that I wrote against him in an attempt to show that the object of thought existed outside the intellect. He made Amelius read this essay to him, and when the reading was finished smiled and said, " You shall have the task of solving these difficulties, Amelius. He has fallen into them because he does not know what we hold." Amelius wrote a lengthy treatise " In Answer to Porphyry's Difficulties " ; I replied to what he had written ; Amelius answered my reply ; and the third time I with difficulty understood the doctrine, changed my mind and wrote a recantation which I read in the meeting of the school. After this I believed in Plotinus's writings, and tried to rouse in the master himself the ambition to organise his doctrine and write it down more at length ; and Amelius also stimulated his desire to write books.

19. The opinion which Longinus,[1] too, had of Plotinus, derived mainly from what I had told him in my letters, will appear from part of a letter written to me, as follows. He is asking me to come from

Ideas, which he thought of as external to the Divine Mind (cp. chs. 18, 20). Plotinus called him " a scholar, not a philosopher " (ch. 14), which may mean that he stuck closer to the text in his interpretation of Plato and objected to Plotinus's speculative flights on the basis of a small number of passages. It is generally agreed by modern scholars, perhaps for not quite conclusive reasons, that he was not the author of the famous extant critical treatise *On the Sublime*.

5 με ἀπὸ τῆς Σικελίας κατιέναι πρὸς αὐτὸν εἰς τὴν
Φοινίκην καὶ κομίζειν τὰ βιβλία τοῦ Πλωτίνου
φησί·

"Καὶ σὺ μὲν ταῦτά τε πέμπειν, ὅταν σοι δοκῇ,
μᾶλλον δὲ κομίζειν· οὐ γὰρ ἂν ἀποσταίην τοῦ
πολλάκις δεῖσθαί σου τὴν πρὸς ἡμᾶς ὁδὸν τῆς
10 ἑτέρωσε προκρῖναι, κἂν εἰ μηδὲν δι' ἄλλο—τί γὰρ
ἂν καὶ σοφὸν παρ' ἡμῶν προσδοκῶν ἀφίκοιο;—
τήν τε παλαιὰν συνήθειαν καὶ τὸν ἀέρα μετριώ-
τατον ὄντα πρὸς ἣν λέγεις τοῦ σώματος ἀσθένειαν·
κἂν ἄλλο τι τύχῃς οἰηθείς, παρ' ἐμοῦ δὲ μηδὲν
προσδοκᾷ καινότερον, μηδ' οὖν τῶν παλαιῶν
15 ὅσα φὴς ἀπολωλεκέναι. Τῶν γὰρ γραψάντων
τοσαύτη σπάνις ἐνταῦθα καθέστηκεν, ὥστε νὴ
τοὺς θεοὺς πάντα τὸν χρόνον τοῦτον τὰ λειπόμενα
τῶν Πλωτίνου κατασκευάζων μόλις αὐτῶν ἐπε-
κράτησα τὸν ὑπογραφέα τῶν μὲν εἰωθότων ἀπάγων
ἔργων, πρὸς ἑνὶ δὲ τούτῳ τάξας γενέσθαι. Καὶ
20 κέκτημαι μὲν ὅσα δοκεῖν πάντα καὶ τὰ νῦν ὑπὸ
σοῦ πεμφθέντα, κέκτημαι δὲ ἡμιτελῶς· οὐ γὰρ
μετρίως ἦν διημαρτημένα, καίτοι τὸν ἑταῖρον
Ἀμέλιον ᾤμην ἀναλήψεσθαι τὰ τῶν γραφέων
πταίσματα· τῷ δ' ἦν ἄλλα προυργιαίτερα τῆς
τοιαύτης προσεδρείας. Οὔκουν ἔχω τίνα χρὴ
25 τρόπον αὐτοῖς ὁμιλῆσαι καίπερ ὑπερεπιθυμῶν τά
τε 'Περὶ ψυχῆς' καὶ τὰ 'Περὶ τοῦ ὄντος'
ἐπισκέψασθαι· ταῦτα γὰρ οὖν καὶ μάλιστα
διημάρτηται. Καὶ πάνυ βουλοίμην ἂν ἐλθεῖν μοι
παρὰ σοῦ τὰ μετ' ἀκριβείας γεγραμμένα τοῦ
παραναγνῶναι μόνον, εἶτα ἀποπέμψαι πάλιν.
30 Αὖθις δὲ τὸν αὐτὸν ἐρῶ λόγον, ὅτι μὴ πέμπειν,

Sicily to join him in Phoenicia and bring Plotinus's works with me. He says:

"Send them when you like, or, better, bring them: for I shall never stop asking you to give the journey to us the preference over any other, if for no other reason—for surely there is no wisdom which you could expect to learn from us as a result of your visit—for the sake of our old friendship and of the climate, which is particularly good for the ill-health of which you speak. Whatever else you think you may find, do not expect anything new from me, or even the old works which you say you have lost. There is such a shortage of copyists here that really all this time I have been trying to complete my set of Plotinus, and have only just managed it by taking my manuscript-writer away from his usual tasks and setting him to this one only. I have everything, as far as I know, including what you have just sent me; but I have it only half complete, because the manuscripts are extremely full of faults. I thought our friend Amelius would have corrected the mistakes of the copyists, but he had other more urgent duties than this sort of supervision. So I do not see how I am to get acquainted with them, though I am extremely anxious to examine *On The Soul*[1] and *On Being*:[2] for it is just these that are the most faulty. I should be very glad if you could send me the accurately written copies, simply to read for the purpose of comparison and then return; though I again repeat my request to you not to send, but to come yourself

[1] Probably the treatise which now appears as *Enneads* IV. 3–5.

[2] Probably *Enneads* VI. 1–3, another single treatise split up by Porphyry.

ἀλλ' αὐτὸν ἥκειν ἔχοντα μᾶλλον ἀξιῶ ταῦτά τε
καὶ τῶν λοιπῶν εἴ τι διαπέφευγε τὸν Ἀμέλιον.
Ἃ μὲν γὰρ ἤγαγεν, ἅπαντα διὰ σπουδῆς ἐκτησάμην.
Πῶς δ' οὐκ ἔμελλον ἀνδρὸς ὑπομνήματα πάσης
ἰδοὺς ἀξίου καὶ τιμῆς κτήσασθαι; Τοῦτο γὰρ
35 οὖν καὶ παρόντι σοι καὶ μακρὰν ἀπόντι καὶ περὶ
τὴν Τύρον διατρίβοντι τυγχάνω δήπουθεν ἐπεσταλ-
κὼς ὅτι τῶν μὲν ὑποθέσεων οὐ πάνυ με τὰς πολλὰς
προσίεσθαι συμβέβηκε· τὸν δὲ τύπον τῆς γραφῆς
καὶ τῶν ἐννοιῶν τἀνδρὸς τὴν πυκνότητα καὶ τὸ
φιλόσοφον τῆς τῶν ζητημάτων διαθέσεως ὑπερβαλ-
40 λόντως ἄγαμαι καὶ φιλῶ καὶ μετὰ τῶν ἐλλογιμω-
τάτων ἄγειν τὰ τούτου βιβλία φαίην ἂν δεῖν τοὺς
ζητητικούς.''
     20. Ταῦτα ἐπιπλέον παρατέθεικα τοῦ καθ' ἡμᾶς
κριτικωτάτου γενομένου καὶ τὰ τῶν ἄλλων
σχεδὸν πάντα τῶν καθ' αὑτὸν διελέγξαντος
δεικνὺς οἷα γέγονεν ἡ περὶ Πλωτίνου κρίσις·
5 καίτοι τὰ πρῶτα ἐκ τῆς τῶν ἄλλων ἀμαθίας
καταφρονητικῶς ἔχων πρὸς αὐτὸν διετέλει. Ἐδόκει δὲ ἃ ἐκτήσατο ἐκ τῶν Ἀμελίου λαβὼν
ἡμαρτῆσθαι διὰ τὸ μὴ νοεῖν τοῦ ἀνδρὸς τὴν
συνήθη ἑρμηνείαν. Εἰ γάρ τινα καὶ ἄλλα, καὶ τὰ
παρ' Ἀμελίῳ διώρθωτο ὡς ἂν ἐκ τῶν αὐτογράφων
10 μετειλημμένα. Ἔτι δὲ τοῦ Λογγίνου ἃ ἐν συγ-
γράμματι γέγραφε περὶ Πλωτίνου τε καὶ Ἀμελίου
καὶ τῶν καθ' ἑαυτὸν γεγονότων φιλοσόφων ἀναγκαῖον παραθεῖναι, ἵνα καὶ πλήρης γένηται ἡ περὶ
αὐτῶν κρίσις οἷα γέγονε τοῦ ἐλλογιμωτάτου ἀνδρὸς
καὶ ἐλεγκτικωτάτου. Ἐπιγράφεται δὲ τὸ βιβλίον
15 Λογγίνου πρὸς Πλωτῖνον καὶ Γεντιλιανὸν Ἀμέλιον
'' Περὶ τέλους.'' Ἔχει δὲ τοιόνδε προοίμιον·

and bring better copies of these and of any others which Amelius may have overlooked. I eagerly acquired all he brought; of course I should want to possess works of Plotinus, who deserves every possible honour and respect. It is true of course that I have given you word, when you were here, when you were far away, and especially at the time when you were staying in Tyre, that I cannot go very far in agreeing with most of his theories; but I feel the utmost admiration and affection for the general character of his writing, the closeness of his thinking, and the philosophical way in which he deals with his enquiries; and I think that seekers after truth must rank his works among the most important."

20. I have inserted at length this judgement by the most discerning critic of our times, a man who subjected practically all the works of his other contemporaries to drastic investigation, to show what conclusion he came to about Plotinus—though at first, as a result of the stupidity of others, he persisted in despising him. He seems to have misjudged the manuscripts which he received from Amelius because he did not understand Plotinus's usual manner of expressing himself; for if there ever were any carefully corrected copies they were those of Amelius, which were transcribed from the author's own originals. I must also insert what Longinus wrote in a book about Plotinus, Amelius, and the philosophers of his time, to give a complete account of the judgement passed on them by this most outstanding man and extremely severe critic. The title of the book is *On The End: by Longinus in answer to Plotinus and Gentilianus Amelius*. This is its preface:

" Πολλῶν καθ' ἡμᾶς, ὦ Μάρκελλε, γεγενημένων
φιλοσόφων οὐχ ἥκιστα παρὰ τοὺς πρώτους τῆς
ἡλικίας ἡμῶν χρόνους· ὁ μὲν γὰρ νῦν καιρὸς
20 οὐδ' εἰπεῖν ἔστιν ὅσην σπάνιν ἔσχηκε τοῦ πράγμα-
τος· ἔτι δὲ μειρακίων ὄντων ἡμῶν οὐκ ὀλίγοι τῶν
ἐν φιλοσοφίᾳ λόγων προέστησαν, οὓς ἅπαντας μὲν
ὑπῆρξεν ἰδεῖν ἡμῖν διὰ τὴν ἐκ παίδων ἐπὶ πολλοὺς
τόπους ἅμα τοῖς γονεῦσιν ἐπιδημίαν, συγγενέσθαι
δὲ αὐτῶν τοῖς ἐπιβιώσασι κατὰ ταὐτὸ συχνοῖς
25 ἔθνεσι καὶ πόλεσιν ἐπιμίξαντας· οἱ μὲν καὶ διὰ
γραφῆς ἐπεχείρησαν τὰ δοκοῦντα σφίσι πραγμα-
τεύεσθαι καταλιπόντες τοῖς ἐπιγιγνομένοις τῆς
παρ' αὐτῶν ὠφελείας μετασχεῖν, οἱ δ' ἀποχρῆναι
σφίσιν ἡγήσαντο τοὺς συνόντας προβιβάζειν εἰς
τὴν τῶν ἀρεσκόντων ἑαυτοῖς κατάληψιν. Ὧν τοῦ
30 μὲν προτέρου γεγόνασι τρόπου Πλατωνικοὶ μὲν
Εὐκλείδης καὶ Δημόκριτος καὶ Προκλῖνος ὁ περὶ
τὴν Τρωάδα διατρίψας οἵ τε μέχρι νῦν ἐν τῇ
Ῥώμῃ δημοσιεύοντες, Πλωτῖνος καὶ Γεντιλιανὸς
Ἀμέλιος ὁ τούτου γνώριμος, Στωικῶν δὲ Θεμι-
στοκλῆς καὶ Φοιβίων οἵ τε μέχρι πρώην ἀκμάσαντες
35 Ἄννιός τε καὶ Μήδιος, Περιπατητικῶν δὲ ὁ
Ἀλεξανδρεὺς Ἡλιόδωρος. Τοῦ δὲ δευτέρου Πλατωνικοὶ μὲν Ἀμμώνιος καὶ Ὠριγένης, οἷς ἡμεῖς
τὸ πλεῖστον τοῦ χρόνου προσεφοιτήσαμεν, ἀνδράσιν
οὐκ ὀλίγῳ τῶν καθ' ἑαυτοὺς εἰς σύνεσιν διενεγ-
κοῦσιν, οἵ τε Ἀθήνησι διάδοχοι Θεόδοτος καὶ
40 Εὔβουλος· καὶ γὰρ εἴ τι τούτων γέγραπταί τισιν,
ὥσπερ Ὠριγένει μὲν τὸ 'Περὶ τῶν δαιμόνων',
Εὐβούλῳ δὲ τὸ 'Περὶ τοῦ Φιλήβου καὶ τοῦ
Γοργίου καὶ τῶν Ἀριστοτέλει πρὸς τὴν Πλάτωνος
πολιτείαν ἀντειρημένων', οὐκ ἐχέγγυα πρὸς τὸ
56

THE LIFE OF PLOTINUS

" There have been in our time, Marcellus, many
philosophers, especially in the early part of our life ; I
say this because at the present moment there is an
indescribable shortage of philosophy. When I was a
boy there were not a few masters of philosophical
argument, all of whom I was enabled to see because
from childhood I travelled to many places with my
parents, and became acquainted in the same way
with those who had lived on later in my intercourse
with a great number of peoples and cities. Some of
them undertook to set down their doctrines in writing, so as to give posterity the chance of deriving
some benefit from them ; others thought that all that
was required of them was to lead the members of their
school to an understanding of what they held. Of
the first kind were the Platonists Eucleides and
Democritus,[1] and Proclinus, who lived in the Troad,
and Plotinus and his friend Gentilianus Amelius,
who are still teaching publicly at Rome, and the
Stoics Themistocles and Phoebion and the two
who were in their prime a little while ago, Annius
and Medius, and the Peripatetic Heliodorus, the
Alexandrian. Of the second were the Platonists
Ammonius and Origen, with whom I studied regularly for a very long time, men who much sur-
passed their contemporaries in wisdom, and the
Successors at Athens, Theodotus and Eubulus.
Some of these did write something, for instance
Origen, *On The Spirits* and Eubulus, *On the
Philebus and the Gorgias and Aristotle's objections
to Plato's ' Republic '* ; but these are not enough to

---

[1] The philosophers contemporary with Plotinus mentioned in
this preface are only names to us.

45 μετὰ τῶν ἐξειργασμένων τὸν λόγον αὐτοὺς
ἀριθμεῖν ἂν γένοιτο πάρεργον τῇ τοιαύτῃ χρησαμέ-
νων σπουδῇ καὶ μὴ προηγουμένην περὶ τοῦ
γράφειν ὁρμὴν λαβόντων. Τῶν δὲ Στωικῶν
Ἑρμῖνος καὶ Λυσίμαχος οἵ τε ἐν ἄστει κατα-
βιώσαντες Ἀθηναῖος καὶ Μουσώνιος, καὶ Περιπατητικῶν Ἀμμώνιος καὶ Πτολεμαῖος φιλολογώ-
50 τατοι μὲν τῶν καθ᾽ ἑαυτοὺς ἄμφω γενόμενοι καὶ
μάλιστα ὁ Ἀμμώνιος· οὐ γὰρ ἔστιν ὅστις ἐκείνῳ
γέγονεν εἰς πολυμαθίαν παραπλήσιος. οὐ μὴν καὶ
γράψαντές γε τεχνικὸν οὐδέν, ἀλλὰ ποιήματα καὶ
λόγους ἐπιδεικτικούς, ἅπερ οὖν καὶ σωθῆναι τῶν
55 ἀνδρῶν τούτων οὐχ ἑκόντων οἶμαι· μὴ γὰρ ἂν
αὐτοὺς δέξασθαι διὰ τοιούτων βιβλίων ὕστερον
γενέσθαι γνωρίμους, ἀφέντας σπουδαιοτέροις συγγράμμασι τὴν ἑαυτῶν ἀποθησαυρίσαι διάνοιαν.
Τῶν δ᾽ οὖν γραψάντων οἱ μὲν οὐδὲν πλέον ἢ
συναγωγὴν καὶ μεταγραφὴν τῶν τοῖς πρεσβυτέροις
60 συντεθέντων ἐποιήσαντο, καθάπερ Εὐκλείδης καὶ
Δημόκριτος καὶ Προκλῖνος, οἱ δὲ μικρὰ κομιδῇ
πράγματα τῆς τῶν παλαιῶν ἱστορίας ἀπομνημο-
νεύσαντες εἰς τοὺς αὐτοὺς τόπους ἐκείνοις ἐπεχείρησαν συντιθέναι βιβλία, καθάπερ Ἄννιός τε καὶ
Μήδιος καὶ Φοιβίων, οὗτος μὲν ἀπὸ τῆς ἐν τῇ
65 λέξει κατασκευῆς γνωρίζεσθαι μᾶλλον ἢ τῆς ἐν
τῇ διανοίᾳ συντάξεως ἀξιῶν· οἷς καὶ τὸν Ἡλιό-
δωρον συγκατανείμειέ τις ἄν, οὐδ᾽ ἐκεῖνον παρὰ
τὰ τοῖς πρεσβυτέροις ἐν ταῖς ἀκροάσεσιν εἰρημένα
πλέον τι συμβαλλόμενον εἰς τὴν τοῦ λόγου
διάρθρωσιν. Οἱ δὲ καὶ πλήθει προβλημάτων ἃ
70 μετεχειρίσαντο τὴν σπουδὴν τοῦ γράφειν ἀποδειξά-

justify us in counting them among those who have written extensively on philosophy; they are occasional works of men whose interest was in teaching, not writing, and who did not make authorship their main concern. Of Stoics in this group there are Herminus and Lysimachus and the two who lived in town,[1] Athenaeus and Musonius, and among Peripatetics Ammonius and Ptolemaeus, both the greatest scholars of their time, especially Ammonius; there has been no one who has come near him in learning: but they did not write any work of professional philosophy, only poems and show-speeches which I believe to have been preserved without their consent; they would not have wanted to be known in later times by works of this kind when they had neglected to store up their thought in more serious treatises. Of those who wrote, some produced nothing except compilations and transcriptions of what their predecessors had composed, like Eucleides and Democritus and Proclinus; others recalled to mind quite small points of the investigations of the ancients and set to work to compose treatises on the same subjects as they, like Annius and Medius and Phoebion; this last chose to be distinguished for elegance of style rather than coherence of thought. One might class Heliodorus with these, for he too contributed nothing to the ordered exposition of philosophical thought beyond what his elders had said in their lectures. Those who have shown the seriousness with which they took their writing by the multitude of problems which

---

[1] ἐν ἄστει: probably at Athens, assuming that Longinus is being a little archaistic and literary in his usage. In Hellenistic Egypt the phrase could mean Alexandria.

μενοι καὶ τρόπῳ θεωρίας ἰδίῳ χρησάμενοι Πλωτῖ-
νός εἰσι καὶ Γεντιλιανὸς Ἀμέλιος· ὃς μὲν τὰς
Πυθαγορείους ἀρχὰς καὶ Πλατωνικάς, ὡς ἐδόκει,
πρὸς σαφεστέραν τῶν πρὸ αὐτοῦ καταστησάμενος
ἐξήγησιν· οὐδὲ γὰρ οὐδὲν ἐγγύς τι τὰ Νουμηνίου
5 καὶ Κρονίου καὶ Μοδεράτου καὶ Θρασύλλου τοῖς
Πλωτίνου περὶ τῶν αὐτῶν συγγράμμασιν εἰς
ἀκρίβειαν· ὁ δὲ Ἀμέλιος κατ᾽ ἴχνη μὲν τούτου
βαδίζειν προαιρούμενος καὶ τὰ πολλὰ μὲν τῶν
αὐτῶν δογμάτων ἐχόμενος, τῇ δὲ ἐξεργασίᾳ
πολὺς ὢν καὶ τῇ τῆς ἑρμηνείας περιβολῇ πρὸς τὸν
80 ἐναντίον ἐκείνῳ ζῆλον ὑπαγόμενος. Ὧν καὶ
μόνων ἡμεῖς ἄξιον εἶναι νομίζομεν ἐπισκοπεῖσθαι
τὰ συγγράμματα. Τοὺς μὲν γὰρ λοιποὺς τί τις
ἂν κινεῖν οἴοιτο δεῖν ἀφεὶς ἐξετάζειν ἐκείνους,
παρ᾽ ὧν ταῦτα λαβόντες οὗτοι γεγράφασιν οὐδὲν
αὐτοὶ παρ᾽ αὐτῶν προσθέντες οὐχ ὅτι τῶν κεφα-
85 λαίων, ἀλλ᾽ οὐδὲ τῶν ἐπιχειρημάτων, οὐδ᾽ οὖν ἢ
συναγωγῆς τῶν παρὰ τοῖς πλείοσιν ἢ κρίσεως
τοῦ βελτίονος ἐπιμεληθέντες; Ἤδη μὲν οὖν καὶ
δι᾽ ἄλλων τουτὶ πεποιήκαμεν, ὥσπερ καὶ τῷ μὲν
Γεντιλιανῷ περὶ τῆς κατὰ Πλάτωνα δικαιοσύνης
ἀντειπόντες, τοῦ δὲ Πλωτίνου τὸ ᾽Περὶ τῶν
90 ἰδεῶν᾽ ἐπισκεψάμενοι· τὸν μὲν γὰρ κοινὸν
ἡμῶν τε κἀκείνων ἑταῖρον ὄντα, Βασιλέα τὸν
Τύριον, οὐδ᾽ αὐτὸν ὀλίγα πεπραγματευμένον κατὰ
τὴν Πλωτίνου μίμησιν, ὃν ἀποδεξάμενος μᾶλλον
τῆς παρ᾽ ἡμῖν ἀγωγῆς ἐπεχείρησε διὰ συγγράμματος ἀποδεῖξαι βελτίω δόξαν περὶ τῶν ἰδεῶν τῆς
95 ἡμῖν ἀρεσκούσης ἔχοντα, μετρίως ἀντιγραφῇ
διελέγξαι δοκοῦμεν οὐκ εὖ παλινῳδήσαντα κἂν
τούτοις οὐκ ὀλίγας τῶν ἀνδρῶν τούτων κεκινη-

they treated and have had an original way of thinking are Plotinus and Gentilianus Amelius. Plotinus, it would seem, has expounded the principles of Pythagorean and Platonic philosophy more clearly than anyone before him. The works of Numenius and Cronius and Moderatus and Thrasyllus come nowhere near the accuracy of Plotinus's treatises on the same subjects. Amelius chooses to walk in his footsteps, and mostly holds the same doctrines, but is diffuse in exposition, and in his roundabout method of explanation is led by an inclination opposed to that of Plotinus. Their treatises are the only ones which I consider worth attention. Why should anyone think he ought to turn over the works of the rest and neglect the authors from whom they derived what they wrote, when they did not add anything of their own, even in the arguments, to say nothing of the chief points, and did not try to do anything but collect the opinions of the majority or select the best?

" I have already expressed my own opinions elsewhere, for instance in my reply to Gentilianus about righteousness in Plato, and my examination of Plotinus, *On The Ideas*:[1] for my friend and theirs, Basileus of Tyre,[2] who has himself written a good deal in the manner of Plotinus, whose direction he has preferred to my own, tried to demonstrate in a treatise that the doctrine of Plotinus about the Ideas was better than that which I approve. I think I showed fairly thoroughly in my reply that his change of mind was a mistake; and I dealt with a con-

---

[1] Possibly *Enneads* VI. 7.
[2] I.e., Porphyry, cp. *Life*, ch. 17.

κότες δόξας, ὥσπερ κἂν τῇ πρὸς τὸν Ἀμέλιον
ἐπιστολῇ, μέγεθος μὲν ἐχούσῃ συγγράμματος,
ἀποκρινομένῃ δὲ πρὸς ἄττα τῶν ὑπ' αὐτοῦ πρὸς
100 ἡμᾶς ἀπὸ τῆς Ῥώμης ἐπεσταλμένων, ἣν αὐτὸς
μὲν ἐπιστολὴν ʽΠερὶ τοῦ τρόπου τῆς Πλωτίνου
φιλοσοφίας᾽ ⟨ἐπ⟩έγραψεν, ἡμεῖς δὲ αὐτὸ μόνον
προσηρκέσθημεν τῇ κοινῇ τοῦ συγγράμματος
ἐπιγραφῇ ʽΠρὸς τὴν Ἀμελίου ἐπιστολὴν᾽ αὐτὸ
προσαγορεύσαντες."

21. Ἐν δὴ τούτοις τότε ὡμολόγησε μὲν πάντων
τῶν ἐπ' αὐτοῦ γεγονότων "πλήθει τε προβλημάτων διενεγκεῖν Πλωτῖνόν τε καὶ Ἀμέλιον, τρόπῳ
δὲ θεωρίας ἰδίῳ μάλιστα τούτους χρήσασθαι, τὰ
5 Νουμηνίου δὲ οὐχ ὅτι ὑποβάλλεσθαι καὶ τἀκείνου
πρεσβεύειν δόγματα, ἀλλὰ τὰ τῶν Πυθαγορείων
αὐτοῦ τε ἑλομένου μετιέναι δόγματα, καὶ οὐδ'
ἐγγὺς εἶναι τὰ Νουμηνίου καὶ Κρονίου καὶ
Μοδεράτου καὶ Θρασύλλου τοῖς Πλωτίνου περὶ
τῶν αὐτῶν συγγράμμασιν εἰς ἀκρίβειαν". Εἰπὼν
10 δὲ περὶ Ἀμελίου, ὅτι "κατ' ἴχνη μὲν τοῦ Πλωτίνου ἐβάδιζε, τῇ δὲ ἐξεργασίᾳ πολὺς ὢν καὶ τῇ
τῆς ἑρμηνείας περιβολῇ πρὸς τὸν ἐναντίον ἐκείνῳ
ζῆλον ὑπήγετο", ὅμως μνησθεὶς ἐμοῦ Πορφυρίου
ἔτι ἀρχὰς ἔχοντος τῆς πρὸς τὸν Πλωτῖνον συνουσίας φησὶν ὅτι "ὁ δὲ κοινὸς ἡμῶν τε κἀκείνων
15 ἑταῖρος Βασιλεὺς ὁ Τύριος οὐδ' αὐτὸς ὀλίγα
πεπραγματευμένος κατὰ τὴν Πλωτίνου μίμησιν."
Συνέθηκε ταῦτα ὄντως κατιδών, ὅτι τῆς Ἀμελίου
περιβολῆς τὸ ἀφιλόσοφον παντελῶς ἐφυλαξάμην
καὶ πρὸς ζῆλον τὸν Πλωτίνου γράφων ἀφεώρων.
Ἀρκεῖ τοίνυν ὁ τοσοῦτος ἀνὴρ καὶ ἐν κρίσει
20 πρῶτος ὢν καὶ ὑπειλημμένος ἄχρι νῦν τοιαῦτα

siderable number of the opinions of these philosophers in this and in my letter to Amelius, which is as long as a book, and answers a number of the points in the letter which he addressed to me from Rome, which he entitled *On The Method of the Philosophy of Plotinus.* I was satisfied to give my treatise the ordinary title, calling it *In Answer to the Letter of Amelius*."

21. Longinus, then, admitted at that time in this preface "that among all his contemporaries Plotinus and Amelius were outstanding in the number of problems which they treated and had a particularly original way of thinking, and were so far from plagiarising from Numenius and giving his views the first place in their system that Plotinus deliberately propounded Pythagorean views, and the works of Numenius and Cronius and Moderatus and Thrasyllus come nowhere near the accuracy of Plotinus's treatises on the same subjects." He said of Amelius that "he walked in Plotinus's footsteps, but was diffuse in exposition and in his roundabout method of exposition was led by an inclination opposed to that of Plotinus"; and at the same time, in referring to me, Porphyry, when I was still at the beginning of my association with Plotinus, he says, "my friend and theirs, Basileus of Tyre, who has himself written a good deal in the manner of Plotinus." He put it in this way because he really recognised that I altogether avoided the unphilosophical circuitousness of Amelius and looked to the manner of Plotinus as my standard in writing. The opinion which so great a man, who is, and is recognised as the foremost critic of our time, expressed in writing like this about

γράφων περὶ Πλωτίνου, ὡς, εἰ καὶ καλοῦντί με
τὸν Πορφύριον συνέβη δυνηθῆναι συμμῖξαι αὐτῷ,
οὐδ' ἂν ἀντέγραψεν, ἃ πρὶν ἀκριβῶσαι τὸ δόγμα
γράψαι ἐπεχείρησεν.

22. Ἀλλὰ τίη μοι ταῦτα περὶ δρῦν ἢ περὶ
πέτραν—φησὶν ὁ Ἡσίοδος—λέγειν; Εἰ γὰρ δεῖ
ταῖς μαρτυρίαις χρῆσθαι ταῖς παρὰ τῶν σοφῶν
γεγενημέναις, τίς ἂν εἴη σοφώτερος θεοῦ, καὶ
5 θεοῦ τοῦ ἀληθῶς εἰρηκότος·

    Οἶδα δ' ἐγὼ ψάμμου τ' ἀριθμὸν καὶ μέτρα
       θαλάσσης
    καὶ κωφοῦ ξυνίημι καὶ οὐ λαλέοντος ἀκούω;

Ὁ γὰρ δὴ Ἀπόλλων ἐρομένου τοῦ Ἀμελίου,
ποῦ ἡ Πλωτίνου ψυχὴ κεχώρηκεν, ὁ τοσοῦτον
10 εἰπὼν περὶ Σωκράτους·

    Ἀνδρῶν ἁπάντων Σωκράτης σοφώτατος,

ἐπάκουσον, ὅσα καὶ οἷα περὶ Πλωτίνου ἐθέσπισεν·

    Ἄμβροτα φορμίζειν ἀναβάλλομαι ὕμνον ἀοιδῆς
    ἀμφ' ἀγανοῖο φίλοιο μελιχροτάτοισιν ὑφαίνων
15   φωναῖς εὐφήμου κιθάρης χρυσέῳ ὑπὸ πλήκτρῳ.
    Κλῄζω καὶ Μούσας ξυνὴν ὄπα γηρύσασθαι
    παμφώνοις ἰαχαῖσι παναρμονίαισί τ' ἐρωαῖς,
    οἷον ἐπ' Αἰακίδῃ στῆσαι χορὸν ἐκλήιχθεν
    ἀθανάτων μανίαισιν Ὁμηρείαισί τ' ἀοιδαῖς.
20   Ἀλλ' ἄγε Μουσάων ἱερὸς χορός, ἀπύσωμεν
    εἰς ἓν ἐπιπνείοντες ἀοιδῆς τέρματα πάσης·
    ὕμμι καὶ ἐν μέσσαισιν ἐγὼ Φοῖβος βαθυ-
       χαίτης·

Plotinus is enough to indicate that if I, Porphyry, had been able to converse with him, as he invited me to, he would not have written in opposition things which he took it upon himself to write before arriving at a sufficiently accurate understanding of the doctrine of Plotinus.

22. But "Why should I talk of oak and rock?"[1] as Hesiod says; for if one wants to appeal to the evidence of the wise, who could be wiser than a god, and that god who truly said,

"I know the number of the sand, the measure of the sea.
I understand the dumb, and hear him who does not speak."[2]

For when Amelius asked where the soul of Plotinus had gone, Apollo, who said of Socrates,

"Socrates is the wisest of men"[3]

—hear what a great and noble oracle he uttered about Plotinus: "I begin to strike upon my lyre an immortal song, in honour of a gentle friend, weaving it of the sweetest notes of the tuneful harp struck by the golden plectrum. And I call the Muses to raise their voices with me in a full-noted crying of triumph, a sweep of universal melody, as when they were summoned to set the dance going for Aeacides with divine inspiration in the verses of Homer. Come, sacred company of Muses, let us unite our voices to accomplish the fullness of all song, I, Phoebus of the thick hair, singing in the midst of you.

[1] *Theogony* 35.   [2] Herodotus I. 47.   [3] Diogenes Laertius II. 5. 37.   Cp. Plato, *Apology* 21A 6–7.

δαῖμον, ἄνερ τὸ πάροιθεν, ἀτὰρ νῦν δαίμονος αἴσῃ
θειοτέρῃ πελάων, ὅτ' ἐλύσαο δεσμὸν ἀνάγκης
25 ἀνδρομέης, ῥεθέων δὲ πολυφλοίσβοιο κυδοιμοῦ
ῥωσάμενος πραπίδεσσιν ἐς ἠόνα νηχύτου ἀκτῆς
νῆχε· ἐπειγόμενος δήμου ἄπο νόσφιν ἀλιτρῶν
στηρίξαι καθαρῆς ψυχῆς εὐκαμπέα οἴμην,
ἧχι θεοῖο σέλας περιλάμπεται, ἧχι θέμιστες
30 ἐν καθαρῷ ἀπάτερθεν ἀλιτροσύνης ἀθεμίστου.
Καὶ τότε μὲν σκαίροντι πικρὸν κῦμ' ἐξυπαλύξαι
αἱμοβότου βιότοιο καὶ ἀσηρῶν εἰλίγγων
ἐν μεσάτοισι κλύδωνος ἀνωίστου τε κυδοιμοῦ
πολλάκις ἐκ μακάρων φάνθη σκοπὸς ἐγγύθι
      ναίων.
35 Πολλάκι σεῖο νόοιο βολὰς λοξῇσιν ἀταρποῖς
ἱεμένας φορέεσθαι ἐρωῇσι σφετέρῃσιν
ὀρθοπόρους ἀνὰ κύκλα καὶ ἄμβροτον οἶμον ἄειραν
ἀθάνατοι θαμινὴν φαέων ἀκτῖνα πορόντες
ὄσσοισιν δέρκεσθαι ἀπαὶ σκοτίης λυγαίης.
40 Οὐδέ σε παμπήδην βλεφάρων ἔχε νήδυμος ὕπνος·
ἀλλ' ἄρ' ἀπὸ βλεφάρων πετάσας κληῖδα βαρεῖαν
ἀχλύος ἐν δίνῃσι φορεύμενος ἔδρακες ὄσσοις
πολλά τε καὶ χαρίεντα, τά κεν ῥέα οὔτις ἴδοιτο
ἀνθρώπων, ὅσσοι σοφίης μαιήτορες ἔπλευν.
45 Νῦν δ' ὅτε δὴ σκῆνος μὲν ἐλύσαο, σῆμα δ'
      ἔλειψας
ψυχῆς δαιμονίης, μεθ' ὁμήγυριν ἔρχεαι ἤδη
δαιμονίην ἐρατοῖσιν ἀναπνείουσαν ἀήταις,

---

[1] The oracle is full of Homeric tags: here we have a reminiscence of Odyssey 5, 399 νῆχε δ' ἐπειγόμενος, and this whole
passage seems to be based on an allegorical interpretation of
Odysseus's swim ashore after the wreck of his raft. For the
interpretation (common in late antiquity and adopted by the

"Spirit, man once, but now nearing the diviner lot of a spirit, as the bond of human necessity has been loosed for you, and strong in heart, you swam swiftly[1] from the roaring surge of the body to that coast where the stream flows strong, far apart from the crowd of the wicked, there to set your steps firm in the easy path of the pure soul, where the splendour of God shines round you and the divine law abides in purity far from lawless wickedness.

"Then too, when you were struggling to escape from the bitter wave of this blood-drinking life, from its sickening whirlpools, in the midst of its billows and sudden surges, often the Blessed Ones showed you the goal ever near. Often when your mind was thrusting out by its own impulse along crooked paths the Immortals raised you by a straight path to the heavenly circuits, the divine way, sending down a solid shaft of light so that your eyes could see out of the mournful darkness. Sweet sleep never held your eyes, but scattering the heavy cloud that would have kept them closed, borne in the whirl you saw many fair sights which are hard for human seekers after wisdom to see.

"But now that you have been freed from this tabernacle[2] and have left the tomb[3] which held your heavenly soul, you come at once to the com-

Christians) of the voyages of Odysseus as a symbol of the journey of the soul cp. *Enneads*, I. 6. 8.

[2] The word σκῆνος is used of the body in a highly pessimistic and dualistic passage of the pseudo-Platonic *Axiochus* 366 A1.

[3] A reference to the σῶμα-σῆμα play on words (of Orphic origin) in Plato *Gorgias* 493 A3, where again it is said that life in the body is really death, and separation from it true life for the soul.

ἔνθ’ ἔνι μὲν φιλότης, ἔνι δ’ ἵμερος ἁβρὸς
  ἰδέσθαι,
εὐφροσύνης πλείων καθαρῆς, πληρούμενος αἰὲν
50 ἀμβροσίων ὀχετῶν θεόθεν ὅθεν ἐστὶν ἐρώτων
πείσματα, καὶ γλυκερὴ πνοιὴ καὶ νήνεμος αἰθήρ,
χρυσείης γενεῆς μεγάλου Διὸς ἧχι νέμονται
Μίνως καὶ Ῥαδάμανθυς ἀδελφεοί, ἧχι δίκαιος
Αἰακός, ἧχι Πλάτων, ἱερὴ ἵς, ἧχί τε καλὸς
55 Πυθαγόρης ὅσσοι τε χορὸν στήριξαν ἔρωτος
ἀθανάτου, ὅσσοι γενεὴν ξυνὴν ἐλάχοντο
δαίμοσιν ὀλβίστοις, ὅθι τοι κέαρ ἐν θαλίησιν
αἰὲν εὐφροσύνησιν τ’ ἰαίνεται. Ἆ μάκαρ, ὅσσους
ὀτλήσας ἀριθμοὺς ἀέθλων μετὰ δαίμονας ἁγνοὺς
60 πωλέεαι ζαμενῇσι κορυσσάμενος ζωῇσι.
Στήσωμεν μολπήν τε χοροῦ τ’ εὐδίνεα κύκλον
Πλωτίνου, Μοῦσαι, πολυγηθέος· αὐτὰρ ἐμεῖο
χρυσείη κιθάρη τόσσον φράσεν εὐαίωνι.

23. Ἐν δὴ τούτοις εἴρηται μὲν ὅτι ἀγανὸς
γέγονε καὶ ἤπιος καὶ πρᾷός γε μάλιστα καὶ
μείλιχος, ἅπερ καὶ ἡμεῖς οὕτως ἔχοντι συνῄδειμεν·
εἴρηται δ’ ὅτι ἄγρυπνος καὶ καθαρὰν τὴν ψυχὴν
5 ἔχων καὶ ἀεὶ σπεύδων πρὸς τὸ θεῖον, οὗ διὰ
πάσης τῆς ψυχῆς ἤρα, ὅτι τε πάντ’ ἐποίει ἀπαλλαγῆναι, πικρὸν κῦμ’ ἐξυπαλύξαι τοῦ αἱμοβότου
τῇδε βίου. Οὕτως δὲ μάλιστα τούτῳ τῷ δαιμονίῳ
φωτὶ πολλάκις ἐνάγοντι ἑαυτὸν εἰς τὸν πρῶτον
10 καὶ ἐπέκεινα θεὸν ταῖς ἐννοίαις καὶ κατὰ τὰς ἐν
τῷ “Συμποσίῳ” ὑφηγημένας ὁδοὺς τῷ Πλάτωνι
ἐφάνη ἐκεῖνος ὁ θεὸς ὁ μήτε μορφὴν μήτε τινὰ
ἰδέαν ἔχων, ὑπὲρ δὲ νοῦν καὶ πᾶν τὸ νοητὸν
ἱδρυμένος. Ὧι δὴ καὶ ἐγὼ Πορφύριος ἅπαξ λέγω

pany of heaven, where winds of delight blow, where is affection and desire that charms the sight, full of pure joy, brimming with streams of immortality from the gods which carry the allurements of the Loves, and sweet breeze and the windless brightness of high heaven. There dwell Minos and Rhadamanthus, brethren of the golden race of great Zeus, there righteous Aeacus and Plato, the sacred power, and noble Pythagoras and all who have set the dance of immortal love and won kinship with spirits most blessed, there where the heart keeps festival in everlasting joy. O blessed one, you have borne so many contests, and now move among holy spirits, crowned with mighty life.

"Muses, let us set going our song and the gracefully winding circle of our dance in honour of Plotinus the happy. My golden lyre has this much to tell of his good fortune."

23. The oracle says that he was mild and kind, most gentle and attractive, and we knew ourselves that he was like this. It says too that he sleeplessly kept his soul pure and ever strove towards the divine which he loved with all his soul, and did everything to be delivered and "escape from the bitter wave of blood-drinking life here." So to this god-like man above all, who often raised himself in thought, according to the ways Plato teaches in the *Banquet*,[1] to the First and Transcendent God, that God appeared who has neither shape nor any intelligible form, but is throned above intellect and all the intelligible. I, Porphyry, who am now in my sixty-

[1] 210-11: the second part of Diotima's speech, the "Greater Mysteries," which describes the ascent of the mind to the Absolute Beauty, identical with the Good.

πλησιάσαι καὶ ἑνωθῆναι ἔτος ἄγων ἑξηκοστόν τε
καὶ ὄγδοον. Ἐφάνη γοῦν τῷ Πλωτίνῳ σκοπὸς
15 ἐγγύθι ναίων. Τέλος γὰρ αὐτῷ καὶ σκοπὸς ἦν
τὸ ἑνωθῆναι καὶ πελάσαι τῷ ἐπὶ πᾶσι θεῷ.
Ἔτυχε δὲ τετράκις που, ὅτε αὐτῷ συνήμην, τοῦ
σκοποῦ τούτου ἐνεργείᾳ ἀρρήτῳ καὶ οὐ δυνάμει.
Καὶ ὅτι λοξῶς φερόμενον πολλάκις οἱ θεοὶ κατ-
εύθυναν θαμινὴν φαέων ἀκτῖνα πορόντες, ὡς
20 ἐπισκέψει τῇ παρ' ἐκείνων καὶ ἐπιβλέψει γραφῆναι
τὰ γραφέντα, εἴρηται. Ἐκ δὲ τῆς ἀγρύπνου
ἔσωθέν τε καὶ ἔξωθεν θέας ἔδρακες, φησίν, ὅσσοις
πολλά τε καὶ χαρίεντα, τά κεν ῥέα οὔτις ἴδοιτο
ἀνθρώπων τῶν φιλοσοφίᾳ προσεχόντων. Ἡ γὰρ
25 δὴ τῶν ἀνθρώπων θεωρία ἀνθρωπίνης μὲν ἂν
γέναιτο ἀμείνων· ὡς δὲ πρὸς τὴν θείαν γνῶσιν
χαρίεσσα μὲν ἂν εἴη, οὐ μὴν ὥστε τὸ βάθος ἑλεῖν
ἂν δυνηθῆναι, ὥσπερ αἱροῦσιν οἱ θεοί. Ταῦτα μὲν
οὖν ὅ τι ἔτι σῶμα περικείμενος ἐνήργει καὶ
τίνων ἐτύγχανε δεδήλωκε. Μετὰ δὲ τὸ λυθῆναι
30 ἐκ τοῦ σώματος ἐλθεῖν μὲν αὐτόν φησιν εἰς τὴν
δαιμονίαν ὁμήγυριν, πολιτεύεσθαι δ' ἐκεῖ φιλότητα,
ἵμερον, εὐφροσύνην, ἔρωτα ἐξημμένον τοῦ θεοῦ,
τετάχθαι δὲ καὶ τοὺς λεγομένους δικαστὰς τῶν
ψυχῶν, παῖδας τοῦ θεοῦ, Μίνω καὶ Ῥαδάμανθυν
καὶ Αἰακόν, πρὸς οὓς οὐ δικασθησόμενον οἴχεσθαι,
35 συνεσόμενον δὲ τούτοις, οἷς καὶ οἱ ἄλλοι ὅσοι
ἄριστοι. Σύνεισι δὲ τοιοῦτοι Πλάτων, Πυθαγόρας
ὁπόσοι τε ἄλλοι χορὸν στήριξαν ἔρωτος ἀθανάτου·
ἐκεῖ δὲ τὴν γένεσιν τοὺς ὀλβίστους δαίμονας ἔχειν
70

eighth year, declare that once I drew near and was
united to him. To Plotinus "the goal ever near was
shown" : for his end and goal was to be united to,
to approach the God who is over all things. Four
times while I was with him he attained that goal,
in an unspeakable actuality and not in potency
only. Also it is said that the gods often set him
straight when he was going on a crooked course
"sending down a solid shaft of light," which means
that he wrote what he wrote under their inspection
and supervision.[1] Through inward and outward
wakefulness, the god says, "you saw many fair
sights, hard to see" for men who study
philosophy. The contemplation of men may certainly become better than human, but as compared with
the divine knowledge it may be fair and fine, but not
enough to be able to grasp the depths as the gods
grasp them. Thus much the oracle has told about
Plotinus's activity and fortunes while he was still in
the body. After his deliverance from the body the
god says that he came to "the company of heaven,"
and that there affection rules and desire and joy and
love kindled by God, and the sons of God hold their
stations, who are judges of the souls, as we are told,
Minos and Rhadamanthus and Aeacus ; to them,
the god says, he went not to be judged but to be
their companion, as are the other noblest
of mankind. Such are their companions, Plato,
Pythagoras, and all who "set the dance of
immortal love." There, he says, the most blessed

[1] Note that Porphyry attributes his master's achievement
predominantly to divine inspiration and guidance. This has
little support from the *Enneads*. Plotinus normally thinks
that the philosopher can attain to the divine level without this
sort of special assistance.

βίον τε μετιέναι τὸν ἐν θαλείαις καὶ εὐφροσύναις
καταπεπυκνωμένον καὶ τοῦτον διατελεῖν καὶ ὑπὸ
40 θεῶν μακαριζόμενον.

24. Τοιοῦτος μὲν οὖν ὁ Πλωτίνου ἡμῖν ἱστόρηται
βίος. Ἐπεὶ δὲ αὐτὸς τὴν διάταξιν καὶ τὴν
διόρθωσιν τῶν βιβλίων ποιεῖσθαι ἡμῖν ἐπέτρεψεν,
ἐγὼ δὲ κἀκείνῳ ζῶντι ὑπεσχόμην καὶ τοῖς ἄλλοις
5 ἑταίροις ἐπηγγειλάμην ποιῆσαι τοῦτο, πρῶτον μὲν
τὰ βιβλία οὐ κατὰ χρόνους ἐᾶσαι φύρδην ἐκδεδομένα
ἐδικαίωσα, μιμησάμενος δ' Ἀπολλόδωρον τὸν
Ἀθηναῖον καὶ Ἀνδρόνικον τὸν Περιπατητικόν,
ὧν ὁ μὲν Ἐπίχαρμον τὸν κωμῳδιογράφον εἰς
δέκα τόμους φέρων συνήγαγεν, ὁ δὲ τὰ Ἀριστοτέ-
10 λους καὶ Θεοφράστου εἰς πραγματείας διεῖλε τὰς
οἰκείας ὑποθέσεις εἰς ταὐτὸν συναγαγών· οὕτω
δὴ καὶ ἐγὼ νδ' ὄντα ἔχων τὰ τοῦ Πλωτίνου βιβλία
διεῖλον μὲν εἰς ἓξ ἐννεάδας τῇ τελειότητι τοῦ ἓξ
ἀριθμοῦ καὶ ταῖς ἐννεάσιν ἀσμένως ἐπιτυχών,
15 ἑκάστῃ δὲ ἐννεάδι τὰ οἰκεῖα φέρων συνεφόρησα
δοὺς καὶ τάξιν πρώτην τοῖς ἐλαφροτέροις προβλή-
μασιν. Ἡ μὲν γὰρ πρώτη ἐννεὰς ἔχει τὰ
ἠθικώτερα τάδε·

I. 1.　α΄ Τί τὸ ζῷον καὶ τίς ὁ ἄνθρωπος·
　　　　οὗ ἡ ἀρχή·　ἡδοναὶ καὶ λῦπαι.

20　I. 2.　β΄ Περὶ ἀρετῶν·
　　　　οὗ ἡ ἀρχή·　ἐπειδὴ τὰ κακὰ ἐνταῦθα.

---

[1] Born c. 180 B.C.: chronologist and scholar; a pupil of the
great Aristarchus.
[2] Of Rhodes; 1st century B.C. It was his edition (c. 40 B.C.)
that brought the mature philosophical works of Aristotle
back into general circulation.

72

spirits have their birth and live a life filled full of festivity and joy; and this life lasts for ever, made blessed by the gods.

24. This, then, is my account of the life of Plotinus. He himself entrusted me with the arrangement and editing of his books, and I promised him in his lifetime and gave undertakings to our other friends that I would carry out this task. So first of all I did not think it right to leave the books in confusion in order of time as they were issued. I followed the example of Apollodorus of Athens,[1] who collected the works of Epicharmus the comedian into ten volumes, and Andronicus the Peripatetic,[2] who classified the works of Aristotle and Theophrastus according to subject, bringing together the discussions of related topics. So I, as I had fifty-four treatises of Plotinus, divided them into six sets of nine (Enneads)—it gave me pleasure to find the perfection of the number six along with the nines. I put related treatises together in each Ennead, giving the first place to the less difficult questions.[3]

The First Ennead contains the treatises mainly concerned with morals, as follows:

I. 1. What is the Living Being, and what is Man?[4]

I. 2. On Virtues.

[3] On Porphyry's editorial methods see Introduction (pp. ix–xi).

[4] Again, as in the chronological list, the first words of the treatise have been omitted in the translation. For the variations of the titles in Porphyry's two lists, in the MSS of the *Enneads* themselves, and in references to the treatises by other authors, see the complete table (with commentary) in P. Henry, *États du Texte de Plotin*, ch. I.

I. 3. γ΄ Περὶ διαλεκτικῆς·

  οὗ ἡ ἀρχή· τίς τέχνη ἢ μέθοδος.

I. 4. δ΄ Περὶ εὐδαιμονίας·

25   οὗ ἡ ἀρχή· τὸ εὖ ζῆν καὶ τὸ εὐδαιμονεῖν.

I. 5. ε΄ Εἰ ἐν παρατάσει χρόνου τὸ εὐδαι-
      μονεῖν·

  οὗ ἡ ἀρχή· εἰ τὸ εὐδαιμονεῖν ἐπίδοσιν.

I. 6. ς΄ Περὶ τοῦ καλοῦ·

  οὗ ἡ ἀρχή· τὸ καλὸν ἔστι μὲν ἐν ὄψει.

30 I. 7. ζ΄ Περὶ τοῦ πρώτου ἀγαθοῦ καὶ τῶν
      ἄλλων ἀγαθῶν·

  οὗ ἡ ἀρχή· ἆρ' ἄν τις ἕτερον εἴποι ἀγαθὸν
  ἑκάστῳ.

I. 8. η΄ Πόθεν τὰ κακά·

  οὗ ἡ ἀρχή· οἱ ζητοῦντες πόθεν τὰ κακά.

I. 9. θ΄ Περὶ τῆς ἐκ τοῦ βίου εὐλόγου
      ἐξαγωγῆς·

35   οὗ ἡ ἀρχή· οὐκ ἐξάξεις ἵνα μὴ ἐξίῃ.

Ἡ μὲν οὖν πρώτη ἐννεὰς τάδε περιέχει ἠθικωτέ-
ρας ὑποθέσεις περιλαβοῦσα. Ἡ δὲ δευτέρα τῶν
φυσικῶν συναγωγὴν ἔχουσα τὰ περὶ κόσμου καὶ
τὰ τῷ κόσμῳ ἐνήκοντα περιέχει. Ἔστι δὲ
ταῦτα·

40 II. 1. α΄ Περὶ τοῦ κόσμου·

  οὗ ἡ ἀρχή· τὸν κόσμον ἀεὶ λέγοντες καὶ πρόσθεν
  εἶναι.

II. 2. β΄ Περὶ τῆς κυκλοφορίας·

  οὗ ἡ ἀρχή· διὰ τί κύκλῳ κινεῖται.

II. 3. γ΄ Εἰ ποιεῖ τὰ ἄστρα·

45   οὗ ἡ ἀρχή· ὅτι ἡ τῶν ἄστρων φορὰ σημαίνει.

I. 3. On Dialectic.

I. 4. On Well-Being.

I. 5. Whether Well-Being depends on Extension of Time.

I. 6. On Beauty.

I. 7. On the First Good and the other goods.

I. 8. On the Origin of Evils.

I. 9. On the Reasonable Departure from Life.

These are the treatises contained in the First Ennead, which includes mainly ethical subject-matter. The Second contains a collection of the treatises on natural philosophy, including those on the physical universe and subjects connected with it. They are:

II. 1. On the Universe.

II. 2. On the Circular Motion.

II. 3. Whether the Stars are Causes.

II. 4. δ′   Περὶ τῶν δύο ὑλῶν·
        οὗ ἡ ἀρχή· τὴν λεγομένην ὕλην.

II. 5. ε′   Περὶ τοῦ δυνάμει καὶ ἐνεργείᾳ·
        οὗ ἡ ἀρχή· λέγεται τὸ μὲν δυνάμει, τὸ δὲ ἐνεργείᾳ.

50   II. 6. ς′   Περὶ ποιότητος καὶ εἴδους·
        οὗ ἡ ἀρχή· ἆρα τὸ ὂν καὶ ἡ οὐσία ἕτερον.

II. 7. ζ′   Περὶ τῆς δι᾽ ὅλων κράσεως·
        οὗ ἡ ἀρχή· περὶ τῆς δι᾽ ὅλων.

II. 8. η′   Πῶς τὰ πόρρω ὁρώμενα μικρὰ
          φαίνεται·
55   οὗ ἡ ἀρχή· ἆρα τὰ πόρρω ἐλάττω φαίνεται.

II. 9. θ′   Πρὸς τοὺς κακὸν τὸν δημιουργὸν τοῦ
          κόσμου καὶ τὸν κόσμον κακὸν
          εἶναι λέγοντας·
        οὗ ἡ ἀρχή· ἐπειδὴ τοίνυν ἐφάνη ἡμῖν.

Ἡ δὲ τρίτη ἐννεὰς ἔτι τὰ περὶ κόσμου ἔχουσα
60 περιείληφε τὰ περὶ τῶν κατὰ τὸν κόσμον θεωρου-
μένων ταῦτα·

III. 1. α′   Περὶ εἱμαρμένης·
        οὗ ἡ ἀρχή· ἅπαντα τὰ γιγνόμενα.

III. 2. β′   Περὶ προνοίας πρῶτον·
        οὗ ἡ ἀρχή· τὸ μὲν τῷ αὐτομάτῳ·

65   III. 3. γ′   Περὶ προνοίας δεύτερον·
        οὗ ἡ ἀρχή· τί τοίνυν δοκεῖ περὶ τούτων.

III. 4. δ′   Περὶ τοῦ εἰληχότος ἡμᾶς δαίμονος·
        οὗ ἡ ἀρχή· τῶν μὲν αἱ ὑποστάσεις.

III. 5. ε′   Περὶ ἔρωτος·
70   οὗ ἡ ἀρχή· περὶ ἔρωτος πότερα θεός τις.

III. 6. ς′   Περὶ τῆς ἀπαθείας τῶν ἀσωμάτων·
        οὗ ἡ ἀρχή· τὰς αἰσθήσεις οὐ λέγοντες πάθη.

II. 4. On the Two Kinds of Matter.

II. 5. On What Exists Potentially and What Actually.

II. 6. On Quality and Form.

II. 7. On Complete Intermingling.

II. 8. How Distant Objects appear Small.

II. 9. Against those who say that the Universe and its Maker are Evil.

The contents of the Third Ennead are still concerned with the physical universe; it includes the following treatises dealing with considerations about the universe:

III. 1. On Destiny.

III. 2. On Providence I.

III. 3. On Providence II.

III. 4. On Our Allotted Guardian Spirit.

III. 5. On Love.

III. 6. On the Impassibility of Beings without Body.

III. 7. ζ′ Περὶ αἰῶνος καὶ χρόνου·
οὗ ἡ ἀρχή· τὸν αἰῶνα καὶ τὸν χρόνον.

75 III. 8. η′ Περὶ φύσεως καὶ θεωρίας καὶ τοῦ
ἑνός·
οὗ ἡ ἀρχή· παίζοντες δὴ τὴν πρώτην.

III. 9. θ′ Ἐπισκέψεις διάφοροι·
οὗ ἡ ἀρχή· νοῦς φησιν ὁρᾷ ἐνούσας.

25. Ταύτας τὰς τρεῖς ἐννεάδας ἡμεῖς ἐν ἑνὶ
σωματίῳ τάξαντες κατεσκευάσαμεν. Ἐν δὲ τῇ
τρίτῃ ἐννεάδι ἐτάξαμεν καὶ τὸ "Περὶ τοῦ εἰληχότος ἡμᾶς δαίμονος", ὅτι καθόλου θεωρεῖται τὰ
5 περὶ αὐτοῦ καὶ ἔστι τὸ πρόβλημα καὶ παρὰ τοῖς
τὰ κατὰ τὰς γενέσεις τῶν ἀνθρώπων σκεπτο-
μένοις. Ὁμοίως δὲ καὶ ὁ "Περὶ ἔρωτος" τόπος.
Τὸ δὲ "Περὶ αἰῶνος καὶ χρόνου" διὰ τὸ περὶ
τοῦ χρόνου ἐνταῦθα ἐτάξαμεν. Τὸ δὲ "Περὶ
10 φύσεως καὶ θεωρίας καὶ τοῦ ἑνὸς" διὰ τὸ περὶ
φύσεως κεφάλαιον ἐνταῦθα τέτακται. Ἡ δὲ
τετάρτη ἐννεὰς μετὰ τὰ περὶ κόσμου τὰ περὶ
ψυχῆς εἴληχε συγγράμματα. Ἔχει δὲ τάδε·

IV. 1. α′ Περὶ οὐσίας ψυχῆς πρῶτον·
οὗ ἡ ἀρχή· τὴν τῆς ψυχῆς οὐσίαν τίς ποτέ
ἐστι.

IV. 2. β′ Περὶ οὐσίας ψυχῆς δεύτερον·
15 οὗ ἡ ἀρχή· ἐν τῷ κόσμῳ τῷ νοητῷ.

IV. 3. γ′ Περὶ ψυχῆς ἀποριῶν πρῶτον·
οὗ ἡ ἀρχή· περὶ ψυχῆς ὅσα ἀπορήσαντας δεῖ εἰς
εὐπορίαν καταστῆναι.

IV. 4. δ′ Περὶ ψυχῆς ἀποριῶν δεύτερον·
20 οὗ ἡ ἀρχή· τί οὖν ἐρεῖ.

III. 7. On Eternity and Time.

III. 8. On Nature and Contemplation and the One.

III. 9. Various Considerations.

25. We have arranged these three Enneads to form a single volume. We placed the treatise *On Our Allotted Guardian Spirit* in the Third Ennead because the subject is treated in a general way and the question is one of those which people consider when dealing with the origins of man. The same applies to the treatise entitled *On Love*. We included *Time and Eternity* here because of the discussion of time. *On Nature and Contemplation and the One* is placed here because of the section on Nature. After the treatises on the physical universe comes the Fourth Ennead, containing those dealing with the soul. Its contents are as follows:

IV. 1. On the Essence of the Soul I.

IV. 2. On the Essence of the Soul II.

IV. 3. On Difficulties about the Soul I.

IV. 4. On Difficulties about the Soul II.

Ἡ μὲν οὖν τετάρτη ἐννεὰς τὰς περὶ ψυχῆς
αὐτῆς ὑποθέσεις πάσας. Ἡ δὲ πέμπτη ἔχει μὲν
τὰς περὶ νοῦ, περιέχει δὲ ἕκαστον τῶν βιβλίων ἔν
τισι καὶ περὶ τοῦ ἐπέκεινα καὶ περὶ τοῦ ἐν ψυχῇ
35   νοῦ καὶ περὶ τῶν ἰδεῶν. Ἔστι δὲ τάδε·

IV. 5. On Difficulties about the Soul III, or On Vision.

IV. 6. On Sense-Perception and Memory.

IV. 7. On the Immortality of the Soul.

IV. 8. On the Descent of the Soul into Bodies.

IV. 9. If All Souls are One.

So the Fourth Ennead contains all the treatises whose subject is the soul itself. The fifth includes those on Intellect, and all books in which there is also reference to That Which is beyond Intellect and to the intellect in the soul, and to the Ideas. They are as follows:

V. 1. On the Three Primary Hypostases.

V. 2. On the Origin and Order of the Beings which came after the First.

V. 3. On the Knowing Hypostases and That Which is Beyond.

V. 4. How That which is after the First comes from the First, and on the One.

45   V. 5.   ε΄   Ὅτι οὐκ ἔξω τοῦ νοῦ τὰ νοητὰ καὶ
περὶ τἀγαθοῦ·

         οὗ ἡ ἀρχή·   τὸν νοῦν τὸν ἀληθῆ νοῦν.

     V. 6.   ς΄   Περὶ τοῦ τὸ ἐπέκεινα τοῦ ὄντος μὴ
νοεῖν καὶ τί τὸ πρώτως νοοῦν καὶ
τί τὸ δευτέρως·

         οὗ ἡ ἀρχή·   τὸ μέν ἐστι νοεῖν.

50   V. 7.   ζ΄   Περὶ τοῦ εἰ καὶ τῶν καθέκαστά ἐστιν
εἴδη·

         οὗ ἡ ἀρχή·   εἰ καὶ τοῦ καθέκαστον.

     V. 8.   η΄   Περὶ τοῦ νοητοῦ κάλλους·

         οὗ ἡ ἀρχή·   ἐπειδή φαμεν τὸν ἐν θέᾳ τοῦ νοητοῦ.

     V. 9.   θ΄   Περὶ νοῦ καὶ τῶν ἰδεῶν καὶ τοῦ ὄντος·

55   οὗ ἡ ἀρχή·   πάντες ἄνθρωποι ἐξ ἀρχῆς γενόμενοι.

26. Καὶ τὴν τετάρτην οὖν καὶ πέμπτην ἐννεάδα
εἰς ἓν σωμάτιον κατελέξαμεν.   Λοιπὴν δὲ τὴν ἕκτην
ἐννεάδα εἰς ἄλλο σωμάτιον, ὡς διὰ τριῶν σωματίων
γεγράφθαι τὰ Πλωτίνου πάντα, ὧν τὸ μὲν
5 πρῶτον σωμάτιον ἔχει τρεῖς ἐννεάδας, τὸ δὲ
δεύτερον δύο, τὸ δὲ τρίτον μίαν.   Ἔστι δὲ τὰ τοῦ
τρίτου σωματίου, ἐννεάδος δὲ ἕκτης, ταῦτα·

     VI. 1.   α΄   Περὶ τῶν γενῶν τοῦ ὄντος πρῶτον·

         οὗ ἡ ἀρχή·   περὶ τῶν ὄντων πόσα καὶ τίνα.

10   VI. 2.   β΄   Περὶ τῶν γενῶν τοῦ ὄντος δεύτερον·

         οὗ ἡ ἀρχή· ἐπειδὴ περὶ τῶν λεγομένων δέκα γενῶν
ἐπέσκεπται.

     VI. 3.   γ΄   Περὶ τῶν γενῶν τοῦ ὄντος τρίτον·

         οὗ ἡ ἀρχή·   περὶ μὲν τῆς οὐσίας ὅπῃ δοκεῖ.

V. 5. That the Intelligibles are not outside the Intellect and on the Good.

V. 6. On the Fact that That Which is beyond Being does not think, and on What is the Primary and What the Secondary Thinking Principle.

V. 7. On whether there are Forms of Particulars.

V. 8. On the Intelligible Beauty.

V. 9. On Intellect, the Forms, and Being.

26. So we arranged the Fourth and Fifth Enneads to form one volume. The remaining, Sixth, Ennead we made into another volume, so that all of Plotinus's writings were distributed in three volumes, of which the first contains three Enneads, the second two, and the third one. The contents of the third volume, the Sixth Ennead, are these:

VI. 1. On the Kinds of Being I.

VI. 2. On the Kinds of Being II.

VI. 3. On the Kinds of Being III.

VI. 4. δ΄ Περὶ τοῦ τὸ ὂν ἓν καὶ ταὐτὸ ὂν ἅμα
πανταχοῦ εἶναι ὅλον πρῶτον·

οὗ ἡ ἀρχή· ἆρά γε ἡ ψυχὴ πανταχοῦ τῷ παντὶ
πάρεστι.

VI. 5. ε΄ Περὶ τοῦ τὸ ὂν ἓν καὶ ταὐτὸ ὂν ἅμα
πανταχοῦ εἶναι ὅλον δεύτερον·

οὗ ἡ ἀρχή· τὸ ἓν καὶ ταὐτὸν ἀριθμῷ πανταχοῦ ἅμα
ὅλον εἶναι.

VI. 6. ς΄ Περὶ ἀριθμῶν·

οὗ ἡ ἀρχή ἄρα ἐστὶ τὸ πλῆθος ἀπόστασις τοῦ
ἑνός.

VI. 7. ζ΄ Πῶς τὸ πλῆθος τῶν ἰδεῶν ὑπέστη
καὶ περὶ τἀγαθοῦ·

οὗ ἡ ἀρχή· εἰς γένεσιν πέμπων ὁ θεός.

VI. 8. η΄ Περὶ τοῦ ἑκουσίου καὶ θελήματος
τοῦ ἑνός·

οὗ ἡ ἀρχή· ἆρα ἐστὶν ἐπὶ θεῶν εἴ τι ἔστιν ἐπ᾽
αὐτοῖς ζητεῖν.

VI. 9. θ΄ Περὶ τἀγαθοῦ ἢ τοῦ ἑνός·

οὗ ἡ ἀρχή· ἅπαντα τὰ ὄντα τῷ ἑνί ἐστιν ὄντα.

Τὰ μὲν οὖν βιβλία εἰς ἓξ ἐννεάδας τοῦτον τὸν
τρόπον κατετάξαμεν τέσσαρα καὶ πεντήκοντα
ὄντα· καταβεβλήμεθα δὲ καὶ εἴς τινα αὐτῶν
ὑπομνήματα ἀτάκτως διὰ τοὺς ἐπείξαντας ἡμᾶς
ἑταίρους γράφειν εἰς ἅπερ αὐτοὶ τὴν σαφήνειαν
αὑτοῖς γενέσθαι ἠξίουν. Ἀλλὰ μὴν καὶ τὰ
κεφάλαια τῶν πάντων πλὴν τοῦ "Περὶ τοῦ
καλοῦ" διὰ τὸ λῖψαι ἡμῖν πεποιήμεθα κατὰ τὴν
χρονικὴν ἔκδοσιν τῶν βιβλίων· ἀλλ᾽ ἐν τούτῳ οὐ
τὰ κεφάλαια μόνον καθ᾽ ἕκαστον ἔκκειται τῶν
βιβλίων, ἀλλὰ καὶ ἐπιχειρήματα, ἃ ὡς κεφάλαια

VI. 4. On the Presence of Being, One and the Same, Everywhere as a Whole I.

VI. 5. On the Presence of Being, One and the Same, Everywhere as a Whole II.

VI. 6. On Numbers.

VI. 7. How the Multitude of the Forms came into being and On the Good

VI. 8. On Free Will and the Will of the One.

VI. 9. On the Good or the One.

So we arranged the fifty-four books in this way in six Enneads; and we have included commentaries on some of them, irregularly, because friends pressed us to write on points they wanted cleared up for them. We also composed headings for all of them except *On Beauty*, because it was not available to us, following the chronological order in which the books were issued; and we have produced not only the headings for each book but also summaries of the arguments, which are numbered

συναριθμεῖται. Νυνὶ δὲ πειρασόμεθα ἕκαστον τῶν
βιβλίων διερχόμενοι τάς τε στιγμὰς αὐτῶν
προσθεῖναι καὶ εἴ τι ἡμαρτημένον εἴη κατὰ λέξιν
40 διορθοῦν· καὶ ὅ τι ἂν ἡμᾶς ἄλλο κινήσῃ, αὐτὸ
σημαίνει τὸ ἔργον.

in the same way as the headings.[1]   Now we shall
try to revise all the books and put in the punctuation and correct any verbal errors: anything else
that may occur to us the work itself will make
clear.

[1] On the attempts of modern scholars to discover traces of
the commentaries, headings, and summaries which Porphyry
mentions here in the text of the Enneads see Schwyzer, art.
cit., col. 495–499.   The marginal numbers which appear in
some MSS may be references to Porphyry's lost commentaries:
cp. Henry, *États du Texte de Plotin*, pp. 312–332 and Henry-
Schwyzer I, Preface, p. xxxvii.   The curious "table of
contents" which forms the second part of the Arabic *Theology
of Aristotle* may be a translation of Porphyry's "headings"
for the first 34 chapters of IV 4: cp. Henry-Schwyzer II,
Preface pp. xxvii–xxviii.   The English translation of these
"headings" is printed under the text of IV 4, 1–34.

PLOTINUS

ENNEAD I

SVMMARIVM

Τάδε ἔνεστιν ἐννεάδος πρώτης Πλωτίνου φιλοσόφου·

ENNEAD I. 1

I. 1. WHAT IS THE LIVING BEING,
AND WHAT IS MAN?

Introductory Note

THIS treatise, though placed first by Porphyry in his edition, is the last but one (No. 53) in his chronological order, and was written by Plotinus shortly before his death (*Life*, ch. 6). Its purpose is to establish the impassibility of our higher soul or true self and its separateness from our animal nature, the compound of body and lower soul, which desires and fears, sins and suffers. This Plotinus does by a critical examination of Peripatetic and Stoic doctrine about the nature and functions of soul and its relationship to body, in which he adopts a great deal of Aristotle's teaching in the *De Anima*, but adapts it to his own views. He concludes by discussing the difficulties which arise for his view from Plato's teaching about the transmigration of souls and their judgement and punishment for sin after death.

Synopsis

What is it in us that feels and thinks—soul or body or a compound of both (ch. 1)? First of all what do we mean by soul? Is it a kind of Form? If so it will be impassible and transcend bodily life, giving to body and receiving nothing from it. How then is soul related to body? Our conclusion, after examining various views that have been put forward, is that our higher soul, our true self, is in fact entirely unaffected by the sensations and passions of bodily life; these belong to the compound of lower soul, a sort of emanation from the higher soul, and body; reason, on the other hand, is an activity of our true self (chs. 2–7). The higher realities, Intellect and God, the One or Good who is beyond Intellect, we possess as "ours" in a sense but yet transcending us (ch. 8). Error and sin belong to our lower nature; and so do the moral virtues which result from habit and training; true reasoning and the intellectual virtues belong to our true, higher self (chs. 9–10). After a brief consideration of children's consciousness and the consciousness of transmigrated human souls in animal bodies (ch. 11) we come to the serious problem of how to reconcile our view of the sinlessness of the true self with Plato's teaching about judgement and punishment after death; we conclude that it is the lower soul, the "image" of the higher soul, which sins and is punished and goes to Hades (ch. 12). This investigation, being a properly intellectual activity, has been carried out by our true self or higher soul, and in carrying it out it has moved with a motion which is not that of bodies but its own life (ch. 13).

I. 1. (53) ΠΕΡΙ ΤΟΥ ΤΙ ΤΟ ΖΩΙΟΝ ΚΑΙ ΤΙΣ Ο ΑΝΘΡΩΠΟΣ

1. Ἡδοναὶ καὶ λῦπαι φόβοι τε καὶ θάρρη ἐπιθυμίαι τε καὶ ἀποστροφαὶ καὶ τὸ ἀλγεῖν τίνος ἂν
εἴεν; Ἢ γὰρ ψυχῆς, ἢ χρωμένης ψυχῆς σώματι,
ἢ τρίτου τινὸς ἐξ ἀμφοῖν. Διχῶς δὲ καὶ τοῦτο· ἢ
5 γὰρ τὸ μῖγμα, ἢ ἄλλο ἕτερον ἐκ τοῦ μίγματος.
Ὁμοίως δὲ καὶ τὰ ἐκ τούτων τῶν παθημάτων
γινόμενα καὶ πραττόμενα καὶ δοξαζόμενα. Καὶ
οὖν καὶ διάνοια καὶ δόξα ζητητέαι, πότερα ὧν τὰ
πάθη, ἢ αἱ μὲν οὕτως, αἱ δὲ ἄλλως. Καὶ τὰς
νοήσεις δὲ θεωρητέον, πῶς καὶ τίνος, καὶ δὴ καὶ
10 αὐτὸ τοῦτο τὸ ἐπισκοποῦν καὶ περὶ τούτων τὴν
ζήτησιν καὶ τὴν κρίσιν ποιούμενον τί ποτ' ἂν εἴη.
Καὶ πρότερον τὸ αἰσθάνεσθαι τίνος; Ἐντεῦθεν
γὰρ ἄρχεσθαι προσήκει, ἐπείπερ τὰ πάθη ἤ εἰσιν
αἰσθήσεις τινὲς ἢ οὐκ ἄνευ αἰσθήσεως.

2. Πρῶτον δὲ ψυχὴν ληπτέον, πότερον ἄλλο μὲν
ψυχή, ἄλλο δὲ ψυχῇ εἶναι. Εἰ γὰρ τοῦτο, σύνθετόν
τι ἡ ψυχὴ καὶ οὐκ ἄτοπον ἤδη δέχεσθαι αὐτὴν καὶ

---

[1] The starting-point of the discussion seems to be a passage
of Aristotle, *De Anima* A. 4. 408b 1 ff., where Aristotle raises
the question whether the soul is really "moved" when it has
these affections. It is possible also that Plotinus has in mind
(as Aristotle most probably has) Plato's description at *Laws*
X 897A of the motions of soul which are prior to and the cause
of the motions of body: this seems more relevant to the present

I. 1. WHAT IS THE LIVING BEING, AND WHAT IS MAN?

1. Pleasures and sadnesses, fears and assurances, desires and aversions and pain—whose are they?[1] They either belong to the soul or the soul using a body or a third thing composed of both (and this can be understood in two ways, either as meaning the mixture or another different thing resulting from the mixture). The same applies to the results of these feelings, both acts and opinions. So we must investigate reasoning and opinion, to see whether they belong to the same as the feelings, or whether this is true of some reasonings and opinions, and something different of others. We must also consider intellectual acts and see how they take place and who or what they belong to, and observe what sort of thing it is that acts as overseer and carries out the investigation and comes to a decision about these matters. And, first of all, who or what does sensation belong to? That is where we ought to begin, as feelings are either a sort of sensations or do not occur without sensation.

2. First we must consider soul. Is soul one thing and essential soulness another? If this is so, soul will be a composite thing and there will be nothing

discussion than the passages (*Republic* 429C–D and 430A–B; *Phaedo* 83B) cited by Henry-Schwyzer in their *apparatus fontium*. (They also cite the Aristotle passage.)

αὐτῆς εἶναι τὰ πάθη τὰ τοιαῦτα, εἰ ἐπιτρέψει καὶ
5 οὕτως ὁ λόγος, καὶ ὅλως ἕξεις καὶ διαθέσεις
χείρους καὶ βελτίους. Ἤ, εἰ ταὐτόν ἐστι ψυχὴ
καὶ τὸ ψυχῇ εἶναι, εἶδός τι ἂν εἴη ψυχὴ ἄδεκτον
τούτων ἁπασῶν τῶν ἐνεργειῶν, ὧν ἐποιστικὸν
ἄλλῳ, ἑαυτῷ δὲ συμφυᾶ ἔχον τὴν ἐνέργειαν ἐν ἑαυτῷ, ἥντινα ἂν φήνῃ ὁ λόγος. Οὕτω γὰρ καὶ τὸ
10 ἀθάνατον ἀληθὲς λέγειν, εἴπερ δεῖ τὸ ἀθάνατον καὶ
ἄφθαρτον ἀπαθὲς εἶναι, ἄλλῳ ἑαυτοῦ πως διδόν,
αὐτὸ δὲ παρ' ἄλλου μηδὲν ἢ ὅσον παρὰ τῶν πρὸ
αὐτοῦ ἔχειν, ὧν μὴ ἀποτέτμηται κρειττόνων
ὄντων. Τί γὰρ ἂν καὶ φοβοῖτο τοιοῦτον ἄδεκτον
15 ὂν παντὸς τοῦ ἔξω; Ἐκεῖνο τοίνυν φοβείσθω, ὃ
δύναται παθεῖν. Οὐδὲ θαρρεῖ τοίνυν· τούτοις γὰρ
θάρρος, οἷς ἂν τὰ φοβερὰ μὴ παρῇ; Ἐπιθυμίαι
τε, αἳ διὰ σώματος ἀποπληροῦνται κενουμένου καὶ
πληρουμένου, ἄλλου τοῦ πληρουμένου καὶ κενουμένου ὄντος; Πῶς δὲ μίξεως; Ἤ τὸ οὐσιῶδες
20 ἄμικτον. Πῶς δὲ ἐπεισαγωγῆς τινων; Οὕτω
γὰρ ἂν σπεύδοι εἰς τὸ μὴ εἶναι ὅ ἐστι. Τὸ δ'
ἀλγεῖν ἔτι πόρρω. Λυπεῖσθαι δὲ πῶς ἢ ἐπὶ τίνι;
Αὔταρκες γὰρ τό γε ἁπλοῦν ἐν οὐσίᾳ, οἷόν ἐστι
μένον ἐν οὐσίᾳ τῇ αὐτοῦ. Ἥδεται δὲ προσγε-
νομένου τινός, οὐδενὸς οὐδ' ἀγαθοῦ προσιόντος;

---

[1] Cp. Aristotle, *Metaphysics* H. 3. 1043 b. 3. Ψυχὴ μὲν γὰρ
καὶ ψυχῇ εἶναι ταὐτόν, ἀνθρώπῳ δὲ καὶ ἄνθρωπος οὐ ταὐτόν, εἰ
μὴ καὶ ἡ ψυχὴ ἄνθρωπος λεχθήσεται. "For 'soul' and 'to
be soul' are the same, but 'to be man' and 'man' are not
the same, unless even the bare soul is to be called man"
(Ross). For Plotinus, on this point in opposition to Aris-

strange in its admitting and possessing feelings of
this kind (if the argument turns out to require this),
and in general better and worse states and dispositions. If on the other hand soul and essential soulness are one and the same,[1] soul will be a kind of
Form, which will not admit of all these activities
which it imparts to something else, but has an
immanent connatural activity of its own, whatever
the discussion reveals that activity to be. If this is
so, we can really call it immortal, if the immortal and
incorruptible must be impassive, giving something
of itself somehow to another thing, but receiving
nothing from anything else, except what it has from
the principles prior to it, those higher principles from
which it is not cut off. What could a thing of this
kind fear, since it admits nothing at all from outside?
Let that fear which is capable of being affected!
Nor does it feel assurance. How can there be
assurance for those who never encounter anything
frightening? And how can there be desires, which
are satisfied by the body when it is emptied and filled,
since that which is emptied and filled is different from
the soul? And how could it admit of mixture?
Substantial being is unmixed. How could there be
any sort of addition? If there was, it would be
hastening to be no more what it is. Pain is far from
it too; and how could it feel sad, and what about?
For that which is essentially simple is sufficient for
itself, inasmuch as it stays set in its own essential
nature. And will it be pleased at any increase, when
nothing, not even any good, can accrue to it? It is

totle, the rational soul *is* the "true man," the "man within" (ch. 10): our lower nature is "another man" which
has attached itself to the first man, our true self (VI. 4. 14).

25 Ὃ γάρ ἐστιν, ἔστιν ἀεί. Καὶ μὴν οὐδὲ αἰσθήσεται
οὐδὲ διάνοια οὐδὲ δόξα περὶ αὐτό· αἴσθησις γὰρ
παραδοχὴ εἴδους ἢ καὶ πάθους σώματος, διάνοια
δὲ καὶ δόξα ἐπ᾽ αἴσθησιν. Περὶ δὲ νοήσεως
ἐπισκεπτέον πῶς, εἰ ταύτην αὐτῇ καταλείψομεν·
30 καὶ περὶ ἡδονῆς αὖ καθαρᾶς, εἰ συμβαίνει περὶ
αὐτὴν μόνην οὖσαν.

3. Ἀλλὰ γὰρ ἐν σώματι θετέον ψυχήν, οὖσαν
εἴτε πρὸ τούτου, εἴτ᾽ ἐν τούτῳ, ἐξ οὗ καὶ αὐτῆς
ζῷον τὸ σύμπαν ἐκλήθη. Χρωμένη μὲν οὖν
σώματι οἷα ὀργάνῳ οὐκ ἀναγκάζεται δέξασθαι τὰ
5 διὰ τοῦ σώματος παθήματα, ὥσπερ οὐδὲ τὰ τῶν
ὀργάνων παθήματα οἱ τεχνῖται· αἴσθησιν δὲ τάχ᾽
ἂν ἀναγκαίως, εἴπερ δεῖ χρῆσθαι τῷ ὀργάνῳ
γινωσκούσῃ τὰ ἔξωθεν παθήματα ἐξ αἰσθήσεως·
ἐπεὶ καὶ τὸ χρῆσθαι ὄμμασίν ἐστιν ὁρᾶν. Ἀλλὰ
καὶ βλάβαι περὶ τὸ ὁρᾶν, ὥστε καὶ λῦπαι καὶ τὸ
10 ἀλγεῖν καὶ ὅλως ὅ τι περ ἂν περὶ τὸ σῶμα πᾶν
γίγνηται· ὥστε καὶ ἐπιθυμίαι ζητούσης τὴν
θεραπείαν τοῦ ὀργάνου. Ἀλλὰ πῶς ἀπὸ τοῦ
σώματος εἰς αὐτὴν ἥξει τὰ πάθη; Σῶμα μὲν γὰρ
σώματι ἄλλῳ μεταδώσει τῶν ἑαυτοῦ. Σῶμα δὲ
ψυχῇ πῶς; Τοῦτο γάρ ἐστιν οἷον ἄλλου παθόντος
15 ἄλλο παθεῖν. Μέχρι γὰρ τοῦ τὸ μὲν εἶναι τὸ
χρώμενον, τὸ δὲ ᾧ χρῆται, χωρίς ἐστιν ἑκάτερον·
χωρίζει γοῦν ὁ τὸ χρώμενον τὴν ψυχὴν διδούς.
Ἀλλὰ πρὸ τοῦ χωρίσαι διὰ φιλοσοφίας αὐτὸ πῶς
εἶχεν; Ἢ ἐμέμικτο. Ἀλλὰ εἰ ἐμέμικτο, ἢ κρᾶσίς

---

[1] This is Aristotelian; cp. *De Anima* B. 12. 24a 18.
[2] The phrase is taken from Plato, *Phaedrus* 246C5: the
idea of the soul using the body as a tool comes from *Alcibiades*
129C–E.

always what it is. Furthermore it will have no sensations and reasoning and opinion will have no connection with it; for sensation is the reception of a form or of an affection of a body,[1] and reasoning and opinion are based on sensation. We must enquire how it is with intelligence, whether we are going to allow this to the soul; and also whether it experiences pure pleasure when it is alone.

3. We must certainly too consider soul as being in body (whether it does in fact exist before it or in it) since it is from the combination of body and soul that "the complete living creature takes its name."[2] Now if soul uses body as a tool it does not have to admit the affections which come through the body; craftsmen are not affected by the affections of their tools. Perhaps one might suggest that it would necessarily have sensation, if a necessary accompaniment of using the tool is knowing by sensation the ways in which it is affected from outside; for using the eyes is just seeing. But there can be harm in seeing, and it can bring sadness and pain and in general anything that may happen to the whole body; and so desire, when the soul seeks the service of its tool. But how will the affections which come from body manage to reach the soul? Body can give of its own to another body, but how can body give to soul? This amounts to saying that if one thing is affected, so must another different thing be. For insofar as one is the user and the other what it uses, they are two separate things. At any rate anyone who states that the soul uses the body as a tool separates the two. But what was their relationship before the separation of soul by philosophy? There was a mixture. But if there was a mixture, there was

20 τις ἦν, ἢ ὡς διαπλακεῖσα, ἢ ὡς εἶδος οὐ
κεχωρισμένον, ἢ εἶδος ἐφαπτόμενον, ὥσπερ ὁ
κυβερνήτης, ἢ τὸ μὲν οὕτως αὐτοῦ, τὸ δὲ ἐκείνως·
λέγω δὲ ἢ τὸ μὲν κεχωρισμένον, ὅπερ τὸ χρώμενον,
τὸ δὲ μεμιγμένον ὁπωσοῦν καὶ αὐτὸ ὂν ἐν τάξει
τοῦ ᾧ χρῆται, ἵνα τοῦτο ἡ φιλοσοφία καὶ αὐτὸ
25 ἐπιστρέφῃ πρὸς τὸ χρώμενον καὶ τὸ χρώμενον
ἀπάγῃ, ὅσον μὴ πᾶσα ἀνάγκη, ἀπὸ τοῦ ᾧ χρῆται,
ὡς μὴ ἀεὶ μηδὲ χρῆσθαι.

4. Θῶμεν τοίνυν μεμῖχθαι. Ἀλλ' εἰ μέμικται,
τὸ μὲν χεῖρον ἔσται βέλτιον, τὸ σῶμα, τὸ δὲ
χεῖρον, ἡ ψυχή· καὶ βέλτιον μὲν τὸ σῶμα ζωῆς
μεταλαβόν, χεῖρον δὲ ἡ ψυχὴ θανάτου καὶ ἀλογίας.
5 Τὸ δὴ ἀφαιρεθὲν ὁπωσοῦν ζωῆς πῶς ἂν προσθήκην
λάβοι τὸ αἰσθάνεσθαι; Τοὐναντίον δ' ἂν τὸ σῶμα
ζωὴν λαβὸν τοῦτο ἂν εἴη τὸ αἰσθήσεως καὶ τῶν ἐξ
αἰσθήσεως παθημάτων μεταλαμβάνον. Τοῦτο τοίνυν καὶ ὀρέξεται—τοῦτο γὰρ καὶ ἀπολαύσει ὧν
ὀρέγεται—καὶ φοβήσεται περὶ αὐτοῦ· τοῦτο γὰρ
10 καὶ οὐ τεύξεται τῶν ἡδέων καὶ φθαρήσεται.
Ζητητέον δὲ καὶ τὸν τρόπον τῆς μίξεως, μήποτε
οὐ δυνατὸς ᾖ, ὥσπερ ἂν εἴ τις λέγοι μεμῖχθαι
λευκῷ γραμμήν, φύσιν ἄλλην ἄλλῃ. Τὸ δὲ
"διαπλακεῖσα" οὐ ποιεῖ ὁμοιοπαθῆ τὰ διαπλακέντα,
ἀλλ' ἔστιν ἀπαθὲς εἶναι τὸ διαπλακὲν καὶ ἔστι

---

[1] So Plato describes the soul of the universe as "woven
through" its body, *Timaeus* 36E2.

either a sort of intermingling, or the soul was in some way "woven through"[1] the body, or it was like a form not separated from the matter, or a form handling the matter as the steersman steers the ship, or one part of it was related in one way and another in another. I mean that one part is separate, the part which uses the body, and the other somehow mixed with body and on a level with that which it uses. In this case philosophy should turn this lower part towards the using part, and draw the using part away from that which it uses, insofar as the connection is not absolutely necessary, so that it may not always have even to use it.

4. Let us assume, then, that there is a mixture. But, if this is so, the worse element, the body, will be improved and the other element, the soul, will be made worse. The body will be improved by sharing in life, the soul made worse by sharing in death and unreason. How then can that which has its life reduced in any way whatever acquire thereby an additional faculty, that of sense-perception? The opposite is true; it is the body which receives life, and so the body which shares in sensation and the affections which come from sensation. So too, it will be the body that desires—for it is the body which is going to enjoy the objects of desire—and is afraid for itself—for it is going to miss its pleasures and be destroyed. And we must investigate the way in which this "mixture" takes place, and see if it is not really impossible; it is like talking about a line being mixed with white, one kind of thing with another kind of thing.

The idea of "being interwoven" does not imply that the things interwoven are affected in the same

15 ψυχὴν διαπεφοιτηκυῖαν μήτοι πάσχειν τὰ ἐκείνου
πάθη, ὥσπερ καὶ τὸ φῶς, καὶ μάλιστα, εἰ οὕτω,
δι' ὅλου ὡς διαπεπλέχθαι· οὐ παρὰ τοῦτο οὖν
πείσεται τὰ σώματος πάθη, ὅτι διαπέπλεκται.
'Αλλ' ὡς εἶδος ἐν ὕλῃ ἔσται ἐν τῷ σώματι; Πρῶτον
μὲν ὡς χωριστὸν εἶδος ἔσται, εἴπερ οὐσία, καὶ
20 μᾶλλον ἂν εἴη κατὰ τὸ χρώμενον. Εἰ δὲ ὡς τῷ
πελέκει τὸ σχῆμα τὸ ἐπὶ τῷ σιδήρῳ, καὶ τὸ
συναμφότερον ὁ πέλεκυς ποιήσει ἃ ποιήσει ὁ
σίδηρος ὁ οὕτως ἐσχηματισμένος, κατὰ τὸ σχῆμα
μέντοι, μᾶλλον ἂν τῷ σώματι διδοῖμεν ὅσα κοινὰ
25 πάθη, τῷ μέντοι τοιούτῳ, τῷ φυσικῷ, ὀργανικῷ,
δυνάμει ζωὴν ἔχοντι. Καὶ γὰρ ἄτοπόν φησι
τὴν ψυχὴν ὑφαίνειν λέγειν, ὥστε καὶ ἐπιθυμεῖν καὶ λυπεῖσθαι· ἀλλὰ τὸ ζῷον μᾶλλον.

5. 'Αλλὰ τὸ ζῷον ἢ τὸ σῶμα δεῖ λέγειν τὸ
τοιόνδε, ἢ τὸ κοινόν, ἢ ἕτερόν τι τρίτον ἐξ
ἀμφοῖν γεγενημένον. "Οπως δ' ἂν ἔχῃ, ἤτοι ἀπαθῆ
δεῖ τὴν ψυχὴν φυλάττειν αὐτὴν αἰτίαν γενομένην
5 ἄλλῳ τοῦ τοιούτου, ἢ συμπάσχειν καὶ αὐτήν· καὶ
ἢ ταὐτὸν πάσχουσαν πάθημα πάσχειν, ἢ ὅμοιόν

---

[1] This comparison is taken from Aristotle, *De Anima* B. 1.
412b. 12.

[2] These phrases are quotations from *De Anima* B. 1. 412a.
27–8. The reference to Aristotle which follows is to the key
passage already quoted, *De Anima* A. 4. 408b. 12–13. Plotinus
is here using Aristotle's doctrine of the soul as the immanent
(and, except for the intellect, inseparable) form of the body as
a starting-point from which to develop his own really very
different doctrine of the relationship of soul and body.

way: it is possible for the principle interwoven to be unaffected and for the soul to pass and repass through the body without being touched by its affections, just like light, especially if it is interwoven right through the whole; this sort of interweaving will not make it subject to the affections of the body. Will it then be in the body like form in matter? First of all, it will be like a separable form, assuming it to be a substantial reality, and so will correspond still more exactly to the conception of it as a "user." But if we assume it to be like the shape of an axe imposed on the iron [1] (in this case it is the compound of matter and form, the axe, which performs its functions, that is to say the iron shaped in this particular way, though it is in virtue of the shape that it does so) we shall attribute all the common affections rather to the body, but to a body "of a specific kind," "formed by nature," "adapted to the use of the soul," "having life potentially." [2] Aristotle says that it is absurd "to talk about the soul weaving," and it follows that it is also absurd to talk about it desiring or grieving; we should attribute these affections rather to the living being.

5. But we must define the living being as either the body of this special kind, or the community of body and soul, or another, third, thing, the product of both. [3] However that may be, the soul must either remain unaffected and only cause affections in something else or must be affected itself along with the body: and, if it is affected, it must either be

[3] The question raised here is discussed in the *Alcibiades* 130A7–C7, a passage which Plotinus seems to have in mind at this point (the word συναμφότερον is used of the compound of body and soul 130A9).

τι, οἷον ἄλλως μὲν τὸ ζῷον ἐπιθυμεῖν, ἄλλως δὲ τὸ
ἐπιθυμητικὸν ἐνεργεῖν ἢ πάσχειν. Τὸ μὲν οὖν
σῶμα τὸ τοιόνδε ὕστερον ἐπισκεπτέον· τὸ δὲ
συναμφότερον οἷον λυπεῖσθαι πῶς; Ἄρα ὅτι τοῦ
10 σώματος οὑτωσὶ διατεθέντος καὶ μέχρις αἰσθήσεως
διελθόντος τοῦ πάθους τῆς αἰσθήσεως εἰς ψυχὴν
τελευτώσης; Ἀλλ' ἡ αἴσθησις οὔπω δῆλον πῶς.
Ἀλλ' ὅταν ἡ λύπη ἀρχὴν ἀπὸ δόξης καὶ κρίσεως
λάβῃ τοῦ κακόν τι παρεῖναι ἢ αὐτῷ ἤ τινι τῶν
οἰκείων, εἶτ' ἐντεῦθεν τροπὴ λυπηρὰ ἐπὶ τὸ
15 σῶμα καὶ ὅλως ἐπὶ πᾶν τὸ ζῷον γένηται; Ἀλλὰ
καὶ τὸ τῆς δόξης οὔπω δῆλον τίνος, τῆς ψυχῆς ἢ
τοῦ συναμφοτέρου· εἶτα ἡ μὲν δόξα ἡ περί του
κακὸν τὸ τῆς λύπης οὐκ ἔχει πάθος· καὶ γὰρ καὶ
δυνατὸν τῆς δόξης παρούσης μὴ πάντως ἐπιγίνε-
20 σθαι τὸ λυπεῖσθαι, μηδ' αὖ τὸ ὀργίζεσθαι δόξης
τοῦ ὀλιγωρεῖσθαι γενομένης, μηδ' αὖ ἀγαθοῦ δόξης
κινεῖσθαι τὴν ὄρεξιν. Πῶς οὖν κοινὰ ταῦτα; Ἤ,
ὅτι καὶ ἡ ἐπιθυμία τοῦ ἐπιθυμητικοῦ καὶ ὁ θυμὸς
τοῦ θυμικοῦ καὶ ὅλως τοῦ ὀρεκτικοῦ ἡ ἐπί τι
ἔκστασις; Ἀλλ' οὕτως οὐκέτι κοινὰ ἔσται, ἀλλὰ
25 τῆς ψυχῆς μόνης· ἢ καὶ τοῦ σώματος, ὅτι δεῖ
αἷμα καὶ χολὴν ζέσαι καί πως διατεθὲν τὸ σῶμα

subjected to the same affection or a similar one (as for instance, if the living being desires in one way, the desiring part of the soul may be active or affected in a different one). We will consider this special kind of body later. But in what way is the compound of body and soul, for instance, capable of grief? Is it that the body is disposed in this particular way, and its affection penetrates to sense-perception, and sense-perception ends in the soul? But this leaves it still obscure how sense-perception comes about. Or alternatively, does grief originate from an opinion, a judgement[1] that there is some evil there for the person concerned himself or something belonging to him, and does this result in an unpleasant change in the body and the living being as a whole? But then it is not yet clear which the opinion belongs to, the soul or the compound. Besides, the opinion about someone's evil does not contain the feeling of grief. It is possible to have the opinion without being grieved at all in consequence, as it is possible not to be angry when we have the opinion that we have been slighted, and for our appetite not to be stirred when we have the opinion that a good is present. How then are affections common to body and soul? Is it because desire belongs to the desiring part of the soul and passion to the passionate part, and in general the movement out towards anything to the appetitive part? But then they are no longer common to body and soul but belong to soul alone. Or do they belong to the body too, because blood and bile must boil and the body be in

[1] This idea of the emotions as judgements or opinions is Stoic (Chrysippus); cp. *Stoicorum Veterum Fragmenta* III. 459.

τὴν ὄρεξιν κινῆσαι, οἷον ἐπὶ ἀφροδισίων. Ἡ δὲ
τοῦ ἀγαθοῦ ὄρεξις μὴ κοινὸν πάθημα ἀλλὰ ψυχῆς
ἔστω, ὥσπερ καὶ ἄλλα, καὶ οὐ πάντα τοῦ κοινοῦ
δίδωσί τις λόγος. Ἀλλὰ ὀρεγομένου ἀφροδισίων
30 τοῦ ἀνθρώπου ἔσται μὲν ὁ ἄνθρωπος ὁ ἐπιθυμῶν,
ἔσται δὲ ἄλλως καὶ τὸ ἐπιθυμητικὸν ἐπιθυμοῦν.
Καὶ πῶς; Ἆρα ἄρξει μὲν ὁ ἄνθρωπος τῆς ἐπιθυμίας,
ἐπακολουθήσει δὲ τὸ ἐπιθυμητικόν; Ἀλλὰ πῶς
ὅλως ἐπεθύμησεν ὁ ἄνθρωπος μὴ τοῦ ἐπιθυμητικοῦ
κεκινημένου; Ἀλλ' ἄρξει τὸ ἐπιθυμητικόν. Ἀλλὰ
35 τοῦ σώματος μὴ πρότερον οὑτωσὶ διατεθέντος
πόθεν ἄρξεται;

6. Ἀλλ' ἴσως βέλτιον εἰπεῖν καθόλου τῷ παρεῖναι τὰς δυνάμεις τὰ ἔχοντα εἶναι τὰ ἐνεργοῦντα
κατ' αὐτάς, αὐτὰς δὲ ἀκινήτους εἶναι χορηγούσας
τὸ δύνασθαι τοῖς ἔχουσιν. Ἀλλ' εἰ τοῦτο, ἔστι
5 πάσχοντος τοῦ ζῴου τὴν αἰτίαν τοῦ ζῆν τῷ
συναμφοτέρῳ δοῦσαν αὐτὴν ἀπαθῆ εἶναι τῶν παθῶν
καὶ τῶν ἐνεργειῶν τοῦ ἔχοντος ὄντων. Ἀλλ' εἰ
τοῦτο, καὶ τὸ ζῆν ὅλως οὐ τῆς ψυχῆς, ἀλλὰ τοῦ
συναμφοτέρου ἔσται. Ἢ τὸ τοῦ συναμφοτέρου
ζῆν οὐ τῆς ψυχῆς ἔσται· καὶ ἡ δύναμις δὲ ἡ
10 αἰσθητικὴ οὐκ αἰσθήσεται, ἀλλὰ τὸ ἔχον τὴν
δύναμιν. Ἀλλ' εἰ ἡ αἴσθησις διὰ σώματος κίνησις
οὖσα εἰς ψυχὴν τελευτᾷ, πῶς ἡ ψυχὴ οὐκ αἰσθήσεται; Ἢ τῆς δυνάμεως τῆς αἰσθητικῆς παρούσης
τῷ ταύτην παρεῖναι αἰσθήσεται ⟨ὅ⟩τι αἰσθήσεται
15 τὸ συναμφότερον. Ἀλλ' εἰ ἡ δύναμις μὴ κινήσε-

a certain state to stir appetite, as in the case of sexual passion? Let us grant anyhow that the appetite for the good is not an affection of both, but of the soul, and this is true of other affections too; a reasoned examination does not attribute them all to the joint entity. But when man has an appetite for sexual pleasures, it will be the man that desires, but in another way it will be the desiring part of the soul that desires. How will this come about? Will the man start the desire and the desiring part of soul follow on? But how could the man manage to desire at all if the desiring part was not moved? Perhaps the desiring part will start. But where will it start from, if the body is not previously disposed in the appropriate way?

6. But perhaps it is better to say that, in general, as a result of the presence of the powers of soul it is their possessors which act by them, and the powers themselves are unmoved and only impart the power to act to their possessors. But if this is so, when the living being is affected, the cause of its life, which gave itself to the compound, can remain unaffected, and the affections and activities belong to the possessor. But if this is so, life will belong altogether, not to the soul, but to the compound. Certainly the life of the compound will not be that of the soul: and the power of sense-perception will not perceive, but that which has the power. But if sense-perception is a movement through the body which ends in the soul, how will the soul not perceive? When the power of sense-perception is present the compound will perceive whatever it perceives by its presence. But if the power is not going to be moved, how will it still be the compound

ται, πῶς ἔτι τὸ συναμφότερον μὴ συναριθμουμένης
ψυχῆς μηδὲ τῆς ψυχικῆς δυνάμεως;

7. Ἢ τὸ συναμφότερον ἔστω τῆς ψυχῆς τῷ
παρεῖναι οὐχ αὑτὴν δούσης τῆς τοιαύτης εἰς τὸ
συναμφότερον ἢ εἰς θάτερον, ἀλλὰ ποιούσης ἐκ τοῦ
σώματος τοῦ τοιούτου καί τινος οἷον φωτὸς τοῦ
5 παρ' αὐτὴν δοθέντος τὴν τοῦ ζῴου φύσιν ἕτερόν
τι, οὗ τὸ αἰσθάνεσθαι καὶ τὰ ἄλλα ὅσα ζῴου πάθη
εἴρηται. Ἀλλὰ πῶς ἡμεῖς αἰσθανόμεθα; Ἢ, ὅτι
οὐκ ἀπηλλάγημεν τοῦ τοιούτου ζῴου, καὶ εἰ ἄλλα
ἡμῖν τιμιώτερα εἰς τὴν ὅλην ἀνθρώπου οὐσίαν ἐκ
πολλῶν οὖσαν πάρεστι. Τὴν δὲ τῆς ψυχῆς τοῦ
10 αἰσθάνεσθαι δύναμιν οὐ τῶν αἰσθητῶν εἶναι δεῖ,
τῶν δὲ ἀπὸ τῆς αἰσθήσεως ἐγγιγνομένων τῷ ζῴῳ
τύπων ἀντιληπτικὴν εἶναι μᾶλλον· νοητὰ γὰρ ἤδη
ταῦτα· ὡς τὴν αἴσθησιν τὴν ἔξω εἴδωλον εἶναι
ταύτης, ἐκείνην δὲ ἀληθεστέραν τῇ οὐσίᾳ οὖσαν
εἰδῶν μόνων ἀπαθῶς εἶναι θεωρίαν. Ἀπὸ δὴ
15 τούτων τῶν εἰδῶν, ἀφ' ὧν ψυχὴ ἤδη παραδέχεται
μόνη τὴν τοῦ ζῴου ἡγεμονίαν, διάνοιαι δὴ καὶ
δόξαι καὶ νοήσεις· ἔνθα δὴ ἡμεῖς μάλιστα. Τὰ δὲ
πρὸ τούτων ἡμέτερα, ἡμεῖς δὴ τὸ ἐντεῦθεν ἄνω
ἐφεστηκότες τῷ ζῴῳ. Κωλύσει δὲ οὐδὲν τὸ
σύμπαν ζῷον λέγειν, μικτὸν μὲν τὰ κάτω, τὸ δὲ
20 ἐντεῦθεν ὁ ἄνθρωπος ὁ ἀληθὴς σχεδόν· ἐκεῖνα δὲ

---

[1] That is "below"; sensation and emotion belong to the
body-soul compound, the "living being"; the true self
begins where thought begins.

that perceives if neither soul nor soul-power are reckoned as included in it?

7. Let us say that it *is* the compound which perceives, and that the soul by its presence does not give itself qualified in a particular way either to the compound or to the other member of it, but makes, out of the qualified body and a sort of light which it gives of itself, the nature of the living creature, another different thing to which belong sense-perception and all other affections which are ascribed to the living body. But then, how is it we who perceive? It is because we are not separated from the living being so qualified, even if other things too, of more value than we are, enter into the composition of the whole essence of man, which is made up of many elements. And soul's power of sense-perception need not be perception of sense-objects, but rather it must be receptive of the impressions produced by sensation on the living being; these are already intelligible entities. So external sensation is the image of this perception of the soul, which is in its essence truer and is a contemplation of forms alone without being affected. From these forms, from which the soul alone receives its lordship over the living being, come reasonings, and opinions and acts of intuitive intelligence; and this precisely is where "we" are. That which comes before[1] this is "ours" but "we," in our presidency over the living being, are what extends from this point upwards. But there will be no objection to calling the whole thing "living being"; the lower parts of it are something mixed, the part which begins on the level of thought is, I suppose, the true man: those lower parts are

τὸ λεοντῶδες καὶ τὸ ποικίλον ὅλως θηρίον.
Συνδρόμου γὰρ ὄντος τοῦ ἀνθρώπου τῇ λογικῇ
ψυχῇ, ὅταν λογιζώμεθα, ἡμεῖς λογιζόμεθα τῷ τοὺς
λογισμοὺς ψυχῆς εἶναι ἐνεργήματα.

8. Πρὸς δὲ τὸν νοῦν πῶς; Νοῦν δὲ λέγω οὐχ ἣν
ἡ ψυχὴ ἔχει ἕξιν οὖσαν τῶν παρὰ τοῦ νοῦ, ἀλλ᾽
αὐτὸν τὸν νοῦν. Ἢ ἔχομεν καὶ τοῦτον ὑπεράνω
ἡμῶν. Ἔχομεν δὲ ἢ κοινὸν ἢ ἴδιον, ἢ καὶ κοινὸν
5 πάντων καὶ ἴδιον· κοινὸν μέν, ὅτι ἀμέριστος καὶ
εἷς καὶ πανταχοῦ ὁ αὐτός, ἴδιον δέ, ὅτι ἔχει καὶ
ἕκαστος αὐτὸν ὅλον ἐν ψυχῇ τῇ πρώτῃ. Ἔχομεν
οὖν καὶ τὰ εἴδη διχῶς, ἐν μὲν ψυχῇ οἷον ἀνειλιγμένα
καὶ οἷον κεχωρισμένα, ἐν δὲ νῷ ὁμοῦ τὰ πάντα.
Τὸν δὲ θεὸν πῶς; Ἢ ὡς ἐποχούμενον τῇ νοητῇ
10 φύσει καὶ τῇ οὐσίᾳ τῇ ὄντως, ἡμᾶς δὲ ἐκεῖθεν
τρίτους ἐκ τῆς ἀμερίστου, φησί, τῆς ἄνωθεν καὶ
ἐκ τῆς περὶ τὰ σώματα μεριστῆς, ἣν δὴ δεῖ
νοεῖν οὕτω μεριστὴν περὶ τὰ σώματα, ὅτι δίδωσιν
ἑαυτὴν τοῖς σώματος μεγέθεσιν, ὁπόσον ἂν ζῷον
15 ᾖ ἕκαστον, ἐπεὶ καὶ τῷ παντὶ ὅλῳ, οὖσα μία· ἤ,
ὅτι φαντάζεται τοῖς σώμασι παρεῖναι ἐλλάμπουσα
εἰς αὐτὰ καὶ ζῷα ποιοῦσα οὐκ ἐξ αὐτῆς καὶ

---

[1] Plotinus is here quoting *Republic* IX 590A9 and 588C7.
The "lion" in Plato symbolises the higher emotions, the
"various beast" (a sort of many-headed dragon) the carnal
lusts and desires. It is noteworthy that the difference in
quality and value of these two lower parts of the soul, which
is so important in the psychology of the *Republic* and *Phaedrus*,
has little significance for Plotinus.

[2] The "true reality" is the world of Forms which is
identical with Intellect. God (the One or Good) is beyond
Intellect and Reality.

[3] Plotinus is again quoting from Plato's description of
the making of the world-soul in *Timaeus* 35A: in what

the "lion-like," and altogether "the various beast."[1] Since man coincides with the rational soul, when we reason it is really we who reason because rational processes are activities of soul.

8. But how are we related to the Intellect? I mean by "Intellect" not that state of the soul, which is one of the things which derive from Intellect, but Intellect itself. We possess this too, as something that transcends us. We have it either as common to all or particular to ourselves, or both common and particular; common because it is without parts and one and everywhere the same, particular to ourselves because each has the whole of it in the primary part of his soul. So we also possess the forms in two ways, in our soul, in a manner of speaking unfolded and separated, in Intellect all together.

But how do we possess God? He rides mounted on the nature of Intellect and true reality—that is how we possess him;[2] "we" are third in order counting from God, being made, Plato says, "from the undivided," that which is above, "and from that which is divided in bodies";[3] we must consider this part of soul as being divided in bodies in the sense that it gives itself to the magnitudes of bodies, in proportion to the size of each living being, since it gives itself to the whole universe, though the soul is one: or because it is pictured as being present to bodies since it shines into them and makes

follows he gives an interpretation of Plato's phrase in terms of his own doctrine of the lower soul and its powers as emanations of the higher soul, which "gives itself" to bodies by illuminating, forming, and vivifying them, remaining itself undiminished and unaffected.

σώματος, ἀλλὰ μένουσα μὲν αὐτή, εἴδωλα δὲ
αὐτῆς διδοῦσα, ὥσπερ πρόσωπον ἐν πολλοῖς
κατόπτροις. Πρῶτον δὲ εἴδωλον αἴσθησις ἡ ἐν
τῷ κοινῷ· εἶτα ἀπὸ ταύτης αὖ πᾶν ⟨ὃ⟩ ἄλλο εἶδος
20 λέγεται ψυχῆς, ἕτερον ἀφ' ἑτέρου ἀεί, καὶ τελευτᾷ
μέχρι γεννητικοῦ καὶ αὐξήσεως καὶ ὅλως ποιήσεως
ἄλλου καὶ ἀποτελεστικοῦ ἄλλου παρ' αὐτὴν τὴν
ποιοῦσαν ἐπεστραμμένης αὐτῆς τῆς ποιούσης πρὸς
τὸ ἀποτελούμενον.

9. Ἔσται τοίνυν ἐκείνης ἡμῖν τῆς ψυχῆς ἡ φύσις
ἀπηλλαγμένη αἰτίας κακῶν, ὅσα ἄνθρωπος ποιεῖ
καὶ πάσχει· περὶ γὰρ τὸ ζῷον ταῦτα, τὸ κοινόν,
[καὶ κοινόν], ὡς εἴρηται. Ἀλλ' εἰ δόξα τῆς ψυχῆς
5 καὶ διάνοια, πῶς ἀναμάρτητος; Ψευδὴς γὰρ δόξα
καὶ πολλὰ κατ' αὐτὴν πράττεται τῶν κακῶν. Ἢ
πράττεται μὲν τὰ κακὰ ἡττωμένων ἡμῶν ὑπὸ τοῦ
χείρονος—πολλὰ γὰρ ἡμεῖς—ἢ ἐπιθυμίας ἢ θυμοῦ
ἢ εἰδώλου κακοῦ· ἡ δὲ τῶν ψευδῶν λεγομένη
10 διάνοια φαντασία οὖσα οὐκ ἀνέμεινε τὴν τοῦ
διανοητικοῦ κρίσιν, ἀλλ' ἐπράξαμεν τοῖς χείροσι
πεισθέντες, ὥσπερ ἐπὶ τῆς αἰσθήσεως πρὶν τῷ
διανοητικῷ ἐπικρῖναι ψευδῆ ὁρᾶν συμβαίνει τῇ
κοινῇ αἰσθήσει. Ὁ δὲ νοῦς ἢ ἐφήψατο ἢ οὔ, ὥστε
ἀναμάρτητος. Ἢ οὕτω δὲ λεκτέον, ὡς ἡμεῖς ἢ
ἐφηψάμεθα τοῦ ἐν τῷ νῷ νοητοῦ ἢ οὔ. Ἢ τοῦ ἐν
15 ἡμῖν· δυνατὸν γὰρ καὶ ἔχειν καὶ μὴ πρόχειρον
ἔχειν. Διείλομεν δὴ τὰ κοινὰ καὶ τὰ ἴδια τῷ τὰ
μὲν σωματικὰ καὶ οὐκ ἄνευ σώματος εἶναι, ὅσα

---

[1] Cp. *Theaetetus* 198D7 (from the comparison, which Plato
afterwards rejects as unsatisfactory, of the mind to an aviary).

living creatures, not of itself and body, but abiding itself and giving images of itself, like a face seen in many mirrors. The first image is the faculty of sensation in the joint entity, and after this comes everything which is called another form of soul, each in its turn proceeding from the other ; the series ends in the powers of generation and growth, and, speaking generally, in the powers which make and perfect other things different from the soul which makes, while the making soul itself stays directed towards its product.

9. The nature of that higher soul of ours will be free from all responsibility for the evils that man does and suffers ; these concern the living being, the joint entity, as has been said. But if opinion and reasoning belong to the soul, how is it free from sin ? For opinion is a cheat and is the cause of much evil-doing. Evil is done when we are mastered by what is worse in us—for we are many—by desire or passion or an evil image. What we call thinking falsities is a making of mind-pictures which has not waited for the judgement of the reasoning faculty—we have acted under the influence of our worse parts, just as in sensation the perception of the joint entity may see falsely before the reasoning faculty has passed judgement on it. The intellect is either in touch with the proceedings or it is not, and so sinless : but we ought rather to say that we are in touch with the intelligible in the intellect or we are not—with the intelligible in ourselves ; for one can have it and not have it available.[1]

So we have distinguished what belongs to the joint entity and what is proper to the soul in this way : what belongs to the joint entity is bodily or not

δὲ οὐ δεῖται σώματος εἰς ἐνέργειαν, ταῦτα ἴδια
ψυχῆς εἶναι, καὶ τὴν διάνοιαν ἐπίκρισιν ποιουμένην
20 τῶν ἀπὸ τῆς αἰσθήσεως τύπων εἴδη ἤδη θεωρεῖν
καὶ θεωρεῖν οἷον συναισθήσει, τήν γε κυρίως τῆς
ψυχῆς τῆς ἀληθοῦς διάνοιαν· νοήσεων γὰρ ἐνέργεια
ἡ διάνοια ἡ ἀληθὴς καὶ τῶν ἔξω πολλάκις πρὸς
τἄνδον ὁμοιότης καὶ κοινωνία. Ἀτρεμήσει οὖν
οὐδὲν ἧττον ἡ ψυχὴ πρὸς ἑαυτὴν καὶ ἐν ἑαυτῇ· αἱ
25 δὲ τροπαὶ καὶ ὁ θόρυβος ἐν ἡμῖν παρὰ τῶν
συνηρτημένων καὶ τῶν τοῦ κοινοῦ, ὅ τι δήποτέ
ἐστι τοῦτο, ὡς εἴρηται, παθημάτων.

10. Ἀλλ᾽ εἰ ἡμεῖς ἡ ψυχή, πάσχομεν δὲ ταῦτα
ἡμεῖς, ταῦτα ἂν εἴη πάσχουσα ἡ ψυχὴ καὶ αὖ
ποιήσει ἃ ποιοῦμεν. Ἢ καὶ τὸ κοινὸν ἔφαμεν
ἡμῶν εἶναι καὶ μάλιστα οὔπω κεχωρισμένων· ἐπεὶ
5 καὶ ἃ πάσχει τὸ σῶμα ἡμῶν ἡμᾶς φαμεν πάσχειν.
Διττὸν οὖν τὸ ἡμεῖς, ἢ συναριθμουμένου τοῦ
θηρίου, ἢ τὸ ὑπὲρ τοῦτο ἤδη· θηρίον δὲ ζωωθὲν
τὸ σῶμα. Ὁ δ᾽ ἀληθὴς ἄνθρωπος ἄλλος ὁ καθαρὸς
τούτων τὰς ἀρετὰς ἔχων τὰς ἐν νοήσει αἳ δὴ ἐν
αὐτῇ τῇ χωριζομένῃ ψυχῇ ἵδρυνται, χωριζομένῃ
10 δὲ καὶ χωριστῇ ἔτι ἐνταῦθα οὔσῃ· ἐπεὶ καί, ὅταν
αὐτὴ παντάπασιν ἀποστῇ, καὶ ἡ ἀπ᾽ αὐτῆς ἐλλαμφ-
θεῖσα ἀπελήλυθε συνεπομένη. Αἱ δ᾽ ἀρεταὶ αἱ μὴ
φρονήσει, ἔθεσι δὲ ἐγγινόμεναι καὶ ἀσκήσεσι,
τοῦ κοινοῦ· τούτου γὰρ αἱ κακίαι, ἐπεὶ καὶ φθόνοι

---

[1] For the " clamour " of the body cp. Phaedo 66D6 and Timaeus 43B6.

[2] Cp. Republic 518E1-2.

without body, but what does not require body for
its operation is proper to the soul.   Reasoning when
it passes judgement on the impressions produced by
sensation is at the same time contemplating forms
and contemplating them by a kind of sympathy—
I mean the reasoning which really belongs to the
true soul: for true reasoning is an operation of acts
of the intelligence, and there is often a resemblance
and community between what is outside and what
is within.   So in spite of everything the soul will be
at peace, turned to itself and resting in itself.   The
changes and the clamour[1] in us come, as we have said,
from what is attached to us and from the affections of
the joint entity, whatever precisely that is.

10. But if we are the soul, and we are affected in
this way, then it would be the soul that is affected in
this way, and again it will be the soul which does
what we do.   Yes, but we said that the joint entity
is part of ourselves, especially when we have not yet
been separated from body: for we say that we are
affected by what affects our body.   So "we" is used
in two senses, either including the beast or referring
to that which even in our present life transcends it.
The beast is the body which has been given life.
But the true man is different, clear of these affections;
he has the virtues which belong to the sphere of intellect and have their seat actually in the separate
soul, separate and separable even while it is still here
below.   (For when it withdraws altogether, the
lower soul which is illumined by it goes away too in
its train.)   But the virtues which result not from
thought but from habit and training[2] belong to the
joint entity; for the vices belong to this, since envy
and jealousy and emotional sympathy are located

καὶ ζῆλοι καὶ ἔλεοι. Φιλίαι δὲ τίνος; Ἢ αἱ μὲν
15 τούτου, αἱ δὲ τοῦ ἔνδον ἀνθρώπου.

11. Παίδων δὲ ὄντων ἐνεργεῖ μὲν τὰ ἐκ τοῦ
συνθέτου, ὀλίγα δὲ ἐλλάμπει ἐκ τῶν ἄνω εἰς αὐτό.
Ὅταν δ᾽ ἀργῇ εἰς ἡμᾶς, ἐνεργεῖ πρὸς τὸ ἄνω· εἰς
ἡμᾶς δὲ ἐνεργεῖ, ὅταν μέχρι τοῦ μέσου ἥκῃ. Τί
5 οὖν; Οὐχ ἡμεῖς καὶ πρὸ τούτου; Ἀλλ᾽ ἀντίληψιν
δεῖ γενέσθαι· οὐ γάρ, ὅσα ἔχομεν, τούτοις χρώμεθα
ἀεί, ἀλλ᾽ ὅταν τὸ μέσον τάξωμεν ἢ πρὸς τὰ ἄνω ἢ
πρὸς τὰ ἐναντία, ἢ ὅσα ἀπὸ δυνάμεως ἢ ἕξεως
εἰς ἐνέργειαν ἄγομεν. Τὰ δὲ θηρία πῶς τὸ ζῷον
ἔχει; Ἢ εἰ μὲν ψυχαὶ εἶεν ἐν αὐτοῖς ἀνθρώπειοι,
10 ὥσπερ λέγεται, ἁμαρτοῦσαι, οὐ τῶν θηρίων γίνεται
τοῦτο, ὅσον χωριστόν, ἀλλὰ παρὸν οὐ πάρεστιν
αὐτοῖς, ἀλλ᾽ ἡ συναίσθησις τὸ τῆς ψυχῆς εἴδωλον
μετὰ τοῦ σώματος ἔχει· σῶμα δὴ τοιόνδε οἷον
ποιωθὲν ψυχῆς εἰδώλῳ· εἰ δὲ μὴ ἀνθρώπου ψυχὴ
εἰσέδυ, ἐλλάμψει ἀπὸ τῆς ὅλης τὸ τοιοῦτον ζῷον
15 γενόμενόν ἐστιν.

12. Ἀλλ᾽ εἰ ἀναμάρτητος ἡ ψυχή, πῶς αἱ δίκαι;
Ἀλλὰ γὰρ οὗτος ὁ λόγος ἀσυμφωνεῖ παντὶ λόγῳ,
ὅς φησιν αὐτὴν καὶ ἁμαρτάνειν καὶ κατορθοῦν καὶ
διδόναι δίκας καὶ ἐν Ἅιδου καὶ μετενσωματοῦσθαι.
5 Προσθετέον μὲν οὖν ὅτῳ τις βούλεται λόγῳ· τάχα
δ᾽ ἄν τις ἐξεύροι καὶ ὅπη μὴ μαχοῦνται. Ὁ μὲν
γὰρ τὸ ἀναμάρτητον διδοὺς τῇ ψυχῇ λόγος ἐν

---

[1] In *Republic* 589A7 the "man within" is the reason, who
should rule the whole man by dominating the "many-
headed beast" with the help of the "lion."

[2] The doctrine of the transmigration of human souls into
animal bodies is accepted by Plotinus on the authority of

there. But which do our loves belong to? Some to the jointd entity, some to the man within.[1]

11. While we are children the powers of the compound are active, and only a few gleams come to it from the higher principles. But when these are inactive as regards us their activity is directed upwards: it is directed towards us when they reach the middle region. But then does not the "we" include what comes before the middle? Yes, but there must be a conscious apprehension of it. We do not always use all that we have, but only when we direct our middle part towards the higher principles or their opposites, or to whatever we are engaged in bringing from potency or state to act.

And how does the living thing include brute beasts? If as it is said[2] there are sinful human souls in them, the separable part of the soul does not come to belong to the beasts but is there without being there for them; their consciousness includes the image of soul and the body: a beast is then a qualified body made, as we may say, by an image of soul. But if a human soul has not entered the beast it becomes a living being of such and such a kind by an illumination from the universal soul.

12. But if the soul is sinless, how is it judged? This line of thought disagrees with all the arguments which maintain that the soul sins and acts rightly and undergoes punishment, punishment in Hades, and passes from body to body. We can accept whichever view we like; and perhaps we can find a point of view where they do not conflict. The argument which concludes that the soul is sinless

Plato: it does not however play any important part in his thought about the nature and destiny of man.

ἁπλοῦν πάντη ἐτίθετο τὸ αὐτὸ ψυχὴν καὶ τὸ ψυχῇ
εἶναι λέγων, ὁ δ' ἁμαρτεῖν διδοὺς συμπλέκει μὲν
καὶ προστίθησιν αὐτῇ καὶ ἄλλο ψυχῆς εἶδος τὸ τὰ
10 δεινὰ ἔχον πάθη· σύνθετος οὖν καὶ τὸ ἐκ πάντων
ἡ ψυχὴ αὐτὴ γίνεται καὶ πάσχει δὴ κατὰ τὸ ὅλον
καὶ ἁμαρτάνει τὸ σύνθετον καὶ τοῦτό ἐστι τὸ
διδὸν δίκην αὐτῷ, οὐκ ἐκεῖνο. Ὅθεν φησί·
τεθεάμεθα γὰρ αὐτήν, ὥσπερ οἱ τὸν θαλάττιον Γλαῦκον ὁρῶντες. Δεῖ δὲ περικρού-
15 σαντας τὰ προστεθέντα, εἴπερ τις ἐθέλει τὴν
φύσιν, φησίν, αὐτῆς ἰδεῖν, εἰς τὴν φιλοσοφίαν
αὐτῆς ἰδεῖν, ὧν ἐφάπτεται καὶ τίσι συγ-
γενὴς οὖσά ἐστιν ὅ ἐστιν. Ἄλλη οὖν ζωὴ καὶ
ἄλλαι ἐνέργειαι καὶ τὸ κολαζόμενον ἕτερον· ἡ δὲ
20 ἀναχώρησις καὶ ὁ χωρισμὸς οὐ μόνον τοῦδε τοῦ
σώματος, ἀλλὰ καὶ ἅπαντος τοῦ προστεθέντος.
Καὶ γὰρ ἐν τῇ γενέσει ἡ προσθήκη· ἢ ὅλως ἡ
γένεσις τοῦ ἄλλου ψυχῆς εἴδους. Τὸ δὲ πῶς ἡ
γένεσις, εἴρηται, ὅτι καταβαινούσης, ἄλλου του
ἀπ' αὐτῆς γινομένου τοῦ καταβαίνοντος ἐν τῇ
νεύσει. Ἆρ' οὖν ἀφίησι τὸ εἴδωλον; Καὶ ἡ νεύσις
25 δὲ πῶς οὐχ ἁμαρτία; Ἀλλ' εἰ ἡ νεύσις ἔλλαμψις
πρὸς τὸ κάτω, οὐχ ἁμαρτία, ὥσπερ οὐδ' ἡ σκιά,
ἀλλ' αἴτιον τὸ ἐλλαμπόμενον· εἰ γὰρ μὴ εἴη, οὐκ
ἔχει ὅπῃ ἐλλάμψει. Καταβαίνειν οὖν καὶ νεύειν
λέγεται τῷ συνεζηκέναι αὐτῇ τὸ ἐλλαμφθὲν παρ'

[1] Here Plotinus is quoting *Republic* X 611D7–612A5, a
passage which expresses extremely clearly that sharp dualism
of rational soul and bodily nature which repeatedly appears
in Plato's thought about the soul (though it is not the whole
of it) and from which Plotinus has developed his own doctrine

assumes that it is a single completely simple thing
and identifies soul and essential soulness; that which
concludes that it sins interweaves with it and adds
to it another form of soul which is affected in this
dreadful way: so the soul itself becomes compound,
the product of all its elements, and is affected as a
whole, and it is the compound which sins, and it is
this which for Plato is punished, not that other single
and simple soul. This is why he says, "We have
seen the soul like the people who see the sea-god
Glaucus." But, he says, if anyone wants to see its
real nature, they must "knock off its encrustations"
and "look at its philosophy,"[1] and see "with what
principles it is in contact" and "by kinship with
what realities it is what it is." So there is another
life of soul, and other activities, and that which is
punished is different. The ascent and the separation
is not only from this body but from all that has been
added. The addition takes place in the process of
coming-to-be; or rather coming-to-be belongs altogether to the other form of soul. We have explained
how the process of coming-to-be takes place; it
results from the descent of the soul, when something
else comes to be from it which comes down in the
soul's inclination. Does it then abandon its image?
And how is this inclination not a sin? If the inclination is an illumination directed to what is below
it is not a sin, just as casting a shadow is not a sin;
what is illuminated is responsible, for if it did not
exist the soul would have nowhere to illuminate.
The soul is said to go down or incline in the sense
that the thing which receives light from it lives with

of the higher and lower self with the help of Aristotelian and
Stoic ideas.

αὐτῆς. Ἀφίησιν οὖν τὸ εἴδωλον, εἰ μὴ ἐγγὺς τὸ
30 ὑποδεξάμενον· ἀφίησι δὲ οὐ τῷ ἀποσχισθῆναι,
ἀλλὰ τῷ μηκέτι εἶναι· οὐκέτι δέ ἐστιν, ἐὰν ἐκεῖ
βλέπῃ ὅλη. Χωρίζειν δὲ ἔοικεν ὁ ποιητὴς τοῦτο
ἐπὶ τοῦ Ἡρακλέους τὸ εἴδωλον αὐτοῦ διδοὺς ἐν
Ἅιδου, αὐτὸν δὲ ἐν θεοῖς εἶναι ὑπ᾽ ἀμφοτέρων τῶν
λόγων κατεχόμενος, καὶ ὅτι ἐν θεοῖς καὶ ὅτι ἐν
35 Ἅιδου· ἐμέρισε δ᾽ οὖν. Τάχα δ᾽ ἂν οὕτω πιθανὸς
ὁ λόγος εἴη· ὅτι δὴ πρακτικὴν ἀρετὴν ἔχων
Ἡρακλῆς καὶ ἀξιωθεὶς διὰ καλοκἀγαθίαν θεὸς
εἶναι, ὅτι πρακτικός, ἀλλ᾽ οὐ θεωρητικὸς ἦν, ἵνα
ἂν ὅλος ἦν ἐκεῖ, ἄνω τέ ἐστι καὶ ἔτι ἐστί τι αὐτοῦ
καὶ κάτω.

13. Τὸ δὲ ἐπισκεψάμενον περὶ τούτων ἡμεῖς ἢ ἡ
ψυχή; Ἢ ἡμεῖς, ἀλλὰ τῇ ψυχῇ. Τὸ δὲ τῇ ψυχῇ
πῶς; Ἆρα τῷ ἔχειν ἐπεσκέψατο; Ἢ ᾗ ψυχή.
Οὐκοῦν κινήσεται; Ἢ κίνησιν τὴν τοιαύτην δοτέον
5 αὐτῇ, ἢ μὴ σωμάτων, ἀλλ᾽ ἐστὶν αὐτῆς ζωή. Καὶ
ἡ νόησις δὲ ἡμῶν οὕτω, ὅτι καὶ νοερὰ ἡ ψυχὴ καὶ
ζωὴ κρείττων ἡ νόησις, καὶ ὅταν ψυχὴ νοῇ, καὶ
ὅταν νοῦς ἐνεργῇ εἰς ἡμᾶς· μέρος γὰρ καὶ οὗτος
ἡμῶν καὶ πρὸς τοῦτον ἄνιμεν.

---

[1] The reference is to *Odyssey* 11. 601-2; the passage (as
Plotinus in the next sentence seems to recognise) is an attempt
to combine two traditions, one which made Heracles a mortal
hero and the other which made him that most exceptional
kind of being in the world of genuine Greek traditional religion, a man who had become a god.

it. It abandons its image if there is nothing at hand to receive it; and it abandons it not in the sense that it is cut off but in that it no longer exists: and the image no longer exists when the whole soul is looking to the intelligible world. The poet seems to be separating the image with regard to Heracles when he says that his shade is in Hades, but he himself among the gods.[1] He was bound to keep to both stories, that he is in Hades and that he dwells among the gods, so he divided him. But perhaps this is the most plausible explanation of the story: because Heracles had this active virtue and in view of his noble character was deemed worthy to be called a god—because he was an active and not a contemplative person (in which case he would have been altogether in that intelligible world), he is above, but there is also still a part of him below.

13. What is it that has carried out this investigation? Is it "we" or the soul? It is "we," but by the soul. And what do we mean by "by the soul"? Did "we" investigate by having soul? No, but in so far as we *are* soul. Will soul move then?[2] Yes, we must allow it this sort of movement, which is not a movement of bodies but its own life. And intellectual activity is ours in the sense that the soul is intellectual and intellectual activity is its higher life, both when the soul operates intellectually and when intellect acts upon us. For intellect too is a part of ourselves and to it we ascend.

[2] Here Plotinus returns to the question raised by Aristotle in the *De Anima* with which he started (cp. the note on ch. 1 of this treatise). But the answer he gives here is Platonic, not Aristotelian; for Aristotle thought is not a movement, as it is for Plato.

ENNEAD I. 2

I. 2. ON VIRTUES

Introductory Note

THIS treatise is No. 19 in Porphyry's chronological order; that is, it belongs to the group of twenty-one treatises which Plotinus had already written by his 59th year, when Porphyry joined him. It is a commentary on the passage from the *Theaetetus* (176A) cited at the beginning of the first chapter, and its object is to determine in what precise sense the virtues can be said to make us godlike. In pursuing this enquiry Plotinus, as often, makes great use of ideas taken from Aristotle, that the gods themselves cannot be said to possess moral virtue (cp. *Nicomachean Ethics* X. 8. 1178b) and that there are two kinds of virtue, intellectual and moral (cp. *Nicomachean Ethics* VI. 2. 1139a ff.)—a doctrine which seems to underlie and be the origin of Plotinus' own rather different doctrine of higher and lower virtue, in which there are also some Stoic elements. In chs. 1–3 Plotinus develops a very interesting and important doctrine of analogy.

Synopsis

We escape from the evils here below by becoming godlike by means of virtue. But what god does virtue make us like?—perhaps the lowest of the three great divine principles, Universal Soul. But does this really possess the cardinal virtues? It does not have civic or moral virtues, but these as well as the higher virtues must play their part in making us godlike (ch. 1). The divinities possess, not virtues as we have them, but the principles from which our virtues derive, and this is sufficient for us to speak of "likeness", which means something different when it is applied to the relationship of a derived thing to its origin from what it means when applied to the relationship of two derived things on the same level (chs. 1–3). The distinction between "civic" and "purifying" virtues (ch. 3). What precisely we mean by "purification" (ch. 4). Its effects on our higher and lower self (ch. 5). What the virtues are in the highest stage of our development, when we are completely free of our lower self, and no longer good men but gods (chs. 6–7).

I. 2. (19) ΠΕΡΙ ΑΡΕΤΩΝ

1. Ἐπειδὴ τὰ κακὰ ἐνταῦθα καὶ τόνδε τὸν
τόπον περιπολεῖ ἐξ ἀνάγκης, βούλεται δὲ ἡ
ψυχὴ φυγεῖν τὰ κακά, φευκτέον ἐντεῦθεν. Τίς
οὖν ἡ φυγή; θεῷ, φησιν, ὁμοιωθῆναι. Τοῦτο
5 δέ, εἰ δίκαιοι καὶ ὅσιοι μετὰ φρονήσεως
γενοίμεθα καὶ ὅλως ἐν ἀρετῇ. Εἰ οὖν ἀρετῇ
ὁμοιούμεθα, ἆρα ἀρετὴν ἔχοντι; Καὶ δὴ καὶ τίνι
θεῷ; Ἆρ' οὖν τῷ μᾶλλον δοκοῦντι ταῦτα ἔχειν
καὶ δὴ τῇ τοῦ κόσμου ψυχῇ καὶ τῷ ἐν ταύτῃ
ἡγουμένῳ ᾧ φρόνησις θαυμαστὴ ὑπάρχει; Καὶ
10 γὰρ εὔλογον ἐνταῦθα ὄντας τούτῳ ὁμοιοῦσθαι.
Ἢ πρῶτον μὲν ἀμφισβητήσιμον, εἰ καὶ τούτῳ
ὑπάρχουσι πᾶσαι· οἷον σώφρονι ἀνδρείῳ εἶναι, ᾧ
μήτε τι δεινόν ἐστιν· οὐδὲν γὰρ ἔξωθεν· μήτε
προσιὸν ἡδὺ οὗ καὶ ἐπιθυμία ἂν γένοιτο μὴ
παρόντος, ἵν' ἔχῃ ἢ ἕλῃ. Εἰ δὲ καὶ αὐτὸς ἐν
15 ὀρέξει ἐστὶ τῶν νοητῶν ὧν καὶ αἱ ἡμέτεραι, δῆλον
ὅτι καὶ ἡμῖν ἐκεῖθεν ὁ κόσμος καὶ αἱ ἀρεταί. Ἆρ'
οὖν ἐκεῖνο ταύτας ἔχει; Ἢ οὐκ εὔλογον τάς γε
πολιτικὰς λεγομένας ἀρετὰς ἔχειν, φρόνησιν μὲν

---

[1] The text which Plotinus is quoting here is Plato, *Theaetetus*
176 A–B. He comments on it again at I. 8. 7, where he is
discussing the necessary existence of evil in this lower world.
[2] Cp. Aristotle, *Nicomachean Ethics* X. 8. 1178b8–18.

I. 2. ON VIRTUES

1. Since it is here that evils are, and "they must necessarily haunt this region," and the soul wants to escape from evils, we must escape from here. What, then, is this escape? "Being made like god," Plato says. And we become godlike "if we become righteous and holy with the help of wisdom," and are altogether in virtue.[1] If then it is virtue which makes us like, it presumably makes us like a being possessing virtue. Then what god would that be? Would it be the one that appears to be particularly characterised by the possession of virtue, that is, the soul of the universe and its ruling principle, in which there is a wonderful wisdom? It is reasonable to suppose that we should become like this principle, as we are here in its universe.

But, first of all, it is debatable whether this principle has all the virtues; whether, for instance, it is self-controlled and brave when it has nothing to frighten it, for there is nothing outside the universe, and nothing attractive can come to it which it has not already got, and produce a desire to have or get it.[2] But if this principle is in a state of aspiration towards the intelligible realities to which our aspirations too are directed, it is clear that our good order and our virtues also come from the intelligible. Has the intelligible, then, virtues? It is at any rate improbable that it has the virtues called "civic,"

περὶ τὸ λογιζόμενον, ἀνδρίαν δὲ περὶ τὸ θυμούμε-
νον, σωφροσύνην δὲ ἐν ὁμολογίᾳ τινὶ καὶ συμφωνίᾳ
ἐπιθυμητικοῦ πρὸς λογισμόν, δικαιοσύνην δὲ τὴν
20 ἑκάστου τούτων ὁμοῦ ο ἰ κ ε ι ο π ρ α γ ί α ν ἀ ρ χ ῆ ς
π έ ρ ι κ α ὶ τ ο ῦ ἄ ρ χ ε σ θ α ι. Ἆρ' οὖν οὐ κατὰ
τὰς πολιτικὰς ὁμοιούμεθα, ἀλλὰ κατὰ τὰς μείζους
τῷ αὐτῷ ὀνόματι χρωμένας; Ἀλλ' εἰ κατ' ἄλλας,
κατὰ τὰς πολιτικὰς ὅλως οὔ; Ἢ ἄλογον μηδ'
ὁπωσοῦν ὁμοιοῦσθαι κατὰ ταύτας—τούτους γοῦν
25 καὶ θείους ἡ φήμη λέγει καὶ λεκτέον ἀμηγέπη
ὡμοιῶσθαι—κατὰ δὲ τὰς μείζους τὴν ὁμοίωσιν
εἶναι. Ἀλλ' ἑκατέρως γε συμβαίνει ἀρετὰς ἔχειν
κἂν εἰ μὴ τοιαύτας. Εἰ οὖν τις συγχωρεῖ[, κἂν
εἰ μὴ τοιαύτας,] ὁμοιοῦσθαι δύνασθαι, ἄλλως ἡμῶν
ἐχόντων πρὸς ἄλλας, οὐδὲν κωλύει, καὶ μὴ πρὸς
30 ἀρετὰς ὁμοιουμένων, ἡμᾶς ταῖς αὐτῶν ἀρεταῖς
ὁμοιοῦσθαι τῷ μὴ ἀρετὴν κεκτημένῳ. Καὶ πῶς;
Ὧδε· εἴ τι θερμότητος παρουσίᾳ θερμαίνεται,
ἀνάγκη καὶ ὅθεν ἡ θερμότης ἐλήλυθε θερμαίνεσθαι;
Καὶ εἴ τι πυρὸς παρουσίᾳ θερμόν ἐστιν, ἀνάγκη
35 καὶ τὸ πῦρ αὐτὸ πυρὸς παρουσίᾳ θερμαίνεσθαι;
Ἀλλὰ πρὸς μὲν τὸ πρότερον εἴποι ἄν τις καὶ ἐν
τῷ πῦρ εἶναι θερμότητα, ἀλλὰ σύμφυτον, ὥστε τὸν
λόγον ποιεῖν τῇ ἀναλογίᾳ ἑπόμενον ἐπακτὸν μὲν
τῇ ψυχῇ τὴν ἀρετήν, ἐκείνῳ δέ, ὅθεν μιμησαμένη
ἔχει, σύμφυτον· πρὸς δὲ τὸν ἐκ τοῦ πυρὸς λόγον

---

[1] This description of the " civic " virtues is based on the
discussion of the virtues in the ideal state in Plato, *Republic* IV
427E–434D.

practical wisdom which has to do with discursive reason, courage which has to do with the emotions, balanced control which consists in a sort of agreement and harmony of passion and reason, justice which makes each of these parts agree in " minding their own business where ruling and being ruled are concerned." [1]   Then are we not made godlike by the civic virtues, but by the greater virtues which have the same names ?   But if by the others, are the civic virtues no help at all to this likeness ?   It is unreasonable to suppose that we are not made godlike in any way by the civic virtues but that likeness comes by the greater ones—tradition certainly calls men of civic virtue godlike and we must say that somehow or other they were made like by this kind of virtue.   It is possible to have virtues on both levels, even if not the same kind of virtues.   If then it is agreed that we can be made like even if we are differently related to different virtues, there is nothing to prevent us, even if we are not made like in regard to virtues, being made like by our own virtues to that which does not possess virtue.   How ?   In this way : if something is made hot by the presence of heat, must that from which the heat comes also be heated ?   And if something is made hot by the presence of fire, must the fire itself be heated by the presence of fire ?   One might object in answer to the first argument that there is heat in fire, but as part of its nature, so that the argument, if it kept to its analogy, would make virtue something extraneous to the soul but part of the nature of that from which the soul receives it by imitation : and in answer to the argument from fire that it would

40 τὸ ἐκεῖνον ἀρετὴν εἶναι· ἀρετῆς δὲ ἀξιοῦμεν εἶναι
μείζονα. Ἀλλ᾽ εἰ μὲν οὗ μεταλαμβάνει ψυχὴ τὸ
αὐτὸ ἦν τῷ ἀφ᾽ οὗ, οὕτως ἔδει λέγειν· νῦν δὲ
ἕτερον μὲν ἐκεῖνο, ἕτερον δὲ τοῦτο. Οὐδὲ γὰρ
οἰκία ἡ αἰσθητὴ τὸ αὐτὸ τῇ νοητῇ, καίτοι ὡμοίωται·
καὶ τάξεως δὲ καὶ κόσμου μεταλαμβάνει ἡ οἰκία ἡ
45 αἰσθητὴ κἀκεῖ ἐν τῷ λόγῳ οὐκ ἔστι τάξις οὐδὲ κόσμος
οὐδὲ συμμετρία. Οὕτως οὖν κόσμου καὶ τάξεως καὶ
ὁμολογίας μεταλαμβάνοντες ἐκεῖθεν καὶ τούτων
ὄντων τῆς ἀρετῆς ἐνθάδε, οὐ δεομένων δὲ τῶν ἐκεῖ
ὁμολογίας οὐδὲ κόσμου οὐδὲ τάξεως, οὐδ᾽ ἂν
50 ἀρετῆς εἴη χρεία, καὶ ὁμοιούμεθα οὐδὲν ἧττον τοῖς
ἐκεῖ δι᾽ ἀρετῆς παρουσίαν. Πρὸς μὲν οὖν τὸ μὴ
ἀναγκαῖον κἀκεῖ ἀρετὴν εἶναι, ἐπείπερ ἡμεῖς
ἀρετῇ ὁμοιούμεθα, ταυτί· δεῖ δὲ πειθὼ ἐπάγειν
τῷ λόγῳ μὴ μένοντας ἐπὶ τῆς βίας.

2. Πρῶτον τοίνυν τὰς ἀρετὰς ληπτέον καθ᾽ ἃς
φαμεν ὁμοιοῦσθαι, ἵν᾽ αὖ τὸ αὐτὸ εὕρωμεν ὃ παρ᾽
ἡμῖν μὲν μίμημα ὂν ἀρετή ἐστιν, ἐκεῖ δὲ οἷον
ἀρχέτυπον ὂν οὐκ ἀρετή, ἐπισημηνάμενοι ὡς ἡ
5 ὁμοίωσις διττή· καὶ ἡ μέν τις ταὐτὸν ἐν τοῖς
ὁμοίοις ἀπαιτεῖ, ὅσα ἐπίσης ὡμοίωται ἀπὸ τοῦ
αὐτοῦ· ἐν οἷς δὲ τὸ μὲν ὡμοίωται πρὸς ἕτερον,
τὸ δὲ ἕτερόν ἐστι πρῶτον, οὐκ ἀντιστρέφον πρὸς
ἐκεῖνο οὐδὲ ὅμοιον αὐτοῦ λεγόμενον, ἐνταῦθα τὴν
10 ὁμοίωσιν ἄλλον τρόπον ληπτέον οὐ ταὐτὸν εἶδος
ἀπαιτοῦντας, ἀλλὰ μᾶλλον ἕτερον, εἴπερ κατὰ τὸν

---

[1] Order, arrangement, and proportion only appear when a form is "extended" in matter, and are not present in the archetypal unity of the intelligible form; they are its expression on a lower level. This is a principle of great importance in Plotinus's theory of art; cp. V. 8. 1.

make that principle virtue; but we consider it greater than virtue. But if that in which the soul participates was the same as the source from which it comes, it would be right to speak in this way; but in fact the two are distinct. The perceptible house is not the same thing as the intelligible house, though it is made in its likeness; the perceptible house participates in arrangement and order, but There, in its formative principle, there is no arrangement or order or proportion.[1] So then, if we participate in order and arrangement and harmony which come from There, and these constitute virtue here, and if the principles There have no need of harmony or order or arrangement, they will have no need of virtue either, and we shall all the same be made like them by the presence of virtue. This is enough to show that it is not necessary for virtue to exist There because we are made like the principles There by virtue. But we must make our argument persuasive, and not be content to force agreement.

2. First then we must consider the virtues by which we assert that we are made like, in order that we may discover this one and the same reality which when we possess it as an imitation is virtue, but There, where it exists as an archetype, is not virtue. We should note that there are two kinds of likeness; one requires that there should be something the same in the things which are alike; this applies to things which derive their likeness equally from the same principle. But in the case of two things of which one is like the other, but the other is primary, not reciprocally related to the thing in its likeness and not said to be like it, likeness must be understood in a different sense; we must not require the

10 ἕτερον τρόπον ὡμοίωται. Τί ποτε οὖν ἐστιν ἡ
ἀρετὴ ἥ τε σύμπασα καὶ ἑκάστη; Σαφέστερος δὲ
ὁ λόγος ἔσται ἐφ᾿ ἑκάστης· οὕτω γὰρ καὶ ὅ τι
κοινόν, καθ᾿ ὃ ἀρεταὶ πᾶσαι, δῆλον ῥαδίως ἔσται.
Αἱ μὲν τοίνυν πολιτικαὶ ἀρεταί, ἃς ἄνω που
15 εἴπομεν, κατακοσμοῦσι μὲν ὄντως καὶ ἀμείνους
ποιοῦσιν ὁρίζουσαι καὶ μετροῦσαι τὰς ἐπιθυμίας
καὶ ὅλως τὰ πάθη μετροῦσαι καὶ ψευδεῖς δόξας
ἀφαιροῦσαι τῷ ὅλως ἀμείνονι καὶ τῷ ὡρίσθαι καὶ
τῶν ἀμέτρων καὶ ἀορίστων ἔξω εἶναι κατὰ τὸ
μεμετρημένον, καὶ αὐταὶ ὁρισθεῖσαι. ᾿Ηι μέτρα
γε ἐν ὕλῃ τῇ ψυχῇ, ὡμοίωνται τῷ ἐκεῖ μέτρῳ καὶ
20 ἔχουσιν ἴχνος τοῦ ἐκεῖ ἀρίστου. Τὸ μὲν γὰρ
πάντη ἄμετρον ὕλη ὂν πάντη ἀνωμοίωται· καθ᾿
ὅσον δὲ μεταλαμβάνει εἴδους, κατὰ τοσοῦτον
ὁμοιοῦται ἀνειδέῳ ἐκείνῳ ὄντι. Μᾶλλον δὲ τὰ
ἐγγὺς μεταλαμβάνει· ψυχὴ δὲ ἐγγυτέρω σώματος
καὶ συγγενέστερον· ταύτῃ καὶ πλέον μεταλαμ-
25 βάνει, ὥστε καὶ ἐξαπατᾶν θεὸς φαντασθεῖσα, μὴ τὸ
πᾶν θεοῦ τοῦτο ᾖ. Οὕτω μὲν οὖν οὗτοι ὁμοιοῦνται.
3. ᾿Αλλ᾿ ἐπεὶ τὴν ὁμοίωσιν ἄλλην ὑποφαίνει ὡς
τῆς μείζονος ἀρετῆς οὔσαν, περὶ ἐκείνης λεκτέον·
ἐν ᾧ καὶ σαφέστερον ἔσται μᾶλλον καὶ τῆς
πολιτικῆς ἡ οὐσία, καὶ ἥτις ἡ μείζων κατὰ τὴν
5 οὐσίαν, καὶ ὅλως, ὅτι ἔστι παρὰ τὴν πολιτικὴν

---

[1] This doctrine of the two kinds of likeness may well have
arisen, as Bréhier suggests, as an answer to the objection of
Parmenides to the view that the Forms are παραδείγματα
(patterns) (Plato, *Parmenides* 132D–133A).

[2] Soul is of course a god for Plotinus, though of the lowest
rank; what we are not to believe is that it is the whole, or the
most important part, of divinity.

same form in both, but rather a different one, since likeness has come about in this different way.[1]

What then is virtue, in general and in particular? Our account of it will be clearer if we deal separately with the particular kinds; in this way that which they have in common, by which they are all virtues, will easily become clear. The civic virtues, which we mentioned above, do genuinely set us in order and make us better by giving limit and measure to our desires, and putting measure into all our experience; and they abolish false opinions, by what is altogether better and by the fact of limitation, and by the exclusion of the unmeasured and indefinite in accord with their measuredness; and they are themselves limited and clearly defined. And so far as they are a measure which forms the matter of the soul, they are made like the measure There and have a trace in them of the Best There. That which is altogether unmeasured is matter, and so altogether unlike: but in so far as it participates in form it becomes like that Good, which is formless. Things which are near participate more. Soul is nearer and more akin to it than body; so it participates more, to the point of deceiving us into imagining that it is a god,[2] and that all divinity is comprised in this likeness. This is how those possessed of political virtue are made like.

3. But, since Plato indicates that likeness is different as belonging to the greater virtue, we must speak about that different likeness. In this discussion the real nature of civic virtue will become clear, and we shall also understand what is the virtue which is greater than it in its real nature, and in general that there is another kind different from civic virtue.

ἑτέρα. Λέγων δὴ ὁ Πλάτων τὴν ὁμοίωσιν τὴν
πρὸς τὸν θεὸν φυγὴν τῶν ἐντεῦθεν εἶναι, καὶ
ταῖς ἀρεταῖς ταῖς ἐν πολιτείᾳ οὐ τὸ ἁπλῶς διδούς,
ἀλλὰ προστιθεὶς πολιτικάς γε, καὶ ἀλλαχοῦ
καθάρσεις λέγων ἁπάσας δῆλός τέ ἐστι διττὰς
10 τιθεὶς καὶ τὴν ὁμοίωσιν οὐ κατὰ τὴν πολιτικὴν
τιθείς. Πῶς οὖν λέγομεν ταύτας καθάρσεις καὶ
πῶς καθαρθέντες μάλιστα ὁμοιούμεθα; Ἢ ἐπειδὴ
κακὴ μέν ἐστιν ἡ ψυχὴ συμπεφυρμένη τῷ
σώματι καὶ ὁμοπαθὴς γινομένη αὐτῷ καὶ πάντα
συνδοξάζουσα, εἴη ἂν ἀγαθὴ καὶ ἀρετὴν ἔχουσα,
15 εἰ μήτε συνδοξάζοι, ἀλλὰ μόνη ἐνεργοῖ—ὅπερ ἐστὶ
νοεῖν τε καὶ φρονεῖν—μήτε ὁμοπαθὴς εἴη—ὅπερ
ἐστὶ σωφρονεῖν—μήτε φοβοῖτο ἀφισταμένη τοῦ
σώματος—ὅπερ ἐστὶν ἀνδρίζεσθαι—ἡγοῖτο δὲ λόγος
καὶ νοῦς, τὰ δὲ μὴ ἀντιτείνοι—δικαιοσύνη δ' ἂν
εἴη τοῦτο. Τὴν δὴ τοιαύτην διάθεσιν τῆς ψυχῆς
20 καθ' ἣν νοεῖ τε καὶ ἀπαθὴς οὕτως ἐστίν, εἴ τις
ὁμοίωσιν λέγοι πρὸς θεόν, οὐκ ἂν ἁμαρτάνοι·
καθαρὸν γὰρ καὶ τὸ θεῖον καὶ ἡ ἐνέργεια τοιαύτη,
ὡς τὸ μιμούμενον ἔχειν φρόνησιν. Τί οὖν οὐ
κἀκεῖνο οὕτω διάκειται; Ἢ οὐδὲ διάκειται, ψυχῆς
δὲ ἡ διάθεσις. Νοεῖ τε ἡ ψυχὴ ἄλλως· τῶν δὲ
25 ἐκεῖ τὸ μὲν ἑτέρως, τὸ δὲ οὐδὲ ὅλως. Πάλιν οὖν

---

[1] The reference here is to the passage of the *Theaetetus*
quoted at the beginning of the first chapter.

ON VIRTUES

Plato, when he speaks of "likeness" as a "flight to God" from existence here below,[1] and does not call the virtues which come into play in civic life just "virtues," but adds the qualification "civic," and elsewhere calls all the virtues "purifications,"[2] makes clear that he postulates two kinds of virtues and does not regard the civic ones as producing likeness. What then do we mean when we call these other virtues "purifications," and how are we made really like by being purified? Since the soul is evil when it is thoroughly mixed with the body and shares its experiences and has all the same opinions, it will be good and possess virtue when it no longer has the same opinions but acts alone—this is intelligence and wisdom—and does not share the body's experiences—this is self-control—and is not afraid of departing from the body—this is courage—and is ruled by reason and intellect, without opposition—and this is justice. One would not be wrong in calling this state of the soul likeness to God, in which its activity is intellectual, and it is free in this way from bodily affections. For the Divine too is pure, and its activity is of such a kind that that which imitates it has wisdom. Well then, why is the Divine itself not in this state? It has no states at all; states belong to the soul. The soul's intellectual activity is different: but of the realities There one thinks differently, and the other does not think at all. Another question then: is "intellectual activity" just a common term covering two different things?

[2] Plato uses the epithet "civic" of virtues at *Republic* IV. 430C, but without any implication of the sort of distinction made here. Virtues are called "purifications" in the *Phaedo*, 69B–C.

τὸ νοεῖν ὁμώνυμον; Οὐδαμῶς· ἀλλὰ τὸ μὲν
πρώτως, τὸ δὲ παρ' ἐκείνου ἑτέρως. Ὡς γὰρ ὁ
ἐν φωνῇ λόγος μίμημα τοῦ ἐν ψυχῇ, οὕτω καὶ ὁ
ἐν ψυχῇ μίμημα τοῦ ἐν ἑτέρῳ. Ὡς οὖν μεμερισμέ-
30 νος ὁ ἐν προφορᾷ πρὸς τὸν ἐν ψυχῇ, οὕτω καὶ ὁ
ἐν ψυχῇ ἑρμηνεὺς ὢν ἐκείνου πρὸς τὸ πρὸ αὐτοῦ.
Ἡ δὲ ἀρετὴ ψυχῆς· νοῦ δὲ οὐκ ἔστιν οὐδὲ τοῦ
ἐπέκεινα.

4. Ζητητέον δέ, εἰ ἡ κάθαρσις ταὐτὸν τῇ
τοιαύτῃ ἀρετῇ, ἢ προηγεῖται μὲν ἡ κάθαρσις,
ἕπεται δὲ ἡ ἀρετή, καὶ πότερον ἐν τῷ καθαίρεσθαι
ἡ ἀρετὴ ἢ ἐν τῷ κεκαθάρθαι. Ἀτελεστέρα τῆς ἐν
5 τῷ κεκαθάρθαι ⟨ἡ ἐν τῷ καθαίρεσθαι· τὸ γὰρ
κεκαθάρθαι⟩ οἷον τέλος ἤδη. Ἀλλὰ τὸ κεκαθάρθαι
ἀφαίρεσις ἀλλοτρίου παντός, τὸ δὲ ἀγαθὸν ἕτερον
αὐτοῦ. Ἤ, εἰ πρὸ τῆς ἀκαθαρσίας ἀγαθὸν ἦν, ἡ
κάθαρσις ἀρκεῖ· ἀλλ' ἀρκέσει μὲν ἡ κάθαρσις, τὸ
δὲ καταλειπόμενον ἔσται τὸ ἀγαθόν, οὐχ ἡ κάθαρ-
10 σις. Καὶ τί τὸ καταλειπόμενόν ἐστι, ζητητέον·
ἴσως γὰρ οὐδὲ τὸ ἀγαθὸν ἦν ἡ φύσις ἡ καταλειπο-
μένη· οὐ γὰρ ἂν ἐγένετο ἐν κακῷ. Ἆρ' οὖν
ἀγαθοειδῆ λεκτέον; Ἤ οὐχ ἱκανὴν πρὸς τὸ μένειν
ἐν τῷ ὄντως ἀγαθῷ· πέφυκε γὰρ ἐπ' ἄμφω. Τὸ
οὖν ἀγαθὸν αὐτῆς τὸ συνεῖναι τῷ συγγενεῖ, τὸ δὲ
15 κακὸν τὸ τοῖς ἐναντίοις. Δεῖ οὖν καθηραμένην
συνεῖναι. Συνέσται δὲ ἐπιστραφεῖσα. Ἆρ' οὖν
μετὰ τὴν κάθαρσιν ἐπιστρέφεται; Ἤ μετὰ τὴν
κάθαρσιν ἐπέστραπται. Τοῦτ' οὖν ἡ ἀρετὴ αὐτῆς;

---

[1] I.e., in Intellect, which is τὸ θεῖον just referred to.

Not at all. It is used primarily of the Divine, and secondarily of that which derives from it. As the spoken word is an imitation of that in the soul, so the word in the soul is an imitation of that in something else: as the uttered word, then, is broken up into parts as compared with that in the soul, so is that in the soul as compared with that before it,[1] which it interprets. And virtue belongs to the soul, but not to Intellect or That which is beyond it.

4. We must investigate whether purification is the same thing as this kind of virtue, or whether purification comes first and virtue follows, and whether virtue consists in the process of being purified or the achieved state of purification. The virtue in the process of purification is less perfect than that in the achieved state, for the achieved state of purification is already a sort of perfection. But being completely purified is a stripping of everything alien, and the good is different from that. If goodness existed before the impurity, purification is enough; but even so, though the purification will be enough, the good will be what is left after purification, not the purification itself. And we must enquire what that which is left is; perhaps the nature which is left was never really the good; for if it was it would not have come into evil. Should we call it something like the good? Yes, but not a nature capable of remaining in the real good, for it has a natural tendency in both directions. So its good will be fellowship with that which is akin to it, and its evil fellowship with its opposites. Then it must attain to this fellowship after being purified; and it will do so by a conversion. Does it then turn itself after the purification? Rather, after the purification it is already turned.

Ἢ τὸ γινόμενον αὐτῇ ἐκ τῆς ἐπιστροφῆς. Τί οὖν
τοῦτο; Θέα καὶ τύπος τοῦ ὀφθέντος ἐντεθεὶς καὶ
20 ἐνεργῶν, ὡς ἡ ὄψις περὶ τὸ ὁρώμενον. Οὐκ ἄρα
εἶχεν αὐτὰ οὐδ' ἀναμιμνήσκεται; Ἢ εἶχεν οὐκ
ἐνεργοῦντα, ἀλλὰ ἀποκείμενα ἀφώτιστα· ἵνα δὲ
φωτισθῇ καὶ τότε γνῷ αὐτὰ ἐνόντα, δεῖ προσβαλεῖν
τῷ φωτίζοντι. Εἶχε δὲ οὐκ αὐτά, ἀλλὰ τύπους·
δεῖ οὖν τὸν τύπον τοῖς ἀληθινοῖς, ὧν καὶ οἱ τύποι,
25 ἐφαρμόσαι. Τάχα δὲ καὶ οὕτω λέγεται ἔχειν, ὅτι
ὁ νοῦς οὐκ ἀλλότριος καὶ μάλιστα δὲ οὐκ ἀλλότριος,
ὅταν πρὸς αὐτὸν βλέπῃ· εἰ δὲ μή, καὶ παρὼν
ἀλλότριος. Ἐπεὶ κἂν[1] ταῖς ἐπιστήμαις· ἐὰν μηδ'
ὅλως ἐνεργῶμεν κατ' αὐτάς, ἀλλότριαι.

5. Ἀλλ' ἐπὶ πόσον κάθαρσις λεκτέον· οὕτω γὰρ
καὶ ἡ ὁμοίωσις τίνι ⟨θεῷ⟩ φανερὰ καὶ ἡ ταυτότης
[τίνι θεῷ]. Τοῦτο δέ ἐστι μάλιστα ζητεῖν θυμὸν
πῶς καὶ ἐπιθυμίαν καὶ τἆλλα πάντα, λύπην καὶ τὰ
5 συγγενῆ, καὶ τὸ χωρίζειν ἀπὸ σώματος ἐπὶ πόσον
δυνατόν. Ἀπὸ μὲν δὴ σώματος ἴσως μὲν καὶ
τοῖς οἷον τόποις συνάγουσαν πρὸς ἑαυτήν, πάντως
μὴν ἀπαθῶς ἔχουσαν καὶ τὰς ἀναγκαίας
τῶν ἡδονῶν αἰσθήσεις μόνον ποιουμένην καὶ
ἰατρεύσεις καὶ ἀπαλλαγὰς πόνων, ἵνα μὴ ἐνοχλοῖτο,
10 τὰς δὲ ἀλγηδόνας ἀφαιροῦσαν καί, εἰ μὴ οἷόν τε,

---

[1] ἐπεὶ κἂν Harder : ἐπεὶ καὶ codd.

---

[1] What the soul sees, the realities which become consciously
present to and active in it after its conversion, are the beings of
the realm of Intellect, the Forms; they were continually present
to it, but it was not conscious of them when it was unpurified
and unconverted.

Is this, then, its virtue? It is rather that which
results for it from the conversion. And what is
this? A sight and the impression of what is seen,[1]
implanted and working in it, like the relationship
between sight and its object. But did it not have
the realities which it sees? Does it not recollect
them? It had them, but not active, lying apart and
unilluminated; if they are to be illuminated and it is
to know that they are present in it, it must thrust
towards that which gives it light. It did not have the
realities themselves but impressions of them; so it
must bring the impressions into accord with the true
realities of which they are impressions. Perhaps, too,
this, they say, is how it is; intellect is not alien and is
particularly not alien when the soul looks towards
it; otherwise it is alien even when it is present. The
same applies to the different branches of knowledge;[2] if we do not act by them at all, they do not
really belong to us.

5. But we must state the extent of the purification;
in this way it will become clear what god we are made
like to and identified with. The question is substantially this; how does the purification deal with
passion and desire and all the rest, pain and its
kindred, and how far is separation from the body
possible? We might say that the soul draws together to itself in a sort of place of its own away from
the body, and is wholly unaffected, and only makes
itself aware of pleasures when it has to, using them as
remedies and reliefs to prevent its activity being
impeded; it gets rid of pains or if it cannot, bears
them quietly and makes them less by not suffer-

[2] I read here κἂν ταῖς ἐπιστήμαις with Harder (*Gnomon* 1952.
188), an emendation now approved by Henry-Schwyzer.

πράως φέρουσαν καὶ ἐλάττους τιθεῖσαν τῷ μὴ
συμπάσχειν· τὸν δὲ θυμὸν ὅσον οἷόν τε ἀφαιροῦσαν
καί, εἰ δυνατόν, πάντη, εἰ δὲ μή, μὴ γοῦν αὐτὴν
συνοργιζομένην, ἀλλ᾽ ἄλλου εἶναι τὸ ἀπροαίρετον,
15 τὸ δὲ ἀπροαίρετον ὀλίγον εἶναι καὶ ἀσθενές· τὸν
δὲ φόβον πάντη· περὶ οὐδενὸς γὰρ φοβήσεται—
τὸ δὲ ἀπροαίρετον καὶ ἐνταῦθα—πλήν γ᾽ ἐν
νουθετήσει. Ἐπιθυμίαν δέ; Ὅτι μὲν μηδενὸς
φαύλου, δῆλον· σίτων δὲ καὶ ποτῶν πρὸς ἄνεσιν
οὐκ αὐτὴ ἕξει· οὐδὲ τῶν ἀφροδισίων δέ· εἰ δ᾽ ἄρα,
20 φυσικῶν, οἶμαι, καὶ οὐδὲ τὸ ἀπροαίρετον ἐχουσῶν·
εἰ δ᾽ ἄρα, ὅσον μετὰ φαντασίας προτυπούς
καὶ ταύτης. Ὅλως δὲ αὕτη μὲν πάντων τούτων
καθαρὰ ἔσται καὶ τὸ ἄλογον δὲ βουλήσεται καὶ
αὐτὸ καθαρὸν ποιῆσαι, ὥστε μηδὲ πλήττεσθαι· εἰ
δ᾽ ἄρα, μὴ σφόδρα, ἀλλ᾽ ὀλίγας τὰς πληγὰς αὐτοῦ
25 εἶναι καὶ εὐθὺς λυομένας τῇ γειτονήσει. ὥσπερ
εἴ τις σοφῷ γειτονῶν ἀπολαύοι τῆς τοῦ σοφοῦ
γειτνιάσεως ἢ ὅμοιος γενόμενος ἢ αἰδούμενος, ὡς
μηδὲν τολμᾶν ποιεῖν ὧν ὁ ἀγαθὸς οὐ θέλει.
Οὔκουν ἔσται μάχη· ἀρκεῖ γὰρ παρὼν ὁ λόγος,
ὃν τὸ χεῖρον αἰδέσεται, ὥστε καὶ αὐτὸ τὸ χεῖρον
30 δυσχερᾶναι, ἐάν τι ὅλως κινηθῇ, ὅτι μὴ ἡσυχίαν
ἦγε παρόντος τοῦ δεσπότου, καὶ ἀσθένειαν αὐτῷ
ἐπιτιμῆσαι.

6. Ἔστι μὲν οὖν οὐδὲν τῶν τοιούτων ἁμαρτία,
ἀλλὰ κατόρθωσις ἀνθρώπῳ· ἀλλ᾽ ἡ σπουδὴ οὐκ

ing with the body. It gets rid of passion as completely as possible, altogether if it can, but if it cannot, at least it does not share its emotional excitement; the involuntary impulse belongs to something else, and is small and weak as well. It does away with fear altogether, for it has nothing to be afraid of—though involuntary impulse comes in here too—except, that is, where fear has a corrective function. What about desire? It will obviously not desire anything bad; it will not itself have the desire of food and drink for the relief of the body, and certainly not of sexual pleasures either. If it does have any of these desires they will, I think, be natural ones with no element of involuntary impulse in them; or if it does have other kinds, only as far as it is with the imagination, which is also prone to these.

The soul will be pure in all these ways and will want to make the irrational part, too, pure, so that this part may not be disturbed; or, if it is, not very much; its shocks will only be slight ones, easily allayed by the neighbourhood of the soul : just as a man living next door to a sage would profit by the sage's neighbourhood, either by becoming like him or by regarding him with such respect as not to dare to do anything of which the good man would not approve. So there will be no conflict : the presence of reason will be enough; the worse part will so respect it that even this worse part itself will be upset if there is any movement at all, because it did not keep quiet in the presence of its master, and will rebuke its own weakness.

6. There is no sin in anything of this sort for a man, but only right action. Our concern, though, is not to

ἔξω ἁμαρτίας εἶναι, ἀλλὰ θεὸν εἶναι. Εἰ μὲν οὖν
τι τῶν τοιούτων ἀπροαίρετον γίνοιτο, θεὸς ἂν εἴη
5 ὁ τοιοῦτος καὶ δαίμων διπλοῦς ὤν, μᾶλλον δὲ
ἔχων σὺν αὐτῷ ἄλλον ἄλλην ἀρετὴν ἔχοντα· εἰ δὲ
μηδέν, θεὸς μόνον· θεὸς δὲ τῶν ἑπομένων τῷ
πρώτῳ. Αὐτὸς μὲν γάρ ἐστιν ὃς ἦλθεν ἐκεῖθεν
καὶ τὸ καθ' αὑτόν, εἰ γένοιτο οἷος ἦλθεν, ἐκεῖ
ἐστιν· ᾧ δὲ συνῳκίσθη ἐνθάδε ἥκων, καὶ τοῦτον
10 αὐτῷ ὁμοιώσει κατὰ δύναμιν τὴν ἐκείνου, ὥστε,
εἰ δυνατόν, ἄπληκτον εἶναι ἢ ἄπρακτόν γε τῶν
μὴ δοκούντων τῷ δεσπότῃ. Τίς οὖν ἑκάστη
ἀρετὴ τῷ τοιούτῳ; Ἡ σοφία μὲν καὶ φρόνησις
ἐν θεωρίᾳ ὧν νοῦς ἔχει· νοῦς δὲ τῇ ἐπαφῇ.
Διττὴ δὲ ἑκατέρα, ἡ μὲν ἐν νῷ οὖσα, ἡ δὲ ἐν
15 ψυχῇ. Κἀκεῖ μὲν οὐκ ἀρετή, ἐν δὲ ψυχῇ ἀρετή.
Ἐκεῖ οὖν τί; Ἐνέργεια αὐτοῦ καὶ ὅ ἐστιν·
ἐνταῦθα δὲ τὸ ἐν ἄλλῳ ἐκεῖθεν ἀρετή. Οὐδὲ γὰρ
αὐτοδικαιοσύνη καὶ ἑκάστη ἀρετή, ἀλλ' οἷον παρά-
δειγμα· τὸ δὲ ἀπ' αὐτῆς ἐν ψυχῇ ἀρετή. Τινὸς

---

[1] The allusion is to the procession of the gods in *Phaedrus*
246E4 ff. In Plato those who follow the first god, Zeus the
leader of the procession, are the philosophical souls (250B7,
252E1); but Plotinus is probably using Plato's language to
express his own thought and means by the First his own
First Principle, the Good, and by the gods who follow, the
divinities of the realm of Intellect.

be out of sin, but to be god.   If, then, there is still any element of involuntary impulse of this sort, a man in this state will be a god or spirit who is double, or rather who has with him someone else who possesses a different kind of virtue: if there is nothing, he will be simply god, and one of those gods who follow the First.[1]   For he himself is the god who came Thence, and his own real nature, if he becomes what he was when he came, is There. When he came here he took up his dwelling with someone else, whom he will make like himself to the best of the powers of his real nature, so that if possible this someone else will be free from disturbance or will do nothing of which his master does not approve. What, then, is each particular virtue when a man is in this state?   Wisdom, theoretical and practical, consists in the contemplation of that which intellect contains; but intellect has it by immediate contact. There are two kinds of wisdom, one in intellect, one in soul.   That which is There [in intellect] is not virtue, that in the soul is virtue.   What is it, then, There?   The act of the self, what it really is; virtue is what comes Thence and exists here in another. For neither absolute justice nor any other moral absolute is virtue, but a kind of exemplar; virtue is what is derived from it in the soul.   Virtue is some-one's virtue; but the exemplar of each particular virtue in the intellect belongs to itself, not to some-one else.

If justice is "minding one's own business" does that mean that it always requires a plurality of parts for its existence?   There is one kind of justice which exists in a plurality, when the parts which it orders are many, and another which is solely and entirely

γὰρ ἡ ἀρετή· αὐτὸ δὲ ἕκαστον αὐτοῦ, οὐχὶ δὲ ἄλλου
20 τινός. Δικαιοσύνη δὲ εἴπερ οἰκειοπραγία, ἆρα αἰεὶ
ἐν πλήθει μερῶν; Ἢ ἡ μὲν ἐν πλήθει, ὅταν πολλὰ
ᾖ τὰ μέρη, ἡ δὲ ὅλως οἰκειοπραγία, κἂν ἑνὸς ᾖ.
Ἡ γοῦν ἀληθὴς αὐτοδικαιοσύνη ἑνὸς πρὸς αὐτό,
ἐν ᾧ οὐκ ἄλλο, τὸ δὲ ἄλλο· ὥστε καὶ τῇ ψυχῇ
δικαιοσύνη ἡ μείζων τὸ πρὸς νοῦν ἐνεργεῖν, τὸ δὲ
25 σωφρονεῖν ἡ εἴσω πρὸς νοῦν στροφή, ἡ δὲ ἀνδρία
ἀπάθεια καθ' ὁμοίωσιν τοῦ πρὸς ὃ βλέπει ἀπαθὲς
ὂν τὴν φύσιν, αὕτη δὲ ἐξ ἀρετῆς, ἵνα μὴ συμπαθῇ
τῷ χείρονι συνοίκῳ.

7. Ἀντακολουθοῦσι τοίνυν ἀλλήλαις καὶ αὗται
αἱ ἀρεταὶ ἐν ψυχῇ, ὥσπερ κἀκεῖ τὰ πρὸ τῆς
ἀρετῆς [αἱ] ἐν νῷ ὥσπερ παραδείγματα. Καὶ γὰρ
ἡ νόησις ἐκεῖ ἐπιστήμη καὶ σοφία, τὸ δὲ πρὸς
5 αὐτὸν ἡ σωφροσύνη, τὸ δὲ οἰκεῖον ἔργον ἡ οἰκειοπραγία, τὸ δὲ οἷον ἀνδρία ἡ αὐλότης καὶ τὸ ἐφ'
αὑτοῦ μένειν καθαρόν. Ἐν ψυχῇ τοίνυν πρὸς νοῦν
ἡ ὅρασις σοφία καὶ φρόνησις, ἀρεταὶ αὐτῆς· οὐ
γὰρ αὐτὴ ταῦτα, ὥσπερ ἐκεῖ. Καὶ τὰ ἄλλα
ὡσαύτως ἀκολουθεῖ· καὶ τῇ καθάρσει δέ, εἴπερ
10 πᾶσαι καθάρσεις κατὰ τὸ κεκαθάρθαι, ἀνάγκη
πάσας· ἢ οὐδεμία τελεία. Καὶ ὁ μὲν ἔχων τὰς

---

[1] Plotinus is here trying to fit Plato's definition of justice as
" minding one's own business " (from the passage in *Republic* IV
referred to in the note on ch. 1) into his own scheme of higher
and lower virtues by means of his principle that the order and
pattern in a lower multiplicity is always the expression of a
higher unity.

[2] The doctrine that the virtues imply one another reciprocally is Stoic. Cp. *Stoicorum Veterum Fragmenta* III. 295
and 299. Plotinus in this treatise, as Bréhier points out in his
introduction, reconciles, by means of his doctrine of

"minding one's own business" even if it is the business of a unity. True absolute justice is the disposition of a unity to itself, a unity in which there are not different parts.[1]

So the higher justice in the soul is its activity towards intellect, its self-control is its inward turning to intellect, its courage is its freedom from affections, according to the likeness of that to which it looks which is free from affections by nature: this freedom from affections in the soul comes from virtue, to prevent its sharing in the affections of its inferior companion.

7. These virtues in the soul, too, imply one another reciprocally, in the same way as the exemplars (so to call them) There in intellect which are prior to virtue.[2] For intuitive thought There is knowledge and wisdom, self-concentration is self-control, its own proper activity is "minding its own business"; its equivalent to courage is immateriality and abiding pure by itself. In the soul, sight directed towards intellect is wisdom, theoretical and practical; these are virtues belonging to soul; for it is not itself they, as is the case There, and the others follow in the same way. And if all virtues are purifications, in the sense that they are the result of a completed process of purification, that process must produce them all, otherwise, [if they are not all present], no single one of them will be perfect. Whoever has the greater virtues

higher and lower virtues, the Stoic view that the virtue of the sage is identical with divine virtue, one and indivisible, with Aristotle's view that the virtues are specifically human excellences, not found in the divine, which is above virtue as the beast is below it (cp. *Nicomachean Ethics* VII 1. 1145a 25–7).

μείζους καὶ τὰς ἐλάττους ἐξ ἀνάγκης δυνάμει, ὁ
δὲ τὰς ἐλάττους οὐκ ἀναγκαίως ἔχει ἐκείνας. Ὁ
μὲν δὴ προηγούμενος τοῦ σπουδαίου βίος οὗτος.
Πότερα δὲ ἐνεργείᾳ ἔχει καὶ τὰς ἐλάττους ὁ τὰς
15 μείζους ἢ ἄλλον τρόπον, σκεπτέον καθ᾽ ἑκάστην·
οἷον φρόνησιν· εἰ γὰρ ἄλλαις ἀρχαῖς χρήσεται,
πῶς ἔτι ἐκείνη μένει κἂν εἰ μὴ ἐνεργοῦσα; Καὶ
εἰ ἡ μὲν φύσει τοσόνδε, ἡ δὲ τοσόνδε, καὶ ἡ
σωφροσύνη ἐκείνη μετροῦσα, ἡ δὲ ὅλως ἀναιροῦσα;
Ταὐτὸν δὲ καὶ ἐπὶ τῶν ἄλλων ὅλως τῆς φρονήσεως
20 κινηθείσης. Ἢ εἰδήσει γε αὐτὰς καὶ ὅσον παρ᾽
αὐτῶν ἕξει; τάχα δέ ποτε περιστατικῶς ἐνεργήσει
κατά τινας αὐτῶν. Ἐπὶ μείζους δὲ ἀρχὰς ἥκων
καὶ ἄλλα μέτρα κατ᾽ ἐκεῖνα πράξει· οἷον τὸ
σωφρονεῖν οὐκ ἐν μέτρῳ ἐκείνῳ τιθείς, ἀλλ᾽ ὅλως
κατὰ τὸ δυνατὸν χωρίζων καὶ ὅλως ζῶν οὐχὶ τὸν
25 ἀνθρώπου βίον τὸν τοῦ ἀγαθοῦ, ὃν ἀξιοῖ ἡ πολιτικὴ
ἀρετή, ἀλλὰ τοῦτον μὲν καταλιπών, ἄλλον δὲ
ἑλόμενος τὸν τῶν θεῶν· πρὸς γὰρ τούτους, οὐ πρὸς
ἀνθρώπους ἀγαθοὺς ἡ ὁμοίωσις. Ὁμοίωσις δὲ ἡ
μὲν πρὸς τούτους, ὡς εἰκὼν εἰκόνι ὡμοίωται ἀπὸ
30 τοῦ αὐτοῦ ἑκατέρα. Ἡ δὲ πρὸς ἄλλον ὡς πρὸς
παράδειγμα.

must necessarily have the lesser ones potentially, but it is not necessary for the possessor of the lesser virtues to have the greater ones. Here, then, we have described the life of the good man in its principal features.

The question whether the possessor of the greater virtues has the lesser ones in act or in some other way must be considered in relation to each individual virtue. Take, for example, practical wisdom. If other principles are in use, how is it still there, even inactive? And if one kind of virtue naturally permits so much, but the other a different amount, and one kind of self-control measures and limits, the other totally abolishes? The same applies to the other virtues, once the question of practical wisdom has been raised. Perhaps the possessor of the virtues will know them, and how much he can get from them, and will act according to some of them as circumstances require. But when he reaches higher principles and different measures he will act according to these. For instance, he will not make self-control consist in that former observance of measure and limit, but will altogether separate himself, as far as possible, from his lower nature and will not live the life of the good man which civic virtue requires. He will leave that behind, and choose another, the life of the gods: for it is to them, not to good men, that we are to be made like. Likeness to good men is the likeness of two pictures of the same subject to each other; but likeness to the gods is likeness to the model, a being of a different kind to ourselves.

ENNEAD I. 3

I. 3. ON DIALECTIC

Introductory Note

THIS treatise is No. 20 in Porphyry's chronological order; it was probably written about the same time as the preceding treatise *On Virtues* (No. 19) and is closely connected with it. It was established in the former treatise that our object is to become godlike, and that this is to be attained by purifying the soul by separating it from the body and ascending in spirit to the intelligible world. *On Dialectic*, as its first words show, is intended to indicate the way of intellectual purification and ascent which we must follow. The first three chapters are an admirable summary of Plato's account of the beginning of the ascent in the *Phaedrus* and the *Symposium*, with two significant (all the more so for being unconscious) alterations: the first is that in Plato φιλόσοφος, μουσικός and ἐρωτικός (*Phaedrus* 248D3) are three different descriptions of the same kind of person, but in Plotinus they are three distinct people: the second is that μουσικός in Plato is used, as always, in the wide classical sense of "cultivated person", one versed in the arts of the Muses; but in Plotinus (as sometimes in Aristotle) it means what we mean by "musician" (in the sense of "music-lover", not specifically composer or performer). The second part of the treatise gives an exposition of Platonic dialectic based on the *Republic*, *Phaedrus* and *Sophist*, asserts its superiority to Aristotelian and Stoic logic, and sketches the relationship to it of natural and moral philosophy.

ON DIALECTIC

Synopsis

What is our way up to the Good, and who is best fitted to start on it? The people best qualified are those of whom Plato speaks, the philosopher, the musician, and the lover. The two stages of the journey, from the sense-world, and in that higher world up to its top (ch. 1). Characteristics of the musician (ch. 1), of the lover (ch. 2) and the philosopher (ch. 3). Description of Platonic dialectic (ch. 4): it is the valuable part of philosophy, concerned with realities (the Forms) and not with words like logic (ch. 5). The dependence on it of natural and moral philosophy and its relationship to moral virtue (ch. 6).

I. 3. (20) ΠΕΡΙ ΔΙΑΛΕΚΤΙΚΗΣ

1. Τίς τέχνη ἢ μέθοδος ἢ ἐπιτήδευσις ἡμᾶς οἷ
δεῖ πορευθῆναι ἀνάγει; Ὅπου μὲν οὖν δεῖ ἐλθεῖν,
ὡς ἐπὶ τἀγαθὸν καὶ τὴν ἀρχὴν τὴν πρώτην,
κείσθω διωμολογημένον καὶ διὰ πολλῶν δεδειγμέ-
5 νον· καὶ δὴ καὶ δι' ὧν τοῦτο ἐδείκνυτο, ἀναγωγή
τις ἦν. Τίνα δὲ δεῖ εἶναι τὸν ἀναχθησόμενον;
Ἆρά γε τὸν πάντα ἢ τὸν πλεῖστά φησιν ἰδόντα,
ὃς ἐν τῇ πρώτῃ γενέσει εἰς γονὴν ἀνδρὸς
ἐσομένου φιλοσόφου μουσικοῦ τινος ἢ
10 ἐρωτικοῦ; Ὁ μὲν δὴ φιλόσοφος τὴν φύσιν καὶ
ὁ μουσικὸς καὶ ὁ ἐρωτικὸς ἀνακτέοι. Τίς οὖν ὁ
τρόπος; Ἆρά γε εἷς καὶ ὁ αὐτὸς ἅπασι τούτοις,
ἢ καθ' ἕνα εἷς τις; Ἔστι μὲν οὖν ἡ πορεία διττὴ
πᾶσιν ἢ ἀναβαίνουσιν ἢ ἄνω ἐλθοῦσιν· ἡ μὲν γὰρ
προτέρα ἀπὸ τῶν κάτω, ἡ δέ γε δευτέρα, οἷς ἤδη
15 ἐν τῷ νοητῷ γενομένοις καὶ οἷον ἴχνος θεῖσιν ἐκεῖ
πορεύεσθαι ἀνάγκη, ἕως ἂν εἰς τὸ ἔσχατον τοῦ
τόπου ἀφίκωνται, ὃ δὴ τέλος τῆς πορείας ὂν
τυγχάνει, ὅταν τις ἐπ' ἄκρῳ γένηται τῷ νοητῷ.
Ἀλλ' ἡ μὲν περιμενέτω, περὶ δὲ τῆς ἀναγωγῆς
πρότερον πειρατέον λέγειν. Πρῶτον δὴ διασταλ-

---

[1] The quotation is from *Phaedrus* 248D1-4 (slightly
adapted). "All or most things" refers to the Forms, seen
by the soul in its heavenly journeying before birth.

I. 3. ON DIALECTIC

1. What art is there, what method or practice, which will take us up there where we must go? Where that is, that it is to the Good, the First Principle, we can take as agreed and established by many demonstrations; and the demonstrations themselves were a kind of leading up on our way. But what sort of person should the man be who is to be led on this upward path? Surely one who has seen all or, as Plato says, "who has seen most things, and in the first birth enters into a human child who is going to be a philosopher, a musician or a lover."[1] The philosopher goes the upward way by nature, the musician and the lover must be led by it. What then is the method of guidance? Is it one and the same for all these, or is there a different one for each? There are two stages of the journey for all, one when they are going up and one when they have arrived above. The first leads from the regions below, the second is for those who are already in the intelligible realm and have gained their footing There, but must still travel till they reach the furthest point of the region; that is the "end of the journey,"[2] when you reach the top of the intelligible. But that can wait. Let us first of all try to speak about the ascent.

[2] From the description of dialectic in *Republic* VII (532E3). The "end of the journey" is the vision of the Good.

20 τέον τοὺς ἄνδρας τούτους ἡμῖν ἀρξαμένους ἀπὸ
τοῦ μουσικοῦ ὅστις ἐστὶ λέγοντας τὴν φύσιν.
Θετέον δὴ αὐτὸν εὐκίνητον καὶ ἐπτοημένον μὲν
πρὸς τὸ καλόν, ἀδυνατώτερον δὲ παρ᾽ αὐτοῦ
κινεῖσθαι, ἕτοιμον δὲ ἐκ τῶν τυχόντων οἷον
ἐκτύπων, ὥσπερ οἱ δειλοὶ πρὸς τοὺς ψόφους,
25 οὕτω καὶ τοῦτον πρὸς τοὺς φθόγγους καὶ τὸ
καλὸν τὸ ἐν τούτοις ἕτοιμον, φεύγοντα δὲ ἀεὶ τὸ
ἀνάρμοστον καὶ τὸ μὴ ἓν ἐν τοῖς ᾀδομένοις καὶ ἐν
τοῖς ῥυθμοῖς καὶ τὸ εὔρυθμον καὶ τὸ εὔσχημον
διώκειν. Μετὰ τοίνυν τοὺς αἰσθητοὺς τούτους
φθόγγους καὶ ῥυθμοὺς καὶ σχήματα οὕτως ἀκτέον·
30 χωρίζοντα τὴν ὕλην ἐφ᾽ ὧν αἱ ἀναλογίαι καὶ οἱ
λόγοι εἰς τὸ κάλλος τὸ ἐπ᾽ αὐτοῖς ἀκτέον καὶ
διδακτέον, ὡς περὶ ἃ ἐπτόητο ἐκεῖνα ἦν, ἡ νοητὴ
ἁρμονία καὶ τὸ ἐν ταύτῃ καλὸν καὶ ὅλως τὸ καλόν,
οὐ τό τι καλὸν μόνον, καὶ λόγους τοὺς φιλοσοφίας
ἐνθετέον· ἀφ᾽ ὧν εἰς πίστιν ἀκτέον ὧν ἀγνοεῖ
35 ἔχων. Τίνες δὲ οἱ λόγοι, ὕστερον.

2. Ὁ δὲ ἐρωτικός, εἰς ὃν μεταπέσοι ἂν καὶ ὁ
μουσικὸς καὶ μεταπεσὼν ἢ μένοι ἂν ἢ παρέλθοι,
μνημονικός ἐστί πως κάλλους· χωρὶς δὲ ὂν
ἀδυνατεῖ καταμαθεῖν, πληττόμενος δὲ ὑπὸ τῶν
5 ἐν ὄψει καλῶν περὶ αὐτὰ ἐπτόηται. Διδακτέον
οὖν αὐτὸν μὴ περὶ ἓν σῶμα πεσόντα ἐπτοῆσθαι,
ἀλλ᾽ ἐπὶ πάντα ἀκτέον τῷ λόγῳ σώματα δεικνύντα
τὸ ἐν πᾶσι ταὐτὸν καὶ ὅτι ἕτερον τῶν σωμάτων

ON DIALECTIC

First of all we must distinguish the characteristics of these men: we will begin by describing the nature of the musician. We must consider him as easily moved and excited by beauty, but not quite capable of being moved by absolute beauty; he is however quick to respond to its images when he comes upon them, and just as nervous people react readily to noises, so does he to articulate sounds and the beauty in them; and he always avoids what is inharmonious and not a unity in songs and verses and seeks eagerly after what is rhythmical and shapely. So in leading him on, these sounds and rhythms and forms perceived by the senses must be made the starting-point. He must be led and taught to make abstraction of the material element in them and come to the principles from which their proportions and ordering forces derive and to the beauty which is in these principles, and learn that this was what excited him, the intelligible harmony and the beauty in it, and beauty universal, not just some particular beauty, and he must have the doctrines of philosophy implanted in him; by these he must be brought to firm confidence in what he possesses without knowing it. We shall explain later what these doctrines are.

2. The lover (into whom the musician may turn, and then either stay at that stage or go on farther) has a kind of memory of beauty. But he cannot grasp it in its separateness, but he is overwhelmingly amazed and excited by visible beauties. So he must be taught not to cling round one body and be excited by that, but must be led by the course of reasoning to consider all bodies and shown the beauty that is the same in all of them, and that it is something

PLOTINUS: ENNEAD I. 3.

καὶ ὅτι ἄλλοθεν λεκτέον καὶ ὅτι ἐν ἄλλοις μᾶλλον,
οἷον ἐ π ι τ η δ ε ύ μ α τ α καλὰ καὶ ν ό μ ο υ ς καλοὺς
10 δεικνύντα—ἐν ἀσωμάτοις γὰρ ὁ ἐθισμὸς τοῦ
ἐρασμίου ἤδη—καὶ ὅτι καὶ ἐν τέχναις καὶ ἐν
ἐ π ι σ τ ή μ α ι ς καὶ ἐν ἀρεταῖς. Εἶτα ἓν ποιητέον
καὶ διδακτέον, ὅπως ἐγγίνονται. Ἀπὸ δὲ τῶν
ἀρετῶν ἤδη ἀναβαίνειν ἐπὶ νοῦν, ἐπὶ τὸ ὄν· κἀκεῖ
βαδιστέον τὴν ἄνω πορείαν.

3. Ὁ δὲ φιλόσοφος τὴν φύσιν ἕτοιμος οὗτος
καὶ οἷον ἐ π τ ε ρ ω μ έ ν ο ς καὶ οὐ δεόμενος χωρίσεως,
ὥσπερ οἱ ἄλλοι οὗτοι, κεκινημένος τὸ ἄνω,
ἀπορῶν δὲ τοῦ δεικνύντος δεῖται μόνον. Δεικτέον
5 οὖν καὶ λυτέον βουλόμενον καὶ αὐτὸν τῇ φύσει καὶ
πάλαι λελυμένον. Τὰ μὲν δὴ μαθήματα δοτέον
πρὸς συνεθισμὸν κατανοήσεως καὶ πίστεως ἀσωμάτου—καὶ γὰρ ῥάδιον δέξεται φιλομαθὴς ὤν—
καὶ φύσει ἐνάρετον πρὸς τελείωσιν ἀρετῶν ἀκτέον
καὶ μετὰ τὰ μαθήματα λόγους διαλεκτικῆς δοτέον
10 καὶ ὅλως διαλεκτικὸν ποιητέον.

4. Τίς δὲ ἡ διαλεκτική, ἣν δεῖ καὶ τοῖς προτέροις
παραδιδόναι; Ἔστι μὲν δὴ ἡ λόγῳ περὶ ἑκάστου
δυναμένη ἕξις εἰπεῖν τί τε ἕκαστον καὶ τί ἄλλων
διαφέρει καὶ τίς ἡ κοινότης ἐν οἷς ἐστι καὶ ποῦ
5 τούτων ἕκαστον καὶ εἰ ἔστιν ὅ ἐστι καὶ τὰ ὄντα

---

[1] This is the ascent of the mind to the vision of Absolute
Beauty in the *Symposium* 210A ff.

[2] The perfect soul is winged in the *Phaedrus* myth (246C1).

[3] The description of dialectic which follows is entirely in
Platonic terms, and there seems no need to assume any Stoic
influence, as Bréhier does. The principal passages from Plato
which Plotinus is using are the descriptions of dialectic in

other than the bodies and must be said to come from elsewhere, and that it is better manifested in other things, by showing him, for instance, the beauty of ways of life and laws—this will accustom him to loveliness in things which are not bodies—and that there is beauty in arts and sciences and virtues.[1] Then all these beauties must be reduced to unity, and he must be shown their origin.   But from virtues he can at once ascend to intellect, to being ; and There he must go the higher way.

3. But the philosopher—he is the one who is by nature ready to respond and " winged,"[2] we may say, and in no need of separation like the others. He has begun to move to the higher world, and is only at a loss for someone to show him the way.   So he must be shown and set free, with his own good will, he who has long been free by nature.   He must be given mathematical studies to train him in philosophical thought and accustom him to firm confidence in the existence of the immaterial—he will take to them easily, being naturally disposed to learning ; he is by nature virtuous, and must be brought to perfect his virtues, and after his mathematical studies instructed in dialectic, and made a complete dialectician.

4. What then is dialectic, which the former kinds of men as well as philosophers must be given ?[3]   It is the science which can speak about everything in a reasoned and orderly way, and say what it is and how it differs from other things and what it has in common with those among which it is and

Republic 531C–535A and *Sophist* 253C–D (with the long discussion which follows) and of the method of division in *Phaedrus* 265D–266A.

ὁπόσα καὶ τὰ μὴ ὄντα αὖ, ἕτερα δὲ ὄντων. Αὕτη
καὶ περὶ ἀγαθοῦ διαλέγεται καὶ περὶ μὴ ἀγαθοῦ
καὶ ὅσα ὑπὸ τὸ ἀγαθὸν καὶ ὅσα ὑπὸ τὸ ἐναντίον
καὶ τί τὸ ἀΐδιον δηλονότι καὶ τὸ μὴ τοιοῦτον,
ἐπιστήμῃ περὶ πάντων, οὐ δόξῃ. Παύσασα δὲ τῆς
10 περὶ τὸ αἰσθητὸν πλάνης ἐνιδρύει τῷ νοητῷ κἀκεῖ
τὴν πραγματείαν ἔχει τὸ ψεῦδος ἀφεῖσα ἐν τῷ
λεγομένῳ ἀληθείας πεδίῳ τὴν ψυχὴν τρέφουσα,
τῇ διαιρέσει τῇ Πλάτωνος χρωμένη μὲν καὶ εἰς
διάκρισιν τῶν εἰδῶν, χρωμένη δὲ καὶ εἰς τὸ τί
ἐστι, χρωμένη δὲ καὶ ἐπὶ τὰ πρῶτα γένη, καὶ τὰ
15 ἐκ τούτων νοερῶς πλέκουσα, ἕως ἂν διέλθῃ πᾶν
τὸ νοητόν, καὶ ἀνάπαλιν ἀναλύουσα, εἰς ὃ ἂν ἐπ᾽
ἀρχὴν ἔλθῃ, τότε δὲ ἡσυχίαν ἄγουσα, ὡς μέχρι γε
τοῦ ἐκεῖ εἶναι ἐν ἡσυχίᾳ οὐδὲν ἔτι πολυπραγμονοῦσα
εἰς ἓν γενομένη βλέπει, τὴν λεγομένην λογικὴν
πραγματείαν περὶ προτάσεως καὶ συλλογισμῶν,
20 ὥσπερ ἂν τὸ εἰδέναι γράφειν, ἄλλῃ τέχνῃ δοῦσα·
ὧν τινα ἀναγκαῖα καὶ πρὸ τέχνης ἡγουμένη,
κρίνουσα δὲ αὐτὰ ὥσπερ καὶ τὰ ἄλλα καὶ τὰ μὲν
χρήσιμα αὐτῶν, τὰ δὲ περιττὰ ἡγουμένη καὶ
μεθόδου τῆς ταῦτα βουλομένης.

5. Ἀλλὰ πόθεν τὰς ἀρχὰς ἔχει ἡ ἐπιστήμη
αὕτη; Ἢ νοῦς δίδωσιν ἐναργεῖς ἀρχάς, εἴ τις
λαβεῖν δύναιτο ψυχή· εἶτα τὰ ἑξῆς καὶ συντίθησι

---

[1] The symbolic place of the Forms in *Phaedrus* 248B6,
where the soul finds its true food.

[2] Plotinus speaks of logic here and in ch. 5 in very general
terms, which apply both to Aristotelian and Stoic logic.
The essential difference for him between logic and dialectic
is that logic deals with words and sentences and their relationships, but dialectic discerns the relationships between

where each of these stands, and if it really is what it is, and how many really existing things there are, and again how many non-existing things, different from real beings. It discusses good and not good, and the things that are classed under good and its opposite, and what is the eternal and what not eternal, with certain knowledge about everything and not mere opinion. It stops wandering about the world of sense and settles down in the world of intellect, and there it occupies itself, casting off falsehood and feeding the soul in what Plato calls "the plain of truth," [1] using his method of division to distinguish the Forms, and to determine the essential nature of each thing, and to find the primary kinds, and weaving together by the intellect all that issues from these primary kinds, till it has traversed the whole intelligible world; then it resolves again the structure of that world into its parts, and comes back to its starting-point; and then, keeping quiet (for it is quiet in so far as it is present There) it busies itself no more, but contemplates, having arrived at unity. It leaves what is called logical activity, about propositions and syllogisms, to another art, as it might leave knowing how to write. Some of the matter of logic it considers necessary, as a preliminary, but it makes itself the judge of this, as of everything else, and considers some of it useful and some superfluous, and belonging to the discipline which wants it. [2]

5. But from where does this science derive its principles? Intellect gives clear principles to any soul which can receive them: and then it combines

things, the only true realities, the Forms, with which the mind of the dialectician is in immediate contact.

καὶ συμπλέκει καὶ διαιρεῖ, ἕως εἰς τέλεον νοῦν
5 ἥκῃ. Ἔστι γάρ, φησιν, αὕτη τὸ καθαρώτατον
νοῦ καὶ φρονήσεως. Ἀνάγκη οὖν τιμιωτάτην
οὖσαν ἕξιν τῶν ἐν ἡμῖν περὶ τὸ ὂν καὶ τὸ τιμιώτατον
εἶναι, φρόνησιν μὲν περὶ τὸ ὄν, νοῦν δὲ περὶ τὸ
ἐπέκεινα τοῦ ὄντος. Τί οὖν; ἡ φιλοσοφία τὸ
τιμιώτατον; ἢ ταὐτὸν φιλοσοφία καὶ διαλεκτική;
Ἢ φιλοσοφίας μέρος τὸ τίμιον. Οὐ γὰρ δὴ
10 οἰητέον ὄργανον τοῦτο εἶναι τοῦ φιλοσόφου· οὐ
γὰρ ψιλὰ θεωρήματά ἐστι καὶ κανόνες, ἀλλὰ περὶ
πράγματά ἐστι καὶ οἷον ὕλην ἔχει τὰ ὄντα· ὁδῷ
μέντοι ἐπ' αὐτὰ χωρεῖ ἅμα τοῖς θεωρήμασι τὰ
πράγματα ἔχουσα· τὸ δὲ ψεῦδος καὶ τὸ σόφισμα
15 κατὰ συμβεβηκὸς γινώσκει ἄλλου ποιήσαντος ὡς
ἀλλότριον κρίνουσα τοῖς ἐν αὐτῇ ἀληθέσι τὸ
ψεῦδος, γινώσκουσα, ὅταν τις προσαγάγῃ, ὅ τι
παρὰ τὸν κανόνα τοῦ ἀληθοῦς. Περὶ προτάσεως
οὖν οὐκ οἶδε—καὶ γὰρ γράμματα—εἰδυῖα δὲ τὸ
ἀληθὲς οἶδεν ὃ καλοῦσι πρότασιν, καὶ καθόλου
20 οἶδε τὰ κινήματα τῆς ψυχῆς, ὅ τε τίθησι καὶ ὃ
αἴρει, καὶ εἰ τοῦτο αἴρει ὃ τίθησιν ἢ ἄλλο, καὶ εἰ
ἕτερα ἢ ταὐτά, προσφερομένων ὥσπερ καὶ ἡ
αἴσθησις ἐπιβάλλουσα, ἀκριβολογεῖσθαι δὲ ἑτέρᾳ
δίδωσι τοῦτο ἀγαπώσῃ.

6. Μέρος οὖν τὸ τίμιον· ἔχει γὰρ καὶ ἄλλα φιλο-
σοφία· καὶ γὰρ καὶ περὶ φύσεως θεωρεῖ βοήθειαν

---

¹ *Philebus* 58D6–7.

and interweaves and distinguishes their consequences, till it arrives at perfect intelligence. For,
Plato says, dialectic is " the purest part of intelligence
and wisdom." [1] So, since it is the most valuable of
our mental abilities, it must be concerned with real
being and what is most valuable; as wisdom it is
concerned with real being, as intelligence with That
which is beyond being. But surely philosophy is
the most valuable thing? Are dialectic and philosophy the same? It is the valuable part of
philosophy. For it must not be thought to be a tool
the philosopher uses. It is not just bare theories
and rules; it deals with things and has real beings
as a kind of material for its activity; it approaches
them methodically and possesses real things along
with its theories. It knows falsehood and sophism
incidentally, as another's product, and judges falsehood as something alien to the truths in itself,
recognising, when anyone brings it forward, something contrary to the rule of truth. So it does not
know about propositions—they are just letters—but
in knowing the truth it knows what they call propositions, and in general it knows the movements of
the soul, what it affirms and what it denies, and
whether it affirms the same thing as it denies or
something else, and if things are different from each
other or the same; whatever is submitted to it it
perceives by directing intuition, as sense-perception
also does, but it hands over petty precisions of
speech to another discipline which finds satisfaction
in them.

6. So dialectic is the valuable part. Philosophy
has other parts; it also surveys the nature of the
physical world with assistance from dialectic, as the

παρὰ διαλεκτικῆς λαβοῦσα, ὥσπερ καὶ ἀριθμητικῇ
προσχρῶνται αἱ ἄλλαι τέχναι· μᾶλλον μέντοι
5 αὕτη ἐγγύθεν κομίζεται παρὰ τῆς διαλεκτικῆς·
καὶ περὶ ἠθῶν ὡσαύτως θεωροῦσα μὲν ἐκεῖθεν,
προστιθεῖσα δὲ τὰς ἕξεις καὶ τὰς ἀσκήσεις, ἐξ ὧν
προίασιν αἱ ἕξεις. Ἴσχουσι δὲ αἱ λογικαὶ ἕξεις
καὶ ὡς ἴδια ἤδη τὰ ἐκεῖθεν· καὶ γὰρ μετὰ τῆς
ὕλης τὰ πλεῖστα· καὶ αἱ μὲν ἄλλαι ἀρεταὶ τοὺς
10 λογισμοὺς ἐν τοῖς πάθεσι τοῖς ἰδίοις καὶ ταῖς
πράξεσιν, ἡ δὲ φρόνησις ἐπιλογισμός τις καὶ τὸ
καθόλου μᾶλλον καὶ εἰ ἀντακολουθοῦσι καὶ εἰ δεῖ
νῦν ἐπισχεῖν ἢ εἰσαῦθις ἢ ὅλως ἄλλο βέλτιον· ἡ
δὲ διαλεκτικὴ καὶ ἡ σοφία ἔτι καθόλου καὶ ἀύλως
πάντα εἰς χρῆσιν προφέρει τῇ φρονήσει. Πότερα
15 δὲ ἔστι τὰ κάτω εἶναι ἄνευ διαλεκτικῆς καὶ
σοφίας; Ἢ ἀτελῶς καὶ ἐλλειπόντως. Ἔστι δὲ
σοφὸν εἶναι καὶ διαλεκτικὸν οὕτως ἄνευ τούτων;
Ἢ οὐδ' ἂν γένοιτο, ἀλλὰ ἢ πρότερον ἢ ἅμα
συναύξεται. Καὶ τάχα ἂν φυσικάς τις ἀρετὰς
ἔχοι, ἐξ ὧν αἱ τέλειαι σοφίας γενομένης. Μετὰ
20 τὰς φυσικὰς οὖν ἡ σοφία· εἶτα τελειοῖ τὰ ἤθη.

---

[1] The idea of the dependence of the other skills on arithmetic comes from *Republic* VII. 522C 1–6. Plotinus is here
claiming for dialectic the same position in relation to natural
and moral philosophy as the Stoics claimed for logic (cp.

other skills use arithmetic to help them;[1] though natural philosophy stands closer to dialectic in its borrowing: in the same way moral philosophy derives from dialectic on its contemplative side, but adds the virtuous dispositions and the exercises which produce them. The intellectual virtues have principles from dialectic almost as their proper possession; although they are with matter most of their principles came from that higher realm.[2] The other virtues apply reasoning to particular experiences and actions, but practical wisdom is a kind of superior reasoning concerned more with the universal; it considers questions of mutual implication, and whether to refrain from action, now or later, or whether an entirely different course would be better. Dialectic and theoretical wisdom provide everything for practical wisdom to use, in a universal and immaterial form.

Can the lower kinds of virtue exist without dialectic and theoretical wisdom? Yes, but only incompletely and defectively. And can one be a wise man and a dialectician without these lower virtues? It would not happen; they must either precede or grow along with wisdom. One might perhaps have natural virtues, from which the perfect ones develop with the coming of wisdom. So wisdom comes after the natural virtue, and then perfects the character; or rather when the natural virtues exist both increase and come to perfection together: as

Diogenes Laertius VII. 83), with the essential differences due to the distinction referred to in the note on ch. 4.

[2] Following Bréhier, Cilento, and Schwyzer, I take καὶ here as concessive and τὰ πλεῖστα as accusative with ἴσχουσι: the intellectual virtues operate in the material world with principles mainly derived from the intelligible world.

Ἡ τῶν φυσικῶν οὐσῶν συναύξεται ἤδη ἄμφω καὶ συντελειοῦται· ἢ προλαβοῦσα ἡ ἑτέρα τὴν ἑτέραν ἐτελείωσεν· ὅλως γὰρ ἡ φυσικὴ ἀρετὴ καὶ ὄμμα ἀτελὲς καὶ ἦθος ἔχει, καὶ αἱ ἀρχαὶ τὸ πλεῖστον ἀμφοτέραις, ἀφ' ὧν ἔχομεν.

the one progresses it perfects the other; for in general natural virtue is imperfect both in vision and character, and the principles from which we derive them are the most important thing both in natural virtue and wisdom.

ENNEAD I. 4

I. 4. ON WELL-BEING

Introductory Note

THIS is a late treatise (No. 46 in the chronological order), written towards the end of Plotinus's life. It is concerned with what was always, and more than ever in his last years, his chief preoccupation, the practical and most urgent question of how we are to live well and attain our true good. The first four chapters are devoted to an establishment of his fundamental position, that the good life is the life of Intellect, independent of all outward circumstances and material and emotional satisfactions of our lower nature, by a critical examination of Aristotelian and Stoic views. The rest of the treatise is a sermon on true well-being; this is very much in the manner of, and deals with the usual themes of, the Stoic–Cynic diatribe: but there are important differences even here between the thought of Plotinus and that of the Stoics due to his different conception of man as a double being, not a single and simple one.

Synopsis

If the good life is simply a matter of successfully performing one's proper functions and attaining one's natural end, as Aristotle thinks, one cannot deny it to other living things, plants included (ch. 1). The Epicurean attempt to make the good life consist in a feeling of pleasure or tranquillity, a particular kind of conscious experience, also breaks down on examination (ch. 2). The Stoic position, that the good life is the life of reason, is nearer the truth, but their doctrine of "primary natural needs" confuses the issue (ch. 2). The good life, the true human good, can only be the highest and most perfect kind of life, that of the Intellect (which depends on the Absolute Good as its cause) (ch. 3). And a man to attain perfection must not only *have* Intellect but *be* Intellect, and so perfectly virtuous; and if he is this he has all he needs for well-being (ch. 4). His well-being will be unaffected by pain, sickness and even the greatest misfortune (chs. 5–8): it will be even independent of consciousness, which is something secondary, the reflection of the life of Intellect on the level of the body–soul composite (chs. 9–10). Outward circumstances and bodily goods will add nothing to his well-being, and if he has too much of them may even detract from it; but he will recognise a responsibility to his body and give it what it really needs (chs. 11–16).

I. 4. (46) ΠΕΡΙ ΕΥΔΑΙΜΟΝΙΑΣ

1. Τὸ εὖ ζῆν καὶ τὸ εὐδαιμονεῖν ἐν τῷ αὐτῷ
τιθέμενοι καὶ τοῖς ἄλλοις ζῴοις ἆρα τούτων μετα-
δώσομεν; Εἰ γὰρ ἔστιν αὐτοῖς ᾗ πεφύκασιν
ἀνεμποδίστως διεξάγειν, κἀκεῖνα τί κωλύει ἐν
5 εὐζωίᾳ λέγειν εἶναι; Καὶ γὰρ εἴτε ἐν εὐπαθείᾳ
τὴν εὐζωίαν τις θήσεται, εἴτε ἐν ἔργῳ οἰκείῳ
τελειουμένῳ, κατ' ἄμφω καὶ τοῖς ἄλλοις ζῴοις
ὑπάρξει. Καὶ γὰρ εὐπαθεῖν ἐνδέχοιτο ἂν καὶ ἐν
τῷ κατὰ φύσιν ἔργῳ εἶναι· οἷον καὶ τὰ μουσικὰ
τῶν ζῴων ὅσα τοῖς τε ἄλλοις εὐπαθεῖ καὶ δὴ καὶ
10 ᾄδοντα ᾗ πέφυκε καὶ ταύτῃ αἱρετὴν αὐτοῖς τὴν
ζωὴν ἔχει. Καὶ τοίνυν καὶ εἰ τέλος τι τὸ εὐδαιμονεῖν τιθέμεθα, ὅπερ ἐστὶν ἔσχατον τῆς ἐν φύσει
ὀρέξεως, καὶ ταύτῃ ἂν αὐτοῖς μεταδοίημεν τοῦ
εὐδαιμονεῖν εἰς ἔσχατον ἀφικνουμένων, εἰς ὃ
ἐλθοῦσιν ἵσταται ἡ ἐν αὐτοῖς φύσις πᾶσαν ζωὴν
15 αὐτοῖς διεξελθοῦσα καὶ πληρώσασα ἐξ ἀρχῆς
τέλος. Εἰ δέ τις δυσχεραίνει τὸ τῆς εὐδαιμονίας

---

[1] I translate εὐδαιμονία and kindred words by "well-
being," "being well off" because this kind of expression,
though inadequate, is at least less misleading than the common
translation "happiness." Happiness, as we normally use
the word, means *feeling* good; but εὐδαιμονία means *being*
in a good state; and Plotinus devotes a great part of this
treatise to showing that one can be εὐδαίμων if one has no

I. 4. ON WELL-BEING[1]

1. Suppose we assume the good life and well-being to be one and the same;[2] shall we then have to allow a share in them to other living things as well as ourselves? If they can live in the way natural to them without impediment,[3] what prevents us from saying that they too are in a good state of life? For whether one considers the good life as consisting in satisfactory experience or accomplishing one's proper work, in either case it will belong to the other living things as well as us. For they can have satisfactory experiences and be engaged in their natural work; musical creatures, for instance, which are otherwise well off and sing in their natural way as well, and so have the life they want. Then again, suppose we make well-being an end,[4] that is, the ultimate term of natural desire; we shall still have to allow other living things a share in well-being when they reach their final state, that where, when they come to it, the nature in them rests, since it has passed through their whole life and fulfilled it from beginning to end. But if anyone dislikes the idea of extending some degree of well-being down to the other

happy emotions and even if one is completely unconscious of one's εὐδαιμονία.

[2] This is Aristotle's position; cp. *Nicomachean Ethics* I. 8 1098b. 21.

[3] Cp. *N.E.* VII. 14. 1153b. 11.

[4] Cp. *N.E.* X. 16. 1176a. 31.

καταφέρειν εἰς τὰ ζῷα τὰ ἄλλα—οὕτω γὰρ ἂν
καὶ τοῖς ἀτιμοτάτοις αὐτῶν μεταδώσειν· μεταδώ-
σειν δὲ καὶ τοῖς φυτοῖς ζῶσι καὶ αὐτοῖς καὶ ζωὴν
ἐξελιττομένην εἰς τέλος ἔχουσι—πρῶτον μὲν ἄτοπος
20 διὰ τί εἶναι οὐ δόξει μὴ ζῆν εὖ τὰ ἄλλα ζῷα λέγων,
ὅτι μὴ πολλοῦ ἄξια αὐτῷ δοκεῖ εἶναι; Τοῖς δὲ
φυτοῖς οὐκ ἀναγκάζοιτο ἂν διδόναι ὃ τοῖς ἅπασι
ζῴοις δίδωσιν, ὅτι μὴ αἴσθησις πάρεστιν αὐτοῖς.
Εἴη δ' ἄν τις ἴσως καὶ ὁ διδοὺς τοῖς φυτοῖς,
25 εἴπερ καὶ τὸ ζῆν· ζωὴ δὲ ἡ μὲν εὖ ἂν εἴη, ἡ δὲ
τοὐναντίον· οἷον ἔστι καὶ ἐπὶ τῶν φυτῶν εὐπαθεῖν
καὶ μή, καρπὸν αὖ φέρειν καὶ μὴ φέρειν. Εἰ μὲν
οὖν ἡδονὴ τὸ τέλος καὶ ἐν τούτῳ τὸ εὖ ζῆν, ἄτοπος
ὁ ἀφαιρούμενος τὰ ἄλλα ζῷα τὸ εὖ ζῆν· καὶ εἰ
ἀταραξία δὲ εἴη, ὡσαύτως· καὶ εἰ τὸ κατὰ φύσιν
30 ζῆν δὲ λέγοιτο τὸ εὖ ζῆν εἶναι.

2. Τοῖς μέντοι φυτοῖς διὰ τὸ μὴ αἰσθάνεσθαι οὐ
διδόντες κινδυνεύσουσιν οὐδὲ ζῴοις ἤδη ἅπασι
διδόναι. Εἰ μὲν γὰρ τὸ αἰσθάνεσθαι τοῦτο λέγουσι,
τὸ τὸ πάθος μὴ λανθάνειν, δεῖ αὐτὸ ἀγαθὸν εἶναι
5 τὸ πάθος πρὸ τοῦ μὴ λανθάνειν, οἷον τὸ κατὰ
φύσιν ἔχειν, κἂν λανθάνῃ, καὶ οἰκεῖον εἶναι, κἂν
μήπω γινώσκῃ ὅτι οἰκεῖον καὶ ὅτι ἡδύ· δεῖ γὰρ
ἡδὺ εἶναι. Ὥστε ἀγαθοῦ τούτου ὄντος καὶ παρόν-

---

[1] Both Hedonists and Epicureans maintained this, in
different senses; but as Epicurus is clearly alluded to in the
next sentence, this is meant to be a reference to the
Hedonists only; cp. Aristippus in Diog. Laert. II. 88.

[2] ἀταραξία, the untroubled peace of mind which was the
Epicurean ideal.

living things—which would involve giving a share in it even to the meanest; one would have to give a share to plants, because they too are alive and have a life which unfolds to its end—first of all, why will it not seem absurd of him to deny that other living things live well just because he does not think them important? Then, one is not compelled to allow to plants what one allows to all other living beings; for plants have no sensations. But there might perhaps be someone who would allow well-being to plants just because they have life; one life can be good, another the opposite, as plants too can be well or badly off, and bear fruit or not bear fruit. If pleasure is the end[1] and the good life is determined by pleasure, it is absurd of anyone to deny the good life to other living things; the same applies to tranquillity,[2] and also if the life according to nature is stated to be the good life.

2. Those who deny it to plants because they have no sensation[3] run the risk of denying it to all living things. For if they mean by sensation being aware of one's experiences, the experience must be good before one is aware of it; for example, to be in a natural state is good, even if one is not aware of it, and so is to be in one's own proper state, even if one does not yet know that it is one's own proper state, and that it is pleasant (as it must necessarily be).

---

[3] As Aristotle did; in *N.E.* X. 8 1178b. 28 he denies it to all living beings except man because they have no share in θεωρία. Plotinus criticises Aristotle because, though he regards εὐδαιμονία as something distinctively human, he often defines it in terms which must necessarily apply to all living things. Both Aristotle and Plotinus place εὐδαιμονία in the life of the intellect, though they conceive that life in very different ways.

τος ἤδη ἐστὶν ἐν τῷ εὖ τὸ ἔχον. Ὥστε τί δεῖ τὴν
αἴσθησιν προσλαμβάνειν, εἰ μὴ ἄρα οὐκ ἐν τῷ
10 γινομένῳ πάθει [ἢ καταστάσει] τὸ ἀγαθὸν διδόασιν,
ἀλλὰ τῇ γνώσει καὶ αἰσθήσει; Ἀλλ' οὕτω γε τὴν
αἴσθησιν αὐτὴν τὸ ἀγαθὸν ἐροῦσι καὶ ἐνέργειαν
ζωῆς αἰσθητικῆς· ὥστε καὶ ὁτουοῦν ἀντιλαμ-
βανομένοις. Εἰ δὲ ἐξ ἀμφοῖν τὸ ἀγαθὸν λέγουσιν,
οἷον αἰσθήσεως τοιούτου, πῶς ἑκατέρου ἀδιαφόρου
15 ὄντος τὸ ἐξ ἀμφοῖν ἀγαθὸν εἶναι λέγουσιν; Εἰ δὲ
ἀγαθὸν μὲν τὸ πάθος, καὶ τὴν τοιάνδε κατάστασιν
τὸ εὖ ζῆν, ὅταν γνῷ τις τὸ ἀγαθὸν αὐτῷ παρόν,
ἐρωτητέον αὐτούς, εἰ γνοὺς τὸ παρὸν δὴ τοῦτο ὅτι
πάρεστιν εὖ ζῇ, ἢ δεῖ γνῶναι οὐ μόνον ὅτι ἡδύ,
ἀλλ' ὅτι τοῦτο τὸ ἀγαθόν. Ἀλλ' εἰ ὅτι τοῦτο τὸ
20 ἀγαθόν, οὐκ αἰσθήσεως τοῦτο ἔργον ἤδη, ἀλλ'
ἑτέρας μείζονος ἢ κατ' αἴσθησιν δυνάμεως. Οὐ
τοίνυν τοῖς ἡδομένοις τὸ εὖ ζῆν ὑπάρξει, ἀλλὰ
τῷ γινώσκειν δυναμένῳ, ὅτι ἡδονὴ τὸ ἀγαθόν.
Αἴτιον δὴ τοῦ εὖ ζῆν οὐχ ἡδονὴ ἔσται, ἀλλὰ τὸ
25 κρίνειν δυνάμενον, ὅτι ἡδονὴ ἀγαθόν. Καὶ τὸ
μὲν κρῖνον βέλτιον ἢ κατὰ πάθος· λόγος γὰρ ἢ
νοῦς· ἡδονὴ δὲ πάθος· οὐδαμοῦ δὲ κρεῖττον
ἄλογον λόγου. Πῶς ἂν οὖν ὁ λόγος αὐτὸν ἀφεὶς
ἄλλο θήσεται ἐν τῷ ἐναντίῳ γένει κείμενον κρεῖττον εἶναι ἑαυτοῦ; Ἀλλὰ γὰρ ἐοίκασιν, ὅσοι τε
τοῖς φυτοῖς οὐ διδόασι καὶ ὅσοι αἰσθήσει τοιάδε
30 τὸ εὖ, λανθάνειν ἑαυτοὺς μεῖζόν τι τὸ εὖ ζῆν

So if something is good and is there its possessor is already well off; so why should we bring sensation into it, unless of course people attribute good not to the actual experience but to the knowledge and perception of it ? But in this way they will be saying that the good is really the sensation, the activity of the sense-life; so that it will be all the same whatever is sensed. But if they say that the good is the product of the two, the sensation of an object of a particular kind, why, when each of the constituents is neutral, do they say that the product is good ? But if it is the experience which is good, and the good life is the special state when someone knows that the good is present to him, we must ask them whether he lives well by knowing that this present thing is present or whether he must know not only that it gives him pleasure but that it is the good. But if he must know that it is the good, this is no longer the business of sensation but of another greater power than that of sense. So the good life will not belong to those who feel pleasure but to the man who is able to know that pleasure is the good. Then the cause of living well will not be pleasure, but the power of judging that pleasure is good. And that which judges is better than mere experience, for it is reason or intellect; but pleasure is an experience; and the irrational is never better than reason. How then can the reason set itself aside and assume that something else which has its place in the contrary kind is better than itself? It looks as if the people who deny well-being to plants, and those who place it in a particular kind of sensation, were unconsciously in search of a good life which is something higher, and were assuming that it is

ζητοῦντες καὶ ἐν τρανοτέρᾳ ζωῇ τὸ ἄμεινον
τιθέντες. Καὶ ὅσοι δὲ ἐν λογικῇ ζωῇ εἶναι
λέγουσιν, ἀλλ᾽ οὐχ ἁπλῶς ζωῇ, οὐδὲ εἰ αἰσθητικὴ
εἴη, καλῶς μὲν ἴσως ἂν λέγοιεν. Διὰ τί δὲ οὕτω
καὶ περὶ τὸ λογικὸν ζῷον μόνον τὸ εὐδαιμονεῖν
35 τίθενται, ἐρωτᾶν αὐτοὺς προσήκει. Ἆρά γε τὸ
λογικὸν προσλαμβάνετε, ὅτι εὐμήχανον μᾶλλον ὁ
λόγος καὶ ῥᾳδίως ἀνιχνεύειν καὶ περιποιεῖν τὰ
πρῶτα κατὰ φύσιν δύναται, ἢ κἂν μὴ δυνατὸς ᾖ
ἀνιχνεύειν μηδὲ τυγχάνειν; Ἀλλ᾽ εἰ μὲν διὰ τὸ
ἀνευρίσκειν μᾶλλον δύνασθαι, ἔσται καὶ τοῖς μὴ
40 λόγον ἔχουσιν, εἰ ἄνευ λόγου φύσει τυγχάνοιεν
τῶν πρώτων κατὰ φύσιν, τὸ εὐδαιμονεῖν· καὶ
ὑπουργὸς ἂν ὁ λόγος καὶ οὐ δι᾽ αὐτὸν αἱρετὸς
γίγνοιτο οὐδ᾽ αὖ ἡ τελείωσις αὐτοῦ, ἥν φαμεν
ἀρετὴν εἶναι. Εἰ δὲ φήσετε μὴ διὰ τὰ κατὰ φύσιν
πρῶτα ἔχειν τὸ τίμιον, ἀλλὰ δι᾽ αὐτὸν ἀσπαστὸν
45 εἶναι, λεκτέον τί τε ἄλλο ἔργον αὐτοῦ καὶ τίς ἡ
φύσις αὐτοῦ καὶ τί τέλειον αὐτὸν ποιεῖ. Ποιεῖν
γὰρ δεῖ αὐτὸν τέλειον οὐ τὴν θεωρίαν τὴν περὶ
ταῦτα, ἀλλὰ ἄλλο τι τὸ τέλειον αὐτῷ εἶναι καὶ
φύσιν ἄλλην εἶναι αὐτῷ καὶ μὴ εἶναι αὐτὸν τούτων
τῶν πρώτων κατὰ φύσιν μηδὲ ἐξ ὧν τὰ πρῶτα
50 κατὰ φύσιν μηδ᾽ ὅλως τούτου τοῦ γένους εἶναι,

---

[1] These are the Stoics, cp. Diog. Laert. VII. 130. The
serious discussion of their position begins here (there has been
a passing allusion to their teaching—"the life according to
nature"—at the end of ch. 1). Plotinus in his criticism of
the Stoics in this chapter fastens upon what was generally
regarded by opponents of the school as the weakest point in
their ethical theory, the difficulty of reconciling their insistence that the life of reason and virtue was the only real good

better the purer and clearer life is. Those who say that it is to be found in a rational life,[1] not simply in life, even life accompanied by sensation, may very likely be right; but we ought to ask them why they posit well-being only in the case of rational living things. "Do you add the 'rational' because reason is more efficient and can easily find out and procure the primary natural needs, or would you require reason even if it was not able to find them out or obtain them? If you require it because it is better able to find them out, then irrational creatures too, if by their nature they can satisfy the primary natural needs without reason, will have well-being; and then reason would be a servant and not worth having for itself, and the same would apply to its perfection, which we say is virtue. But if you say that reason has not its place of honour because of the primary natural needs, but is welcome for its own sake, you must tell us what other work it has and what is its nature and what makes it perfect." For it cannot be the study of these primary natural needs which perfects reason; its perfection is something else, and its nature is different, and it is not itself one of these primary natural needs or of the sources from which the primary natural needs derive; it does not belong to this class of beings at all, but is

for man with their doctrine of the importance of τὰ πρῶτα κατὰ φύσιν, the primary natural needs. For criticism of Stoic ethics on these lines cp. Cicero, *De Finibus*, Book IV, and Plutarch, *De Communibus Notitiis* (especially chs. 23 and 26). Plotinus however is closer to the Stoic position than its earlier critics; he agrees completely with them that external goods and natural advantages are indifferent, and that true well-being lies in the life of reason and virtue alone; but, he says, the Stoics cannot explain *why* this is so.

ἀλλὰ κρείττονα τούτων ἁπάντων· ἢ πῶς τὸ τίμιον
αὐτῷ οὐκ οἶμαι ἕξειν αὐτοὺς λέγειν. Ἀλλ' οὗτοι
μέν, ἕως ἂν κρείττονα εὕρωσι φύσιν τῶν περὶ ἃ
νῦν ἵστανται, ἐατέοι ἐνταυθοῖ εἶναι, οὗπερ μένειν
55 ἐθέλουσιν, ἀπόρως ἔχοντες ὅπῃ τὸ εὖ ζῆν, οἷς
δυνατόν ἐστι τούτων.

3. Ἡμεῖς δὲ λέγωμεν ἐξ ἀρχῆς τί ποτε τὸ
εὐδαιμονεῖν ὑπολαμβάνομεν εἶναι. Τιθέμενοι δὴ
τὸ εὐδαιμονεῖν ἐν ζωῇ, εἰ μὲν συνώνυμον τὸ ζῆν
ἐποιούμεθα, πᾶσι μὲν ἂν τοῖς ζῶσιν ἀπέδομεν
5 δεκτικοῖς εὐδαιμονίας εἶναι, εὖ δὲ ζῆν ἐνεργείᾳ
ἐκεῖνα, οἷς παρῆν ἕν τι καὶ ταὐτόν, οὗ ἐπεφύκει
δεκτικὰ πάντα τὰ ζῷα εἶναι, καὶ οὐκ ἂν τῷ μὲν
λογικῷ ἔδομεν δύνασθαι τοῦτο, τῷ δὲ ἀλόγῳ
οὐκέτι· ζωὴ γὰρ ἦν τὸ κοινόν, ὃ δεκτικὸν τοῦ
αὐτοῦ πρὸς τὸ εὐδαιμονεῖν ἔμελλεν εἶναι, εἴπερ ἐν
10 ζωῇ τινι τὸ εὐδαιμονεῖν ὑπῆρχεν. Ὅθεν, οἶμαι,
καὶ οἱ ἐν λογικῇ ζωῇ λέγοντες τὸ εὐδαιμονεῖν
γίνεσθαι οὐκ ἐν τῇ κοινῇ ζωῇ τιθέντες ἠγνόησαν
τὸ εὐδαιμονεῖν οὐδὲ ζωὴν ὑποτιθέμενοι. Ποιότητα
δὲ τὴν λογικὴν δύναμιν, περὶ ἣν ἡ εὐδαιμονία
συνίσταται, ἀναγκάζοιντο ἂν λέγειν. Ἀλλὰ τὸ
15 ὑποκείμενον αὐτοῖς λογική ἐστι ζωή· περὶ γὰρ
τὸ ὅλον τοῦτο ἡ εὐδαιμονία συνίσταται· ὥστε περὶ
ἄλλο εἶδος ζωῆς. Λέγω δὲ οὐχ ὡς ἀντιδιῃρημένον
τῷ λόγῳ, ἀλλ' ὡς ἡμεῖς φαμεν πρότερον, τὸ δὲ
ὕστερον εἶναι. Πολλαχῶς τοίνυν τῆς ζωῆς λεγο-

---

[1] Plotinus is distinguishing here between a simple classi-
fication, by dichotomy or genus and species, of the sort of
which ἀντιδιῃρῆσθαι is used by Aristotle (*Categories* 13.
14b33 ff.), and the recognition of a hierarchical order of reality,

better than all these; otherwise I do not think they would be able to explain its place of honour. But until these people find a better nature than the things at which they now stop, we must let them stay where they are, which is where they want to be, unable to answer the question how the good life is possible for the beings which are capable of it.

3. We, however, intend to state what we understand by well-being, beginning at the beginning. Suppose we assume that it is to be found in life; then if we make "life" a term which applies to all living things in exactly the same sense, we allow that all of them are capable of well-being, and that those of them actually live well who possess one and the same thing, something which all living beings are naturally capable of acquiring; we do not on this assumption grant the ability to live well to rational beings, but not to irrational. Life is common to both, and it is life which by the same acquisition [in both cases] tends towards well-being, if well-being is to be found in a kind of life. So I think that those who say that well-being is to be found in rational life are unaware that, since they do not place it in life in general, they are really assuming that it is not a life at all. They would have to say that the rational power on which well-being depends is a quality. But their starting-point is rational *life*. Well-being depends on this as a whole; that is, on another kind of life. I do not mean "another kind" in the sense of a logical distinction, but in the sense in which we Platonists speak of one thing as prior and another as posterior.[1] The term "life" is used in many

in which one kind of life is dependent on another higher kind and the image of it.

μένης καὶ τὴν διαφορὰν ἐχούσης κατὰ τὰ πρῶτα καὶ
20 δεύτερα καὶ ἐφεξῆς καὶ ὁμωνύμως τοῦ ζῆν
λεγομένου ἄλλως μὲν τοῦ φυτοῦ, ἄλλως δὲ τοῦ
ἀλόγου καὶ τρανότητι καὶ ἀμυδρότητι τὴν διαφορὰν
ἐχόντων, ἀνάλογον δηλονότι καὶ τὸ εὖ. Καὶ εἰ
εἴδωλον ἄλλο ἄλλου, δηλονότι καὶ τὸ εὖ ὡς εἴδωλον
αὖ τοῦ εὖ. Εἰ δὲ ὅτῳ ἄγαν ὑπάρχει τὸ ζῆν—
25 τοῦτο δέ ἐστιν ὃ μηδενὶ τοῦ ζῆν ἐλλείπει—
τὸ εὖ, μόνῳ ἂν τῷ ἄγαν ζῶντι τὸ εὐδαιμονεῖν ὑπάρχοι· τούτῳ γὰρ καὶ τὸ ἄριστον, εἴπερ
ἐν τοῖς οὖσι τὸ ἄριστον τὸ ὄντως ἐν ζωῇ καὶ ἡ
τέλειος ζωή· οὕτω γὰρ ἂν οὐδὲ ἐπακτὸν τὸ ἀγαθὸν
ὑπάρχοι, οὐδ' ἄλλο τὸ ὑποκείμενον ἀλλαχόθεν
30 γενόμενον παρέξει αὐτὸ ἐν ἀγαθῷ εἶναι. Τί γὰρ
τῇ τελείᾳ ζωῇ ἂν προσγένοιτο εἰς τὸ ἀρίστη
εἶναι; Εἰ δέ τις τὴν τοῦ ἀγαθοῦ φύσιν ἐρεῖ,
οἰκεῖος μὲν ὁ λόγος ἡμῖν, οὐ μὴν τὸ αἴτιον, ἀλλὰ
τὸ ἐνυπάρχον ζητοῦμεν. Ὅτι δ' ἡ τελεία ζωὴ
καὶ ἡ ἀληθινὴ καὶ ὄντως ἐν ἐκείνῃ τῇ νοερᾷ
35 φύσει, καὶ ὅτι αἱ ἄλλαι ἀτελεῖς καὶ ἰνδάλματα
ζωῆς καὶ οὐ τελείως οὐδὲ καθαρῶς καὶ οὐ μᾶλλον
ζωαὶ ἢ τοὐναντίον, πολλάκις μὲν εἴρηται· καὶ νῦν
δὲ λελέχθω συντόμως ὡς, ἕως ἂν πάντα τὰ ζῶντα
ἐκ μιᾶς ἀρχῆς ᾖ, μὴ ἐπίσης δὲ τὰ ἄλλα ζῇ,
40 ἀνάγκη τὴν ἀρχὴν τὴν πρώτην ζωὴν καὶ τὴν
τελειοτάτην εἶναι.

4. Εἰ μὲν οὖν τὴν τελείαν ζωὴν ἔχειν οἷός τε
ἄνθρωπος, καὶ ἄνθρωπος ὁ ταύτην ἔχων τὴν ζωὴν
εὐδαίμων. Εἰ δὲ μή, ἐν θεοῖς ἄν τις τὸ εὐδαιμονεῖν
θεῖτο, εἰ ἐν ἐκείνοις μόνοις ἡ τοιαύτη ζωή. Ἐπειδὴ

different senses, distinguished according to the rank of the things to which it is applied, first, second and so on ; and " living " means different things in different contexts ; it is used in one way of plants, in another of irrational animals, in various ways of things distinguished from each other by the clarity or dimness of their life ; so obviously the same applies to " living well." And if one thing is an image of another, obviously its good life is the image of another good life. If then the good life belongs to what has a superabundance of life (this means what is in no way deficient in life), well-being will belong only to the being which lives superabundantly : this will have the best, if the best among realities is being really alive, is perfect life. So its good will not be something brought in from outside, nor will the basis of its goodness come from somewhere else and bring it into a good state ; for what could be added to the perfect life to make it into the best life ? If anyone says " The Absolute Good," that is our own way of talking, but at present we are not looking for the cause, but for the immanent element.

We have often said that the perfect life, the true, real life, is in that transcendent intelligible reality, and that other lives are incomplete, traces of life, not perfect or pure and no more life than its opposite. Let us put it shortly ; as long as all living things proceed from a single origin, but have not life to the same degree as it, the origin must be the first and most perfect life.

4. If then man can have the perfect life, the man who has this life is well off. If not, one would have to attribute well-being to the gods, if among them alone this kind of life is to be found. But since we

5 τοίνυν φαμὲν εἶναι καὶ ἐν ἀνθρώποις τὸ εὐδαιμονεῖν
τοῦτο, σκεπτέον πῶς ἔστι τοῦτο. Λέγω δὲ ὧδε·
ὅτι μὲν οὖν ἔχει τελείαν ζωὴν ἄνθρωπος οὐ τὴν
αἰσθητικὴν μόνον ἔχων, ἀλλὰ καὶ λογισμὸν καὶ
νοῦν ἀληθινόν, δῆλον καὶ ἐξ ἄλλων. Ἀλλ' ἆρά γε
ὡς ἄλλος ὢν ἄλλο τοῦτο ἔχει; Ἢ οὐδ' ἐστὶν ὅλως
10 ἄνθρωπος μὴ οὐ καὶ τοῦτο ἢ δυνάμει ἢ ἐνεργείᾳ
ἔχων, ὃν δὴ καί φαμεν εὐδαίμονα εἶναι. Ἀλλ'
ὡς μέρος αὐτοῦ τοῦτο φήσομεν ἐν αὐτῷ τὸ εἶδος
τῆς ζωῆς τὸ τέλειον εἶναι; Ἢ τὸν μὲν ἄλλον
ἄνθρωπον μέρος τι τοῦτο ἔχειν δυνάμει ἔχοντα,
τὸν δὲ εὐδαίμονα ἤδη, ὃς δὴ καὶ ἐνεργείᾳ ἐστὶ
15 τοῦτο καὶ μεταβέβηκε πρὸς τὸ αὐτό, εἶναι τοῦτο·
περικεῖσθαι δ' αὐτῷ τὰ ἄλλα ἤδη, ἃ δὴ οὐδὲ μέρη
αὐτοῦ ἄν τις θεῖτο οὐκ ἐθέλοντι περικείμενα· ἦν
δ' ἂν αὐτοῦ κατὰ βούλησιν συνηρτημένα. Τούτῳ
τοίνυν τί ποτ' ἐστὶ τὸ ἀγαθόν; Ἢ αὐτὸς αὑτῷ
ὅπερ ἔχει· τὸ δὲ ἐπέκεινα αἴτιον τοῦ ἐν αὐτῷ καὶ
20 ἄλλως ἀγαθόν, αὐτῷ παρὸν ἄλλως. Μαρτύριον
δὲ τοῦ τοῦτο εἶναι τὸ μὴ ἄλλο ζητεῖν τὸν οὕτως
ἔχοντα. Τί γὰρ ἂν καὶ ζητήσειε; Τῶν μὲν γὰρ
χειρόνων οὐδέν, τῷ δὲ ἀρίστῳ σύνεστιν. Αὐτάρκης
οὖν ὁ βίος τῷ οὕτως ζωὴν ἔχοντι. Κἂν σπουδαῖος
25 ᾖ, αὐτάρκης εἰς εὐδαιμονίαν καὶ εἰς κτῆσιν ἀγαθοῦ·
οὐδὲν γὰρ ἔστιν ἀγαθὸν ὃ μὴ ἔχει. Ἀλλ' ὃ ζητεῖ
ὡς ἀναγκαῖον ζητεῖ, καὶ οὐχ αὑτῷ, ἀλλά τινι τῶν
αὐτοῦ. Σώματι γὰρ προσηρτημένῳ ζητεῖ· κἂν
ζῶντι δὲ σώματι, τὰ αὐτοῦ ζῶντι τούτῳ, οὐχ ἃ
τοιούτου τοῦ ἀνθρώπου ἐστί. Καὶ γινώσκει ταῦτα
30 καὶ δίδωσιν ἃ δίδωσιν οὐδὲν τῆς αὐτοῦ παραιρού-
μενος ζωῆς. Οὐδ' ἐν τύχαις τοίνυν ἐναντίαις

maintain that this well-being is to be found among men we must consider how it is so. What I mean is this; it is obvious from what has been said elsewhere that man has perfect life by having not only sense-life but reasoning and true intelligence. But is he different from this when he has it? No, he is not a man at all unless he has this, either potentially or actually (and if he has it actually we say that he is in a state of well-being). But shall we say that he has this perfect kind of life in him as a part of himself? Other men, we maintain, who have it poten- tially, have it as a part, but the man who is well off, who actually is this and has passed over into identity with it, [does not have it but] *is* it. Everything else is just something he wears; you could not call it part of him because he wears it without wanting to; it would be his if he united it to him by an act of the will. What then is the good for him? He is what he has, his own good. The Transcendent Good is Cause of the good in him; the fact that It is good is different from the fact that It is present to him. There is evidence for this in the fact that the man in this state does not seek for anything else; for what could he seek? Certainly not anything worse, and he has the best with him. The man who has a life like this has all he needs in life. If he is virtuous, he has all he needs for well-being and the acquisition of good; for there is no good that he has not got. What he seeks he seeks as a necessity, not for himself but for something that belongs to him; that is, he seeks it for the body which is joined to him; and even grant- ing that this is a living body, it lives its own life and not the life which is that of the good man. He knows its needs, and gives it what he gives it without

183

ἐλαττώσεται εἰς τὸ εὐδαιμονεῖν· μένει γὰρ καὶ
ὡς ἡ τοιαύτη ζωή· ἀποθνησκόντων τε οἰκείων
καὶ φίλων οἶδε τὸν θάνατον ὅ τι ἐστίν, ἴσασι δὲ
καὶ οἱ πάσχοντες σπουδαῖοι ὄντες. Οἰκεῖοι δὲ καὶ
35 προσήκοντες τοῦτο πάσχοντες κἂν λυπῶσιν, οὐκ
αὐτόν, τὸ δ' ἐν αὐτῷ νοῦν οὐκ ἔχον, οὗ τὰς λύπας
οὐ δέξεται.

5. Ἀλγηδόνες δὲ τί καὶ νόσοι καὶ τὰ ὅλως
κωλύοντα ἐνεργεῖν; Εἰ δὲ δὴ μηδ' ἑαυτῷ παρακολουθοῖ; Γένοιτο γὰρ ἂν καὶ ἐκ φαρμάκων καί
τινων νόσων. Πῶς δὴ ἐν τούτοις ἅπασι τὸ ζῆν
5 εὖ καὶ τὸ εὐδαιμονεῖν ἂν ἔχοι; Πενίας γὰρ καὶ
ἀδοξίας ἐατέον. Καίτοι καὶ πρὸς ταῦτα ἄν τις
ἀποβλέψας ἐπιστήσειε καὶ πρὸς τὰς πολυθρυλλή-
τους αὖ μάλιστα Πριαμικὰς τύχας· ταῦτα γὰρ εἰ
καὶ φέροι καὶ ῥαδίως φέροι, ἀλλ' οὐ βουλητά γε
10 ἦν αὐτῷ· δεῖ δὲ βουλητὸν τὸν εὐδαίμονα βίον
εἶναι· ἐπεὶ οὐδὲ τοῦτον εἶναι τὸν σπουδαῖον
ψυχὴν τοιάνδε, μὴ συναριθμεῖσθαι δ' αὐτοῦ τῇ
οὐσίᾳ τὴν σώματος φύσιν. Ἑτοίμως γὰρ τοῦτο
φαῖεν ἂν λαμβάνειν, ἕως ἂν αἱ τοῦ σώματος
πείσεις πρὸς αὐτὸν ἀναφέρωνται καὶ αὖ καὶ αἱ
αἱρέσεις καὶ φυγαὶ διὰ τοῦτο γίγνωνται αὐτῷ.
15 Ἡδονῆς δὲ συναριθμουμένης τῷ εὐδαίμονι βίῳ,
πῶς ἂν λυπηρὸν διὰ τύχας καὶ ὀδύνας ἔχων
εὐδαίμων εἴη, ὅτῳ ταῦτα σπουδαίῳ ὄντι γίγνοιτο;
Ἀλλὰ θεοῖς μὲν ἡ τοιαύτη διάθεσις εὐδαίμων καὶ

---

[1] Cp. Aristotle, *Nicomachean Ethics* I. 10. 1100a8 and 11.
1101a8. Plotinus in this section of the treatise is defending the
essential Stoic position, that the good man is absolutely

taking away anything from his own life. His well-being will not be reduced even when fortune goes against him; the good life is still there even so. When his friends and relations die he knows what death is—as those who die do also if they are virtuous. Even if the death of friends and relations causes grief, it does not grieve him but only that in him which has no intelligence, and he will not allow the distresses of this to move him.

5. But what about pain and sickness and everything that hinders activity? And suppose the good man is not even conscious? That could happen as the result of drugs and some kinds of illness. How could he in all these circumstances have a good life and well-being? We need not consider poverty and disgrace; though someone might raise an objection in regard of these too, and especially that "fate of Priam" that people are always talking about.[1] For even if he bore them and bore them lightly, he would not want them; and the life of well-being must be something one wants. This good man, it might be objected, is not a good soul, without reckoning his bodily nature as part of his essential being. Our opponents might say that they willingly accept our point of view, as long as the bodily affections are referred to the man himself, and it is he himself who chooses and avoids for reasons connected with the body. But if pleasure is counted as part of the life of well-being, how can a man be well off when chance and pain bring distress, even if it is a good man that these things happen to? This kind of state of self-sufficient well-being belongs to the

independent of external circumstances, against an attack on Peripatetic lines.

αὐτάρκης, ἀνθρώποις δὲ προσθήκην τοῦ χείρονος
λαβοῦσι περὶ ὅλον χρὴ τὸ γενόμενον τὸ εὔδαιμον
20 ζητεῖν, ἀλλὰ μὴ περὶ μέρος, ὃ ἐκ θατέρου κακῶς
ἔχοντος ἀναγκάζοιτο ἂν καὶ θάτερον τὸ κρεῖττον
ἐμποδίζεσθαι πρὸς τὰ αὑτοῦ, ὅτι μὴ καὶ τὰ τοῦ
ἑτέρου καλῶς ἔχει. Ἢ ἀπορρήξαντα δεῖ σῶμα ἢ
καὶ αἴσθησιν τὴν σώματος οὕτω τὸ αὔταρκες
ζητεῖν πρὸς τὸ εὐδαιμονεῖν ἔχειν.

6. ’Αλλ’ εἰ μὲν τὸ εὐδαιμονεῖν ἐν τῷ μὴ ἀλγεῖν
μηδὲ νοσεῖν μηδὲ δυστυχεῖν μηδὲ συμφοραῖς μεγά-
λαις περιπίπτειν ἐδίδου ὁ λόγος, οὐκ ἦν τῶν ἐναντίων
παρόντων εἶναι ὁντινοῦν εὐδαίμονα· εἰ δ’ ἐν τῇ τοῦ
5 ἀληθινοῦ ἀγαθοῦ κτήσει τοῦτό ἐστι κείμενον, τί δεῖ
παρέντας τοῦτο καὶ τὸ πρὸς τοῦτο βλέποντας κρίνειν
τὸν εὐδαίμονα τὰ ἄλλα ζητεῖν, ἃ μὴ ἐν τῷ εὐδαιμονεῖν
ἠρίθμηται; Εἰ μὲν γὰρ συμφόρησις ἦν ἀγαθῶν
καὶ ἀναγκαίων ἢ καὶ οὐκ ἀναγκαίων, ἀλλ’ ἀγαθῶν
10 καὶ τούτων λεγομένων, ἐχρῆν καὶ ταῦτα παρεῖναι
ζητεῖν· εἰ δὲ τὸ τέλος ἕν τι εἶναι ἀλλ’ οὐ πολλὰ
δεῖ—οὕτω γὰρ ἂν οὐ τέλος, ἀλλὰ τέλη ἂν ζητοῖ—
ἐκεῖνο χρὴ λαμβάνειν μόνον, ὃ ἔσχατόν τέ ἐστι καὶ
τιμιώτατον καὶ ὃ ἡ ψυχὴ ζητεῖ ἐν αὑτῇ ἐγκολπίσασ-
θαι. Ἡ δὲ ζήτησις αὕτη καὶ ἡ βούλησις οὐχὶ τὸ
15 μὴ ἐν τούτῳ εἶναι· ταῦτα γὰρ οὐκ αὐτῇ φύσει,
ἀλλὰ παρόντα μόνον φεύγει ὁ λογισμὸς ἀποικο-
νομούμενος ἢ καὶ προσλαμβάνων ζητεῖ· αὐτὴ δὲ
ἡ ἔφεσις πρὸς τὸ κρεῖττον αὑτῆς, οὗ ἐγγενομένου

gods; since men have a supplement of lower nature one must look for well-being in the whole of what has come into existence, and not in a part; for if one part is in a bad state the other, higher, part must necessarily be hindered in its proper work if the affairs of the lower part are not going well. Otherwise one must cut off the body, and even perception of the body, from human nature, and in this way try to find self-sufficiency in the matter of well-being.

6. But [we should answer], if our argument made well-being consist in freedom from pain and sickness and ill-luck and falling into great misfortunes, it would be impossible for anyone to be well off when any of these circumstances opposed to well-being was present. But if well-being is to be found in possession of the true good, why should we disregard this and omit to use it as a standard to which to look in judging well-being, and look for other things which are not reckoned as a part of well-being? If it was a collection of goods and necessities, or things as well which are not necessities but even so are called goods, we should have to try and see that these were there too. But if the end at which we aim must be one and not many—otherwise one would not be aiming at an end but at ends—one must gain that alone which is of ultimate and highest value, and which the soul seeks to clasp close within itself. This search and willing is not directed to not being in this condition. These things are not of our very nature, but only [incidentally] present, and it is our reasoning power that avoids and manages to get rid of them, or also sometimes seeks to acquire them. But the real drive of desire of our soul is towards that which is better than itself. When that is present

ἀποπεπλήρωται καὶ ἔστη, καὶ οὗτος ὁ βουλητὸς
ὄντως βίος. Τῶν δ' ἀναγκαίων τι παρεῖναι οὐ
20 βούλησις ἂν εἴη, εἰ κυρίως τὴν βούλησιν ὑπολαμ-
βάνοι, ἀλλὰ μὴ καταχρώμενος ἄν τις λέγοι, ἐπειδὴ
καὶ ταῦτα παρεῖναι ἀξιοῦμεν. Ἐπεὶ καὶ ὅλως τὰ
κακὰ ἐκκλίνομεν, καὶ οὐ δήπου βουλητὸν τὸ τῆς
ἐκκλίσεως τῆς τοιαύτης· μᾶλλον γὰρ βουλητὸν τὸ
μηδὲ δεηθῆναι τῆς ἐκκλίσεως τῆς τοιαύτης.
25 Μαρτυρεῖ δὲ καὶ αὐτά, ὅταν παρῇ· οἷον ὑγίεια
καὶ ἀνωδυνία. Τί γὰρ τούτων ἐπαγωγόν ἐστι;
Καταφρονεῖται γοῦν ὑγίεια παροῦσα καὶ τὸ μὴ
ἀλγεῖν. Ἃ δὲ παρόντα μὲν οὐδὲν ἐπαγωγὸν ἔχει
οὐδὲ προστίθησί τι πρὸς τὸ εὐδαιμονεῖν, ἀπόντα δὲ
διὰ τὴν τῶν λυπούντων παρουσίαν ζητεῖ⟨ται⟩,
30 εὔλογον ἀναγκαῖα, ἀλλ' οὐκ ἀγαθὰ φάσκειν εἶναι.
Οὐδὲ συναριθμητέα τοίνυν τῷ τέλει, ἀλλὰ καὶ
ἀπόντων αὐτῶν καὶ τῶν ἐναντίων παρόντων ἀκέραιον
τὸ τέλος τηρητέον.

7. Διὰ τί οὖν ὁ εὐδαιμονῶν ταῦτα ἐθέλει
παρεῖναι καὶ τὰ ἐναντία ἀπωθεῖται; Ἢ φήσομεν
οὐχ ὅτι πρὸς τὸ εὐδαιμονεῖν εἰσφέρεταί τινα
μοῖραν, ἀλλὰ μᾶλλον πρὸς τὸ εἶναι· τὰ δ' ἐναντία
5 τούτων ἢ πρὸς τὸ μὴ εἶναι ἢ ὅτι ἐνοχλεῖ τῷ τέλει
παρόντα, οὐχ ὡς ἀφαιρούμενα αὐτό, ἀλλ' ὅτι ὁ
ἔχων τὸ ἄριστον αὐτὸ μόνον βούλεται ἔχειν, οὐκ
ἄλλο τι μετ' αὐτοῦ, ὃ ὅταν παρῇ, οὐκ ἀφήρηται
μὲν ἐκεῖνο, ἔστι δ' ὅμως κἀκείνου ὄντος. Ὅλως
δὲ οὐκ, εἴ τι ὁ εὐδαίμων μὴ ἐθέλοι, παρείη δὲ
188

within it, it is fulfilled and at rest, and this is the way of living it really wills. We cannot be said to " will " the presence of necessities, if " willing " is used in its proper sense and not misapplied to the occasions when we prefer the necessities also to be there: for we generally avoid evils, but this sort of avoidance is not, I suppose, a matter of willing, for we should will rather not to have occasion for this sort of avoidance. The necessities themselves provide evidence of this when we have them, health and freedom from pain, for instance. What attraction have they for us? We despise health when we have it, and freedom from pain as well. But these things, which have no attraction for us when they are there and do not contribute anything to our well-being, but which we seek in their absence because of the presence of things which distress us, can reasonably be called necessities, but not goods. So they must not be reckoned as part of the end we aim at; even when they are absent and their opposites are present, the end must be kept intact.

7. Why then does the man who is in a state of well-being want these necessities to be there and reject their opposites? We shall answer that it is not because they make any contribution to his well-being, but rather, to his existence: and he rejects their opposites either because they help towards non-existence or because they get in the way of his aim by their presence, not by taking anything away from it but because he who has the best wants to have it alone, and not something else with it, something which when it is there has not made away with the best, but, still, exists alongside it. But even if something which the man who is well off does not

10 τοῦτο, ἤδη παραιρεῖταί τι τῆς εὐδαιμονίας· ἢ
οὕτω γε καθ᾽ ἑκάστην τὴν ἡμέραν μεταπίπτοι ἂν
καὶ ἐκπίπτοι τῆς εὐδαιμονίας· οἷον εἰ καὶ παῖδα
ἀποβάλλοι ἢ καὶ ὁτιοῦν τῶν κτημάτων. Καὶ
μυρία ἂν εἴη ἃ οὐ κατὰ γνώμην ἐκβάντα οὐδέν τι
15 παρακινεῖ τοῦ παρόντος τέλους αὐτῷ. Ἀλλὰ τὰ
μεγάλα, φασί, καὶ οὐ τὰ τυχόντα. Τί δ᾽ ἂν εἴη
τῶν ἀνθρωπίνων μέγα, ὥστ᾽ ἂν μὴ καταφρονηθῆναι
ὑπὸ τοῦ ἀναβεβηκότος πρὸς τὸ ἀνωτέρω ἁπάντων
τούτων καὶ οὐδενὸς ἔτι τῶν κάτω ἐξηρτημένου;
Διὰ τί γὰρ τὰς μὲν εὐτυχίας, ἡλικαιοῦν ἂν ὦσιν,
οὐ μεγάλας ἡγεῖται, οἷον βασιλείας καὶ πόλεων
20 καὶ ἐθνῶν ἀρχάς, οὐδὲ οἰκίσεις καὶ κτίσεις πόλεων,
οὐδ᾽ εἰ ὑπ᾽ αὐτοῦ γίγνοιντο, ἐκπτώσεις δὲ ἀρχῶν
καὶ πόλεως αὐτοῦ κατασκαφὴν ἡγήσεταί τι εἶναι
μέγα; Εἰ δὲ δὴ καὶ κακὸν μέγα ἢ ὅλως κακόν,
γελοῖος ἂν εἴη τοῦ δόγματος καὶ οὐκ ἂν ἔτι
σπουδαῖος εἴη ξύλα καὶ λίθους καὶ νὴ Δία θανάτους
25 θνητῶν μέγα ἡγούμενος, ᾧ φαμεν δεῖν δόγμα
παρεῖναι περὶ θανάτου τὸ ἄμεινον ζωῆς τῆς μετὰ
σώματος εἶναι. Αὐτὸς δὲ εἰ τυθείη, κακὸν οἰήσε-
ται αὐτῷ τὸν θάνατον, ὅτι παρὰ βωμοῖς τέθνηκεν;
Ἀλλ᾽ εἰ μὴ ταφείη, πάντως που καὶ ὑπὲρ γῆς καὶ
ὑπὸ γῆν τεθὲν τὸ σῶμα σαπείη. Εἰ δ᾽ ὅτι μὴ
30 πολυδαπάνως, ἀλλ᾽ ἀνωνύμως τέθαπται οὐκ ἀξιωθεὶς ὑψηλοῦ μνήματος, τῆς μικρολογίας. Ἀλλ᾽ εἰ
αἰχμάλωτος ἄγοιτο, πάρ τοί ἐστιν ὁδὸς ἐξιέναι,

---

[1] In the last days of St. Augustine's life, while the Vandals
were besieging Hippo he comforted himself with these words;
see Possidius, *Vita Augustini* XXVIII: et se inter haec mala

want is there all the same, nothing at all of his well-being is taken away; otherwise he would change every day and fall from his well-being—if he lost a servant, for instance, or any one of his possessions: there are thousands of things which, if they do not turn out according to his mind, disturb in no way the final good which he has attained.   But, people say, consider great disasters, not ordinary chances! What human circumstance is so great that a man will not think little of it who has climbed higher than all this and depends on nothing below?   He does not think any piece of good fortune great, however important it may be, kingship, for instance, and rule over cities and peoples, or founding of colonies and states (even if he founds them himself).   Why then should he think that falling from power and the ruin of his city are great matters?   If he thought that they were great evils, or evils at all, he would deserve to be laughed at for his opinion; there would be no virtue left in him if he thought that wood and stones, and (God help us!) the death of mortals, were important,[1] this man who, we say, ought to think about death that it is better than life with the body!   If he himself is offered in sacrifice, will he think his death an evil, because he dies by the altars?   If he is not buried, his body will rot anyhow, on the earth or under it.   If he is distressed because he does not have an expensive funeral but is buried without a name and not thought worth a lofty monument—the pettiness of it!   If he is taken away as a war-slave, "the way lies open" to depart,

cuiusdam sapientis sententia consolabatur dicentis: *Non erit magnus magnum putans, quod cadunt ligna et lapides et moriuntur mortales.*

εἰ μὴ εἴη εὐδαιμονεῖν. Εἰ δὲ οἰκεῖοι αὐτῷ
αἰχμάλωτοι, οἷον ἑλκόμεναι νυοὶ καὶ θυγα-
τέρες— τί οὖν, φήσομεν, εἰ ἀποθνήσκοι μηδὲν
35 τοιοῦτον ἑωρακώς ; Ἆρ' ἂν οὕτω δόξῃς ἔχοι
ἀπιών, ὡς μὴ ἂν τούτων ἐνδεχομένων γενέσθαι ;
'Αλλ' ἄτοπος ἂν εἴη. Οὐκ ἂν οὖν δοξάσειεν, ὡς
ἐνδέχεται τοιαύταις τύχαις τοὺς οἰκείους περιπε-
σεῖν ; Ἆρ' οὖν διὰ τὸ οὕτως ἂν δόξαι ὡς καὶ
γενησομένου ἂν οὐκ εὐδαίμων ; Ἢ καὶ δοξάζων
40 οὕτως εὐδαίμων· ὥστε καὶ γινομένου. 'Ενθυμοῖτο
γὰρ ἄν, ὡς ἡ τοῦδε τοῦ παντὸς φύσις τοιαύτη, οἷα
καὶ τὰ τοιαῦτα φέρειν, καὶ ἕπεσθαι χρή. Καὶ
πολλοὶ δὴ καὶ ἄμεινον αἰχμάλωτοι γενόμενοι
πράξουσι. Καὶ ἐπ' αὐτοῖς δὲ βαρυνομένοις ἀπελ-
θεῖν·[1] ἢ μένοντες ἢ εὐλόγως μένουσι καὶ οὐδὲν
45 δεινόν, ἢ ἀλόγως μένοντες, δέον μή, αὐτοῖς αἴτιοι.
Οὐ γὰρ δὴ διὰ τὴν τῶν ἄλλων ἄνοιαν οἰκείων
ὄντων αὐτὸς ἐν κακῷ ἔσται καὶ εἰς ἄλλων εὐτυχίας
καὶ δυστυχίας ἀναρτήσεται.

8. Τὸ δὲ τῶν ἀλγηδόνων αὐτοῦ, ὅταν σφοδραὶ
ὦσιν, ἕως δύναται φέρειν, οἴσει· εἰ δὲ ὑπερβάλ-
λουσιν, ἐξοίσουσι. Καὶ οὐκ ἐλεεινὸς ἔσται ⟨καὶ⟩ ἐν
τῷ ἀλγεῖν, ἀλλὰ τὸ αὐτοῦ [καίεται] ἔνδον φέγγος
5 οἷον ἐν λαμπτῆρι φῶς πολλοῦ ἔξωθεν πνέοντος ἐν
πολλῇ ζάλῃ ἀνέμων καὶ χειμῶνι. 'Αλλ' εἰ μὴ
παρακολουθοῖ, ἢ παρατείνοι τὸ ἀλγεῖν ἐπὶ τοσοῦτον
αἰρόμενον, ὥστε ἐν τῷ σφοδρῷ ὅμως μὴ ἀποκτιν-

---

[1] This means suicide, which Plotinus admitted as legitimate,
though only in absolutely desperate circumstances ; cp. the next
chapter and I. 9. 11–14, and 17.
[2] Again an allusion to Priam, cp. *Iliad* 22. 65.

if it is not possible to live well.[1] If his relatives are captured in war, " his daughters-in-law and daughters dragged off " [2]—well, suppose he had died without seeing anything of the sort ; would he then leave the world in the belief that it was impossible that it should happen ? If so, he would be a fool. So will he not think that it is possible for his relatives to fall into such misfortune ? And does his belief that this may happen prevent his well-being ? Then neither does the fact of its happening. For he will think that the nature of this universe is of a kind to bring these sorts of misfortunes, and we must follow it obediently. Anyhow, many people will do better by becoming war-slaves ; and it is in their own power to depart if they find the burden heavy. If they stay, either it is reasonable for them to stay and there is nothing terrible about it, or if they stay unreasonably, when they ought not to, it is their own fault. The good man will not be involved in evil because of the stupidity of others, even if they are his relatives ; he will not be dependent on the good or bad fortune of other people.

8. As far as his own pains go, when they are very great, he will bear them as long as he can ; when they are too much for him, they will bear him off.[3] He is not to be pitied even in his pain ; his light within is like the light in a lantern when it is blowing hard outside with a great fury of wind and storm.[4] But suppose the pain brings delirium, or goes on at such a height that, though it is extreme it does not

    [3] Cp. Epicurus fr. V. B64–65 Bailey.
    [4] There may be a reminiscence here of Empedocles fr. B 84, Diels, but the context there is quite different—the storm-lantern is only an analogy for the structure of the eye.

νύναι; Ἀλλ' εἰ μὲν παρατείνοι, τί χρὴ ποιεῖν
βουλεύσεται· οὐ γὰρ ἀφῄρηται τὸ αὐτεξούσιον ἐν
10 τούτοις. Χρὴ δὲ εἰδέναι, ὡς οὐχ, οἷα τοῖς ἄλλοις
φαίνεται, τοιαῦτα καὶ τῷ σπουδαίῳ φανεῖται
ἕκαστα, καὶ οὐ μέχρι τοῦ εἴσω ἕκαστα οὔτε τὰ
ἄλλα, [οὔτε ἀλγεινὰ] οὔτε τὰ λυπηρά. Καὶ ὅταν
περὶ ἄλλους τὰ ἀλγεινά; ἀσθένεια γὰρ εἴη ψυχῆς
ἡμετέρας. Καὶ τοῦτο μαρτυρεῖ, ὅταν λανθάνειν
15 ἡμᾶς κέρδος ἡγώμεθα καὶ ἀποθανόντων ἡμῶν, εἰ
γίγνοιτο, κέρδος εἶναι τιθεμένων καὶ οὐ τὸ ἐκείνων
ἔτι σκοπουμένων, ἀλλὰ τὸ αὑτῶν, ὅπως μὴ
λυποίμεθα. Τοῦτο δὲ ἡμετέρα ἤδη ἀσθένεια, ἣν
δεῖ περιαιρεῖν, ἀλλὰ μὴ ἐῶντας φοβεῖσθαι μὴ
γένηται. Εἰ δέ τις λέγοι οὕτως ἡμᾶς πεφυκέναι,
20 ὥστε ἀλγεῖν ἐπὶ ταῖς τῶν οἰκείων συμφοραῖς,
γιγνωσκέτω, ὅτι οὐ πάντες οὕτω, καὶ ὅτι τῆς
ἀρετῆς τὸ κοινὸν τῆς φύσεως πρὸς τὸ ἄμεινον
ἄγειν καὶ πρὸς τὸ κάλλιον παρὰ τοὺς πολλούς·
κάλλιον δὲ τὸ μὴ ἐνδιδόναι τοῖς νομιζομένοις τῇ
κοινῇ φύσει δεινοῖς εἶναι. Οὐ γὰρ ἰδιωτικῶς δεῖ,
25 ἀλλ' οἷον ἀθλητὴν μέγαν διακεῖσθαι τὰς τῆς τύχης
πληγὰς ἀμυνόμενον, γινώσκοντα μὲν ὅτι τινὶ φύσει
ταῦτα οὐκ ἀρεστά, τῇ δὲ αὑτοῦ φύσει οἰστά, οὐχ
ὡς δεινά, ἀλλ' ὡς παισὶ φοβερά. Ταῦτ' οὖν
ἤθελεν; Ἡ καὶ πρὸς τὰ μὴ θελητά, ὅταν παρῇ,
ἀρετὴν καὶ πρὸς ταῦτα ἔχει δυσκίνητον καὶ
30 δυσπαθῆ τὴν ψυχὴν παρέχουσαν.

9. Ἀλλ' ὅταν μὴ παρακολουθῇ βαπτισθεὶς ἢ
νόσοις ἢ μάγων τέχναις; Ἀλλ' εἰ μὲν φυλάξουσιν

---

[1] Plotinus's view, expounded in this and the next chapter,
of the secondary and relatively inferior status of consciousness

kill? If it goes on, he will consider what he ought to do; the pain has not taken away his power of self-disposal. One must understand that things do not look to the good man as they look to others; none of his experiences penetrate to the inner self, griefs no more than any of the others. And when the pains concern others? [To sympathise with them] would be a weakness in our soul. There is evidence for this in the fact that we think it something gained if we do not know about other people's sufferings, and even regard it as a good thing if we die first, not considering it from their point of view but from our own, trying to avoid being grieved. This is just our weakness, which we must get rid of and not leave it there and then be afraid of its coming over us. If anyone says that it is our nature to feel pain at the misfortunes of our own people, he should know that this does not apply to everybody, and that it is the business of virtue to raise ordinary nature to a higher level, something better than most people are capable of; and it is better not to give in to what ordinary nature normally finds terrible. One must not behave like someone untrained, but stand up to the blows of fortune like a great trained fighter, and know that, though some natures may not like them, one's own can bear them, not as terrors but as children's bogeys. Does the good man, then, want misfortune? No, but when what he does not want comes he sets virtue against it, which makes his soul hard to disturb or distress.

9. But suppose he is unconscious, his mind swamped by sickness or magic arts?[1] If they maintain that

is entirely un-Stoic and based (see ch. 10) on a most original development of his own double-self psychology.

αὐτὸν σπουδαῖον εἶναι οὕτως ἔχοντα καὶ οἷα ἐν
ὕπνῳ κιομώμενον, τί κωλύει εὐδαίμονα αὐτὸν
5 εἶναι; Ἐπεὶ οὐδὲ ἐν τοῖς ὕπνοις ἀφαιροῦνται τῆς
εὐδαιμονίας αὐτόν, οὐδ' ὑπὸ λόγον ποιοῦνται τὸν
χρόνον τοῦτον, ὡς μὴ πάντα τὸν βίον εὐδαιμονεῖν
λέγειν· εἰ δὲ μὴ σπουδαῖον φήσουσιν, οὐ περὶ τοῦ
σπουδαίου ἔτι τὸν λόγον ποιοῦνται. Ἡμεῖς δὲ
ὑποθέμενοι σπουδαῖον, εἰ εὐδαιμονεῖ, ἕως ἂν εἴη
10 σπουδαῖος, ζητοῦμεν. Ἀλλ' ἔστω σπουδαῖος,
φασί· μὴ αἰσθανόμενος μηδ' ἐνεργῶν κατ' ἀρετήν,
πῶς ἂν εὐδαίμων εἴη; Ἀλλ' εἰ μὲν μὴ αἰσθάνοιτο
ὅτι ὑγιαίνοι, ὑγιαίνει οὐδὲν ἧττον, καὶ εἰ μὴ ὅτι
καλός, οὐδὲν ἧττον καλός· εἰ δὲ ὅτι σοφὸς μὴ
αἰσθάνοιτο, ἧττον σοφὸς ἂν εἴη; Εἰ μή πού τις
15 λέγοι ὡς ἐν τῇ σοφίᾳ γὰρ δεῖ τὸ αἰσθάνεσθαι καὶ
παρακολουθεῖν αὐτῷ παρεῖναι· ἐν γὰρ τῇ κατ'
ἐνέργειαν σοφίᾳ καὶ τὸ εὐδαιμονεῖν παρεῖναι.
Ἐπακτοῦ μὲν οὖν ὄντος τοῦ φρονεῖν καὶ τῆς
σοφίας λέγοι ἄν τι ἴσως ὁ λόγος οὗτος· εἰ δ' ἡ
τῆς σοφίας ὑπόστασις ἐν οὐσίᾳ τινί, μᾶλλον δὲ ἐν
20 τῇ οὐσίᾳ, οὐκ ἀπόλωλε δὲ αὕτη ἡ οὐσία ἔν τε τῷ
κοιμωμένῳ καὶ ὅλως ἐν τῷ λεγομένῳ μὴ παρακολουθεῖν ἑαυτῷ, καὶ ἔστιν ἡ τῆς οὐσίας αὐτὴ
ἐνέργεια ἐν αὐτῷ καὶ ἡ τοιαύτη ἄϋπνος ἐνέργεια,
ἐνεργοῖ μὲν ἂν καὶ τότε ὁ σπουδαῖος ἢ τοιοῦτος·
λανθάνοι δ' ἂν αὕτη ἡ ἐνέργεια οὐκ αὐτὸν πάντα,
25 ἀλλά τι μέρος αὐτοῦ· οἷον καὶ τῆς φυτικῆς
ἐνεργείας ἐνεργούσης οὐκ ἔρχεται εἰς τὸν ἄλλον
ἄνθρωπον ἡ τῆς τοιαύτης ἐνεργείας ἀντίληψις τῷ

---

[1] Contrast Aristotle *Nicomachean Ethics* X. 6. 1176a33–35.

he is a good man when he is in this state, only fallen
into a sort of sleep, what prevents him from being
well off? After all, they do not remove him from
well-being when he is asleep, or reckon the time he
spends asleep so as to show that he is not well off
for his whole life.[1] But if they say that he is not
good when he is in this state, then they are not any
longer discussing the good man. But we are taking
the good man as our starting-point, and enquiring
if he is well off as long as he is good. "But," they
say, "granted that he is good, if he is not conscious
of it or engaged in virtuous activity, how can he be
in a state of well-being?" But if he does not know
that he is healthy, he *is* healthy just the same, and
if he does not know that he is handsome, he *is*
handsome just the same. So if he does not know
that he is wise, will he be any the less wise? Perhaps
someone might say that wisdom requires awareness
and consciousness of its presence, because it is in
actual and active wisdom that well-being is to be
found. If intelligence and wisdom were something
brought in from outside, this argument would
perhaps make sense: but if wisdom essentially
consists in a substance, or rather in *the* substance,
and this substance does not cease to exist in someone
who is asleep or what is called unconscious; if the
real activity of the substance goes on in him, and this
activity is unsleeping; then the good man, in that
he is a good man, will be active even then. It will
not be the whole of him that is unaware of this
activity, but only a part of him. In the same way
when our growth-activity is active no perception of
it reaches the rest of the man through our sense-
faculties; and, if that in us which grows were our-

197

αἰσθητικῷ, καί, εἴπερ ἦμεν τὸ φυτικὸν ἡμῶν
ἡμεῖς, ἡμεῖς ἂν ἐνεργοῦντες ἦμεν· νῦν δὲ τοῦτο
μὲν οὐκ ἐσμέν, ἡ δὲ τοῦ νοοῦντος ἐνέργεια· ὥστε
30 ἐνεργοῦντος ἐκείνου ἐνεργοῖμεν ἂν ἡμεῖς.

10. Λανθάνει δὲ ἴσως τῷ μὴ περὶ ὁτιοῦν τῶν
αἰσθητῶν· διὰ γὰρ τῆς αἰσθήσεως ὥσπερ μέσης
περὶ ταῦτα ἐνεργεῖν δοκεῖ καὶ περὶ τούτων.
Αὐτὸς δὲ ὁ νοῦς διὰ τί οὐκ ἐνεργήσει καὶ ἡ ψυχὴ
5 περὶ αὐτὸν ἡ πρὸ αἰσθήσεως καὶ ὅλως ἀντιλήψεως;
Δεῖ γὰρ τὸ πρὸ ἀντιλήψεως ἐνέργημα εἶναι, εἴπερ
τὸ αὐτὸ τὸ νοεῖν καὶ εἶναι. Καὶ ἔοικεν ἡ
ἀντίληψις εἶναι καὶ γίνεσθαι ἀνακάμπτοντος τοῦ
νοήματος καὶ τοῦ ἐνεργοῦντος τοῦ κατὰ τὸ ζῆν
τῆς ψυχῆς οἷον ἀπωσθέντος πάλιν, ὥσπερ ἐν
10 κατόπτρῳ περὶ τὸ λεῖον καὶ λαμπρὸν ἡσυχάζον.
Ὡς οὖν ἐν τοῖς τοιούτοις παρόντος μὲν τοῦ κατόπτ-
ρου ἐγένετο τὸ εἴδωλον, μὴ παρόντος δὲ ἢ μὴ
οὕτως ἔχοντος ἐνεργείᾳ πάρεστιν οὗ τὸ εἴδωλον
ἦν ἄν, οὕτω καὶ περὶ ψυχὴν ἡσυχίαν μὲν ἄγοντος
τοῦ ἐν ἡμῖν τοιούτου, ᾧ ἐμφαίνεται τὰ τῆς
15 διανοίας καὶ τοῦ νοῦ εἰκονίσματα, ἐνορᾶται ταῦτα
καὶ οἷον αἰσθητῶς γινώσκεται μετὰ τῆς προτέρας
γνώσεως, ὅτι ὁ νοῦς καὶ ἡ διάνοια ἐνεργεῖ.
Συγκλασθέντος δὲ τούτου διὰ τὴν τοῦ σώματος
ταραττομένην ἁρμονίαν ἄνευ εἰδώλου ἡ διάνοια καὶ
ὁ νοῦς νοεῖ καὶ ἄνευ φαντασίας ἡ νόησις τότε·

---

[1] Parmenides fr. B3 Diels. What Parmenides may have
really meant by these words is not relevant here. Plotinus,

selves, it would be ourselves that would be active [irrespective of the fact that we were unconscious of it]. Actually, however, we are not it, but we *are* the activity of the intellect; so that when that is active, we are active.

10. Perhaps we do not notice it because it is not concerned with any object of sense; for our minds, by means of sense-perception—which is a kind of intermediary when dealing with sensible things—do appear to work on the level of sense and think about sense-objects. But why should not intellect itself be active [without perception], and also its attendant soul, which comes before sense-perception and any sort of awareness? There must be an activity prior to awareness if "thinking and being are the same."[1] It seems as if awareness exists and is produced when intellectual activity is reflexive and when that in the life of the soul which is active in thinking is in a way projected back, as happens with a mirror-reflection when there is a smooth, bright, untroubled surface. In these circumstances when the mirror is there the mirror-image is produced, but when it is not there or is not in the right state the object of which the image would have been is [all the same] actually there. In the same way as regards the soul, when that kind of thing in us which mirrors the images of thought and intellect is undisturbed, we see them and know them in a way parallel to sense-perception, along with the prior knowledge that it is intellect and thought that are active. But when this is broken because the harmony of the body is upset, thought and intellect

as his citation of them at V. 1. 8. 17 makes clear, interprets them as referring to his own doctrine of the unity of Real Being and Intellect.

20 ὥστε καὶ τοιοῦτον ἄν τι νοοῖτο μετὰ φαντασίας
τὴν νόησιν γίνεσθαι οὐκ οὔσης τῆς νοήσεως
φαντασίας. Πολλὰς δ' ἄν τις εὕροι καὶ ἐγρηγο-
ρότων καλὰς ἐνεργείας καὶ θεωρίας καὶ πράξεις,
ὅτε θεωροῦμεν καὶ ὅτε πράττομεν, τὸ παρακολουθεῖν ἡμᾶς αὐταῖς οὐκ ἐχούσας. Οὐ γὰρ τὸν
25 ἀναγινώσκοντα ἀνάγκη παρακολουθεῖν ὅτι ἀνα-
γινώσκει καὶ τότε μάλιστα, ὅτε μετὰ τοῦ συντόνου
ἀναγινώσκοι· οὐδὲ ὁ ἀνδριζόμενος ὅτι ἀνδρίζεται
καὶ κατὰ τὴν ἀνδρίαν ἐνεργεῖ ὅσῳ ἐνεργεῖ· καὶ
ἄλλα μυρία· ὥστε τὰς παρακολουθήσεις κινδυ-
νεύειν ἀμυδροτέρας αὐτὰς τὰς ἐνεργείας αἷς
30 παροκολουθοῦσι ποιεῖν, μόνας δὲ αὐτὰς οὔσας
καθαρὰς τότε εἶναι καὶ μᾶλλον ἐνεργεῖν καὶ μᾶλλον
ζῆν καὶ δὴ καὶ ἐν τῷ τοιούτῳ πάθει τῶν σπουδαίων
γενομένων μᾶλλον τὸ ζῆν εἶναι, οὐ κεχυμένον εἰς
αἴσθησιν, ἀλλ' ἐν τῷ αὐτῷ ἐν ἑαυτῷ συνηγμένον.

11. Εἰ δέ τινες μηδὲ ζῆν λέγοιεν τὸν τοιοῦτον,
ζῆν μὲν αὐτὸν φήσομεν, λανθάνειν δ' αὐτοὺς τὴν
εὐδαιμονίαν τοῦ τοιούτου, ὥσπερ καὶ τὸ ζῆν. Εἰ
δὲ μὴ πείθοιντο, ἀξιώσομεν αὐτοὺς ὑποθεμένους
5 τὸν ζῶντα καὶ τὸν σπουδαῖον οὕτω ζητεῖν εἰ
εὐδαίμων, μηδὲ τὸ ζῆν αὐτοῦ ἐλαττώσαντας τὸ
εὖ ζῆν ζητεῖν εἰ πάρεστι μηδὲ ἀνελόντας τὸν
ἄνθρωπον περὶ εὐδαιμονίας ἀνθρώπου ζητεῖν μηδὲ
τὸν σπουδαῖον συγχωρήσαντας εἰς τὸ εἴσω ἐπεστρά-
φθαι ἐν ταῖς ἔξωθεν ἐνεργείαις αὐτὸν ζητεῖν μηδὲ
10 ὅλως τὸ βουλητὸν αὐτοῦ ἐν τοῖς ἔξω. Οὕτω γὰρ

---

[1] φαντασία is here used in its Aristotelian sense, for which
see *De Anima* III. 3. 427b–429a.

operate without an image, and then intellectual activity takes place without a mind-picture.[1] So one might come to this sort of conclusion, that intellectual activity is [normally] accompanied by a mind-picture but is not a mind-picture. One can find a great many valuable activities, theoretical and practical, which we carry on both in our contemplative and active life even when we are fully conscious, which do not make us aware of them. The reader is not necessarily aware that he is reading, least of all when he is really concentrating: nor the man who is being brave that he is being brave and that his action conforms to the virtue of courage; and there are thousands of similar cases. Conscious awareness, in fact, is likely to enfeeble the very activities of which there is consciousness; only when they are alone are they pure and more genuinely active and living; and when good men are in this state their life is increased, when it is not spilt out into perception, but gathered together in one in itself.

11. If some people were to say that a man in this state is not even alive, we shall maintain that he is alive, but they fail to observe his well-being just as they do his life. If they will not believe us, we shall ask them to take as their starting-point a living man and a good man and so to pursue the enquiry into his well-being, and not to minimise his life and then to enquire if he has a good life, or to take away his humanity and then enquire about human well-being, or to agree that the good man has his attention directed inward and then to look for him in external activities, still less to seek the object of his desire in outward things. There would not be any possibility

ἂν οὐδὲ ὑπόστασις εὐδαιμονίας εἴη, εἰ τὰ ἔξω
βουλητὰ λέγοι καὶ τὸν σπουδαῖον βούλεσθαι ταῦτα.
Ἐθέλοι γὰρ ἂν καὶ πάντας ἀνθρώπους εὖ πράττειν
καὶ μηδὲν τῶν κακῶν περὶ μηδένα εἶναι· ἀλλὰ μὴ
γινομένων ὅμως εὐδαίμων. Εἰ δέ τις παράλογον
15 ἂν αὐτὸν ποιήσειν φήσει, εἰ ταῦτα ἐθελήσει—μὴ
γὰρ οἷόν τε τὰ κακὰ μὴ εἶναι—δῆλον ὅτι συγχωρή-
σει ἡμῖν ἐπιστρέφουσιν αὐτοῦ τὴν βούλησιν εἰς τὸ
εἴσω.

12. Τὸ δὲ ἡδὺ τῷ βίῳ τοιούτῳ ὅταν ἀπαιτῶ-
σιν, οὐ τὰς τῶν ἀκολάστων οὐδὲ τὰς τοῦ σώματος
ἡδονὰς ἀξιώσουσι παρεῖναι—αὗται γὰρ ἀδύνατοι
παρεῖναι καὶ τὸ εὐδαιμονεῖν ἀφανιοῦσιν—οὐδὲ μὴν
5 τὰς περιχαρίας—διὰ τί γάρ;—ἀλλὰ τὰς συνούσας
παρουσίᾳ ἀγαθῶν οὐκ ἐν κινήσεσιν οὔσας, οὐδὲ
γινομένας τοίνυν· ἤδη γὰρ τὰ ἀγαθὰ πάρεστι, καὶ
αὐτὸς αὑτῷ πάρεστι· καὶ ἕστηκε τὸ ἡδὺ καὶ τὸ
ἵλεων τοῦτο· ἵλεως δὲ ὁ σπουδαῖος ἀεὶ καὶ
κατάστασις ἥσυχος καὶ ἀγαπητὴ ἡ διάθεσις ἣν
10 οὐδὲν τῶν λεγομένων κακῶν παρακινεῖ, εἴπερ
σπουδαῖος. Εἰ δέ τις ἄλλο εἶδος ἡδονῆς περὶ τὸν
[σπουδαῖον] βίον ζητεῖ, οὐ τὸν σπουδαῖον βίον
ζητεῖ.

13. Οὐδ' αἱ ἐνέργειαι δὲ διὰ τὰς τύχας ἐμποδί-
ζοιντο ἄν, ἀλλὰ ἄλλαι ἂν κατ' ἄλλας γίγνοιντο
τύχας, πᾶσαι δὲ ὅμως καλαὶ καλλίους ἴσως ὅσῳ
περιστατικαί. Αἱ δὲ κατὰ τὰς θεωρίας ἐνέργειαι

of the existence of well-being if one said that outward things were to be desired and that the good man desired them. He would like all men to prosper and no one to be subject to any sort of evil ; but if this does not happen, he is all the same well off. But if anyone maintains that it will make the good man absurd to suppose him wanting anything like this—for it is impossible that evils should not exist—then the person who maintains this will obviously agree with us in directing the good man's desire inwards.

12. When they demand to be shown what is pleasant in a life of this kind, they will not be requiring the presence of the pleasures of debauchees, or of bodily pleasures at all—these could not be there and would abolish well-being—or of violent emotions of pleasure—why should the good man have any ?—but only those pleasures which accompany the presence of goods, pleasures not consisting in movements, which are not the results of any process : for the goods are there already, and the good man is present to himself ; his pleasure and happiness are at rest. The good man is always happy ; his state is tranquil, his disposition contented and undisturbed by any so-called evils—if he is really good. If anyone looks for another kind of pleasure in life it is not the life of virtue he is looking for.

13. The good man's activities will not be hindered by changes of fortune, but will vary according to what change and chance brings ; but they will all be equally fine, and, perhaps, finer for being adapted to circumstances. As for his speculative activities, some of them which are concerned with particular points will possibly be hindered by circumstances,

5 αἱ μὲν καθ' ἕκαστα τάχα ἄν, οἷον ἃς ζητήσας ἂν
καὶ σκεψάμενος προφέροι· τὸ δὲ μέγιστον
μάθημα πρόχειρον ἀεὶ καὶ μετ' αὐτοῦ καὶ τοῦτο
μᾶλλον, κἂν ἐν τῷ Φαλάριδος ταύρῳ λεγομένῳ
ᾖ, ὃ μάτην λέγεται ἡδὺ δὶς ἢ καὶ πολλάκις
λεγόμενον. Ἐκεῖ μὲν γὰρ τὸ φθεγξάμενον τοῦτο
10 αὐτό ἐστι τὸ ἐν τῷ ἀλγεῖν ὑπάρχον, ἐνταῦθα δὲ τὸ
μὲν ἀλγοῦν ἄλλο, τὸ δὲ ἄλλο, ὃ συνὸν ἑαυτῷ, ἕως
ἂν ἐξ ἀνάγκης συνῇ, οὐκ ἀπολελείψεται τῆς τοῦ
ἀγαθοῦ ὅλου θέας.

14. Τὸ δὲ μὴ συναμφότερον εἶναι τὸν ἄνθρωπον
καὶ μάλιστα τὸν σπουδαῖον μαρτυρεῖ καὶ ὁ
χωρισμὸς ὁ ἀπὸ τοῦ σώματος καὶ ἡ τῶν λεγομένων
ἀγαθῶν τοῦ σώματος καταφρόνησις. Τὸ δὲ καθό-
5 σον ἀξιοῦν τὸ ζῷον τὴν εὐδαιμονίαν εἶναι γελοῖον
εὐζωίας τῆς εὐδαιμονίας οὔσης, ἣ περὶ ψυχὴν
συνίσταται, ἐνεργείας ταύτης οὔσης καὶ ψυχῆς οὐ
πάσης—οὐ γὰρ δὴ τῆς φυτικῆς, ἵν' ἂν καὶ ἐφήψατο
σώματος· οὐ γὰρ δὴ τὸ εὐδαιμονεῖν τοῦτο ἦν
σώματος μέγεθος καὶ εὐεξία—οὐδ' αὖ ἐν τῷ
10 αἰσθάνεσθαι εὖ, ἐπεὶ καὶ κινδυνεύσουσιν αἱ τούτων
πλεονεξίαι βαρύνασαι πρὸς αὐτὰς φέρειν τὸν
ἄνθρωπον. Ἀντισηκώσεως δὲ οἷον ἐπὶ θάτερα
πρὸς τὰ ἄριστα γενομένης μινύθειν καὶ χείρω τὰ
σώματα ποιεῖν, ἵνα δεικνύοιτο οὗτος ὁ ἄνθρωπος
15 ἄλλος ὢν ἢ τὰ ἔξω. Ὁ δὲ τῶν τῇδε ἄνθρωπος
ἔστω καὶ καλὸς καὶ μέγας καὶ πλούσιος καὶ

---

[1] The "greatest study" is for both Plato and Plotinus that
of the Good; cp. *Republic* VI. 505A2 and *Enn.* VI. 7. 36.

[2] The paradox that the wise and good man would be
εὐδαίμων on the rack or while being roasted in the brazen
bull of Phalaris was common to Stoics and Epicureans.

those for instance which require research and investigation. But the "greatest study"[1] is always ready to hand and always with him, all the more if he is in the so-called "bull of Phalaris"—which it is silly to call pleasant, though people keep on saying that it is;[2] for according to their philosophy that which says that its state is pleasant is the very same thing which is in pain; according to ours that which suffers pain is one thing, and there is another which, even while it is compelled to accompany that which suffers pain, remains in its own company and will not fall short of the vision of the universal good.

14. Man, and especially the good man, is not the composite of soul and body; separation from the body and despising of its so-called goods make this plain. It is absurd to maintain that well-being extends as far as the living body, since well-being is the good life, which is concerned with soul and is an activity of soul, and not of all of it—for it is not an activity of the growth-soul, which would bring it into connexion with body. This state of well-being is certainly not in the body's size or health, nor again does it consist in the excellence of the senses, for too much of these advantages is liable to weigh man down and bring him to their level. There must be a sort of counterpoise on the other side, towards the best, to reduce the body and make it worse, so that it may be made clear that the real man is other than his outward parts. The man who belongs to this world may be handsome and tall and rich and the

Plotinus argues that it makes no sense on their assumptions about the nature of man, but does on his, for he distinguishes the lower self (which really suffers) from the higher self (which remains unaffected).

πάντων ἀνθρώπων ἄρχων ὡς ἂν ὢν τοῦδε τοῦ
τόπου, καὶ οὐ φθονητέον αὐτῷ τῶν τοιούτων
ἠπατημένῳ. Περὶ δὲ σοφὸν ταῦτα ἴσως μὲν ἂν
οὐδὲ τὴν ἀρχὴν γένοιτο, γενομένων δὲ ἐλαττώσει
αὐτός, εἴπερ αὐτοῦ κήδεται. Καὶ ἐλαττώσει μὲν
20 καὶ μαρανεῖ ἀμελείᾳ τὰς τοῦ σώματος πλεονεξίας,
ἀρχὰς δὲ ἀποθήσεται. Σώματος δὲ ὑγίειαν φυλάτ-
των οὐκ ἄπειρος νόσων εἶναι παντάπασι βουλήσε-
ται· οὐδὲ μὴ οὐδὲ ἄπειρος εἶναι ἀλγηδόνων·
ἀλλὰ καὶ μὴ γινομένων νέος ὢν μαθεῖν βουλήσεται,
ἤδη δὲ ἐν γήρᾳ ὢν οὔτε ταύτας οὔτε ἡδονὰς
25 ἐνοχλεῖν οὐδέ τι τῶν τῇδε οὔτε προσηνὲς οὔτε
ἐναντίον, ἵνα μὴ πρὸς τὸ σῶμα βλέπῃ. Γινόμενος
δ' ἐν ἀλγηδόσι τὴν πρὸς ταύτας αὐτῷ πεπορισμένην
δύναμιν ἀντιτάξει οὔτε προσθήκην ἐν ταῖς ἡδοναῖς
καὶ ὑγιείαις καὶ ἀπονίαις πρὸς τὸ εὐδαιμονεῖν
λαμβάνων οὔτε ἀφαίρεσιν ἢ ἐλάττωσιν ταύτης ἐν
30 τοῖς ἐναντίοις τούτων. Τοῦ γὰρ ἐναντίου μὴ
προστιθέντος τῷ αὐτῷ πῶς ἂν τὸ ἐναντίον
ἀφαιροῖ;

15. Ἀλλ' εἰ δύο εἶεν σοφοί, τῷ δὲ ἑτέρῳ παρείη
ὅσα κατὰ φύσιν λέγεται, τῷ δὲ τὰ ἐναντία, ἴσον
φήσομεν τὸ εὐδαιμονεῖν αὐτοῖς παρεῖναι; Φήσομεν,
εἴπερ ἐπίσης σοφοί. Εἰ δὲ καλὸς τὸ σῶμα ὁ
5 ἕτερος καὶ πάντα τὰ ἄλλα ὅσα μὴ πρὸς σοφίαν
μηδὲ ὅλως πρὸς ἀρετὴν καὶ τοῦ ἀρίστου θέαν καὶ
τὸ ἄριστον εἶναι, τί τοῦτο ἂν εἴη; Ἐπεὶ οὐδὲ
αὐτὸς ὁ ταῦτα ἔχων σεμνυνεῖται ὡς μᾶλλον
εὐδαίμων τοῦ μὴ ἔχοντος· οὐδὲ γὰρ ἂν πρὸς

ruler of all mankind (since he is essentially of this region), and we ought not to envy him for things like these, by which he is beguiled. The wise man will perhaps not have them at all, and if he has them will himself reduce them, if he cares for his true self. He will reduce and gradually extinguish his bodily advantages by neglect, and will put away authority and office. He will take care of his bodily health, but will not wish to be altogether without experience of illness, nor indeed also of pain. Rather, even if these do not come to him he will want to learn them when he is young, but when he is old he will not want either pains or pleasures to hinder him, or any earthly thing, pleasant or the reverse, so that he may not have to consider the body. When he finds himself in pain he will oppose to it the power which he has been given for the purpose; he will find no help to his well-being in pleasure and health and freedom from pain and trouble, nor will their opposites take it away or diminish it. For if one thing adds nothing to a state, how can its opposite take anything away?

15. But suppose there were two wise men, one of whom had all of what are called natural goods and the other their opposites, shall we say that they both have well-being equally? Yes, if they are equally wise. Even if one is good-looking and has all the other advantages which have nothing to do with wisdom, or in any way with virtue and the vision of the best, or with the best itself, what does that amount to? After all, even the man who has these advantages will not give himself airs about them as if he was better off than the one who has not got them; to have more of them than others would be no help

αὐλητικὸν τέλος ἡ τούτων πλεονεξία συμβάλλοιτο.
10 Ἀλλὰ γὰρ θεωροῦμεν τὸν εὐδαίμονα μετὰ τῆς
ἡμετέρας ἀσθενείας φρικτὰ καὶ δεινὰ νομίζοντες,
ἃ μὴ ἂν ὁ εὐδαίμων νομίσειεν· ἢ οὔπω οὔτε
σοφὸς οὔτε εὐδαίμων εἴη μὴ τὰς περὶ τούτων
φαντασίας ἁπάσας ἀλλαξάμενος καὶ οἷον ἄλλος
παντάπασι γενόμενος πιστεύσας ἑαυτῷ, ὅτι μηδέν
15 ποτε κακὸν ἕξει· οὕτω γὰρ καὶ ἀδεὴς ἔσται περὶ
πάντα. Ἢ δειλαίνων περί τινα οὐ τέλεος πρὸς
ἀρετήν, ἀλλὰ ἥμισύς τις ἔσται. Ἐπεὶ καὶ τὸ
ἀπροαίρετον αὐτῷ καὶ τὸ γινόμενον πρὸ κρίσεως
δέος κἂν ποτε πρὸς ἄλλοις ἔχοντι γένηται, προσελ-
θὼν ὁ σοφὸς ἀπώσεται καὶ τὸν ἐν αὑτῷ κινηθέντα
20 οἷον πρὸς λύπας παῖδα καταπαύσει ἢ ἀπειλῇ ἢ
λόγῳ· ἀπειλῇ δὲ ἀπαθεῖ, οἷον εἰ ἐμβλέψαντος
σεμνὸν μόνον παῖς ἐκπλαγείη. Οὐ μὴν διὰ ταῦτα
ἄφιλος οὐδὲ ἀγνώμων ὁ τοιοῦτος· τοιοῦτος γὰρ
καὶ περὶ αὑτὸν καὶ ἐν τοῖς ἑαυτοῦ. Ἀποδιδοὺς
οὖν ὅσα αὑτῷ καὶ τοῖς φίλοις φίλος ἂν εἴη μάλιστα
25 μετὰ τοῦ νοῦν ἔχειν.

16. Εἰ δέ τις μὴ ἐνταῦθα ἐν τῷ νῷ τούτῳ ἄρας
θήσειε τὸν σπουδαῖον, κατάγοι δὲ πρὸς τύχας καὶ
ταύτας φοβήσεται περὶ αὑτὸν γενέσθαι, οὔτε
σπουδαῖον τηρήσει, οἷον ἀξιοῦμεν εἶναι, ἀλλ'
5 ἐπιεικῆ ἄνθρωπον, καὶ μικτὸν ἐξ ἀγαθοῦ καὶ
κακοῦ διδοὺς μικτὸν βίον ἔκ τινος ἀγαθοῦ καὶ
κακοῦ ἀποδώσει τῷ τοιούτῳ, καὶ οὐ ῥᾴδιον
γενέσθαι. Ὃς εἰ καὶ γένοιτο, οὐκ ἂν ὀνομάζεσθαι
εὐδαίμων εἴη ἄξιος οὐκ ἔχων τὸ μέγα οὔτε ἐν

even towards becoming a piper. But we bring our own weakness into it when we are considering whether a man is well off, and regard things as frightening and terrible which the man in a state of well-being would not so regard. He would not yet have attained to wisdom or well-being if he had not freed himself of all imaginations about this sort of thing, and become in a way quite a different man, with confidence in himself that evil can never touch him. In this state of mind he will be without fear of anything. If he is afraid at all he is not perfect in virtue, but a kind of half-man. If sometimes when he is concerned with other things an involuntary fear comes upon him before he has time to reflect, the wise man [in him] will come and drive it away and quiet the child in him which is stirred to a sort of distress, by threatening or reasoning; the threatening will be unemotional, as if the child was shocked into quietness just by a severe look. A man of this sort will not be unfriendly or unsympathetic; he will be like this to himself and in dealing with his own affairs: but he will render to his friends all that he renders to himself, and so will be the best of friends as well as remaining intelligent.

16. If anyone does not set the good man up on high in this world of intellect, but brings him down to chance events and fears their happening to him, he is not keeping his mind on the good man as we consider he must be, but assuming an ordinary man, a mixture of good and bad, and assigning to him a life which is also a mixture of good and bad and of a kind which cannot easily occur. Even if a person of this sort did exist, he would not be worth calling well off; he would have no greatness in him, either of the

ἀξίᾳ σοφίας οὔτε ἐν καθαρότητι ἀγαθοῦ. Οὐκ
10 ἔστιν οὖν ἐν τῷ κοινῷ εὐδαιμόνως ζῆν. Ὀρθῶς
γὰρ καὶ Πλάτων ἐκεῖθεν ἄνωθεν τὸ ἀγαθὸν ἀξιοῖ
λαμβάνειν καὶ πρὸς ἐκεῖνο βλέπειν τὸν μέλλοντα
σοφὸν καὶ εὐδαίμονα ἔσεσθαι καὶ ἐκείνῳ ὁμοιοῦσθαι
καὶ κατ' ἐκεῖνο ζῆν. Τοῦτο οὖν δεῖ ἔχειν μόνον
πρὸς τὸ τέλος, τὰ δ' ἄλλα ὡς ἂν καὶ τόπους
15 μεταβάλλοι οὐκ ἐκ τῶν τόπων προσθήκην πρὸς τὸ
εὐδαιμονεῖν ἔχων, ἀλλ' ὡς στοχαζόμενος καὶ τῶν
ἄλλων περικεχυμένων αὐτόν, οἷον εἰ ὡδὶ κατακείσε-
ται ἢ ὡδί, διδοὺς μὲν τούτῳ ὅσα πρὸς τὴν χρείαν
καὶ δύναται, αὐτὸς δὲ ὢν ἄλλος οὐ κωλυόμενος
καὶ τοῦτον ἀφεῖναι, καὶ ἀφήσων δὲ ἐν καιρῷ
20 φύσεως, κύριος δὲ καὶ αὐτὸς ὢν τοῦ βουλεύσασθαι
περὶ τούτου. Ὥστε αὐτῷ τὰ ἔργα τὰ μὲν πρὸς
εὐδαιμονίαν συντείνοντα ἔσται, τὰ δ' οὐ τοῦ τέλους
χάριν καὶ ὅλως οὐκ αὐτοῦ ἀλλὰ τοῦ προσεζευγμέ-
νου, οὗ φροντιεῖ καὶ ἀνέξεται, ἕως δυνατόν, οἷον
εἰ μουσικὸς λύρας, ἕως οἷόν τε χρῆσθαι· εἰ δὲ
25 μή, ἄλλην ἀλλάξεται, ἢ ἀφήσει τὰς λύρας χρήσεις
καὶ τοῦ εἰς λύραν ἐνεργεῖν ἀφέξεται ἄλλο ἔργον
ἄνευ λύρας ἔχων καὶ κειμένην πλησίον περιόψεται
ᾄδων ἄνευ ὀργάνων. Καὶ οὐ μάτην αὐτῷ ἐξ
ἀρχῆς τὸ ὄργανον ἐδόθη· ἐχρήσατο γὰρ αὐτῷ ἤδη
πολλάκις.

dignity of wisdom or the purity of good. The common life of body and soul cannot possibly be the life of well-being. Plato was right in maintaining that the man who intends to be wise and in a state of well-being must take his good from There, from above, and look to that good and be made like it and live by it.[1] He must hold on to this only as his goal, and change his other circumstances as he changes his dwelling-place, not because he derives any advantage in the point of well-being from one dwelling-place or another, but guessing, as it were, how his alien covering will be affected if he lodges here or there. He must give to this bodily life as much as it needs and he can, but he is himself other than it and free to abandon it, and he will abandon it in nature's good time, and, besides, has the right to decide about this for himself. So some of his activities will tend towards well-being; others will not be directed to the goal and will really not belong to him but to that which is joined to him, which he will care for and bear with as long as he can, like a musician with his lyre, as long as he can use it; if he cannot use it he will change to another, or give up using the lyre and abandon the activities directed to it. Then he will have something else to do which does not need the lyre, and will let it lie unregarded beside him while he sings without an instrument. Yet the instrument was not given him at the beginning without good reason. He has used it often up till now.

---

[1] Plotinus is referring to *Symposium* 212A1 and the *Theaetetus* passage (176B1) quoted at the beginning of the treatise *On Virtue* (I. 2).

ENNEAD I. 5

I. 5. ON WHETHER WELL-BEING INCREASES WITH TIME

Introductory Note

THIS short treatise is No. 36 in the chronological order; its subject is one that had been much discussed in the philosophical schools since Aristotle (see *Nicomachean Ethics* I. ch. 10), and, for once, Peripatetics, Stoics and Epicureans were substantially in agreement that the length of time a man was well off made no essential difference to his well-being. Plotinus's own original contribution to the discussion is his argument (ch. 7) that the life of well-being is really lived in eternity, not in time, and so the passage of time cannot affect it.

Synopsis

Well-being must consist in an actual present state, not in memory or anticipation (chs. 1–2). Short refutations of opposing arguments (chs. 2–5). The case of the man who is badly off (ch. 6). Well-being, time, and eternity (ch. 7). Memory of past goodness and pleasure can add nothing to well-being (chs. 8–9). Well-being a matter, not primarily of good external acts but of a good interior disposition (ch. 10).

I. 5. (36) ΠΕΡΙ ΤΟΥ ΕΙ ΤΟ ΕΥΔΑΙΜΟΝΕΙΝ
ΕΠΙΔΟΣΙΝ ΧΡΟΝΩΙ ΛΑΜΒΑΝΕΙ

1. Εἰ τὸ εὐδαιμονεῖν ἐπίδοσιν τῷ χρόνῳ λαμβάνει τοῦ εὐδαιμονεῖν ἀεὶ κατὰ τὸ ἐνεστὼς καμβανομένου; Οὐδὲ γὰρ ἡ μνήμη τοῦ εὐδαιμονῆσαι ποιοῖ ἄν τι, οὐδ' ἐν τῷ λέγειν, ἀλλ' ἐν τῷ διακεῖσθαί
5 πως τὸ εὐδαιμονεῖν. Ἡ δὲ διάθεσις ἐν τῷ παρεῖναι καὶ ἡ ἐνέργεια τῆς ζωῆς.

2. Εἰ δ' ὅτι ἐφιέμεθα ἀεὶ τοῦ ζῆν καὶ τοῦ ἐνεργεῖν, τὸ τυγχάνειν τοῦ τοιούτου εὐδαιμονεῖν λέγοι μᾶλλον, πρῶτον μὲν οὕτω καὶ ἡ αὔριον εὐδαιμονία μείζων ἔσται καὶ ἡ ἑξῆς ἀεὶ τῆς προτέ
5 ρας, καὶ οὐκέτι μετρηθήσεται τὸ εὐδαιμονεῖν τῇ ἀρετῇ. Ἔπειτα καὶ οἱ θεοὶ νῦν μᾶλλον εὐδαιμονήσουσιν ἢ πρότερον καὶ οὔπω τέλεον καὶ οὐδέποτε τέλεον. Ἔπειτα καὶ ἡ ἔφεσις λαβοῦσα τὴν τεῦξιν τὸ παρὸν εἴληφε καὶ ἀεὶ τὸ παρὸν καὶ ζητεῖ τὸ ἕως ἂν ᾖ τὸ εὐδαιμονεῖν ἔχειν. Ἡ δ' ἔφεσις τοῦ
10 ζῆν τὸ εἶναι ζητοῦσα τοῦ παρόντος ἂν εἴη, εἰ τὸ εἶναι ἐν τῷ παρόντι. Εἰ δὲ τὸ μέλλον καὶ τὸ ἐφεξῆς θέλοι, ὃ ἔχει θέλει καὶ ὅ ἐστιν, οὐχ ὃ παρελήλυθεν οὐδ' ὃ μέλλει, ἀλλ' ὃ ἤδη ἐστὶ τοῦτο εἶναι, οὐ τὸ εἰσαεὶ ζητοῦσα, ἀλλὰ τὸ παρὸν ἤδη εἶναι ἤδη.

3. Τί οὖν τὸ "πλείονα χρόνον εὐδαιμόνησε καὶ πλείονα χρόνον εἶδε τοῖς ὄμμασι τὸ αὐτό"; Εἰ

I. 5. ON WHETHER WELL-BEING
INCREASES WITH TIME

1. Does well-being increase with time, though it is understood always to refer to our present state? Memory, surely, can play no part in well-being; nor is it a matter of talking, but of being in a particular state. And a state is something present, and so is actuality of life.

2. But if it is said that, because we are always aiming at life and actuality, attaining [progressively] to this is greater well-being; first of all tomorrow's well-being will always be greater, and that which comes after greater than what was before it, and well-being will no longer be measured by virtue. Even the gods will be better off now than they were before, but they will not be perfectly well off; they will never be perfectly well off. And then, desire when it attains its end attains something present, something present at each particular moment, and seeks to possess well-being as long as it exists. Then too, since the desire of life seeks existence, it will be desire of the present, if existence is in the present. Even if it does want the future and what comes after, it wants what it has and what it is, not what it has been or is going to be; it wants what is already to exist; it is not seeking for the everlasting but wants what is present now to exist now.

3. What, then, about the statement " he has been well off for longer and had the same thing before his

217

μὲν γὰρ ἐν τῷ πλείονι τὸ ἀκριβέστερον εἶδε, πλέον
ἄν τι ὁ χρόνος αὐτῷ εἰργάσατο· εἰ δὲ ὁμοίως διὰ
5 παντὸς εἶδε, τὸ ἴσον καὶ ὁ ἅπαξ θεασάμενος ἔχει.

4. Ἀλλὰ πλείονα ἅτερος ἥσθη χρόνον. Ἀλλὰ
τοῦτο οὐκ ἂν ὀρθῶς ἔχοι ἀριθμεῖν εἰς τὸ εὐδαιμονεῖν. Εἰ δὲ τὴν ἡδονὴν λέγοι τις τὴν ἐνέργειαν τὴν
ἀνεμπόδιστον, τὸ αὐτὸ τῷ ζητουμένῳ λέγει. Καὶ
5 ἡ ἡδονὴ δὲ ἡ πλείων ἀεὶ τὸ παρὸν μόνον ἔχει, τὸ
δὲ παρεληλυθὸς αὐτῆς οἴχεται.

5. Τί οὖν; Εἰ ὁ μὲν ἐξ ἀρχῆς εὐδαιμόνησεν εἰς
τέλος, ὁ δὲ τὸν ὕστερον χρόνον, ὁ δὲ πρότερον
εὐδαιμονήσας μετέβαλεν, ἔχουσι τὸ ἴσον; Ἡ
ἐνταῦθα ἡ παραβολὴ οὐκ εὐδαιμονούντων γεγένηται
5 πάντων, ἀλλὰ μὴ εὐδαιμονούντων, ὅτε μὴ εὐδαιμό-
νουν, πρὸς εὐδαιμονοῦντα. Εἴ τι οὖν πλέον ἔχει,
τοῦτο ἔχει, ὅσον ὁ εὐδαίμων πρὸς οὐκ εὐδαίμονας,
ᾧ καὶ συμβαίνει πλεονεκτεῖν αὐτοὺς τῷ παρόντι.

6. Τί οὖν ὁ κακοδαίμων; Οὐ μᾶλλον κακοδαίμων
τῷ πλείονι; Καὶ τὰ ἄλλα δὲ ὅσα δυσχερῆ οὐκ ἐν
τῷ πλείονι χρόνῳ πλείω τὴν συμφορὰν δίδωσιν,
οἷον ὀδύναι πολυχρόνιοι καὶ λῦπαι καὶ πάντα τὰ
5 τούτου τοῦ τύπου; Ἀλλ᾽ εἰ ταῦτα οὕτω τῷ
χρόνῳ τὸ κακὸν ἐπαύξει, διὰ τί οὐ καὶ τὰ ἐναντία
καὶ τὸ εὐδαιμονεῖν ὡσαύτως; Ἡ ἐπὶ μὲν τῶν
λυπῶν καὶ ὀδυνῶν ἔχοι ἄν τις λέγειν, ὡς προσθήκην

---

[1] Cp. Aristotle, *Nicomachean Ethics* VII. 14. 1153b. 10–12.

eyes for longer"? If in the longer time he gained a more accurate knowledge of it, then the time would have done something more for him. But if he knows it just the same all the time, the man who has seen it once has as much.

4. "But the first man had a longer period of pleasure." But it is not right to count pleasure in reckoning well-being. But if someone says that pleasure is "unhindered activity,"[1] he is stating just the conclusion we are seeking. And anyhow this longer-lasting pleasure at any moment only has what is present; past pleasure is gone and done with.

5. Well then, if one man has been well off from beginning to end, and another in the latter part of his life, and yet another has been well off at first and then changed his state, do they have equal shares? Here the comparison is not being made between people who are all in a state of well-being; it is a comparison of those who are not well off, at the time when they are not well off, with a man who is well off. So if this latter has anything more, he has just what the man in a state of well-being has in comparison with those who are not; and that means that his advantage is by something in the present.

6. Then what about the man who is badly off? Is he not worse off the longer his bad fortune lasts? And do not all other troubles make the misfortune worse the longer they last, long-lasting pains and griefs for instance, and other things of that stamp? But if these troubles in this way make the evil increase with the passage of time, why do not their opposites in the same way cause an increase of well-being? One could, certainly, say in the case of griefs and pains that time brings about an increase,

ὁ χρόνος δίδωσιν, οἷον τὸ ἐπιμένειν τὴν νόσον·
ἕξις γὰρ γίνεται, καὶ κακοῦται μᾶλλον τῷ χρόνῳ
10 τὸ σῶμα. Ἐπεί, εἴ γε τὸ αὐτὸ μένοι καὶ μὴ
μείζων ἡ βλάβη, καὶ ἐνταῦθα τὸ παρὸν ἀεὶ τὸ
λυπηρὸν ἔσται, εἰ μὴ τὸ παρεληλυθὸς προσαριθμοῖ
ἀφορῶν εἰς τὸ γενόμενον καὶ μένον· ἐπί τε τῆς
κακοδαίμονος ἕξεως τὸ κακὸν ἐς τὸν πλείονα
χρόνον ἐπιτείνεσθαι αὐξανομένης καὶ τῆς κακίας
15 τῷ ἐμμόνῳ. Τῇ γοῦν προσθήκῃ τοῦ μᾶλλον, οὐ
τῷ πλείονι ἴσῳ τὸ μᾶλλον κακοδαιμονεῖν γίνεται.
Τὸ δὲ πλεῖον ἴσον οὐχ ἅμα ἐστὶν οὐδὲ δὴ πλεῖον
ὅλως λεκτέον τὸ μηκέτι ὂν τῷ ὄντι συναριθμοῦντα.
Τὸ δὲ τῆς εὐδαιμονίας ὅρον τε καὶ πέρας ἔχει καὶ
ταὐτὸν ἀεί. Εἰ δέ τις καὶ ἐνταῦθα ἐπίδοσις παρὰ
20 τὸν πλείονα χρόνον, ὥστε μᾶλλον εὐδαιμονεῖν εἰς
ἀρετὴν ἐπιδιδόντα μείζονα, οὐ τὴν πολυετῆ
εὐδαιμονίαν ἀριθμῶν ἐπαινεῖ, ἀλλὰ τὴν μᾶλλον
γενομένην τότε, ὅτε μᾶλλόν ἐστιν.

7. Ἀλλὰ διὰ τί, εἰ τὸ παρὸν θεωρεῖν δεῖ μόνον
καὶ μὴ συναριθμεῖν τῷ γενομένῳ, οὐ κἀπὶ τοῦ
χρόνου τὸ αὐτὸ ποιοῦμεν, ἀλλὰ καὶ τὸν παρεληλυ-
θότα τῷ παρόντι συναριθμοῦντες πλείω λέγομεν;
5 Διὰ τί οὖν οὐχ, ὅσος ὁ χρόνος, τοσαύτην καὶ τὴν
εὐδαιμονίαν ἐροῦμεν; Καὶ διαιροῖμεν ἂν κατὰ τὰς
τοῦ χρόνου διαιρέσεις καὶ τὴν εὐδαιμονίαν· καὶ
γὰρ αὖ τῷ παρόντι μετροῦντες ἀδιαίρετον αὐτὴν

for instance in chronic illness; it becomes a permanent state, and as time goes on the condition of the
body grows worse. For if it remains the same and
the damage is no greater, then here too it will be the
present state always which is painful, if one does not
add on what is past in consideration of the persistence of the illness once it has come into existence; in the case of a state of ill-being, too, the evil
will grow worse the longer it lasts since the badness
of the state will be increased by its persistence. So
the greater misfortune will be due to the addition of
the increase, not to the persistence for a longer time
in the same state. That which lasts longer in the
same state is not all present at once; one ought not
really to talk about " longer " at all, because it means
reckoning that which does not any longer exist along
with that which does. But as regards well-being,
it has a boundary and a limit and is always the
same. But if here too there is an increase with
greater length of time, so that as a man progresses to
greater virtue he is better off, one is not counting the
many years of well-being and praising it for lasting so
long, but praising it for being greater at the time
when it is greater.

7. But why, if we ought only to consider the
present and not to count it along with the past, do
we not do the same with time? Why do we count
the past along with the present and say that it is
more? Why, then, should we not say that well-
being is equal in quantity to the time its lasts? We
should then divide well-being according to the divi-
sions of time; of course if we measure it by the
present we shall make it indivisible. Now it is not

ποιήσομεν. Ἡ τὸν μὲν χρόνον ἀριθμεῖν καὶ
μηκέτι ὄντα οὐκ ἄτοπον, ἐπείπερ καὶ τῶν γενομέ-
10 νων μέν, μηκέτι δὲ ὄντων, ἀριθμὸν ἂν ποιησαίμεθα,
οἷον τῶν τετελευτηκότων· εὐδαιμονίαν δὲ μηκέτι
οὖσαν [παρεῖναι] λέγειν τῆς παρούσης πλείονα
ἄτοπον. Τὸ μὲν γὰρ εὐδαιμονεῖν συμμεμενηκέναι
ἀξιοῖ, ὁ δὲ χρόνος ὁ πλείων παρὰ τὸν παρόντα τὸ
μηκέτι εἶναι. Ὅλως δὲ τοῦ χρόνου τὸ πλέον
15 σκέδασιν βούλεται ἑνός τινος ἐν τῷ παρόντι
ὄντος. Διὸ καὶ εἰκὼν αἰῶνος εἰκότως λέγεται
ἀφανίζειν βουλομένη ἐν τῷ σκιδναμένῳ αὐτῆς τὸ
ἐκείνου μένον. Ὅθεν κἂν ἀπὸ τοῦ αἰῶνος ἀφέληται
τὸ ἐν ἐκείνῳ μεῖναν ἂν καὶ αὐτῆς ποιήσηται,
ἀπώλεσεν αὐτό, σωζόμενον τέως ἐκείνῳ τρόπον
20 τινά, ἀπολόμενον δέ, ἐν αὐτῇ εἰ πᾶν γένοιτο.
Εἴπερ οὖν τὸ εὐδαιμονεῖν κατὰ ζωὴν ἀγαθήν,
δηλονότι κατὰ τὴν τοῦ ὄντος αὐτὴν θετέον ζωήν·
αὕτη γὰρ ἀρίστη. Οὐκ ἄρα ἀριθμητέα χρόνῳ,
ἀλλ' αἰῶνι· τοῦτο δὲ οὔτε πλέον οὔτε ἔλαττον
οὔτε μήκει τινί, ἀλλὰ τὸ τοῦτο καὶ τὸ ἀδιάστατον
25 καὶ τὸ οὐ χρονικὸν εἶναι. Οὐ συναπτέον τοίνυν
τὸ ὂν τῷ μὴ ὄντι οὐδὲ [τῷ αἰῶνι] τὸν χρόνον οὐδὲ
τὸ χρονικὸν δὲ ἀεὶ τῷ αἰῶνι οὐδὲ παρεκτατέον τὸ
ἀδιάστατον, ἀλλὰ πᾶν ὅλον ληπτέον, εἴ ποτε
λαμβάνοις, λαμβάνων οὐ τοῦ χρόνου τὸ ἀδιαίρετον,
ἀλλὰ τοῦ αἰῶνος τὴν ζωὴν τὴν οὐκ ἐκ πολλῶν
30 χρόνων, ἀλλὰ τὴν ἐκ παντὸς χρόνου πᾶσαν
ὁμοῦ.

8. Εἰ δέ τις λέγοι τὴν μνήμην τῶν παρεληλυθότων ἐν τῷ ἐνεστηκότι μένουσαν παρέχεσθαι τὸ
πλέον τῷ πλείονα χρόνον ἐν τῷ εὐδαιμονεῖν
γεγενημένῳ, τί ἂν τὸ τῆς μνήμης λέγοι; Ἡ γὰρ

unreasonable to count time even when it does not
exist any longer, since we reckon the number of
things which have been there in the past but no
longer exist, the dead for instance; but it is unreasonable to say that well-being which no longer
exists is more than that which is present. For well-
being requires to persist, but time over and above the
present admits of existing no longer. In general
extension of time means the dispersal of a single
present. That is why it is properly called "the
image of eternity,"[1] since it intends to bring about
the disappearance of what is permanent in eternity
by its own dispersion. So if it takes from eternity
what would be permanent in it and makes it its own,
it destroys it—it is preserved, up to a point, by
eternity, in one way, but destroyed if it passes
altogether into temporal dispersion. So if well-
being is a matter of good life, obviously the life
concerned must be that of real being; for this is the
best. So it must not be counted by time but by
eternity; and this is neither more nor less nor of any
extension, but is a "this here," unextended and
timeless. So one must not join being to non-being or
time or everlastingness of time to eternity nor must
one extend the unextended; one must take it all as a
whole, if one takes it at all, and apprehend, not the
undividedness of time but the life of eternity, which is
not made up of many times, but is all together from
the whole of time.

8. But if someone says that the memory of the past
remaining in the present gives more to the man who
has been longer in a state of well-being, what does he
mean by memory? If it is memory of previous

---

[1] Plato, *Timaeus* 37D5.

5 φρονήσεως μνήμη τῆς πρόσθεν γεγενημένης, ὥστε
φρονιμώτερον ἂν λέγοι καὶ οὐκ ἂν τηροῖ τὴν
ὑπόθεσιν· ἢ τῆς ἡδονῆς τὴν μνήμην, ὥσπερ
πολλῆς περιχαρίας δεομένου τοῦ εὐδαίμονος καὶ
οὐκ ἀρκουμένου τῇ παρούσῃ. Καίτοι τί ἂν ἡδὺ
ἡ μνήμη τοῦ ἡδέος ἔχοι; Ὥσπερ ἄν, εἰ μνημονεύοι
10 τις ὅτι ἐχθὲς ἐπὶ ὄψῳ ἥσθη· ἢ εἰς δέκατον ἔτος
ἔτι ἂν εἴη γελοιότερος· τὸ δὲ τῆς φρονήσεως. ὅτι
πέρυσιν ἐφρόνουν.

9. Εἰ δὲ τῶν καλῶν εἴη ἡ μνήμη, πῶς οὐκ
ἐνταῦθα λέγοιτο ἄν τι; Ἀλλὰ ἀνθρώπου ἐστὶ
τοῦτο ἐλλείποντος τοῖς καλοῖς ἐν τῷ παρόντι καὶ
τῷ μὴ ἔχειν νυνὶ ζητοῦντος τὴν μνήμην τῶν
γεγενημένων.

10. Ἀλλ᾽ ὁ πολὺς χρόνος πολλὰς ποιεῖ καλὰς
πράξεις, ὧν ἄμοιρος ὁ πρὸς ὀλίγον εὐδαίμων· εἰ
δεῖ λέγειν ὅλως εὐδαίμονα τὸν οὐ διὰ πολλῶν τῶν
καλῶν. Ἢ ὃς ἐκ πολλῶν τὸ εὐδαιμονεῖν καὶ
5 χρόνων καὶ πράξεων λέγει, ἐκ τῶν μηκέτι ὄντων ἀλλ᾽
ἐκ τῶν παρεληλυθότων καὶ ἑνός τινος τοῦ παρόντος
τὸ εὐδαιμονεῖν συνίστησι. Διὸ κατὰ τὸ παρὸν
ἐθέμεθα τὸ εὐδαιμονεῖν, εἶτα ἐζητοῦμεν εἰ μᾶλλόν
⟨ἐστι⟩ τὸ ἐν πλείονι εὐδαιμονῆσαι [μᾶλλόν ἐστι].
Τοῦτο οὖν ζητητέον, εἰ ταῖς πράξεσι ταῖς πλείοσι
10 πλεονεκτεῖ τὸ ἐν πολλῷ χρόνῳ εὐδαιμονεῖν.
Πρῶτον μὲν οὖν ἔστι καὶ μὴ ἐν πράξεσι γενόμενον
εὐδαιμονεῖν καὶ οὐκ ἔλαττον ἀλλὰ μᾶλλον τοῦ
πεπραγότος· ἔπειτα αἱ πράξεις οὐκ ἐξ αὐτῶν τὸ

virtue and intelligence, he will be saying that the man is more virtuous and intelligent [not better off] and so will not be keeping to the point; if it is memory of pleasure, he will be representing the man in a state of well-being as needing a great deal of extra enjoyment and not being satisfied with what he has. And besides what pleasure is there in the memory of pleasantness—for instance, if someone remembers that yesterday he enjoyed some nice food? And if it was ten years ago that he enjoyed it, he would be even more ridiculous. The same applies to the memory that one was virtuous and intelligent last year.

9. But if it is memory of excellence that is in question, is there not some sense in this? This is the idea of a man whose life is without excellence in the present, and because he has not got it now is seeking for memories of past excellences.

10. But length of time brings many excellent actions, in which the man who has only been well off for a short time has no share; if indeed we can call anyone well off who is not so as the result of much well-doing. Anyone who says that the state of well-being is produced by many times and actions is putting it together out of pieces which no longer exist but are past and one which is present. That is why we started by positing well-being in the present, and then enquired whether longer duration of well-being meant an increase. So we must enquire whether well-being which lasts for a long time is increased by a greater number of actions. First of all, it is possible for someone who is not active to be well off, and better off than the active man; then, actions do not produce goodness of themselves, but

225

εὖ διδόασιν, ἀλλ' αἱ διαθέσεις καὶ τὰς πράξεις
καλὰς ποιοῦσι καρποῦταί τε ὁ φρόνιμος τὸ ἀγαθὸν
15 καὶ πράττων, οὐχ ὅτι πράττει οὐδ' ἐκ τῶν συμβαι-
νόντων, ἀλλ' ἐξ οὗ ἔχει. Ἐπεὶ καὶ ἡ σωτηρία
τῆς πατρίδος γένοιτο ἂν καὶ παρὰ φαύλου, καὶ τὸ
ἐπὶ σωτηρίᾳ τῆς πατρίδος ἡδὺ καὶ ἄλλου πράξαντος
γένοιτο ἂν αὐτῷ. Οὐ τοίνυν τοῦτό ἐστι τὸ ποιοῦν
τὴν τοῦ εὐδαίμονος ἡδονήν, ἀλλ' ἡ ἕξις καὶ τὴν
20 εὐδαιμονίαν καὶ εἴ τι ἡδὺ δι' αὐτὴν ποιεῖ. Τὸ δὲ
ἐν ταῖς πράξεσι τὸ εὐδαιμονεῖν τίθεσθαι ἐν τοῖς
ἔξω τῆς ἀρετῆς καὶ τῆς ψυχῆς ἐστι τιθέντος· ἡ
γὰρ ἐνέργεια τῆς ψυχῆς ἐν τῷ φρονῆσαι καὶ ἐν
ἑαυτῇ ὡδὶ ἐνεργῆσαι. Καὶ τοῦτο τὸ εὐδαιμόνως.

it is men's dispositions which make actions excellent, and the wise and good man gets the benefit of goodness in his action, not from the fact that he acts nor the circumstances of his action, but from what he has.   Even a bad man can save his country; and the good man's pleasure that his country is saved will be there even if someone else saves it.   So it is not this which causes the pleasure of well-being; it is one's inner state which produces both well-being and any pleasure that results from it.   To place well-being in actions is to locate it in something outside virtue and the soul; the activity of the soul lies in thought, and action of this kind within itself; and this is the state of well-being.

ENNEAD I. 6

I. 6. ON BEAUTY

Introductory Note

THIS treatise is the first in Porphyry's chronological order (which does not necessarily mean that it was the first which Plotinus wrote). It has been perhaps the best known and most read treatise in the *Enneads*, both in ancient and modern times. It should be read with the later treatise *On the Intelligible Beauty* (V. 8). The two together give a fairly complete view of Plotinus's most original and important aesthetic philosophy and of how he understands the relationship of physical to moral beauty and of both to their origin in the intelligible beauty of the World of Forms and its principle, the Good. The object of the treatise *On Beauty*, as becomes clear in the later chapters, is not to provide its readers with an aesthetic philosophy but to exhort them to ascend through all the visible and invisible beauties of derived reality to the source of all beauty, the Good, on that journey of the mind to God which was always Plotinus's main concern.

Synopsis

What is it that makes things beautiful? We will start our enquiry by considering the beauty of bodies. The Stoic view that it is entirely a matter of good proportion will not do (ch. 1). It is due to the presence of form from the intelligible world (ch. 2) and we recognise and appreciate it by our inward knowledge of intelligible form (ch. 3). The beauty of virtue (ch. 4). It is the beauty of true reality in its transcendent purity, and its opposite, moral ugliness, is due to admixture with body (ch. 5). We attain to it by purifying ourselves (ch. 6). The supreme and absolute beauty, the Good (ch. 7). The way to it (ch. 8). The power of inner sight and how to develop it (ch. 9).

I. 6. (1) ΠΕΡΙ ΤΟΥ ΚΑΛΟΥ

1. Τὸ καλὸν ἔστι μὲν ἐν ὄψει πλεῖστον, ἔστι δ᾽
ἐν ἀκοαῖς κατά τε λόγων συνθέσεις, ἔστι δὲ καὶ
ἐν μουσικῇ καὶ ἁπάσῃ· καὶ γὰρ μέλη καὶ ῥυθμοί
εἰσι καλοί· ἔστι δὲ καὶ προιοῦσι πρὸς τὸ ἄνω
5 ἀπὸ τῆς αἰσθήσεως καὶ ἐπιτηδεύματα καλὰ καὶ
πράξεις καὶ ἕξεις καὶ ἐπιστῆμαί τε καὶ τὸ τῶν
ἀρετῶν κάλλος. Εἰ δέ τι καὶ πρὸ τούτων, αὐτὸ
δείξει. Τί οὖν δὴ τὸ πεποιηκὸς καὶ τὰ σώματα
καλὰ φαντάζεσθαι καὶ τὴν ἀκοὴν ἐπινεύειν ταῖς
φωναῖς, ὡς καλαί; Καὶ ὅσα ἐφεξῆς ψυχῆς ἔχεται,
10 πῶς ποτε πάντα καλά; Καὶ ἆρά γε ἑνὶ καὶ τῷ
αὐτῷ καλῷ τὰ πάντα, ἢ ἄλλο μὲν ἐν σώματι τὸ
κάλλος, ἄλλο δὲ ἐν ἄλλῳ; Καὶ τίνα ποτὲ ταῦτα ἢ
τοῦτο; Τὰ μὲν γὰρ οὐ παρ᾽ αὐτῶν τῶν ὑποκειμέ-
νων καλά, οἷον τὰ σώματα, ἀλλὰ μεθέξει, τὰ δὲ
κάλλη αὐτά, ὥσπερ ἀρετῆς ἡ φύσις. Σώματα μὲν
15 γὰρ τὰ αὐτὰ ὁτὲ μὲν καλά, ὁτὲ δὲ οὐ καλὰ
φαίνεται, ὡς ἄλλου ὄντος τοῦ σώματα εἶναι,
ἄλλου δὲ τοῦ καλά. Τί οὖν ἐστι τοῦτο τὸ παρὸν
τοῖς σώμασι; Πρῶτον γὰρ περὶ τούτου σκεπτέον.
Τί οὖν ἐστιν, ὃ κινεῖ τὰς ὄψεις τῶν θεωμένων καὶ
ἐπιστρέφει πρὸς αὐτὸ καὶ ἕλκει καὶ εὐφραίνεσθαι
τῇ θέᾳ ποιεῖ; Τοῦτο γὰρ εὑρόντες τάχ᾽ ἂν
20 ἐπιβάθρᾳ αὐτῷ χρώμενοι καὶ τὰ ἄλλα θεασαί-

---

[1] Cf. Plato, *Symposium* 211C3.

I. 6. ON BEAUTY

1. Beauty is mostly in sight, but it is to be found too in things we hear, in combinations of words and also in music, and in all music [not only in songs]; for tunes and rhythms are certainly beautiful: and for those who are advancing upwards from sense-perception ways of life and actions and characters and intellectual activities are beautiful, and there is the beauty of virtue. If there is any beauty prior to these, it itself will reveal it.

Very well then, what is it which makes us imagine that bodies are beautiful and attracts our hearing to sounds because of their beauty? And how are all the things which depend on soul beautiful? Are they all made beautiful by one and the same beauty or is there one beautifulness in bodies and a different one in other things? And what are they, or what is it? Some things, bodies for instance, are not beautiful from the nature of the objects themselves, but by participation, others are beauties themselves, like the nature of virtue. The same bodies appear sometimes beautiful, sometimes not beautiful, so that their being bodies is one thing, their being beautiful another. What is this principle, then, which is present in bodies? We ought to consider this first. What is it that attracts the gaze of those who look at something, and turns and draws them to it and makes them enjoy the sight? If we find this perhaps we can use it as a stepping-stone [1] and get

μεθα. Λέγεται μὲν δὴ παρὰ πάντων, ὡς εἰπεῖν,
ὡς συμμετρία τῶν μερῶν πρὸς ἄλληλα καὶ πρὸς
τὸ ὅλον τό τε τῆς εὐχροίας προστεθὲν τὸ πρὸς τὴν
ὄψιν κάλλος ποιεῖ καὶ ἔστιν αὐτοῖς καὶ ὅλως τοῖς
ἄλλοις πᾶσι τὸ καλοῖς εἶναι τὸ συμμέτροις καὶ
25 μεμετρημένοις ὑπάρχειν· οἷς ἁπλοῦν οὐδέν, μόνον
δὲ τὸ σύνθετον ἐξ ἀνάγκης καλὸν ὑπάρξει· τό τε
ὅλον ἔσται καλὸν αὐτοῖς, τὰ δὲ μέρη ἕκαστα οὐχ
ἕξει παρ' ἑαυτῶν τὸ καλὰ εἶναι, πρὸς δὲ τὸ ὅλον
συντελοῦντα, ἵνα καλὸν ᾖ· καίτοι δεῖ, εἴπερ ὅλον,
30 καὶ τὰ μέρη καλὰ εἶναι· οὐ γὰρ δὴ ἐξ αἰσχρῶν,
ἀλλὰ πάντα κατειληφέναι τὸ κάλλος. Τά τε
χρώματα αὐτοῖς τὰ καλά, οἷον καὶ τὸ τοῦ ἡλίου
φῶς, ἁπλᾶ ὄντα, οὐκ ἐκ συμμετρίας ἔχοντα τὸ
κάλλος ἔξω ἔσται τοῦ καλὰ εἶναι. Χρωσός τε δὴ
πῶς καλόν; Καὶ νυκτὸς ἡ ἀστραπὴ ἢ ἄστρα
35 ὁρᾶσθαι τῷ καλά; Ἐπί τε τῶν φωνῶν ὡσαύτως
τὸ ἁπλοῦν οἰχήσεται, καίτοι ἑκάστου φθόγγου
πολλαχῇ τῶν ἐν τῷ ὅλῳ καλῷ καλοῦ καὶ αὐτοῦ
ὄντος. Ὅταν δὲ δὴ τῆς αὐτῆς συμμετρίας
μενούσης ὁτὲ μὲν καλὸν τὸ αὐτὸ πρόσωπον, ὁτὲ
δὲ μὴ φαίνηται, πῶς οὐκ ἄλλο δεῖ ἐπὶ τῷ συμ-
40 μέτρῳ λέγειν τὸ καλὸν εἶναι, καὶ τὸ σύμμετρον
καλὸν εἶναι δι' ἄλλο; Εἰ δὲ δὴ μεταβαίνοντες καὶ
ἐπὶ τὰ ἐπιτηδεύματα καὶ τοὺς λόγους τοὺς καλοὺς
τὸ σύμμετρον καὶ ἐπ' αὐτῶν αἰτιῶντο, τίς ἂν

---

[1] That good proportion was an essential part of beauty was
a general Greek conviction, accepted by Plato and Aristotle;
but it was the Stoics who defined beauty strictly and exclusively in these terms, cp. Cicero, *Tusculans* IV. 31, *et ut
corporis est quaedam apta figura membrorum cum coloris*

a sight of the rest. Nearly everyone says that it is good proportion of the parts to each other and to the whole, with the addition of good colour,[1] which produces visible beauty, and that with the objects of sight and generally with everything else, being beautiful is being well-proportioned and measured. On this theory nothing single and simple but only a composite thing will have any beauty. It will be the whole which is beautiful, and the parts will not have the property of beauty by themselves, but will contribute to the beauty of the whole. But if the whole is beautiful the parts must be beautiful too; a beautiful whole can certainly not be composed of ugly parts; all the parts must have beauty. For these people, too, beautiful colours, and the light of the sun as well, since they are simple and do not derive their beautifulness from good proportion, will be excluded from beauty. And how do they think gold manages to be beautiful? And what makes lightning in the night and stars beautiful to see? And in sounds in the same way the simple will be banished, though often in a composition which is beautiful as a whole each separate sound is beautiful. And when, though the same good proportion is there all the time, the same face sometimes appears beautiful and sometimes does not, surely we must say that being beautiful is something else over and above good proportion, and good proportion is beautiful because of something else? But if when these people pass on to ways of life and beautiful expressions of thought they allege good proportion as the cause of

quadam suavitate eaque dicitur pulchritudo..., repeated by S. Augustine with only slight variation in *De Civitate Dei* XXII. 19.

λέγοιτο ἐν ἐπιτηδεύμασι συμμετρία καλοῖς ἢ
νόμοις ἢ μαθήμασιν ἢ ἐπιστήμαις; Θεωρήματα
45 γὰρ σύμμετρα πρὸς ἄλληλα πῶς ἂν εἴη; Εἰ δ'
ὅτι σύμφωνά ἐστι, καὶ κακῶν ἔσται ὁμολογία τε
καὶ συμφωνία. Τῷ γὰρ τὴν σωφροσύνην ἠλι-
θιότητα εἶναι τὸ τὴν δικαιοσύνην γενναίαν
εἶναι εὐήθειαν σύμφωνον καὶ συνῳδὸν καὶ
ὁμολογεῖ πρὸς ἄλληλα. Κάλλος μὲν οὖν ψυχῆς
50 ἀρετὴ πᾶσα καὶ κάλλος ἀληθινώτερον ἢ τὰ
πρόσθεν· ἀλλὰ πῶς σύμμετρα; Οὔτε γὰρ ὡς
μεγέθη οὔτε ὡς ἀριθμὸς σύμμετρα· καὶ πλειόνων
μερῶν τῆς ψυχῆς ὄντων, ἐν ποίῳ γὰρ λόγῳ ἡ
σύνθεσις ἢ ἡ κρᾶσις τῶν μερῶν ἢ τῶν θεωρημάτων;
Τὸ δὲ τοῦ νοῦ κάλλος μονουμένου τί ἂν εἴη;

2. Πάλιν οὖν ἀναλαβόντες λέγωμεν τί δῆτά ἐστι
τὸ ἐν τοῖς σώμασι καλὸν πρῶτον. Ἔστι μὲν
γάρ τι καὶ βολῇ τῇ πρώτῃ αἰσθητὸν γινόμενον
καὶ ἡ ψυχὴ ὥσπερ συνεῖσα λέγει καὶ ἐπιγνοῦσα
5 ἀποδέχεται καὶ οἷον συναρμόττεται. Πρὸς δὲ τὸ
αἰσχρὸν προσβαλοῦσα ἀνίλλεται καὶ ἀρνεῖται
καὶ ἀνανεύει ἀπ' αὐτοῦ οὐ συμφωνοῦσα καὶ
ἀλλοτριουμένη. Φαμὲν δή, ὡς τὴν φύσιν οὖσα
ὅπερ ἐστὶ καὶ πρὸς τῆς κρείττονος ἐν τοῖς οὖσιν
οὐσίας, ὅ τι ἂν ἴδῃ συγγενὲς ἢ ἴχνος τοῦ συγγενοῦς,
10 χαίρει τε καὶ διεπτόηται καὶ ἀναφέρει πρὸς
ἑαυτὴν καὶ ἀναμιμνήσκεται ἑαυτῆς καὶ τῶν ἑαυτῆς.
Τίς οὖν ὁμοιότης τοῖς τῇδε πρὸς τὰ ἐκεῖ καλά;

---

[1] Cicero, in the *Tusculans* passage quoted above, goes on to
draw a precise parallel between the beauty of body, which
consists in good proportion with pleasant colour, and beauty
of soul.

beauty in these too,[1] what can be meant by good proportion in beautiful ways of life or laws or studies or branches of knowledge? How can speculations be well-proportioned in relation to each other? If it is because they agree, there can be concord and agreement between bad ideas. The statement that "righteousness is a fine sort of silliness" agrees with and is in tune with the saying that "morality is stupidity";[2] the two fit perfectly. Again, every sort of virtue is a beauty of the soul, a truer beauty than those mentioned before; but how is virtue well-proportioned? Not like magnitudes or a number. We grant that the soul has several parts, but what is the formula for the composition or mixture in the soul of parts or speculations? And what [on this theory] will the beauty of the intellect alone by itself be?

2. So let us go back to the beginning and state what the primary beauty in bodies really is. It is something which we become aware of even at the first glance; the soul speaks of it as if it understood it, recognises and welcomes it and as it were adapts itself to it. But when it encounters the ugly it shrinks back and rejects it and turns away from it and is out of tune and alienated from it. Our explanation of this is that the soul, since it is by nature what it is and is related to the higher kind of reality in the realm of being, when it sees something akin to it or a trace of its kindred reality, is delighted and thrilled and returns to itself and remembers itself and its own possessions. What likeness, then, is there between beautiful things here and There? If

[2] Cp. Plato, *Republic* 348C11–12 and 560D2–3.

καὶ γάρ, εἰ ὁμοιότης, ὅμοια μὲν ἔστω· πῶς δὲ
καλὰ κἀκεῖνα καὶ ταῦτα; Μετοχῇ εἴδους φαμὲν
ταῦτα.   Πᾶν μὲν γὰρ τὸ ἄμορφον πεφυκὸς μορφὴν
15 καὶ εἶδος δέχεσθαι ἄμοιρον ὂν λόγου καὶ εἴδους
αἰσχρὸν καὶ ἔξω θείου λόγου· καὶ τὸ πάντη
αἰσχρὸν τοῦτο.   Αἰσχρὸν δὲ καὶ τὸ μὴ κρατηθὲν
ὑπὸ μορφῆς καὶ λόγου οὐκ ἀνασχομένης τῆς ὕλης
τὸ πάντη κατὰ τὸ εἶδος μορφοῦσθαι.   Προσιὸν
20 οὖν τὸ εἶδος τὸ μὲν ἐκ πολλῶν ἐσόμενον μερῶν ἓν
συνθέσει συνέταξέ τε καὶ εἰς μίαν συντέλειαν
ἤγαγε καὶ ἓν τῇ ὁμολογίᾳ πεποίηκεν, ἐπείπερ ἓν
ἦν αὐτὸ ἕν τε ἔδει τὸ μορφούμενον εἶναι ὡς
δυνατὸν αὐτῷ ἐκ πολλῶν ὄντι.   Ἵδρυται οὖν ἐπ'
αὐτοῦ τὸ κάλλος ἤδη εἰς ἓν συναχθέντος καὶ τοῖς
μέρεσι διδὸν ἑαυτὸ καὶ τοῖς ὅλοις.   Ὅταν δὲ ἕν
25 τι καὶ ὁμοιομερὲς καταλάβῃ, εἰς ὅλον δίδωσι τὸ
αὐτό·   οἷον ὁτὲ μὲν πάσῃ οἰκίᾳ μετὰ τῶν μερῶν,
ὁτὲ δὲ ἑνὶ λίθῳ διδοίη τις φύσις τὸ κάλλος, τῇ
δὲ ἡ τέχνη.   Οὕτω μὲν δὴ τὸ καλὸν σῶμα γίγνεται
λόγου ἀπὸ θείων ἐλθόντος κοινωνία.

3. Γινώσκει δὲ αὐτὸ ἡ ἐπ' αὐτῷ δύναμις
τεταγμένη, ἧς οὐδὲν κυριώτερον εἰς κρίσιν τῶν
ἑαυτῆς, ὅταν καὶ ἡ ἄλλη συνεπικρίνῃ ψυχή, τάχα
δὲ καὶ αὕτη λέγῃ συναρμόττουσα τῷ παρ' αὐτῇ
εἴδει κἀκείνῳ πρὸς τὴν κρίσιν χρωμένη ὥσπερ
238

there is a likeness, let us agree that they are alike.
But how are both the things in that world and the
things in this beautiful? We maintain that the
things in this world are beautiful by participating in
form; for every shapeless thing which is naturally
capable of receiving shape and form is ugly and outside the divine formative power as long as it has no
share in formative power and form. This is absolute ugliness. But a thing is also ugly when it is
not completely dominated by shape and formative
power, since its matter has not submitted to be
completely shaped according to the form. The
form, then, approaches and composes that which is to
come into being from many parts into a single
ordered whole; it brings it into a completed unity
and makes it one by agreement of its parts; for since
it is one itself, that which is shaped by it must also
be one as far as a thing can be which is composed of
many parts. So beauty rests upon the material thing
when it has been brought into unity, and gives itself
to parts and wholes alike. When it comes upon
something that is one and composed of like parts it
gives the same gift to the whole; as sometimes art
gives beauty to a whole house with its parts, and
sometimes a nature gives beauty to a single stone.
So then the beautiful body comes into being by
sharing in a formative power which comes from the
divine forms.

3. The power ordained for the purpose recognises
this, and there is nothing more effective for judging
its own subject-matter, when the rest of the soul
judges along with it; or perhaps the rest of the soul
too pronounces the judgement by fitting the beautiful body to the form in itself and using this for judg-

5 κανόνι τοῦ εὐθέος. Πῶς δὲ συμφωνεῖ τὸ περὶ
σῶμα τῷ πρὸ σώματος; Πῶς δὲ τὴν ἔξω οἰκίαν
τῷ ἔνδον οἰκίας εἴδει ὁ οἰκοδομικὸς συναρμόσας
καλὴν εἶναι λέγει; ῞Η ὅτι ἐστὶ τὸ ἔξω, εἰ χωρίσειας
τοὺς λίθους, τὸ ἔνδον εἶδος μερισθὲν τῷ ἔξω ὕλης
ὄγκῳ, ἀμερὲς ὂν ἐν πολλοῖς φανταζόμενον.
10 ῞Οταν οὖν καὶ ἡ αἴσθησις τὸ ἐν σώμασιν εἶδος
ἴδῃ συνδησάμενον καὶ κρατῆσαν τῆς φύσεως τῆς
ἐναντίας ἀμόρφου οὔσης καὶ μορφὴν ἐπὶ ἄλλαις
μορφαῖς ἐκπρεπῶς ἐποχουμένην, συνελοῦσα ἀθρόον
αὐτὸ τὸ πολλαχῇ ἀνήνεγκέ τε καὶ εἰσήγαγεν εἰς
τὸ εἴσω ἀμερὲς ἤδη καὶ ἔδωκε τῷ ἔνδον σύμφωνον
15 καὶ συναρμόττον καὶ φίλον· οἷα ἀνδρὶ ἀγαθῷ
προσηνὲς ἐπιφαινόμενον ἀρετῆς ἴχνος ἐν νέῳ
συμφωνοῦν τῷ ἀληθεῖ τῷ ἔνδον. Τὸ δὲ τῆς χρόας
κάλλος ἁπλοῦν μορφῇ καὶ κρατήσει τοῦ ἐν ὕλῃ
σκοτεινοῦ παρουσίᾳ φωτὸς ἀσωμάτου καὶ λόγου
καὶ εἴδους ὄντος. ῞Οθεν καὶ τὸ πῦρ αὐτὸ παρὰ
20 τὰ ἄλλα σώματα καλόν, ὅτι τάξιν εἴδους πρὸς τὰ
ἄλλα στοιχεῖα ἔχει, ἄνω μὲν τῇ θέσει, λεπτότατον
δὲ τῶν ἄλλων σωμάτων, ὡς ἐγγὺς ὂν τοῦ ἀσωμάτου, μόνον δὲ αὐτὸ οὐκ εἰσδεχόμενον τὰ ἄλλα· τὰ
δ' ἄλλα δέχεται αὐτό. Θερμαίνεται γὰρ ἐκεῖνα,
οὐ ψύχεται δὲ τοῦτο, κέχρωσταί τε πρώτως, τὰ δ'
25 ἄλλα παρὰ τούτου τὸ εἶδος τῆς χρόας λαμβάνει.
Λάμπει οὖν καὶ στίλβει, ὡς ἂν εἶδος ὄν. Τὸ δὲ

ing beauty as we use a ruler for judging straightness. But how does the bodily agree with that which is before body? How does the architect declare the house outside beautiful by fitting it to the form of house within him? The reason is that the house outside, apart from the stones, is the inner form divided by the external mass of matter, without parts but appearing in many parts. When sense-perception, then, sees the form in bodies binding and mastering the nature opposed to it, which is shapeless, and shape riding gloriously upon other shapes, it gathers into one that which appears dispersed and brings it back and takes it in, now without parts, to the soul's interior and presents it to that which is within as something in tune with it and fitting it and dear to it; just as when a good man sees a trace of virtue in the young, which is in tune with his own inner truth, the sight delights him. And the simple beauty of colour comes about by shape and the mastery of the darkness in matter by the presence of light which is incorporeal[1] and formative power and form. This is why fire itself is more beautiful than all other bodies, because it has the rank of form in relation to the other elements; it is above them in place and is the finest and subtlest of all bodies, being close to the incorporeal.[2] It alone does not admit the others; but the others admit it: for it warms them but is not cooled itself; it has colour primarily and all other things take the form of colour from it. So it shines and glitters as if it was a form. The inferior

[1] For Plotinus light is the incorporeal ἐνέργεια of the luminous body; cp. IV. 5, chs. 6 and 7.
[2] This seems to be a Platonic adaptation of the Stoic doctrine of fire as the divine formative principle.

μὴ κρατοῦν ἐξίτηλον τῷ φωτὶ γινόμενον οὐκέτι
καλόν, ὡς ἂν τοῦ εἴδους τῆς χρόας οὐ μετέχον
ὅλου. Αἱ δὲ ἁρμονίαι αἱ ἐν ταῖς φωναῖς αἱ
ἀφανεῖς τὰς φανερὰς ποιήσασαι καὶ ταύτῃ τὴν
30 ψυχὴν σύνεσιν καλοῦ λαβεῖν ἐποίησαν, ἐν ἄλλῳ τὸ
αὐτὸ δείξασαι. Παρακολουθεῖ δὲ ταῖς αἰσθηταῖς
μετρεῖσθαι ἀριθμοῖς ἐν λόγῳ οὐ παντί, ἀλλ' ὃς
ἂν ᾖ δουλεύων εἰς ποίησιν εἴδους εἰς τὸ κρατεῖν.
Καὶ περὶ μὲν τῶν ἐν αἰσθήσει καλῶν, ἃ δὴ εἴδωλα
35 καὶ σκιαὶ οἷον ἐκδραμοῦσαι εἰς ὕλην ἐλθοῦσαι
ἐκόσμησάν τε καὶ διεπτόησαν φανεῖσαι, τοσαῦτα.

4. Περὶ δὲ τῶν προσωτέρω καλῶν, ἃ οὐκέτι
αἴσθησις ὁρᾶν εἴληχε, ψυχὴ δὲ ἄνευ ὀργάνων ὁρᾷ
καὶ λέγει, ἀναβαίνοντας δεῖ θεάσασθαι καταλιπόν-
τας τὴν αἴσθησιν κάτω περιμένειν. Ὥσπερ δὲ
5 ἐπὶ τῶν τῆς αἰσθήσεως καλῶν οὐκ ἦν περὶ αὐτῶν
λέγειν τοῖς μήτε ἑωρακόσι μήθ' ὡς καλῶν ἀντει-
λημμένοις, οἷον εἴ τινες ἐξ ἀρχῆς τυφλοὶ γεγονότες,
τὸν αὐτὸν τρόπον οὐδὲ περὶ κάλλους ἐπιτηδευμάτων
τοῖς μὴ ἀποδεξαμένοις τὸ τῶν ἐπιτηδευμάτων καὶ
ἐπιστημῶν καὶ τῶν ἄλλων τῶν τοιούτων κάλλος,
10 οὐδὲ περὶ ἀρετῆς φέγγους τοῖς μηδὲ φαντασθεῖσιν
ὡς καλὸν τὸ τῆς δικαιοσύνης καὶ σωφροσύνης
πρόσωπον, καὶ οὔτε ἕσπερος οὔτε ἑῷος

---

[1] τὸ μὴ κρατοῦν in this sense is very odd, and unparalleled,
but not quite impossible. I take the point of the sentence to
be that Plotinus had noticed that dull, ugly colours sometimes
look uglier and not more beautiful in a bright light and is
trying to explain this in terms of his own theory; the matter
of the thing is incapable of receiving enough of the form of
colour which the light gives it to look beautiful. Another

thing[1] which becomes faint and dull by the fire's light
is not beautiful any more, as not participating in the
whole form of colour. The melodies in sounds, too,
the imperceptible ones which make the perceptible
ones, make the soul conscious of beauty in the same
way, showing the same thing in another medium.
It is proper to sensible melodies to be measured by
numbers, not according to any and every sort of
formula but one which serves for the production of
form so that it may dominate. So much, then, for
the beauties in the realm of sense, images and
shadows which, so to speak, sally out and come into
matter and adorn it and excite us when they appear.

4. But about the beauties beyond, which it is no
more the part of sense to see, but the soul sees them
and speaks of them without instruments—we must
go up to them and contemplate them and leave sense
to stay down below. Just as in the case of the
beauties of sense it is impossible for those who have
not seen them or grasped their beauty—those born
blind, for instance—to speak about them, in the
same way only those can speak about the beauty of
ways of life who have accepted the beauty of ways
of life and kinds of knowledge and everything else
of the sort; and people cannot speak about the
splendour of virtue who have never even imagined
how fair is the face of justice and moral order;
"neither the evening nor the morning star are as

possible translation is "fire that is overcome and vanishes in
the sunlight." This has been suggested by Professor Post, who
cites for comparison Plutarch *De Facie in Orbe Lunae* 933 D.
It has obviously very much to commend it; my only reason
for hesitation about adopting it is that there is nothing about
the sun and its relationship to earthly fires in the context.

οὕτω καλά. Ἀλλὰ δεῖ ἰδόντας μὲν εἶναι ᾧ ψυχὴ
τὰ τοιαῦτα βλέπει, ἰδόντας δὲ ἡσθῆναι καὶ
ἔκπληξιν λαβεῖν καὶ πτοηθῆναι πολλῷ μᾶλλον ἢ
15 ἐν τοῖς πρόσθεν, ἅτε ἀληθινῶν ἤδη ἐφαπτομένους.
Ταῦτα γὰρ δεῖ τὰ πάθη γενέσθαι περὶ τὸ ὅ τι ἂν
ᾖ καλόν, θάμβος καὶ ἔκπληξιν ἡδεῖαν καὶ πόθον
καὶ ἔρωτα καὶ πτόησιν μεθ' ἡδονῆς. Ἔστι δὲ
ταῦτα παθεῖν καὶ πάσχουσιν αἱ ψυχαὶ καὶ περὶ τὰ
μὴ ὁρώμενα πᾶσαι μέν, ὡς εἰπεῖν, μᾶλλον μέντοι
20 αἱ τούτων ἐρωτικώτεραι, ὥσπερ καὶ ἐπὶ τῶν
σωμάτων πάντες μὲν ὁρῶσι, κεντοῦνται δ' οὐκ
ἴσα, ἀλλ' εἰσὶν οἳ μάλιστα, οἳ καὶ λέγονται ἐρᾶν.

5. Τῶν δὴ καὶ περὶ τὰ ἐν οὐκ αἰσθήσει ἐρωτικῶν
ἀναπυνθάνεσθαι δεῖ· τί πάσχετε περὶ τὰ λεγόμενα
ἐπιτηδεύματα καλὰ καὶ τρόπους καλοὺς καὶ ἤθη
σώφρονα καὶ ὅλως ἔργα ἀρετῆς καὶ διαθέσεις καὶ
5 τὸ τῶν ψυχῶν κάλλος; Καὶ ἑαυτοὺς δὲ ἰδόντες τὰ
ἔνδον καλοὺς τί πάσχετε; Καὶ πῶς ἀναβακχεύεσθε
καὶ ἀνακινεῖσθε καὶ ἑαυτοῖς συνεῖναι ποθεῖτε
συλλεξάμενοι αὑτοὺς ἀπὸ τῶν σωμάτων; Πάσχουσι
μὲν γὰρ ταῦτα οἱ ὄντως ἐρωτικοί. Τί δέ ἐστι,
10 περὶ ὃ ταῦτα πάσχουσιν; Οὐ σχῆμα, οὐ χρῶμα,
οὐ μέγεθός τι, ἀλλὰ περὶ ψυχήν, ἀχρώματον
μὲν αὐτήν, ἀχρώματον δὲ καὶ τὴν σωφροσύνην
ἔχουσαν καὶ τὸ ἄλλο τῶν ἀρετῶν φέγγος, ὅταν
ἢ ἐν αὑτοῖς ἴδητε, ἢ καὶ ἐν ἄλλῳ θεάσησθε μέγεθος

---

[1] Aristotle applies this quotation, probably from the
Melanippe of Euripides (fr. 486 Nauck), to justice in *Nicomachean Ethics* V. 3. 1129b 28–9. Plotinus recalls the passage
again at VI. 6. 6. 39.

[2] Cp. Plato, *Symposium* 210B–C.

ON BEAUTY

fair."[1] But there must be those who see this
beauty by that with which the soul sees things of this
sort, and when they see it they must be delighted
and overwhelmed and excited much more than by
those beauties we spoke of before, since now it is
true beauty they are grasping. These experiences
must occur whenever there is contact with any sort of
beautiful thing, wonder and a shock of delight and
longing and passion and a happy excitement. One
can have these experiences by contact with invisible
beauties, and souls do have them, practically all, but
particularly those who are more passionately in love
with the invisible, just as with bodies all see them,
but all are not stung as sharply, but some, who are
called lovers, are most of all.

5. Then we must ask the lovers of that which is
outside sense "What do you feel about beautiful
ways of life, as we call them, and beautiful habits
and well-ordered characters and in general about
virtuous activities and dispositions and the beauty
of souls?[2] What do you feel when you see your
own inward beauty?[3] How are you stirred to wild
exultation, and long to be with yourselves, gathering
your selves together away from your bodies?"
For this is what true lovers feel. But what is it
which makes them feel like this? Not shape or
colour[4] or any size, but soul, without colour itself
and possessing a moral order without colour and possessing all the other light of the virtues; you feel
like this when you see, in yourself or in someone else,

[3] Socrates prays for "inward beauty" at the end of the
Phaedrus, 279B9.
[4] Plato's real being, the World of Forms, is described as
"without colour or shape" at *Phaedrus* 247C6.

ψυχῆς καὶ ἦθος δίκαιον καὶ σωφροσύνην καθαρὰν
καὶ ἀνδρίαν βλοσυρὸν ἔχουσαν πρόσωπον καὶ
15 σεμνότητα καὶ αἰδῶ ἐπιθέουσαν ἐν ἀτρεμεῖ καὶ
ἀκύμονι καὶ ἀπαθεῖ διαθέσει, ἐπὶ πᾶσι δὲ τούτοις
τὸν θεοειδῆ νοῦν ἐπιλάμποντα. Ταῦτα οὖν ἀγάμε-
νοι καὶ φιλοῦντες πῶς αὐτὰ λέγομεν καλά; Ἔστι
μὲν γὰρ καὶ φαίνεται καὶ οὐ μήποτε ὁ ἰδὼν ἄλλο
20 τι φῇ ἢ τὰ ὄντως ὄντα ταῦτα εἶναι. Τί ὄντα
ὄντως; Ἦ καλά. Ἀλλ' ἔτι ποθεῖ ὁ λόγος, τί
ὄντα πεποίηκε τὴν ψυχὴν εἶναι ἐράσμιον· τί τὸ
ἐπὶ πάσαις ἀρεταῖς διαπρέπον οἷον φῶς; Βούλει
δὴ καὶ τὰ ἐναντία λαβών, τὰ περὶ ψυχὴν αἰσχρὰ
γινόμενα, ἀντιπαραθεῖναι; Τάχα γὰρ ἂν συμβάλ-
25 λοιτο πρὸς ὃ ζητοῦμεν τὸ αἰσχρὸν ὅ τί ποτέ ἐστι
καὶ διότι φανέν. Ἔστω δὴ ψυχὴ αἰσχρά, ἀκόλασ-
τός τε καὶ ἄδικος, πλείστων μὲν ἐπιθυμιῶν
γέμουσα, πλείστης δὲ ταραχῆς ἐν φόβοις διὰ
δειλίαν, ἐν φθόνοις διὰ μικροπρέπειαν, πάντα
φρονοῦσα ἃ δὴ καὶ φρονεῖ θνητὰ καὶ ταπεινά,
30 σκολιὰ πανταχοῦ, ἡδονῶν οὐ καθαρῶν φίλη, ζῶσα
ζωὴν τοῦ ὅ τι ἂν πάθῃ διὰ σώματος ὡς ἡδὺ
λαβοῦσα αἶσχος. Αὐτὸ τοῦτο τὸ αἶσχος αὐτῇ ἆρα
οὐ προσγεγονέναι οἷον ἐπακτὸν καλὸν φήσομεν, ὃ
ἐλωβήσατο μὲν αὐτῇ, πεποίηκε δὲ αὐτὴν ἀκάθαρτον
καὶ πολλῷ τῷ κακῷ συμπεφυρμένην, οὐδὲ
35 ζωὴν ἔτι ἔχουσαν οὐδὲ αἴσθησιν καθαράν, ἀλλὰ
τῷ μίγματι τοῦ κακοῦ ἀμυδρᾷ τῇ ζωῇ κεχρημένην
καὶ πολλῷ τῷ θανάτῳ κεκραμένην, οὐκέτι μὲν
ὁρῶσαν ἃ δεῖ ψυχὴν ὁρᾶν, οὐκέτι δὲ ἐωμένην ἐν

---

[1] The phrase is taken from the description of Ajax advancing to battle in *Iliad* 7. 212.

greatness of soul, a righteous life, a pure morality, courage with its noble look,[1] and dignity and modesty advancing in a fearless, calm and unperturbed disposition, and the godlike light of intellect shining upon all this. We love and delight in these qualities, but why do we call them beautiful? They exist and appear to us and he who sees them cannot possibly say anything else except that they are what really exists. What does "really exists" mean? That they exist as beauties. But the argument still requires us to explain why real beings make the soul lovable. What is this kind of glorifying light on all the virtues? Would you like to take the opposites, the uglinesses in soul, and contrast them with the beauties? Perhaps a consideration of what ugliness is and why it appears so will help us to find what we are looking for. Suppose, then, an ugly soul, dissolute and unjust, full of all lusts, and all disturbance, sunk in fears by its cowardice and jealousies by its pettiness, thinking mean and mortal thoughts as far as it thinks at all, altogether distorted, loving impure pleasures, living a life which consists of bodily sensations and finding delight in its ugliness. Shall we not say that its ugliness came to it as a "beauty"[2] brought in from outside, injuring it and making it impure and "mixed with a great deal of evil,"[3] with its life and perceptions no longer pure, but by the admixture of evil living a dim life and diluted with a great deal of death, no longer seeing what a soul ought to see, no longer left in

[2] A beauty, that is, to the soul's corrupt perception; its perversion makes it apprehend αἶσχος as καλὸν as well as ἡδύ.

[3] From a violently dualistic passage in the *Phaedo* 66B5.

αὐτῇ μένειν τῷ ἕλκεσθαι ἀεὶ πρὸς τὸ ἔξω καὶ τὸ
κάτω καὶ τὸ σκοτεινόν; Ἀκάθαρτος δή, οἶμαι,
40 οὖσα καὶ φερομένη πανταχοῦ ὁλκαῖς πρὸς τὰ τῇ
αἰσθήσει προσπίπτοντα, πολὺ τὸ τοῦ σώματος
ἔχουσα ἐγκεκραμένον, τῷ ὑλικῷ πολλῷ συνοῦσα
καὶ εἰς αὐτὴν εἰσδεξαμένη εἶδος ἕτερον ἠλλάξατο
κράσει τῇ πρὸς τὸ χεῖρον· οἷον εἴ τις δὺς εἰς
πηλὸν ἢ βόρβορον τὸ μὲν ὅπερ εἶχε κάλλος μηκέτι
45 προφαίνοι, τοῦτο δὲ ὁρῷτο, ὃ παρὰ τοῦ πηλοῦ ἢ
βορβόρου ἀπεμάξατο· ᾧ δὴ τὸ αἰσχρὸν προσθήκῃ
τοῦ ἀλλοτρίου προσῆλθε καὶ ἔργον αὐτῷ, εἴπερ
ἔσται πάλιν καλός, ἀπονιψαμένῳ καὶ καθηραμένῳ
ὅπερ ἦν εἶναι. Αἰσχρὰν δὴ ψυχὴν λέγοντες μίξει
καὶ κράσει καὶ νεύσει τῇ πρὸς τὸ σῶμα καὶ ὕλην
50 ὀρθῶς ἂν λέγοιμεν. Καὶ ἔστι τοῦτο αἶσχος ψυχῇ
μὴ καθαρᾷ μηδὲ εἰλικρινεῖ εἶναι ὥσπερ χρυσῷ,
ἀναπεπλῆσθαι δὲ τοῦ γεώδους, ὃ εἴ τις ἀφέλοι,
καταλέλειπται χρυσὸς καὶ ἔστι καλός, μονούμενος
μὲν τῶν ἄλλων, αὑτῷ δὲ συνὼν μόνῳ. Τὸν αὐτὸν
δὴ τρόπον καὶ ψυχή, μονωθεῖσα μὲν ἐπιθυμιῶν,
55 ἃς διὰ τὸ σῶμα ἔχει, ᾧ ἄγαν προσωμίλει,
ἀπαλλαγεῖσα δὲ τῶν ἄλλων παθῶν καὶ καθαρθεῖσα ἃ ἔχει σωματωθεῖσα, μείνασα μόνη τὸ
αἰσχρὸν τὸ παρὰ τῆς ἑτέρας φύσεως ἅπαν ἀπεθή-
κατο.

6. Ἔστι γὰρ δή, ὡς ὁ παλαιὸς λόγος, καὶ ἡ
σωφροσύνη καὶ ἡ ἀνδρία καὶ πᾶσα ἀρετὴ
κάθαρσις καὶ ἡ φρόνησις αὐτή. Διὸ καὶ αἱ
τελεταὶ ὀρθῶς αἰνίττονται τὸν μὴ κεκαθαρμέ-
νον καὶ εἰς Ἅιδου κείσεσθαι ἐν βορβόρῳ,
5 ὅτι τὸ μὴ καθαρὸν βορβόρῳ διὰ κάκην φίλον· οἷα

peace in itself because it keeps on being dragged out, and down, and to the dark? Impure, I think, and dragged in every direction towards the objects of sense, with a great deal of bodily stuff mixed into it, consorting much with matter and receiving a form other than its own it has changed by a mixture which makes it worse; just as if anyone gets into mud or filth he does not show any more the beauty which he had: what is seen is what he wiped off on himself from the mud and filth; his ugliness has come from an addition of alien matter, and his business, if he is to be beautiful again, is to wash and clean himself and so be again what he was before. So we shall be right in saying that the soul becomes ugly by mixture and dilution and inclination towards the body and matter. This is the soul's ugliness, not being pure and unmixed, like gold, but full of earthiness; if anyone takes the earthy stuff away the gold is left, and is beautiful, when it is singled out from other things and is alone by itself. In the same way the soul too, when it is separated from the lusts which it has through the body with which it consorted too much, and freed from its other affections, purged of what it gets from being embodied, when it abides alone has put away all the ugliness which came from the other nature.

6. For, as was said in old times, self-control, and courage and every virtue, is a purification, and so is even wisdom itself. This is why the mysteries are right when they say riddlingly that the man who has not been purified will lie in mud when he goes to Hades, because the impure is fond of mud by reason of its badness;[1] just as pigs, with their unclean

[1] Cp. Plato, *Phaedo* 69C1–6.

δὴ καὶ ὕες, οὐ καθαραὶ τὸ σῶμα, χαίρουσι τῷ
τοιούτῳ. Τί γὰρ ἂν καὶ εἴη σωφροσύνη ἀληθὴς
ἢ τὸ μὴ προσομιλεῖν ἡδοναῖς τοῦ σώματος,
φεύγειν δὲ ὡς οὐ καθαρὰς οὐδὲ καθαροῦ; Ἡ δὲ
ἀνδρία ἀφοβία θανάτου. Ὁ δέ ἐστιν ὁ θάνατος
10 χωρὶς εἶναι τὴν ψυχὴν τοῦ σώματος. Οὐ φοβεῖται
δὲ τοῦτο, ὃς ἀγαπᾷ μόνος γενέσθαι. Μεγαλοψυχία
δὲ δὴ ὑπεροψία τῶν τῇδε. Ἡ δὲ φρόνησις νόησις
ἐν ἀποστροφῇ τῶν κάτω, πρὸς δὲ τὰ ἄνω τὴν
ψυχὴν ἄγουσα. Γίνεται οὖν ἡ ψυχὴ καθαρθεῖσα
15 εἶδος καὶ λόγος καὶ πάντη ἀσώματος καὶ νοερὰ
καὶ ὅλη τοῦ θείου, ὅθεν ἡ πηγὴ τοῦ καλοῦ καὶ τὰ
συγγενῆ πάντα τοιαῦτα. Ψυχὴ οὖν ἀναχθεῖσα
πρὸς νοῦν ἐπὶ τὸ μᾶλλόν ἐστι καλόν. Νοῦς δὲ
καὶ τὰ παρὰ νοῦ τὸ κάλλος αὐτῇ οἰκεῖον καὶ οὐκ
ἀλλότριον, ὅτι τότε ἐστὶν ὄντως μόνον ψυχή.
Διὸ καὶ λέγεται ὀρθῶς τὸ ἀγαθὸν καὶ καλὸν τὴν
20 ψυχὴν γίνεσθαι ὁμοιωθῆναι εἶναι θεῷ, ὅτι ἐκεῖθεν
τὸ καλὸν καὶ ἡ μοῖρα ἡ ἑτέρα τῶν ὄντων. Μᾶλλον
δὲ τὰ ὄντα ἡ καλλονή ἐστιν, ἡ δ' ἑτέρα φύσις τὸ
αἰσχρόν, τὸ δ' αὐτὸ καὶ πρῶτον κακόν, ὥστε
κἀκείνῳ ταὐτὸν ἀγαθόν τε καὶ καλόν, ἢ τἀγαθόν
τε καὶ καλλονή. Ὁμοίως οὖν ζητητέον καλόν τε
25 καὶ ἀγαθὸν καὶ αἰσχρόν τε καὶ κακόν. Καὶ τὸ
πρῶτον θετέον τὴν καλλονήν, ὅπερ καὶ τἀγαθόν·
ἀφ' οὗ νοῦς εὐθὺς τὸ καλόν· ψυχὴ δὲ νῷ καλόν·

---

[1] Diels, followed by Henry-Schwyzer, thinks that there is
an allusion here to a remark Heraclitus appears to have made
about pigs liking mud (fr. B13): but it seems to me at least
possible that Plotinus might have thought of pigs at this point
for himself, without any assistance from earlier philosophy.
[2] Cp. *Phaedo* 64C5–7.

bodies, like that sort of thing.[1] For what can true
self-control be except not keeping company with
bodily pleasures, but avoiding them as impure and
belonging to something impure? Courage, too, is
not being afraid of death. And death is the separation of body and soul;[2] and a man does not fear this
if he welcomes the prospect of being alone. Again,
greatness of soul is despising the things here: and
wisdom is an intellectual activity which turns away
from the things below and leads the soul to those
above. So the soul when it is purified becomes form
and formative power, altogether bodiless and intellectual and entirely belonging to the divine,
whence beauty springs and all that is akin to it.
Soul, then, when it is raised to the level of intellect
increases in beauty. Intellect and the things of
intellect are its beauty, its own beauty and not
another's, since only then [when it is perfectly conformed to intellect] is it truly soul. For this reason
it is right to say that the soul's becoming something
good and beautiful is its being made like to God,
because from Him come beauty and all else which
falls to the lot of real beings. Or rather, beautifulness is reality, and the other kind of thing is the
ugly, and this same is the primary evil; so for God
the qualities of goodness and beauty are the same,
or the realities, the good and beauty.[3] So we must
follow the same line of enquiry to discover beauty
and goodness, and ugliness and evil. And first we
must posit beauty which is also the good; from this
immediately comes intellect, which is beauty; and

[3] God, the First Principle of reality, has no qualities, but is
absolutely single and simple, at once Absolute Good and
Absolute Beauty.

τὰ δὲ ἄλλα ἤδη παρὰ ψυχῆς μορφούσης καλά, τά
τε ἐν ταῖς πράξεσι τά τε ἐν τοῖς ἐπιτηδεύμασι.
30 Καὶ δὴ καὶ τὰ σώματα, ὅσα οὕτω λέγεται, ψυχὴ
ἤδη ποιεῖ· ἅτε γὰρ θεῖον οὖσα καὶ οἷον μοῖρα
τοῦ καλοῦ, ὧν ἂν ἐφάψηται καὶ κρατῇ, καλὰ ταῦτα,
ὡς δυνατὸν αὐτοῖς μεταλαβεῖν, ποιεῖ.

7. Ἀναβατέον οὖν πάλιν ἐπὶ τὸ ἀγαθόν, οὗ
ὀρέγεται πᾶσα ψυχή. Εἴ τις οὖν εἶδεν αὐτό, οἶδεν
ὃ λέγω, ὅπως καλόν. Ἐφετὸν μὲν γὰρ ὡς
ἀγαθὸν καὶ ἡ ἔφεσις πρὸς τοῦτο, τεῦξις δὲ αὐτοῦ
5 ἀναβαίνουσι πρὸς τὸ ἄνω καὶ ἐπιστραφεῖσι καὶ
ἀποδυομένοις ἃ καταβαίνοντες ἠμφιέσμεθα· οἷον
ἐπὶ τὰ ἅγια τῶν ἱερῶν τοῖς ἀνιοῦσι καθάρσεις τε
καὶ ἱματίων ἀποθέσεις τῶν πρὶν καὶ τὸ γυμνοῖς
ἀνιέναι· ἕως ἄν τις παρελθὼν ἐν τῇ ἀναβάσει πᾶν
ὅσον ἀλλότριον τοῦ θεοῦ αὐτῷ μόνῳ αὐτὸ μόνον
10 ἴδῃ εἰλικρινές, ἁπλοῦν, καθαρόν, ἀφ᾽ οὗ πάντα
ἐξήρτηται καὶ πρὸς αὐτὸ βλέπει καὶ ἔστι καὶ ζῇ
καὶ νοεῖ· ζωῆς γὰρ αἴτιος καὶ νοῦ καὶ τοῦ εἶναι.
Τοῦτο οὖν εἴ τις ἴδοι, ποίους ἂν ἴσχοι ἔρωτας,
ποίους δὲ πόθους, βουλόμενος αὐτῷ συγκερασθῆναι,
15 πῶς δ᾽ ἂν ⟨οὐκ⟩ ἐκπλαγείη μεθ᾽ ἡδονῆς; Ἔστι γὰρ
τῷ μὲν μήπω ἰδόντι ὀρέγεσθαι ὡς ἀγαθοῦ· τῷ δὲ
ἰδόντι ὑπάρχει ἐπὶ καλῷ ἄγασθαί τε καὶ θάμβους
πίμπλασθαι μεθ᾽ ἡδονῆς καὶ ἐκπλήττεσθαι ἀβλαβῶς
καὶ ἐρᾶν ἀληθῆ ἔρωτα καὶ δριμεῖς πόθους καὶ τῶν
ἄλλων ἐρώτων καταγελᾶν καὶ τῶν πρόσθεν νομι-
ζομένων καλῶν καταφρονεῖν· ὁποῖον πάσχουσιν
20 ὅσοι θεῶν εἴδεσιν ἢ δαιμόνων προστυχόντες οὐκέτ᾽
ἂν ἀποδέχοιντο ὁμοίως ἄλλων κάλλη σωμάτων.

---

[1] Cp. *Symposium* 211E1.

soul is given beauty by intellect.   Everything else is
beautiful by the shaping of soul, the beauties in
actions and in ways of life.   And soul makes beautiful the bodies which are spoken of as beautiful;
for since it is a divine thing and a kind of part of
beauty, it makes everything it grasps and masters
beautiful, as far as they are capable of participation.

7. So we must ascend again to the good, which
every soul desires.   Anyone who has seen it knows
what I mean when I say that it is beautiful.   It is
desired as good, and the desire for it is directed to
good, and the attainment of it is for those who go
up to the higher world and are converted and strip
off what we put on in our descent; (just as for those
who go up to the celebrations of sacred rites there
are purifications, and strippings off of the clothes
they wore before, and going up naked) until, passing
in the ascent all that is alien to the God, one sees
with one's self alone That alone, simple, single and
pure,[1] from which all depends and to which all look
and are and live and think: for it is cause of life and
mind and being.   If anyone sees it, what passion
will he feel, what longing in his desire to be united
with it, what a shock of delight!   The man who has
not seen it may desire it as good, but he who has
seen it glories in its beauty and is full of wonder and
delight, enduring a shock which causes no hurt,
loving with true passion and piercing longing; he
laughs at all other loves and despises what he thought
beautiful before; it is like the experience of those
who have met appearances of gods or spirits and do
not any more appreciate as they did the beauty of
other bodies.   "What then are we to think, if any-

Τί δῆτα οἰόμεθα, εἴ τις αὐτὸ τὸ καλὸν
θεῶτο αὐτὸ ἐφ' ἑαυτοῦ καθαρόν, μὴ σαρκῶν,
μὴ σώματος ἀνάπλεων, μὴ ἐν γῇ, μὴ ἐν οὐρανῷ,
ἵν' ᾖ καθαρόν; Καὶ γὰρ ἐπακτὰ πάντα ταῦτα καὶ
25 μέμικται καὶ οὐ πρῶτα, παρ' ἐκείνου δέ. Εἰ οὖν
ἐκεῖνο, ὃ χορηγεῖ μὲν ἅπασιν, ἐφ' ἑαυτοῦ δὲ μένον
δίδωσι καὶ οὐ δέχεταί τι εἰς αὐτό, ἴδοι, μένων ἐν
τῇ θέᾳ τοῦ τοιούτου καὶ ἀπολαύων αὐτοῦ ὁμοιούμε-
νος, τίνος ἂν ἔτι δέοιτο καλοῦ; Τοῦτο γὰρ αὐτὸ
μάλιστα κάλλος ὂν αὐτὸ καὶ τὸ πρῶτον ἐργάζεται
30 τοὺς ἐραστὰς αὐτοῦ καλοὺς καὶ ἐραστοὺς ποιεῖ.
Οὗ δὴ καὶ ἀγὼν μέγιστος καὶ ἔσχατος
ψυχαῖς πρόκειται, ὑπὲρ οὗ καὶ ὁ πᾶς πόνος,
μὴ ἀμοίρους γενέσθαι τῆς ἀρίστης θέας, ἧς ὁ μὲν
τυχὼν μακάριος ὄψιν μακαρίαν τεθεαμένος·
ἀτυχὴς δὲ [οὗτος] ὁ μὴ τυχών. Οὐ γὰρ ὁ χρωμάτων
35 ἢ σωμάτων καλῶν μὴ τυχὼν οὐδὲ δυνάμεως οὐδὲ
ἀρχῶν οὐδὲ ὁ βασιλείας μὴ τυχὼν ἀτυχής, ἀλλ'
ὁ τούτου καὶ μόνου, ὑπὲρ οὗ τῆς τεύξεως καὶ
βασιλείας καὶ ἀρχὰς γῆς ἁπάσης καὶ θαλάττης καὶ
οὐρανοῦ προέσθαι χρεών, εἰ καταλιπών τις ταῦτα
καὶ ὑπεριδὼν εἰς ἐκεῖνο στραφεὶς ἴδοι.

8. Τίς οὖν ὁ τρόπος; Τίς μηχανή; Πῶς τις
θεάσηται κάλλος ἀμήχανον οἷον ἔνδον ἐν ἁγίοις
ἱεροῖς μένον οὐδὲ προϊὸν εἰς τὸ ἔξω, ἵνα τις καὶ
βέβηλος ἴδῃ; Ἴτω δὴ καὶ συνεπέσθω εἰς τὸ εἴσω
5 ὁ δυνάμενος ἔξω καταλιπὼν ὄψιν ὀμμάτων μηδ'

---

[1] Cp. *Symposium* 211A8 and D8–E2 (this is not an exact
quotation but is amplified by Plotinus).

[2] A partial quotation from *Phaedrus*, 247B5–6.

one contemplates the absolute beauty which exists
pure by itself, uncontaminated by flesh or body, not
in earth or heaven, that it may keep its purity?"[1]
All these other things are external additions and
mixtures and not primary, but derived from it. If
then one sees That which provides for all and remains
by itself and gives to all but receives nothing into
itself, if he abides in the contemplation of this kind
of beauty and rejoices in being made like it, how
can he need any other beauty? For this, since it is
beauty most of all, and primary beauty, makes its
lovers beautiful and lovable. Here the greatest, the
ultimate contest is set before our souls;[2] all our
toil and trouble is for this, not to be left without a
share in the best of visions. The man who attains
this is blessed in seeing that "blessed sight", and he
who fails to attain it has failed utterly. A man has
not failed if he fails to win beauty of colours or
bodies, or power or office or kingship even, but if he
fails to win this and only this. For this he should
give up the attainment of kingship and of rule over
all earth and sea and sky, if only by leaving and over-
looking them he can turn to That and see.

8. But how shall we find the way?[3] What
method can we devise? How can one see the "in-
conceivable beauty"[4] which stays within the holy
sanctuary and does not come out where the profane
may see it? Let him who can, follow and come
within, and leave outside the sight of his eyes and

[3] This chapter made a deep impression on the mind of S.
Augustine, and he uses phrases from it more than once in
speaking of the return of the soul to God; cp. *De Civitate Dei*
IX. 17 and *Confessions* I. 18 and VIII. 8.
[4] *Symposium* 218E2.

ἐπιστρέφων αὐτὸν εἰς τὰς προτέρας ἀγλαίας
σωμάτων. Ἰδόντα γὰρ δεῖ τὰ ἐν σώμασι καλὰ
μήτοι προστρέχειν, ἀλλὰ γνόντας ὡς εἰσιν εἰκόνες
καὶ ἴχνη καὶ σκιαὶ φεύγειν πρὸς ἐκεῖνο οὗ ταῦτα
εἰκόνες. Εἰ γάρ τις ἐπιδράμοι λαβεῖν βουλόμενος
10 ὡς ἀληθινόν, οἷα εἰδώλου καλοῦ ἐφ' ὕδατος
ὀχουμένου, ὁ λαβεῖν βουληθείς, ὥς πού τις
μῦθος, δοκῶ μοι, αἰνίττεται, δὺς εἰς τὸ κάτω τοῦ
ῥεύματος ἀφανὴς ἐγένετο, τὸν αὐτὸν δὴ τρόπον ὁ
ἐχόμενος τῶν καλῶν σωμάτων καὶ μὴ ἀφιεὶς οὐ
τῷ σώματι, τῇ δὲ ψυχῇ καταδύσεται εἰς σκοτεινὰ
15 καὶ ἀτερπῆ τῷ νῷ βάθη, ἔνθα τυφλὸς ἐν Ἅιδου
μένων καὶ ἐνταῦθα κἀκεῖ σκιαῖς συνέσται. Φεύ-
γωμεν δὴ φίλην ἐς πατρίδα, ἀληθέστερον ἄν
τις παρακελεύοιτο. Τίς οὖν ἡ φυγὴ καὶ πῶς;
ἀναξόμεθα οἷον ἀπὸ μάγου Κίρκης (φησὶν) ἢ
Καλυψοῦς Ὀδυσσεὺς (αἰνιττόμενος, δοκεῖ μοι)
20 μεῖναι οὐκ ἀρεσθείς, καίτοι ἔχων ἡδονὰς δι'
ὀμμάτων καὶ κάλλει πολλῷ αἰσθητῷ συνών.
Πατρὶς δὴ ἡμῖν, ὅθεν παρήλθομεν, καὶ πατὴρ
ἐκεῖ. Τίς οὖν ὁ στόλος καὶ ἡ φυγή; Οὐ ποσὶ δεῖ
διανύσαι· πανταχοῦ γὰρ φέρουσι πόδες ἐπὶ γῆν
ἄλλην ἀπ' ἄλλης· οὐδέ σε δεῖ ἵππων ὄχημα ἤ τι

not turn back to the bodily splendours which he saw
before. When he sees the beauty in bodies he must
not run after them; we must know that they are
images, traces, shadows, and hurry away to that
which they image. For if a man runs to the image
and wants to seize it as if it was the reality (like a
beautiful reflection playing on the water, which
some story somewhere, I think, said riddlingly a
man wanted to catch and sank down into the stream
and disappeared) then this man who clings to beautiful bodies and will not let them go, will, like the man
in the story, but in soul, not in body, sink down into
the dark depths where intellect has no delight, and
stay blind in Hades, consorting with shadows there
and here. This would be truer advice " Let us fly
to our dear country." ¹ What then is our way of
escape, and how are we to find it? We shall put
out to sea, as Odysseus did, from the witch Circe or
Calypso—as the poet says (I think with a hidden
meaning)—and was not content to stay though he
had delights of the eyes and lived among much
beauty of sense. Our country from which we came
is there, our Father is there. How shall we travel
to it, where is our way of escape? We cannot get
there on foot; for our feet only carry us everywhere
in this world, from one country to another. You

---

¹ The quotation is from *Iliad* 2. 140 (of course from a quite
irrelevant context). But Plotinus's mind turns immediately to
reminiscences of *Odyssey* 9. 29 ff. and 10. 483-4, where
Odysseus tells Alcinous how Calypso and Circe had loved him
and tried to detain him on his journey home. Odysseus became
in late antiquity, for Christians as well as pagans, the type of the
soul journeying to its true home and overcoming all difficulties
and temptations on the way.

25 θαλάττιον παρασκευάσαι, ἀλλὰ ταῦτα πάντα ἀφεῖναι δεῖ καὶ μὴ βλέπειν, ἀλλ' οἷον μύσαντα ὄψιν
ἄλλην ἀλλάξασθαι καὶ ἀνεγεῖραι, ἣν ἔχει μὲν πᾶς,
χρῶνται δὲ ὀλίγοι.

9. Τί οὖν ἐκείνη, ἢ ἔνδον βλέπει; Ἄρτι μὲν
ἐγειρομένη οὐ πάνυ τὰ λαμπρὰ δύναται βλέπειν.
Ἐθιστέον οὖν τὴν ψυχὴν αὐτὴν πρῶτον μὲν τὰ
καλὰ βλέπειν ἐπιτηδεύματα· εἶτα ἔργα καλά,
5 οὐχ ὅσα αἱ τέχναι ἐργάζονται, ἀλλ' ὅσα οἱ ἄνδρες
οἱ λεγόμενοι ἀγαθοί· εἶτα ψυχὴν ἴδε τῶν τὰ ἔργα
τὰ καλὰ ἐργαζομένων. Πῶς ἂν οὖν ἴδοις ψυχὴν
ἀγαθὴν οἷον τὸ κάλλος ἔχει; Ἄναγε ἐπὶ σαυτὸν
καὶ ἴδε· κἂν μήπω σαυτὸν ἴδῃς καλόν, οἷα ποιητὴς
ἀγάλματος, ὃ δεῖ καλὸν γενέσθαι, τὸ μὲν ἀφαιρεῖ,
10 τὸ δὲ ἀπέξεσε, τὸ δὲ λεῖον, τὸ δὲ καθαρὸν ἐποίησεν,
ἕως ἔδειξε καλὸν ἐπὶ τῷ ἀγάλματι πρόσωπον,
οὕτω καὶ σὺ ἀφαίρει ὅσα περιττὰ καὶ ἀπεύθυνε
ὅσα σκολιά, ὅσα σκοτεινὰ καθαίρων ἐργάζου εἶναι
λαμπρὰ καὶ μὴ παύσῃ τεκταίνων τὸ σὸν
ἄγαλμα, ἕως ἂν ἐκλάμψειέ σοι τῆς ἀρετῆς ἡ
15 θεοειδὴς ἀγλαΐα, ἕως ἂν ἴδῃς σωφροσύνην ἐν
ἁγνῷ βεβῶσαν βάθρῳ. Εἰ γέγονας τοῦτο καὶ
εἶδες αὐτὸ καὶ σαυτῷ καθαρὸς συνεγένου οὐδὲν
ἔχων ἐμπόδιον πρὸς τὸ εἰς οὕτω γενέσθαι
οὐδὲ σὺν αὐτῷ ἄλλο τι ἐντὸς μεμιγμένον ἔχων,
ἀλλ' ὅλος αὐτὸς φῶς ἀληθινὸν μόνον, οὐ μεγέθει
μεμετρημένον οὐδὲ σχήματι εἰς ἐλάττωσιν περι-
20 γραφὲν οὐδ' αὖ εἰς μέγεθος δι' ἀπειρίας αὐξηθέν,
ἀλλ' ἀμέτρητον πανταχοῦ, ὡς ἂν μεῖζον παντὸς

must not get ready a carriage, either, or a boat. Let all these things go, and do not look. Shut your eyes, and change to and wake another way of seeing, which everyone has but few use.

9. And what does this inner sight see? When it is just awakened it is not at all able to look at the brilliance before it. So that the soul must be trained, first of all to look at beautiful ways of life: then at beautiful works, not those which the arts produce, but the works of men who have a name for goodness: then look at the souls of the people who produce the beautiful works. How then can you see the sort of beauty a good soul has? Go back into yourself and look; and if you do not yet see yourself beautiful, then, just as someone making a statue which has to be beautiful cuts away here and polishes there and makes one part smooth and clears another till he has given his statue a beautiful face, so you too must cut away excess and straighten the crooked and clear the dark and make it bright, and never stop "working on your statue"[1] till the divine glory of virtue shines out on you, till you see "self-mastery enthroned upon its holy seat."[2] If you have become this, and see it, and are at home with yourself in purity, with nothing hindering you from becoming in this way one, with no inward mixture of anything else, but wholly yourself, nothing but true light, not measured by dimensions, or bounded by shape into littleness, or expanded to size by unboundedness, but everywhere unmeasured, because greater than all measure and

[1] A reference to *Phaedrus* 252D7; but in Plato it is the lover who works on the soul of his beloved, fashioning it into the likeness of the god they once followed together.
[2] *Phaedrus* 254B7.

μέτρου καὶ παντὸς κρεῖσσον ποσοῦ· εἰ τοῦτο
γενόμενον σαυτὸν ἴδοις, ὄψις ἤδη γενόμενος
θαρσήσας περὶ σαυτῷ καὶ ἐνταῦθα ἤδη ἀναβε-
βηκὼς μηκέτι τοῦ δεικνύντος δεηθεὶς ἀτενίσας
25 ἴδε· οὗτος γὰρ μόνος ὁ ὀφθαλμὸς τὸ μέγα κάλλος
βλέπει. Ἐὰν δὲ ἴῃ ἐπὶ τὴν θέαν λημῶν κακίαις
καὶ οὐ κεκαθαρμένος ἢ ἀσθενής, ἀνανδρίᾳ οὐ
δυνάμενος τὰ πάνυ λαμπρὰ βλέπειν, οὐδὲν βλέπει,
κἂν ἄλλος δεικνύῃ παρὸν τὸ ὁραθῆναι δυνάμενον.
Τὸ γὰρ ὁρῶν πρὸς τὸ ὁρώμενον συγγενὲς καὶ
30 ὅμοιον ποιησάμενον δεῖ ἐπιβάλλειν τῇ θέᾳ. Οὐ
γὰρ ἂν πώποτε εἶδεν ὀφθαλμὸς ἥλιον ἡλιοειδὴς
μὴ γεγενημένος, οὐδὲ τὸ καλὸν ἂν ἴδοι ψυχὴ μὴ
καλὴ γενομένη. Γενέσθω δὴ πρῶτον θεοειδὴς
πᾶς καὶ καλὸς πᾶς, εἰ μέλλει θεάσασθαι θεόν τε
καὶ καλόν. Ἥξει γὰρ πρῶτον ἀναβαίνων ἐπὶ τὸν
35 νοῦν κἀκεῖ πάντα εἴσεται καλὰ τὰ εἴδη καὶ φήσει
τὸ κάλλος τοῦτο εἶναι, τὰς ἰδέας· πάντα γὰρ
ταύταις καλά, τοῖς νοῦ γεννήμασι καὶ οὐσίας. Τὸ
δὲ ἐπέκεινα τούτου τὴν τοῦ ἀγαθοῦ λέγομεν φύσιν
προβεβλημένον τὸ καλὸν πρὸ αὐτῆς ἔχουσαν.
40 Ὥστε ὁλοσχερεῖ μὲν λόγῳ τὸ πρῶτον καλόν·
διαιρῶν δὲ τὰ νοητὰ τὸ μὲν νοητὸν καλὸν τὸν τῶν
εἰδῶν φήσει τόπον, τὸ δ᾽ ἀγαθὸν τὸ ἐπέκεινα καὶ

260

superior to all quantity; when you see that you have become this, then you have become sight; you can trust yourself then; you have already ascended and need no one to show you; concentrate your gaze and see. This alone is the eye that sees the great beauty. But if anyone comes to the sight blear-eyed with wickedness, and unpurified, or weak and by his cowardice unable to look at what is very bright, he sees nothing, even if someone shows him what is there and possible to see. For one must come to the sight with a seeing power made akin and like to what is seen. No eye ever saw the sun without becoming sun-like,[1] nor can a soul see beauty without becoming beautiful. You must become first all godlike and all beautiful if you intend to see God and beauty. First the soul will come in its ascent to intellect and there will know the Forms, all beautiful, and will affirm that these, the Ideas, are beauty; for all things are beautiful by these, by the products of intellect and essence. That which is beyond this we call the nature of the Good, which holds beauty as a screen before it. So in a loose and general way of speaking the Good is the primary beauty; but if one distinguishes the intelligibles [from the Good] one will say that the place of the Forms [2] is the intelligible beauty, but the Good is That which is beyond, the " spring and

---

[1] Cp. *Republic* VI. 508B3 and 509A1. Plato's point in these passages is, however, not that the eye must become sun-like in order to see the sun, but that the eye (the symbol of knowledge) is sun-like but *not* the sun (the symbol of the Good). This Platonic context may perhaps be relevant to the correct interpretation of Plotinus's thought here and elsewhere where he speaks of the vision of the Good.

[2] Cp. *Republic* VII. 517B5.

πηγὴν καὶ ἀρχὴν τοῦ καλοῦ. Ἢ ἐν τῷ αὐτῷ
τἀγαθὸν καὶ καλὸν πρῶτον θήσεται· πλὴν ἐκεῖ τὸ
καλόν.

---

[1] Cp. *Phaedrus* 245C9: the context of the phrase there is,
however, quite different.

[2] Plotinus in these last sentences is discussing questions of
language; he is very conscious of the inadequacy of all human

origin "[1] of beauty; or one will place the Good and the primal beauty on the same level: in any case, however, beauty is in the intelligible world.[2]

language to describe the realities here under discussion, and is prepared to tolerate a variety of ways of expressing the relationship of beauty to the Good; cp. the discussions of the same subject in V. 5. 12 and VI. 7. 22. The one thing he insists on is that true beauty is only to be found in the intelligible world, not in that of sense-perception.

ENNEAD I. 7

I. 7. ON THE PRIMAL GOOD

Introductory Note

THIS short treatise is the last which Plotinus wrote before his death; in it we find the essentials of his moral and religious teaching in their simplest form. In the first chapter he establishes briefly the necessity of accepting the transcendent Platonic Good, refuting Aristotle's rejection of it according to Aristotle's own principles. Then, after stating that life is a way of sharing in the Good and so a good, he shows that death, the death he himself saw approaching, is a greater good than life in the body.

Synopsis

If, as Aristotle says, a thing's proper good is its full natural activity, then that to which the soul directs its best activity will be the Absolute Good; this has no activity directed towards other things but is the source and goal of all activities; it is, in a truer sense than Aristotle's Unmoved Mover, the supreme object of desire (ch. 1). Unity, existence, form, life, intellect are all in their degree ways of sharing in the Good, and soul approaches the Good through its life and intellect (ch. 2). But if life, then, is a good, is not death an evil? No, for life in the body is only good in so far as the soul separates itself from the body by virtue, and death, the separation of soul and body, brings the soul to a better life (ch. 3).

I. 7. (54) ΠΕΡΙ ΤΟΥ ΠΡΩΤΟΥ ΑΓΑΘΟΥ ΚΑΙ ΤΩΝ ΑΛΛΩΝ ΑΓΑΘΩΝ

1. Ἆρ' ἄν τις ἕτερον εἴποι ἀγαθὸν ἑκάστῳ εἶναι
ἢ τὴν κατὰ φύσιν τῆς ζωῆς ἐνέργειαν, καὶ εἴ τι ἐκ
πολλῶν εἴη, τούτῳ εἶναι ἀγαθὸν τὴν τοῦ ἀμείνονος
ἐν αὐτῷ ἐνέργειαν οἰκείαν καὶ κατὰ φύσιν ἀεὶ
5 μηδὲν ἐλλείπουσαν; Ψυχῆς δὴ ἐνέργεια τὸ κατὰ
φύσιν ἀγαθὸν αὐτῇ. Εἰ δὲ καὶ πρὸς τὸ ἄριστον
ἐνεργοῖ ἀρίστη οὖσα, οὐ μόνον πρὸς αὐτὴν τὸ
ἀγαθόν, ἀλλὰ καὶ ἁπλῶς τοῦτο ἀγαθὸν ἂν εἴη.
Εἰ οὖν τι μὴ πρὸς ἄλλο ἐνεργοῖ ἄριστον ὂν τῶν
ὄντων καὶ ἐπέκεινα τῶν ὄντων, πρὸς αὐτὸ δὲ τὰ
10 ἄλλα, δῆλον, ὡς τοῦτο ἂν εἴη τὸ ἀγαθόν, δι' ὃ
καὶ τοῖς ἄλλοις ἀγαθοῦ μεταλαμβάνειν ἔστι· τὰ
δὲ ἄλλα διχῶς ἂν ἔχοι, ὅσα οὕτω τὸ ἀγαθόν, καὶ τῷ
πρὸς αὐτὸ ὡμοιῶσθαι καὶ τῷ πρὸς αὐτὸ τὴν
ἐνέργειαν ποιεῖσθαι. Εἰ οὖν ἔφεσις καὶ ἐνέργεια
15 πρὸς τὸ ἄριστον ἀγαθόν, δεῖ τὸ ἀγαθὸν μὴ πρὸς
ἄλλο βλέπον μηδ' ἐφιέμενον ἄλλου ἐν ἡσύχῳ οὖσαν
πηγὴν καὶ ἀρχὴν ἐνεργειῶν κατὰ φύσιν οὖσαν
καὶ τὰ ἄλλα ἀγαθοειδῆ ποιοῦσαν οὐ τῇ πρὸς
ἐκεῖνα ἐνεργείᾳ—ἐκεῖνα γὰρ πρὸς αὐτήν—οὐ τῇ
ἐνεργείᾳ οὐδὲ τῇ νοήσει τἀγαθὸν εἶναι, ἀλλ' αὐτῇ

---

[1] These first lines are a compressed summary of Aristotelian
and Stoic views about the good of the individual which are

I. 7. ON THE PRIMAL GOOD AND
THE OTHER GOODS

1. Could one say that the good for a thing was anything else than the full natural activity of its life? If the thing was made up of many parts, would not its good be the proper, natural, and never-failing activity of the better part of it? So the soul's activity will be its natural good.[1] Now if it is of the best sort itself and its activity is directed towards the best, this best will not only be the good for it but it will be the good absolutely. Then if something does not direct its activity towards another thing, since it is the best of beings and transcends all beings, and all other things direct their activities towards it, it is obvious that this will be the Good, through which other things are enabled to participate in good. All the other things which have the good like this will have it in two ways, by being made like it and by directing their activity towards it. So if the aspiration and activity towards the best is good, the Good must not look or aspire to something else, but stay quiet and be the "spring and origin" of natural activities, and give other things the form of good, not by its activity directed to them—for they are directed to it, their source. It must not be the Good by activity or thought, but by reason of its

made in what follows to lead up to a Platonic view of the Absolute Good.

μονῇ τἀγαθὸν εἶναι. Καὶ γὰρ ὅτι ἐπέκεινα
20 οὐσίας, ἐπέκεινα καὶ ἐνεργείας καὶ ἐπέκεινα νοῦ
καὶ νοήσεως. Καὶ γὰρ αὖ τοῦτο δεῖ τἀγαθὸν
τίθεσθαι, εἰς ὃ πάντα ἀνήρτηται, αὐτὸ δὲ εἰς
μηδέν· οὕτω γὰρ καὶ ἀληθὲς τὸ οὗ πάντα
ἐφίεται. Δεῖ οὖν μένειν αὐτό, πρὸς αὐτὸ δὲ
ἐπιστρέφειν πάντα, ὥσπερ κύκλον πρὸς κέντρον
25 ἀφ' οὗ πᾶσαι γραμμαί. Καὶ παράδειγμα ὁ ἥλιος
ὥσπερ κέντρον ὢν πρὸς τὸ φῶς τὸ παρ' αὐτοῦ
ἀνηρτημένον πρὸς αὐτόν· πανταχοῦ γοῦν μετ'
αὐτοῦ καὶ οὐκ ἀποτέτμηται· κἂν ἀποτεμεῖν
ἐθελήσῃς ἐπὶ θάτερα, πρὸς τὸν ἥλιόν ἐστι τὸ φῶς.

2. Τὰ δὲ ἄλλα πάντα πρὸς αὐτὸ πῶς; Ἢ τὰ
μὲν ἄψυχα πρὸς ψυχήν, ψυχὴ δὲ πρὸς αὐτὸ διὰ
νοῦ. Ἔχει δέ τι αὐτοῦ τῷ ἕν πως καὶ τῷ ὄν πως
ἕκαστον εἶναι. Καὶ μετέχει δὲ καὶ εἴδους· ὡς
οὖν μετέχει τούτων, οὕτω καὶ τοῦ ἀγαθοῦ.
5 Εἰδώλου ἄρα· ὧν γὰρ μετέχει, εἴδωλα ὄντος καὶ
ἑνός, καὶ τὸ εἶδος ὡσαύτως. Ψυχῇ δὲ τὸ ζῆν,
τῇ μὲν πρώτῃ τῇ μετὰ νοῦν, ἐγγυτέρω ἀληθείας,
καὶ διὰ νοῦ ἀγαθειδὲς αὕτη· ἔχοι δ' ἂν τὸ
ἀγαθόν, εἰ πρὸς ἐκεῖνο βλέποι· νοῦς δὲ μετὰ
τἀγαθόν. Ζωὴ τοίνυν, ὅτῳ τὸ ζῆν, τὸ ἀγαθόν,

---

[1] The famous phrase in Plato, *Republic* VI. 509B9, which is one of the foundations of Neo-Platonic theology.

very abiding. For because it is " beyond being," [1] it transcends activity and transcends mind and thought. For, to put it another way, one must assume the Good to be that on which everything else depends and which itself depends on nothing ; for so the statement is true that it is that " to which everything aspires." [2] So it must stay still, and all things turn back to it, as a circle does to the centre from which all the radii come. The sun, too, is an example, since it is like a centre in relation to the light which comes from it and depends on it ; for the light is everywhere with it and is not cut off from it ; even if you want to cut it off on one side, the light remains with the sun.

2. And how is everything else directed towards it ? Soulless things are directed towards soul, and soul to the Good through intellect. But soulless things too have something of it, because each particular thing is one somehow and is existent somehow. Soulless things, too, share in form ; and as they share in unity, existence and form so they share in the Good. In an image of the Good, that is to say ; for what they share in are images of existence and the One, and their form is an image too. But the life of soul, of the first soul which comes next after intellect, is nearer to truth, and this first soul has through intellect the form of good. It can have the Good if it looks to it (Intellect comes after the Good). Life, then, is the good to that which

---

[2] Aristotle's definition of the Good (*Nicomachean Ethics* I. 1094a3) here applied to the transcendent Platonic Good, probably not without some remembrance of Aristotle's Unmoved Mover in *Metaphysics* Λ 7. 1072a–b, which moves all things as the object of desire.

10 καὶ νοῦς, ὅτῳ νοῦ μέτεστιν· ὥστε ὅτῳ ζωὴ μετὰ
νοῦ, διχῶς καὶ ἐπ' αὐτό.

3. Εἰ δ' ἡ ζωὴ ἀγαθόν, ὑπάρχει τοῦτο ζῶντι
παντί; Ἢ οὔ· χωλεύει γὰρ ἡ ζωὴ τῷ φαύλῳ,
ὥσπερ ὄμμα τῷ μὴ καθαρῶς ὁρῶντι· οὐ γὰρ ποιεῖ
τὸ ἔργον αὐτοῦ. Εἰ δὴ ἡ ζωὴ ἡμῖν, ᾗ μέμικται
5 κακόν, ἀγαθόν, πῶς οὐχ ὁ θάνατος κακόν; Ἢ τίνι;
Τὸ γὰρ κακὸν συμβεβηκέναι δεῖ τῳ· ὃ δ' οὐκ ἔστιν
ἔτι ὄν, ἤ, εἰ ἔστιν, ἐστερημένον ζωῆς, οὐδ' οὕτω
κακὸν ⟨οὐδέν, ὥσπερ οὐδὲν κακὸν⟩ τῷ λίθῳ. Εἰ δ'
ἔστι ζωὴ καὶ ψυχὴ μετὰ θάνατον, ἤδη ἂν εἴη ἀγαθόν,
ὅσῳ μᾶλλον ἐνεργεῖ τὰ αὐτῆς ἄνευ σώματος. Εἰ δὲ
10 τῆς ὅλης γίνεται, τί ἂν ἐκεῖ οὔσῃ εἴη κακόν; Καὶ
ὅλως ὥσπερ τοῖς θεοῖς ἀγαθὸν μέν ἐστι, κακὸν δὲ
οὐδέν, οὕτως οὐδὲ τῇ ψυχῇ τῇ σωζούσῃ τὸ καθαρὸν
αὐτῆς· εἰ δὲ μὴ σώζοι, οὐχ ὁ θάνατος ἂν εἴη
κακὸν αὐτῇ, ἀλλ' ἡ ζωή. Εἰ δὲ καὶ ἐν Ἅιδου
δίκαι, πάλιν αὐτῇ ἡ ζωὴ κἀκεῖ κακόν, ὅτι μὴ ζωὴ
μόνον. Ἀλλ' εἰ σύνοδος μὲν ψυχῆς καὶ σώματος
15 ζωή, θάνατος δὲ διάλυσις τούτων, ἡ ψυχὴ ἔσται
ἀμφοτέρων δεκτική. Ἀλλ' εἰ ἀγαθὴ ἡ ζωή, πῶς
ὁ θάνατος οὐ κακόν; Ἢ ἀγαθὴ μὲν ἡ ζωὴ οἷς
ἐστιν, ἀγαθὸν οὐ καθόσον σύνοδος, ἀλλ' ὅτι δι'
ἀρετῆς ἀμύνεται τὸ κακόν· ὁ δὲ θάνατος μᾶλλον
20 ἀγαθόν. Ἢ λεκτέον αὐτὴν μὲν τὴν ἐν σώματι
ζωὴν κακὸν παρ' αὐτῆς, τῇ δὲ ἀρετῇ ἐν ἀγαθῷ
γίνεσθαι τὴν ψυχὴν οὐ ζῶσαν τὸ σύνθετον, ἀλλ'
ἤδη χωρίζουσαν ἑαυτήν.

lives, and intellect to that which has a share in intellect; so that if something has life and intellect, it has a twofold approach to the Good.

3. If life is a good, does every living thing have this good? No; in the bad, life limps; it is like an eye in one who does not see clear; it is not doing its proper work. But if our life, with its mixture of evil, is good, why is not death an evil? Evil for whom? Evil must happen to *someone*; and as for what does not exist any more or, if it exists, is deprived of life, there is nothing evil for this, just as nothing is evil for a stone. But if life and soul exist after death, then there is good, in proportion as it pursues its proper activity better without the body. If it becomes part of the universal soul, what evil can there be for it there? And altogether, just as the gods have good and no evil, so there is no evil for the sould which keeps its purity; and if it does not keep pure, it is not death that is an evil for it, but life. Even if there are punishments in Hades, it will be again life that is an evil for it, there too, because it is not simply life. But if life is a union of soul and body, and death is their separation, then the soul will be adapted to both. But if life is good, how can death not be an evil? Life is good to those for whom it is a good, not in so far as it is a union but because by virtue it keeps away evil; and death is a greater good. We must say that life in a body is an evil in itself, but the soul comes into good by its virtue, by not living the life of the compound but separating itself even now.

ENNEAD I. 8

I. 8. ON WHAT ARE AND WHENCE COME EVILS

Introductory Note

THIS is again a very late treatise (No. 51 in Porphyry's chronological order). Its primary object appears to be to provide a solid metaphysical foundation for Plotinus's moral teaching about the necessity of purifying the soul by separating it from the material: this it does by showing that evil is not an imperfection or weakness of the soul but has an independent quasi-existence and is identical with matter. The treatise falls into three parts; the first (chs. 1–5) is intended to show that there is an absolute evil and that it is identical with matter, absolute formlessness; the second (chs. 6–7) is a commentary on Plotinus's favourite text from the *Theaetetus* (176A), coupled in ch. 7 with others from the *Timaeus* (47E–48A and 41B), in which two important objections to the idea of an absolute contrary to good, drawn from Aristotle's logic, are refuted; they are, that the existence of a term does not necessarily imply the existence of its contrary and that substance has no contrary; the third part (chs. 8 to 15) deals with a series of objections to the idea of matter as absolute evil, which come from various sources, mostly Aristotelian and Stoic.

The genuineness of various parts of the treatise has been attacked by Thedinga and Heinemann. Bréhier refutes their arguments briefly but adequately in the introduction to the treatise in his edition.

Synopsis

What is evil and how do we know it (ch. 1)? It cannot be included in what exists or in what is beyond existence;

ON WHAT ARE EVILS

there is no evil in the Good, Intellect or Soul (ch. 2).
It must, then, be absolute non-existence, formlessness and
unmeasuredness (ch. 3).   Bodies are evil in the second
degree, not absolute evil, and soul is not evil in itself at
all; its evil comes from matter (ch. 4).   Matter is absolute
deficiency, not any particular evil but the source of them
all (ch. 5).   Commentary on a text from the *Theaetetus*,
with refutation of objections drawn from Aristotle's
logic (ch. 6).   Linking of the *Theaetetus* text with texts
from the *Timaeus* (ch. 7).   It is never pure form, but
form in matter and corrupted by matter which causes
particular evils like ignorance and bad desires (ch. 8).
We know particular evils by measuring them against good
and seeing the falling short, but absolute evil by a process
of extreme abstraction which leads to a "seeing which is
not seeing" (ch. 9).   Matter is evil by its very absence
of quality (ch. 10).   Refutation of arguments which
make evil a privation, an impediment, or a weakness in the
soul (chs. 11–14).   The relationship between matter and
soul and the nature of the soul's fall into matter (ch. 14).
Summing-up, with emphasis on the moral implications
of the doctrine (ch. 15).

I. 8. (51) ΠΕΡΙ ΤΟΥ ΤΙΝΑ ΚΑΙ ΠΟΘΕΝ ΤΑ ΚΑΚΑ

1. Οἱ ζητοῦντες, πόθεν τὰ κακά, εἴτ᾽ οὖν εἰς τὰ ὄντα εἴτε περὶ γένος τῶν ὄντων παρελήλυθεν, ἀρχὴν ἂν προσήκουσαν τῆς ζητήσεως ποιοῖντο, εἰ τί ποτ᾽ ἐστὶ τὸ κακὸν καὶ ἡ κακοῦ φύσις πρότερον
5 ὑποθεῖντο. Οὕτω γὰρ καὶ ὅθεν ἐλήλυθε καὶ ὅπου ἵδρυται καὶ ὅτῳ συμβέβηκε γνωσθείη, καὶ ὅλως εἰ ἔστιν ἐν τοῖς οὖσιν ὁμολογηθείη. Κακοῦ δὲ φύσιν τίνι ποτὲ δυνάμει τῶν ἐν ἡμῖν γνοίημεν ἄν, τῆς γνώσεως ἑκάστων δι᾽ ὁμοιότητος γιγνομένης, ἄπορον ἂν εἴη. Νοῦς μὲν γὰρ καὶ ψυχὴ εἴδη ὄντα
10 εἰδῶν καὶ τὴν γνῶσιν ἂν ποιοῖντο, καὶ πρὸς αὐτὰ ἂν ἔχοιεν τὴν ὄρεξιν· εἶδος δὲ τὸ κακὸν πῶς ἄν τις φαντάζοιτο ἐν ἀπουσίᾳ παντὸς ἀγαθοῦ ἰνδαλλόμενον; Ἀλλ᾽ εἰ, ὅτι τῶν ἐναντίων ἡ αὐτὴ γένοιτ᾽ ἂν ἐπιστήμη καὶ τῷ ἀγαθῷ ἐναντίον τὸ κακόν, ἤπερ τοῦ ἀγαθοῦ, καὶ τοῦ κακοῦ ἔσται,
15 ἀναγκαῖον περὶ ἀγαθοῦ διιδεῖν τοῖς μέλλουσι τὰ κακὰ γνώσεσθαι, ἐπείπερ προηγούμενα τὰ ἀμείνω τῶν χειρόνων καὶ εἴδη, τὰ δ᾽ οὔ, ἀλλὰ στέρησις μᾶλλον. Ζήτημα δ᾽ ὅμως καὶ πῶς ἐναντίον τὸ ἀγαθὸν τῷ κακῷ· εἰ μὴ ἄρα, ὡς τὸ μὲν ἀρχή, τὸ δὲ ἔσχατον, ἢ τὸ μὲν ὡς εἶδος, τὸ δὲ ὡς στέρησις.
20 Ἀλλὰ ταῦτα μὲν ὕστερον.

I. 8. ON WHAT ARE AND WHENCE COME EVILS

1. Those who enquire whence evils come, either into reality as a whole or to a particular kind of reality, would make an appropriate beginning of their enquiry if they proposed the question first, what evil is and what is its nature. In this way one would know whence it came and where its seat is and what it affects, and one would be able to decide the general question whether it really exists. But there would be no way to decide by which of the powers in us we know evil, if knowledge of everything comes by likeness. For intellect and soul, since they are Forms, would produce knowledge of Forms and have a natural tendency towards them. But how could anyone imagine that evil is a Form when it appears in the absence of every sort of good? But if, because opposites are known by one and the same kind of knowledge and evil is opposite to good, the knowledge of good will also be knowledge of evil, then those who mean to know evils must have a clear perception of good, since the better precedes the worse, and the better is Form, and the worse is not, but rather privation of form. How good is the opposite of evil is also something to investigate—perhaps one is the beginning, the other the end, and one is Form, the other privation. But we shall discuss this later.

2. Νῦν δὲ λεγέσθω, τίς ἡ τοῦ ἀγαθοῦ φύσις,
καθ᾽ ὅσον τοῖς παροῦσι λόγοις προσήκει. Ἔστι
δὲ τοῦτο, εἰς ὃ πάντα ἀνήρτηται καὶ οὗ πάντα
τὰ ὄντα ἐφίεται ἀρχὴν ἔχοντα αὐτὸ κἀκείνου
5 δεόμενα· τὸ δ᾽ ἐστὶν ἀνενδεές, ἱκανὸν ἑαυτῷ,
μηδενὸς δεόμενον, μέτρον πάντων καὶ πέρας, δοὺς
ἐξ αὐτοῦ νοῦν καὶ οὐσίαν καὶ ψυχὴν καὶ ζωὴν καὶ
περὶ νοῦν ἐνέργειαν. Καὶ μέχρι μὲν τούτου καλὰ
πάντα· αὐτός τε γὰρ ὑπέρκαλος καὶ ἐπέκεινα τῶν
ἀρίστων βασιλεύων ἐν τῷ νοητῷ, νοῦ ἐκείνου
10 ὄντος οὐ κατὰ νοῦν, ὃν οἰηθείη ἄν τις κατὰ τοὺς
παρ᾽ ἡμῖν λεγομένους νοῦς εἶναι τοὺς ἐκ προτάσεων
συμπληρουμένους καὶ τῶν λεγομένων συνιέναι
δυναμένους λογιζομένους τε καὶ τοῦ ἀκολούθου
θεωρίαν ποιουμένους ὡς ἐξ ἀκολουθίας τὰ ὄντα
θεωμένους ὡς πρότερον οὐκ ἔχοντας, ἀλλὰ κενοὺς
15 ἔτι πρὶν μαθεῖν ὄντας, καίτοι νοῦς ὄντας. Οὐ δὴ
ἐκεῖνος ὁ νοῦς τοιοῦτος, ἀλλ᾽ ἔχει πάντα καὶ ἔστι
πάντα καὶ σύνεστιν αὐτῷ συνὼν καὶ ἔχει πάντα
οὐκ ἔχων. Οὐ γὰρ ἄλλα, ὁ δὲ ἄλλος· οὐδὲ χωρὶς
ἕκαστον τῶν ἐν αὐτῷ· ὅλον τε γάρ ἐστιν ἕκαστον
καὶ πανταχῇ πᾶν· καὶ οὐ συγκέχυται, ἀλλὰ αὖ
20 χωρίς. Τὸ γοῦν μεταλαμβάνον οὐχ ὁμοῦ πάντων,
ἀλλ᾽ ὅτου δύναται μεταλαμβάνει. Καὶ ἔστι πρώτη
ἐνέργεια ἐκείνου καὶ πρώτη οὐσία ἐκείνου μένοντος
ἐν ἑαυτῷ· ἐνεργεῖ μέντοι περὶ ἐκεῖνον οἷον περὶ
ἐκεῖνον ζῶν. Ἡ δὲ ἔξωθεν περὶ τοῦτον χορεύουσα
ψυχὴ ἐπὶ αὐτὸν βλέπουσα καὶ τὸ εἴσω αὐτοῦ
25 θεωμένη τὸν θεὸν δι᾽ αὐτοῦ βλέπει. Καὶ οὗτος
θεῶν ἀπήμων καὶ μακάριος βίος καὶ τὸ κακὸν

---

[1] The Aristotelian definition of the Good; cp. I. 7. 1.

ON WHAT ARE EVILS

2. Now we must state what is the nature of the Good, as far as the present argument requires. It is that on which everything depends and "to which all beings aspire";[1] they have it as their principle and need it: but it is without need, sufficient to itself, lacking nothing, the measure and bound of all things, giving from itself intellect and real being and soul and life and intellectual activity. Up to it all things are beautiful. But he is beautiful beyond all beauty, and is king in the intelligible realm, transcending the best—intellect there is not the sort one might conceive on the analogy of our so-called intellects which get their content from premises and are able to understand what is said, and reason discursively and observe what follows, contemplating reality as the result of a process of reasoning since they did not have it before but were empty before they learnt, though they were intellects. Intellect there is not like this, but has all things and is all things, and is with them when it is with itself and has all things without having them. For it is not one thing and they another; nor is each individual thing in it separate; for each is the whole and in all ways all, and yet they are not confused, but each is in a different sense separate; at any rate what participates in it does not participate in everything at once, but in what it is capable of. That intellect is the first act of the Good and the first substance; the Good stays still in himself; but intellect moves about him in its activity, as also it lives around him. And soul dances round intellect outside, and looks to it, and in contemplating its interior sees God through it. "This is the life of the gods,"[2] without

[2] *Phaedrus* 248A1.

οὐδαμοῦ ἐνταῦθα καὶ εἰ ἐνταῦθα ἔστη, κακὸν οὐδὲν
ἂν ἦν, ἀλλὰ πρῶτον καὶ δεύτερα τἀγαθὰ καὶ
τρίτα· περὶ τὸν πάντων βασιλέα πάντα ἐστί,
30 καὶ ἐκεῖνο αἴτιον πάντων καλῶν, καὶ πάντα
ἐστὶν ἐκείνου, καὶ δεύτερον περὶ τὰ δεύτερα
καὶ τρίτον περὶ τὰ τρίτα.

3. Εἰ δὴ ταῦτά ἐστι τὰ ὄντα καὶ τὸ ἐπέκεινα
τῶν ὄντων, οὐκ ἂν ἐν τοῖς οὖσι τὸ κακὸν ἐνείη,
οὐδ' ἐν τῷ ἐπέκεινα τῶν ὄντων· ἀγαθὰ γὰρ ταῦτα.
Λείπεται τοίνυν, εἴπερ ἔστιν, ἐν τοῖς μὴ οὖσιν
5 εἶναι οἷον εἶδός τι τοῦ μὴ ὄντος ὂν καὶ περί τι τῶν
μεμιγμένων τῷ μὴ ὄντι ἢ ὁπωσοῦν κοινωνούντων
τῷ μὴ ὄντι. Μὴ ὂν δὲ οὔτι τὸ παντελῶς μὴ ὄν,
ἀλλ' ἕτερον μόνον τοῦ ὄντος· οὐχ οὕτω δὲ μὴ ὂν
ὡς κίνησις καὶ στάσις ἡ περὶ τὸ ὄν, ἀλλ' ὡς
εἰκὼν τοῦ ὄντος ἢ καὶ ἔτι μᾶλλον μὴ ὄν. Τοῦτο
10 δ' ἐστὶ τὸ αἰσθητὸν πᾶν καὶ ὅσα περὶ τὸ αἰσθητὸν
πάθη ἢ ὕστερόν τι τούτων καὶ ὡς συμβεβηκὸς
τούτοις ἢ ἀρχὴ τούτων ἢ ἕν τι τῶν συμπλη-
ρούντων τοῦτο τοιοῦτον ὄν. Ἤδη γὰρ ἄν τις εἰς
ἔννοιαν ἤκοι αὐτοῦ οἷον ἀμετρίαν εἶναι πρὸς μέτρον
καὶ ἄπειρον πρὸς πέρας καὶ ἀνείδεον πρὸς εἰδο-
15 ποιητικὸν καὶ ἀεὶ ἐνδεὲς πρὸς αὔταρκες, ἀεὶ
ἀόριστον, οὐδαμῇ ἑστώς, παμπαθές, ἀκόρητον,
πενία παντελής· καὶ οὐ συμβεβηκότα ταῦτα

---

[1] This passage from the doubtfully genuine Platonic
Second Letter (312E1–4) is one of the foundation-texts of
Neo-Platonic theology.

[2] Cp. V. 8. 7. 22, where matter is called εἶδός τι ἔσχατον.

[3] Plotinus is alluding to the discussion in Plato, *Sophist*,
250 ff. The point he is making is that he is not using " non-
being " here in the sense in which it could be applied to a term

sorrow and blessed; evil is nowhere here, and if things had stopped here there would not have been any evil, only a First and the second and third goods. "All things are around the King of all, and That is the cause of all good and beautiful things, and all things belong to That, and the second things are around the Second and the third around the Third."[1]

3. If, then, these are what really exists and what is beyond existence, then evil cannot be included in what really exists or in what is beyond existence; for these are good. So it remains that if evil exists, it must be among non-existent things, as a sort of form of non-existence,[2] and pertain to one of the things that are mingled with non-being or somehow share in non-being. Non-being here does not mean absolute non-being but only something other than being; not non-being in the same way as the movement and rest which affect being,[3] but like an image of being or something still more non-existent. The whole world of sense is non-existent in this way, and also all sense-experience and whatever is posterior or incidental to this, or its principle, or one of the elements which go to make up the whole which is of this non-existent kind. At this point one might be able to arrive at some conception of evil as a kind of unmeasuredness in relation to measure, and unboundedness in relation to limit, and formlessness in relation to formative principle, and perpetual neediness in relation to what is self-sufficient; always undefined, nowhere stable, subject to every sort of influence, insatiate, complete poverty: and

logically distinct from being ("motion" means something different from "being") but to refer to matter as a pseudo-being, something which really is not being, a real unreality.

αὐτῷ, ἀλλ' οἷον οὐσία αὐτοῦ ταῦτα, καὶ ὅ τι ἂν
αὐτοῦ μέρος ἴδῃς, καὶ αὐτὸ πάντα ταῦτα· τὰ δ'
ἄλλα, ὅσα ἂν αὐτοῦ μεταλάβῃ καὶ ὁμοιωθῇ, κακὰ
20 μὲν γίνεσθαι, οὐχ ὅπερ δὲ κακὰ εἶναι. Τίνι οὖν
ὑποστάσει ταῦτα πάρεστιν οὐχ ἕτερα ὄντα ἐκείνης,
ἀλλ' ἐκείνη; Καὶ γὰρ εἰ ἑτέρῳ συμβαίνει τὸ κακόν,
δεῖ τι πρότερον αὐτὸ εἶναι, κἂν μὴ οὐσία τις ᾖ.
Ὡς γὰρ ἀγαθὸν τὸ μὲν αὐτό, τὸ δὲ ὃ συμβέβηκεν,
οὕτω καὶ κακὸν τὸ μὲν αὐτό, τὸ δὲ ἤδη κατ' ἐκεῖνο
25 συμβεβηκὸς ἑτέρῳ. Τίς οὖν ἀμετρία, εἰ μὴ ἐν
τῷ ἀμέτρῳ; [Τί δὲ "μέτρον μὴ ἐν τῷ μεμετρημένῳ";] Ἀλλ' ὥσπερ ἐστὶ μέτρον μὴ ἐν τῷ
μεμετρημένῳ, οὕτω καὶ ἀμετρία οὐκ ἐν ἀμέτρῳ.
Εἰ γὰρ ἐν ἄλλῳ, ἢ ἐν ἀμέτρῳ—ἀλλ' οὐ δεῖ αὐτῷ
ἀμετρίας αὐτῷ ἀμέτρῳ ὄντι—ἢ ἐν μεμετρημένῳ·
30 ἀλλ' οὐχ οἷόν τε τὸ μεμετρημένον ἀμετρίαν ἔχειν
καθ' ὃ μεμέτρηται. Καὶ οὖν εἶναί τι καὶ ἄπειρον
καθ' αὑτὸ καὶ ἀνείδεον αὖ αὐτὸ καὶ τὰ ἄλλα τὰ
πρόσθεν, ἃ τὴν τοῦ κακοῦ ἐχαρακτήριζε φύσιν,
καὶ εἴ τι μετ' ἐκεῖνο τοιοῦτον, ἢ μεμιγμένον ἔχει
τοῦτο ἢ βλέπον πρὸς αὐτό ἐστι τοιοῦτον ἢ ποιητι-
35 κόν ἐστι τοιούτου. Τὴν δ' ὑποκειμένην σχήμασι
καὶ εἴδεσι καὶ μορφαῖς καὶ μέτροις καὶ πέρασι καὶ
ἀλλοτρίῳ κόσμῳ κοσμουμένην, μηδὲν παρ' αὐτῆς
ἀγαθὸν ἔχουσαν, εἴδωλον δὲ ὡς πρὸς τὰ ὄντα,

---

[1] These words seem to be a rather stupid gloss on the sentence which follows. Plotinus speaks of both Intellect (VI.
5. 11, VI. 6. 18) and the One (V. 5. 4) as "measure which is
not measured," the absolute standard of measurement which
transcends all that is measured or numbered and is the source
of measure or number.

all this is not accidental to it but in a sort of way its essence; whatever part of it you see, it is all this; and everything which participates in it and is made like it becomes evil, though not essential evil.   What sort of entity, then, is it, in which all this is present, not as something different from itself but as itself? For if evil occurs accidentally in something else, it must be something itself first, even if it is not a substance.   Just as there is absolute good and good as a quality, so there must be absolute evil and the evil derived from it which inheres in something else. What then is unmeasuredness, if it is not in what is unmeasured?   [But what about "measure which is not in that which is measured?"][1]   But just as there is measure which is not in that which is measured, so there is unmeasuredness which is not in the unmeasured.   If it is in something else, it is either in something unmeasured—and then this something will have no need of unmeasuredness if it is unmeasured itself—or in something measured; but it is not possible for that which is measured to have unmeasuredness in the respect in which it is measured.   So there must be something which is unbounded in itself and absolutely formless and has all the other attributes which we mentioned before as characterising the nature of evil; and if there is anything of the same sort posterior to this, it either has an admixture of this or is of the same sort because it directs its attention towards it, or because it is pro-ductive of something of this kind.   So that which underlies figures and forms and shapes and measures and limits, decked out with an adornment which belongs to something else, having no good of its own, only a shadow in comparison with real being,

κακοῦ δὴ οὐσίαν, εἴ τις καὶ δύναται κακοῦ οὐσία
εἶναι, ταύτην ἀνευρίσκει ὁ λόγος κακὸν εἶναι
40 πρῶτον καὶ καθ' αὑτὸ κακόν.

4. Σωμάτων δὲ φύσις, καθόσον μετέχει ὕλης,
κακὸν ἂν οὐ πρῶτον εἴη· ἔχει μὲν γὰρ εἶδός τι
οὐκ ἀληθινὸν ἐστέρηταί τε ζωῆς φθείρει τε ἄλληλα
φορά τε παρ' αὐτῶν ἄτακτος ἐμπόδιά τε ψυχῆς
5 πρὸς τὴν αὐτῆς ἐνέργειαν φεύγει τε οὐσίαν ἀεὶ
ῥέοντα, δεύτερον κακόν· ψυχὴ δὲ καθ' ἑαυτὴν μὲν
οὐ κακὴ οὐδ' αὖ πᾶσα κακή. Ἀλλὰ τίς ἡ κακή;
Οἷόν φησι· δουλωσάμενοι μὲν ᾧ πέφυκε
κακία ψυχῆς ἐγγίγνεσθαι, ὡς τοῦ ἀλόγου τῆς
ψυχῆς εἴδους τὸ κακὸν δεχομένου, ἀμετρίαν καὶ
10 ὑπερβολὴν καὶ ἔλλειψιν, ἐξ ὧν καὶ ἀκολασία καὶ
δειλία καὶ ἡ ἄλλη ψυχῆς κακία, ἀκούσια παθήματα,
δόξας ψευδεῖς ἐμποιοῦντα κακά τε νομίζειν καὶ
ἀγαθὰ ἃ φεύγει τε καὶ διώκει. Ἀλλὰ τί τὸ
πεποιηκὸς τὴν κακίαν ταύτην καὶ πῶς εἰς ἀρχὴν
ἐκείνην καὶ αἰτίαν ἀνάξεις; Ἢ πρῶτον μὲν οὐκ
15 ἔξω ὕλης οὐδὲ καθ' αὑτὴν εἶναι ἡ ψυχὴ ἡ τοιαύτη.
Μέμικται οὖν ἀμετρίᾳ καὶ ἄμοιρος εἴδους τοῦ
κοσμοῦντος καὶ εἰς μέτρον ἄγοντος· σώματι γὰρ
ἐγκέκραται ὕλην ἔχοντι. Ἔπειτα δὲ καὶ τὸ λογιζόμενον εἰ βλάπτοιτο, ὁρᾶν κωλύεται καὶ τοῖς
πάθεσι καὶ τῷ ἐπισκοτεῖσθαι τῇ ὕλῃ καὶ πρὸς
20 ὕλην νενευκέναι καὶ ὅλως οὐ πρὸς οὐσίαν, ἀλλὰ
πρὸς γένεσιν ὁρᾶν, ἧς ἀρχὴ ἡ ὕλης φύσις οὕτως

---

[1] *Phaedrus* 256B2–3.

is the substance of evil (if there really can be a substance of evil); this is what our argument discovers to be the primal evil, absolute evil.

4. The nature of bodies, in so far as it participates in matter, will be an evil, not the primal evil. For bodies have a sort of form which is not true form, and they are deprived of life, and in their disorderly motion they destroy each other, and they hinder the soul in its proper activity, and they evade reality in their continual flow, being secondary evil. The soul is not in itself evil, nor is it all evil. Which, then, is the evil soul? It is the sort of thing which Plato means when he says "those in whom the part of the soul in which evil naturally resides has been brought into subjection,"[1] that is, it is the irrational part of the soul which is receptive of evil, that is of unmeasuredness and excess and defect, from which come unrestrained wickedness and cowardice and all the rest of the soul's evil, involuntary affections which produce false opinions, making it think that the things which it shuns and seeks after are evil and good respectively. But what is it which produces this evil, and how are you going to trace it back to the source and cause of evil which you have just described? First of all, this kind of soul is not outside matter or by itself. So it is mixed with unmeasuredness and without a share in the form which brings order and reduces to measure, since it is fused with a body which has matter. And then its reasoning part, if that is damaged, is hindered in its seeing by the passions and by being darkened by matter, and inclined to matter, and altogether by looking towards becoming, not being; and the principle of becoming is the nature of matter, which is so evil

οὖσα κακὴ ὡς καὶ τὸ μήπω ἐν αὐτῇ, μόνον δὲ
βλέψαν εἰς αὐτήν, ἀναπιμπλάναι κακοῦ ἑαυτῆς.
Ἄμοιρος γὰρ παντελῶς οὖσα ἀγαθοῦ καὶ στέρησις
τούτου καὶ ἄκρατος ἔλλειψις ἐξομοιοῖ ἑαυτῇ πᾶν
25 ὅ τι ἂν αὐτῆς προσάψηται ὁπωσοῦν. Ἡ μὲν οὖν
τελεία καὶ πρὸς νοῦν νεύουσα ψυχὴ ἀεὶ καθαρὰ καὶ
ὕλην ἀπέστραπται καὶ τὸ ἀόριστον ἅπαν καὶ τὸ
ἄμετρον καὶ κακὸν οὔτε ὁρᾷ οὔτε πελάζει· καθαρὰ
οὖν μένει ὁρισθεῖσα νῷ παντελῶς. Ἡ δὲ μὴ
μείνασα τοῦτο, ἀλλ' ἐξ αὐτῆς προελθοῦσα τῷ μὴ
30 τελείῳ μηδὲ πρώτῳ οἷον ἴνδαλμα ἐκείνης τῷ
ἐλλείμματι καθόσον ἐνέλιπεν ἀοριστίας πληρωθεῖσα
σκότος ὁρᾷ καὶ ἔχει ἤδη ὕλην βλέπουσα εἰς ὃ μὴ
βλέπει, ὡς λεγόμεθα ὁρᾶν καὶ τὸ σκότος.

5. Ἀλλ' εἰ ἡ ἔλλειψις τοῦ ἀγαθοῦ αἰτία τοῦ
ὁρᾶν καὶ συνεῖναι τῷ σκότει, τὸ κακὸν εἴη ἂν ἐν
τῇ ἐλλείψει [ἢ τῷ σκότῳ] τῇ ψυχῇ καὶ πρῶτον—
δεύτερον δὲ ἔστω τὸ σκότος—καὶ ἡ φύσις τοῦ
5 κακοῦ οὐκέτι ἐν τῇ ὕλῃ, ἀλλὰ καὶ πρὸ τῆς ὕλης.
Ἢ οὐκ ἐν τῇ ὁπωσοῦν ἐλλείψει, ἀλλ' ἐν τῇ
παντελεῖ τὸ κακόν· τὸ γοῦν ἐλλεῖπον ὀλίγῳ τοῦ
ἀγαθοῦ οὐ κακόν, δύναται γὰρ καὶ τέλεον εἶναι ὡς
πρὸς φύσιν τὴν αὑτοῦ. Ἀλλ' ὅταν παντελῶς
ἐλλείπῃ, ὅπερ ἐστὶν ἡ ὕλη, τοῦτο τὸ ὄντως κακὸν
10 μηδεμίαν ἔχον ἀγαθοῦ μοῖραν. Οὐδὲ γὰρ τὸ εἶναι
ἔχει ἡ ὕλη, ἵνα ἀγαθοῦ ταύτῃ μετεῖχεν, ἀλλ'
ὁμώνυμον αὐτῇ τὸ εἶναι, ὡς ἀληθὲς εἶναι λέγειν
αὐτὸ μὴ εἶναι. Ἡ οὖν ἔλλειψις ἔχει μὲν τὸ μὴ

that it infects with its own evil that which is not in it but only directs its gaze to it. For since it is altogether without any share in good and is a privation of good and a pure lack of it, it makes everything which comes into contact with it in any way like itself. The perfect soul, then, which directs itself to intellect is always pure and turns away from matter and neither sees nor approaches anything undefined and unmeasured and evil. It remains, therefore, pure, completely defined by intellect. That which does not stay like this, but goes out from itself because it is not perfect or primary but is a sort of ghost of the first soul, because of its deficiency, as far as it extends, is filled with indefiniteness and sees darkness, and has matter by looking at that which it does not look at (as we say that we see darkness as well as the things we really see).

5. But if lack of good is the cause of seeing and keeping company with darkness, then evil for the soul will lie in the lack [or the dark] and this will be primary evil—the darkness can be put second—and the nature of evil will no longer be in matter but before matter. Yes, but evil is not in any sort of deficiency but in absolute deficiency; a thing which is only slightly deficient in good is not evil, for it can even be perfect on the level of its own nature. But when something is absolutely deficient—and this is matter—this is essential evil without any share in good. For matter has not even being—if it had it would by this means have a share in good; when we say it "is" we are just using the same word for two different things, and the true way of speaking is to say it "is not." Deficiency, then, involves being not good, but

289

ἀγαθὸν εἶναι, ἡ δὲ παντελὴς τὸ κακόν· ἡ δὲ
πλείων τὸ πεσεῖν εἰς τὸ κακὸν δύνασθαι καὶ ἤδη
15 κακόν. Τῷ χρὴ [δὴ] τὸ κακὸν νοεῖσθαι μὴ τόδε τὸ
κακόν, οἷον ἀδικίαν ἢ ἄλλην τινὰ κακίαν, ἀλλ᾿
ἐκεῖνο ὃ οὐδὲν μέν πω τούτων, ταῦτα δὲ οἷον
εἴδη ἐκείνου προσθήκαις εἰδοποιούμενα· οἷον ἐν
μὲν ψυχῇ πονηρίαν καὶ ταύτης αὖ εἴδη ἢ ὕλη περὶ
20 ἢν, ἢ τοῖς μέρεσι τῆς ψυχῆς, ἢ τῷ τὸ μὲν οἷον
ὁρᾶν εἶναι, τὸ δὲ ὁρμᾶν ἢ πάσχειν. Εἰ δέ τις
θεῖτο καὶ τὰ ἔξω ψυχῆς κακὰ εἶναι, πῶς ἐπ᾿
ἐκείνην τὴν φύσιν ἀνάξει, οἷον νόσον, πενίαν; Ἢ
νόσον μὲν ἔλλειψιν καὶ ὑπερβολὴν σωμάτων ἐνύλων
τάξιν καὶ μέτρον οὐκ ἀνεχομένων, αἶσχος δὲ
ὕλην οὐ κρατηθεῖσαν εἴδει, πενίαν δὲ ἔνδειαν
25 καὶ στέρησιν ὧν ἐν χρείᾳ ἐσμὲν διὰ τὴν ὕλην ᾗ
συνεζεύγμεθα φύσιν ἔχουσαν χρησμοσύνην εἶναι.
Εἰ δὴ ταῦτα ὀρθῶς λέγεται, οὐ θετέον ἡμᾶς
ἀρχὴν κακῶν εἶναι κακοὺς παρ᾿ αὐτῶν ὄντας,
ἀλλὰ πρὸ ἡμῶν ταῦτα· ἃ δ᾿ ἂν ἀνθρώπους
κατάσχῃ, κατέχειν οὐχ ἑκόντας, ἀλλ᾿ εἶναι μὲν
30 ἀποφυγὴν κακῶν τῶν ἐν ψυχῇ τοῖς δυνηθεῖσι,
πάντας δὲ οὐ δύνασθαι. Θεοῖς¹ δὲ ὕλης παρούσης
τοῖς αἰσθητοῖς τὸ κακὸν μὴ παρεῖναι, τὴν κακίαν
ἢν ἄνθρωποι ἔχουσιν, μηδ᾿ ἀνθρώποις ἅπασι·
κρατεῖν γὰρ αὐτῆς—ἀμείνους δέ, οἷς μὴ πάρεστι—
καὶ τούτῳ κρατεῖν δὲ τῷ μὴ ἐν ὕλῃ ἐν αὐτοῖς ὄντι.

6. Ἐπισκεπτέον δὲ καὶ πῶς λέγεται μὴ ἂν
ἀπολέσθαι τὰ κακά, ἀλλ᾿ εἶναι ἐξ ἀνάγκης·
καὶ ἐν θεοῖς μὲν οὐκ εἶναι, περιπολεῖν δὲ τὴν

---

¹ θεοῖς (Heintz) seems a certain correction for the MSS θέσις or
θέσεις.

absolute deficiency evil; great deficiency involves the possibility of falling into evil and is already an evil in itself. On this principle one must not think of evil as this or that particular kind of evil, injustice for instance or any other vice, but that which is not yet any of these particular evils; these are a sort of species of evil, specified by their own particular additions; as wickedness in the soul and its species are specified by the matter which they concern or the parts of the soul, or by the fact that one is like a sort of seeing, another like an impulse or experience.

But if one considers that things external to the soul are evils, illness or poverty for instance, how will one trace them back to the nature of matter? Illness is defect and excess of material bodies which do not keep order and measure; ugliness is matter not mastered by form; poverty is lack and deprivation of things which we need because of the matter with which we are coupled, whose very nature is to be need. If this is true, then we must not be assumed to be the principle of evil as being evil by and from ourselves; evils are prior to us, and those that take hold on men do not do so with their good will, but there is an "escape from the evils in the soul" for those who are capable of it, though not all men are. Though there is matter with the visible gods [1], evil is not there, not the vice which men have—since not even all men have it; the visible gods master matter,—yet the gods with whom there is no matter are better—and they master it by that in them which is not in matter.

6. We must consider, too, what Plato means when he says "Evils can never be done away with," but exist "of necessity"; and that "they have no

θνητὴν φύσιν καὶ τόνδε τὸν τόπον ἀεί.
Ἆρ᾽ οὖν οὕτως εἴρηται, ὡς τοῦ μὲν οὐρανοῦ
5 καθαροῦ κακῶν ὄντος ἀεὶ ἐν τάξει ἰόντος καὶ
κόσμῳ φερομένου καὶ μήτε ἀδικίας ἐκεῖ οὔσης
μήτε ἄλλης κακίας μήτε ἀδικοῦντα ἄλληλα, κόσμῳ
δὲ φερόμενα, ἐν γῇ δὲ τῆς ἀδικίας καὶ τῆς ἀταξίας
οὔσης; Τοῦτο γάρ ἐστιν ἡ θνητὴ φύσις καὶ ὅδε ὁ
τόπος. Ἀλλὰ τὸ ἐντεῦθεν φεύγειν δεῖ οὐκέτι
10 περὶ τῶν ἐπὶ γῆς λέγεται. Φυγὴ γάρ, φησιν,
οὐ τὸ ἐκ γῆς ἀπελθεῖν, ἀλλὰ καὶ ὄντα ἐπὶ γῆς
δίκαιον καὶ ὅσιον εἶναι μετὰ φρονήσεως, ὡς
εἶναι τὸ λεγόμενον φεύγειν κακίαν δεῖν, ὥστε τὰ
κακὰ αὐτῷ ἡ κακία καὶ ὅσα ἐκ κακίας· καὶ τοῦ
προσδιαλεγομένου δὲ ἀναίρεσιν λέγοντος κακῶν
15 ἔσεσθαι, εἰ πείθοι τοὺς ἀνθρώπους ἃ λέγει,
ὁ δέ φησι μὴ δύνασθαι τοῦτο γενέσθαι· τὰ γὰρ
κακὰ εἶναι ἀνάγκη, ἐπείπερ τοὐναντίον τι δεῖ
εἶναι τῷ ἀγαθῷ. Τὴν μὲν οὖν κακίαν τὴν περὶ
ἄνθρωπον πῶς οἷόν τε ἐναντίον εἶναι ἐκείνῳ τῷ
ἀγαθῷ; Ἐναντίον γὰρ τοῦτο τῇ ἀρετῇ, αὕτη δὲ οὐ
20 τὸ ἀγαθόν, ἀλλὰ ἀγαθόν, ὃ κρατεῖν τῆς ὕλης
ποιεῖ. Ἐκείνῳ δὲ τῷ ἀγαθῷ πῶς ἄν τι εἴη
ἐναντίον; Οὐ γὰρ δὴ ποιόν. Εἶτα τίς ἀνάγκη
πανταχοῦ, εἰ θάτερον τῶν ἐναντίων, καὶ θάτερον;
Ἐνδεχέσθω μὲν γὰρ καὶ ἔστω γε καὶ τὸ ἐναντίον
τοῦ ἐναντίου αὐτῷ ὄντος—οἷον ὑγιείας οὔσης
25 ἐνδέχεται καὶ νόσον εἶναι—οὐ μὴν ἐξ ἀνάγκης.

---

[1] Here again we have *Theaetetus* 176A (cp. I. 2. 1).
[2] Plotinus clearly means to reject the suggested interpretation of Plato in terms of the spatial other-worldliness common
in his own day; which would make earth the place of evil

place among the gods, but haunt our mortal nature and this region for ever."[1] Is it meant that heaven is "clean of evil" because it always moves regularly and goes on in order, and there is no injustice or other vice there, nor do the heavenly bodies do injustice to each other, but go on in order, but on earth there is injustice and disorder? For this is what is meant by "mortal nature" and "this place." But when he says "we must take flight from thence" he is no longer referring to life on earth.[2] For "flight," he says, is not going away from earth but being on earth "just and holy with the help of wisdom"; what he means is that we must fly from wickedness; so evil for him is wickedness and all that comes from wickedness; and when the answering speaker in the dialogue says that there would be an end of evils "if he convinced men of the truth of his words" Socrates answers that "this cannot be; evils must exist of necessity, since the good must have its contrary." But how can human wickedness be the contrary of that transcendent Good? Human wickedness is contrary to virtue, and virtue is not the Good, but a good, which enables us to master matter. How can anything be contrary to the transcendent Good? It is not of a particular quality; and then what universal necessity is there, that if one of a pair of contraries exists, the other must also exist? Granted that it is possible, and may in fact be the case, that when one contrary exists, the other does also—as when health exists sickness can also exist— all the same it is not necessarily so. But Plato does

and the visible heavens above the moon altogether good and pure. The quotations here and in what follows are all from *Theaetetus*, 176–7.

Ἦ οὐκ ἀνάγκη λέγειν αὐτόν, ὡς ἐπὶ παντὸς
ἐναντίου τοῦτο ἀληθές, ἀλλ' ἐπὶ τοῦ ἀγαθοῦ εἴρηται. Ἀλλ' εἰ οὐσία τἀγαθόν, πῶς ἐστιν αὐτῷ τι
ἐναντίον; ἢ τῷ ἐπέκεινα οὐσίας; Τὸ μὲν οὖν μὴ
εἶναι μηδὲν οὐσίᾳ ἐναντίον ἐπὶ τῶν καθ' ἕκαστα
30 οὐσιῶν ἐστι πιστὸν τῇ ἐπαγωγῇ δεδειγμένον·
ὅλως δὲ οὐσίᾳ οὐκ ἔστι δεδειγμένον. Ἀλλὰ τί τῇ
καθόλου οὐσίᾳ ἔσται ἐναντίον καὶ ὅλως τοῖς
πρώτοις; Ἦ τῇ μὲν οὐσίᾳ ἡ μὴ οὐσία, τῇ δὲ
ἀγαθοῦ φύσει ἥτις ἐστὶ κακοῦ φύσις καὶ ἀρχή·
ἀρχαὶ γὰρ ἄμφω, ἡ μὲν κακῶν, ἡ δὲ ἀγαθῶν· καὶ
35 πάντα τὰ ἐν τῇ φύσει ἑκατέρᾳ ἐναντία· ὥστε καὶ
τὰ ὅλα ἐναντία καὶ μᾶλλον ἐναντία ἢ τὰ ἄλλα.
Τὰ μὲν γὰρ ἄλλα ἐναντία ἢ ἐν τῷ αὐτῷ εἴδει ὄντα
ἢ ἐν τῷ αὐτῷ γένει καὶ κοινοῦ τινός ἐστι μετειλη-
φότα ἐν οἷς ἐστιν· ὅσα δὲ χωρίς ἐστι, καὶ ἃ τῷ
ἑτέρῳ ἐστὶ συμπληρώσει τοῦ ὅ ἐστι, τούτων τὰ
40 ἐναντία ἐν τῷ ἑτέρῳ ἐστί, πῶς οὐ μάλιστα ἂν εἴη
ἐναντία, εἴπερ ἐναντία τὰ πλεῖστον ἀλλήλων ἀφε-
στηκότα; Πέρατι δὴ καὶ μέτρῳ καὶ [τὰ ἄλλα,] ὅσα
ἔνεστιν ἐν τῇ θείᾳ φύσει, ἀπειρία καὶ ἀμετρία καὶ
τὰ ἄλλα, ὅσα ἔχει ἡ κακὴ φύσις, ἐναντία· ὥστε
καὶ τὸ ὅλον τῷ ὅλῳ ἐναντίον. Καὶ τὸ εἶναι δὲ
45 ψευδόμενον ἔχει καὶ πρώτως καὶ ὄντως ψεῦδος·
τῷ δὲ τὸ εἶναι τὸ ἀληθῶς εἶναι· ὥστε καὶ καθὰ τὸ
ψεῦδος τῷ ἀληθεῖ ἐναντίον καὶ τὸ ⟨μὴ⟩ κατ' οὐσίαν
τῷ κατ' οὐσίαν αὐτῆς ἐναντίον. Ὥστε ἡμῖν ἀνα-

not necessarily mean that this is true in the case of every contrary; he is only referring to the Good. But if the Good is substance, or something which transcends substance, how can it have any contrary? That there is nothing contrary to substance is established by inductive demonstration in the case of particular substances; but it has not been demonstrated that this applies in general. But what can there be contrary to universal substance and, in general, to the first principles? Non-substance is contrary to substance, and that which is the nature and principle of evil to the nature of good: for both are principles, one of evils, the other of goods; and all the things which are included in each nature are contrary to those in the other; so that the wholes are contrary, and more contrary to each other than are the other contraries. For the other contraries belong to the same species or the same genus and have something in common as a result of this belonging. But things which are completely separate, and in which there are present in one the contraries to whatever is necessary for the fulfilment of the being of the other, must surely be most of all contraries, if by contraries we mean things that are furthest of all removed from each other. Indefiniteness and unmeasuredness and all the other characteristics which the evil nature has are contrary to the definition and measure and all the characteristics present in the divine nature; so the whole, too, is contrary to the whole. The evil nature, too, has a false being, primary and absolute falsehood; the being of the divine is true being; so that as falsehood is contrary to truth, so is the non-substantiality of the evil nature contrary to the substantial reality of

πέφανται τὸ μὴ πανταχοῦ οὐσίᾳ μηδὲν εἶναι
ἐναντίον· ἐπεὶ καὶ ἐπὶ πυρὸς καὶ ὕδατος ἐδεξάμεθα
50 ἂν εἶναι ἐναντία, εἰ μὴ κοινὸν ἦν ἡ ὕλη ἐν αὐτοῖς,
ἐφ᾽ ἧς τὸ θερμὸν καὶ ξηρὸν καὶ ὑγρὸν καὶ ψυχρὸν
συμβεβηκότα ἐγίνετο· εἰ δ᾽ ἐπ᾽ αὐτῶν ἦν μόνα
τὴν οὐσίαν αὐτῶν συμπληροῦντα ἄνευ τοῦ κοινοῦ,
ἐγίγνετο ἂν ἐναντίον καὶ ἐνταῦθα, οὐσία οὐσίᾳ
ἐναντίον. Τὰ ἄρα πάντη κεχωρισμένα καὶ μηδὲν
55 ἔχοντα κοινὸν καὶ πλείστην ἀπόστασιν ἔχοντα ἐν
τῇ φύσει αὐτῶν ἐναντία· ἐπείπερ ἡ ἐναντίωσις
οὐχ ᾗ ποιόν τι οὐδὲ ὅλως ὁτιοῦν γένος τῶν ὄντων,
ἀλλ᾽ ᾗ πλεῖστον ἀλλήλων κεχώρισται καὶ ἐξ
ἀντιθέτων συνέστηκε καὶ τὰ ἐναντία ποιεῖ.

7. Ἀλλὰ πῶς οὖν ἐξ ἀνάγκης, εἰ τὸ ἀγαθόν, καὶ
τὸ κακόν; Ἆρ᾽ οὖν οὕτως ὅτι ἐν τῷ παντὶ δεῖ
τὴν ὕλην εἶναι; Ἐξ ἐναντίων γὰρ ἐξ ἀνάγκης τόδε
τὸ πᾶν· ἢ οὐδ᾽ ἂν εἴη μὴ ὕλης οὔσης. Μεμιγ-
5 μένη γὰρ οὖν δὴ ἡ τοῦδε τοῦ κόσμου φύσις
ἔκ τε νοῦ καὶ ἀνάγκης, καὶ ὅσα παρὰ θεοῦ εἰς
αὐτὸν ἥκει, ἀγαθά, τὰ δὲ κακὰ ἐκ τῆς ἀρχαίας
φύσεως, τὴν ὕλην λέγων τὴν ὑποκειμένην οὔπω
κοσμηθεῖσαν [εἰ θεῷτο]. Ἀλλὰ πῶς θνητὴν

---

[1] *Timaeus* 47E5–48A1.
[2] There is an allusion here to *Politicus* 273B5 and D4.
[3] *Timaeus* 41B2–4. If the material universe is never to be
dissolved, then matter-evil is a permanent element in our mortal
life, from which we cannot escape by getting into a

the divine. So we have shown that it is not universally true that there is nothing contrary to substance. Besides, even in the case of fire and water, we should accept that they were contraries if they did not have matter as a common element in them, in which hot and dry and wet and cold occurred as accidents. If they only had the things which go to make up their substantial forms without what they have in common, there would be here too a contrariety of substance to substance. So things which are altogether separate, and have nothing in common, and are as far apart as they can be, are contrary in their very nature: for their contrariety does not depend on quality or any other category of being, but on their furthest possible separation from each other, and on their being made up of opposites and on their contrary action.

7. But how then is it necessary that if the Good exists, so should evil? Is it because there must be matter in the All? This All must certainly be composed of contrary principles; it would not exist at all if matter did not exist. "For the generation of this universe was a mixed result of the combination of intellect and necessity." [1] What comes into it from God is good; the evil comes from the "ancient nature" (Plato means the underlying matter, not yet set in order).[2] But what does he mean by "mortal nature," granted that "this place" refers to the All? The answer is given where he says "Since you have come into being, you are not immortal, but you shall by no means be dissolved" through me.[3] If this is so, the statement is

superior part of the universe but only by a radical inner detachment from the body.

φύσιν; Τὸ μὲν γὰρ τόνδε τὸν τόπον ἔστω
δεικνύειν τὸ πᾶν. Ἢ τὸ ἀλλ᾽ ἐπείπερ ἐγένεσθε,
10 ἀθάνατοι μὲν οὔκ ἐστε, οὔτι γε μὴν λυθή-
σεσθε δι᾽ ἐμέ. Εἰ δὴ οὕτως, ὀρθῶς ἂν λέγοιτο
μὴ ἂν ἀπολέσθαι τὰ κακά. Πῶς οὖν ἐκφεύξε-
ται; Οὐ τῷ τόπῳ, φησίν, ἀλλ᾽ ἀρετὴν κτησάμενος
καὶ τοῦ σώματος αὐτὸν χωρίσας· οὕτω γὰρ καὶ
ὕλης· ὡς ὅ γε συνὼν τῷ σώματι καὶ ὕλῃ σύνεστι.
15 Τὸ δὲ χωρίσαι καὶ μὴ δῆλόν που αὐτὸς ποιεῖ· τὸ
δ᾽ ἐν θεοῖς εἶναι, ἐν τοῖς νοητοῖς· οὗτοι γὰρ
ἀθάνατοι. Ἔστι δὲ τοῦ κακοῦ λαβεῖν καὶ οὕτω
τὴν ἀνάγκην. Ἐπεὶ γὰρ οὐ μόνον τὸ ἀγαθόν,
ἀνάγκη τῇ ἐκβάσει τῇ παρ᾽ αὐτό, ἤ, εἰ οὕτω τις
ἐθέλοι λέγειν, τῇ ἀεὶ ὑποβάσει καὶ ἀποστάσει, τὸ
20 ἔσχατον, καὶ μεθ᾽ ὃ οὐκ ἦν ἔτι γενέσθαι ὁτιοῦν,
τοῦτο εἶναι τὸ κακόν. Ἐξ ἀνάγκης δὲ εἶναι τὸ
μετὰ τὸ πρῶτον, ὥστε καὶ τὸ ἔσχατον· τοῦτο δὲ
ἡ ὕλη μηδὲν ἔτι ἔχουσα αὐτοῦ. Καὶ αὕτη ἡ
ἀνάγκη τοῦ κακοῦ.

8. Εἰ δέ τις λέγοι μὴ διὰ τὴν ὕλην ἡμᾶς γενέσθαι
κακούς—μήτε γὰρ τὴν ἄγνοιαν διὰ τὴν ὕλην εἶναι
μήτε τὰς ἐπιθυμίας τὰς πονηράς· καὶ γάρ, εἰ διὰ
σώματος κακίαν ἡ σύστασις γίνοιτο, μὴ τὴν ὕλην,
5 ἀλλὰ τὸ εἶδος ποιεῖν, οἷον θερμότητας, ψυχρότητας,
πικρόν, ἁλμυρὸν καὶ ὅσα χυμῶν εἴδη, ἔτι πληρώσεις, κενώσεις, καὶ πληρώσεις οὐχ ἁπλῶς, ἀλλὰ
πληρώσεις τοιῶνδε, καὶ ὅλως τὸ τοιόνδε εἶναι τὸ
ποιοῦν τὴν διαφορὰν τῶν ἐπιθυμιῶν καί, εἰ βούλει,
δοξῶν ἐσφαλμένων, ὥστε τὸ εἶδος μᾶλλον ἢ τὴν
10 ὕλην τὸ κακὸν εἶναι—καὶ οὗτος οὐδὲν ἧττον τὴν
ὕλην συγχωρεῖν ἀναγκασθήσεται τὸ κακὸν εἶναι.

correct that "evils will never be done away with."
How then is one to escape? Not by movement in
place, Plato says, but by winning virtue and separating oneself from the body: for in this way one
separates oneself from matter as well, since the man
who lives in close connection with the body is also
closely connected with matter. Plato himself
explains somewhere about separating or not separating oneself: but being "among the gods" means
"among the beings of the world of intellect"; for
these are immortal.

One can grasp the necessity of evil in this way too.
Since not only the Good exists, there must be the
last end to the process of going out past it, or if one
prefers to put it like this, going down or going away:
and this last, after which nothing else can come into
being, is evil. Now it is necessary that what comes
after the First should exist, and therefore that the
Last should exist; and this is matter, which possesses
nothing at all of the Good. And in this way too evil
is necessary.

8. But if someone says that we do not become evil
because of matter—giving as a reason that ignorance
is not caused by matter, nor are bad desires; even
supposing that their coming into existence is caused
by the badness of body, it is not the matter but the
form that causes them, heat, cold, bitter, salt and all
the forms of flavour, and also fillings and emptyings,
and not just fillings, but fillings with bodies of a
particular quality; and in general it is the qualified
thing which produces the distinction of desires, and,
if you like, of falsified opinions, so that form rather
than matter is evil—he too will be compelled all the
same to admit that matter is evil. For what the

Ἅ τε γὰρ ποιεῖ ἡ ἐν ὕλῃ ποιότης, οὐ χωρὶς οὖσα
ποιεῖ, ὥσπερ οὐδὲ τὸ σχῆμα τοῦ πελέκεως ἄνευ
σιδήρου ποιεῖ· εἶτα καὶ τὰ ἐν τῇ ὕλῃ εἴδη οὐ
ταὐτά ἐστιν, ἅπερ ἦν, εἰ ἐφ' αὑτῶν ὑπῆρχεν, ἀλλὰ
15 λόγοι ἔνυλοι φθαρέντες ἐν ὕλῃ καὶ τῆς φύσεως
τῆς ἐκείνης ἀναπλησθέντες· οὐδὲ γὰρ τὸ πῦρ
αὐτὸ καίει οὐδὲ ἄλλο τι τῶν ἐφ' ἑαυτῶν ταῦτα
ἐργάζεται, ἃ ἐν τῇ ὕλῃ γενόμενα λέγεται ποιεῖν.
Γενομένη γὰρ κυρία τοῦ εἰς αὑτὴν ἐμφαντασθέντος
20 φθείρει αὐτὸ καὶ διόλλυσι τὴν αὑτῆς παραθεῖσα
φύσιν ἐναντίαν οὖσαν, οὐ τῷ θερμῷ τὸ ψυχρὸν
προσφέρουσα, ἀλλὰ τῷ εἴδει τοῦ θερμοῦ τὸ αὑτῆς
ἀνείδεον προσάγουσα καὶ τὴν ἀμορφίαν τῇ μορφῇ
καὶ ὑπερβολὴν καὶ ἔλλειψιν τῷ μεμετρημένῳ, ἕως
25 ἂν αὐτὸ ποιήσῃ τῆς, ἀλλὰ μὴ αὑτοῦ ἔτι εἶναι,
ὥσπερ ἐν τροφῇ ζῴων τὸ εἰσενεχθὲν μηκέτι εἶναι
ὅπερ προσελήλυθεν, ἀλλ' αἷμα κυνὸς καὶ πᾶν
κύνιον, καὶ χυμοὶ πάντες οἵπερ τοῦ δεξαμένου
ἐκείνου. Εἰ δὴ σῶμα αἴτιον τῶν κακῶν, ὕλη ἂν
εἴη καὶ ταύτῃ αἴτιον τῶν κακῶν. Ἀλλὰ κρατεῖν
ἔδει, ἄλλος ἂν εἴποι. Ἀλλ' οὐ καθαρὸν τὸ
30 δυνάμενον κρατεῖν, εἰ μὴ φύγοι. Καὶ σφοδρότεραι
δέ αἱ ἐπιθυμίαι κράσει τοιᾷδε σωμάτων, ἄλλαι δὲ
ἄλλων, ὥστε μὴ κρατεῖν τὸ ἐν ἑκάστῳ, ἀμβλύτεροι
δὲ καὶ πρὸς τὸ κρίνειν διὰ σωμάτων κάκην
κατεψυγμένοι καὶ ἐμπεποδισμένοι, αἱ δ' ἐναντίαι
ποιοῦσιν ἀνερματίστους. Μαρτυροῦσι δὲ ταῦτα καὶ
35 αἱ πρὸς καιρὸν ἕξεις. Πλήρεις μὲν γὰρ ἄλλοι καὶ

---

[1] Cp. Aristotle, *De Anima* B. 1. 412b12. This is good
Aristotelian doctrine used to lead to a very un-Aristotelian
conclusion.

quality in matter does, it does not do when it is separate, as the shape of the axe does not do anything without the iron.[1] Then, too, the forms in matter are not the same as they would be if they were by themselves; they are formative forces immanent in matter, corrupted in matter and infected with its nature. Essential fire does not burn, nor do any other forms existing by themselves do what they are said to do when they come to exist in matter. For matter masters what is imaged in it and corrupts and destroys it by applying its own nature which is contrary to form, not bringing cold to hot but putting its own formlessness to the form of heat and its shapelessness to the shape and its excess and defect to that which is measured, till it has made the form belong to matter and no longer to itself; just as when animals feed that which is taken in is no longer as it came but becomes dog's blood and everything doggish, and all the juices become like those of the animal which receives them. If then the body is the cause of evils, matter would be in this way too the cause, of evils.

But, someone else might say, we have to get the better of it. But that which could get the better of it is not in a pure state unless it escapes. And the passions are stronger because of a corresponding mixture of bodies, and some people's passions are stronger than others', so that the individual's power cannot get the better of them, and some people have their powers of judgement dulled because bodily badness has chilled and restricted them; the opposite vices of bodily constitution make them unstable. The variations in our state of mind at different times are evidence of this too. When we

ταῖς ἐπιθυμίαις καὶ ταῖς διανοίαις, κενοὶ δὲ ἄλλοι,
καὶ ταδὶ πληρωθέντες ἄλλοι, ταδὶ δὲ ἄλλοι.
Ἔστω δὴ πρώτως μὲν τὸ ἄμετρον κακόν, τὸ δ' ἐν
ἀμετρίᾳ γενόμενον ἢ ὁμοιώσει ἢ μεταλήψει τῷ
40 συμβεβηκέναι αὐτῷ δευτέρως κακόν· καὶ πρώτως
μὲν τὸ σκότος, τὸ δὲ ἐσκοτισμένον δευτέρως
ὡσαύτως. Κακία δὴ ἄγνοια οὖσα καὶ ἀμετρία
περὶ ψυχὴν δευτέρως κακὸν καὶ οὐκ αὐτοκακόν·
οὐδὲ γὰρ ἀρετὴ πρῶτον ἀγαθόν, ἀλλ' ὅ τι ὡμοίωται
ἢ μετείληφεν αὐτοῦ.

9. Τίνι οὖν ἐγνωρίσαμεν ταῦτα; Καὶ πρῶτον
κακίαν τίνι; Ἀρετὴν μὲν γὰρ νῷ αὐτῷ καὶ
φρονήσει· αὐτὴν γὰρ γνωρίζει· κακίαν δὲ πῶς;
Ἢ ὥσπερ κανόνι τὸ ὀρθὸν καὶ μή, οὕτω καὶ τὸ
5 μὴ ἐναρμόζον τῇ ἀρετῇ [κακίαν]. Βλέποντες οὖν
αὐτὸ ἢ μὴ βλέποντες, τὴν κακίαν λέγω; Ἢ τὴν
μὲν παντελῆ κακίαν οὐ βλέποντες· καὶ γὰρ
ἄπειρον· ἀφαιρέσει οὖν τὸ μηδαμοῦ τοῦτο· τὴν
δὲ μὴ παντελῆ τῷ ἐλλείπειν τούτῳ. Μέρος οὖν
ὁρῶντες τῷ παρόντι μέρει τὸ ἀπὸν λαμβάνοντες,
10 ὅ ἐστι μὲν ἐν τῷ ὅλῳ εἴδει, ἐκεῖ δὲ ἄπεστιν, οὕτω
κακίαν λέγομεν, ἐν ἀορίστῳ τὸ ἐστερημένον
καταλιπόντες. Καὶ δὴ ἐπὶ τῆς ὕλης οἷον αἰσχρόν
τι πρόσωπον ἰδόντες, οὐ κρατήσαντος ἐν αὐτῷ τοῦ
λόγου, ὥστε κρύψαι τὸ τῆς ὕλης αἶσχος, αἰσχρὸν
φανταζόμεθα τῇ τοῦ εἴδους ἐλλείψει. Ὁ δὲ

are full we are different, both in our desires and our thoughts, from what we are when we are empty, and when we have eaten our fill of one kind of food we are different from what we are when we are filled with another.

So then, let unmeasure be the primary evil, and that which is in a state of unmeasuredness by likeness or participation evil in a secondary sense, because its unmeasuredness is accidental. Primary evil is the darkness, secondary evil the darkened, in the same way. Vice, which is ignorance and unmeasuredness in the soul, is evil secondarily, not absolute evil : just as virtue is not primary good, but that which is made like to or participates in it.

9. With what, then, do we know good and evil? First, of all, with what do we know vice? We know virtue by our very intellect and power of thought ; it knows itself : but how do we know vice? Just as with a ruler we know what is straight and also what is not straight, so we know what does not fit with virtue. Do we see it then or do we not see it when we know it, vice I mean? We do not see absolute wickedness, because it is unbounded ; we know it by removal, as what is in no way virtue ; but we know vice which is not absolute by its falling short of virtue. So we see a part, and by the part which is there we grasp what is not there, which is in the complete form but missing in that particular thing, and so we speak of vice, leaving the missing part in indefiniteness. So too, when for instance we see an ugly face in matter, because the formative principle in it has not got the better of the matter so as to hide its ugliness, we picture it to ourselves as ugly because it falls short of the form.

15 μηδαμῇ εἴδους τετύχηκε, πῶς; Ἢ τὸ ⟨πᾶν⟩ πάρά-
παν εἶδος ἀφαιροῦντες [πᾶν εἶδος], ᾧ μὴ ταῦτα
πάρεστι, λέγομεν εἶναι ὕλην, ἀμορφίαν καὶ αὐτοὶ
ἐν ἡμῖν λαβόντες ἐν τῷ πᾶν εἶδος ἀφελεῖν, εἰ
ἐμέλλομεν ὕλην θεάσασθαι. Διὸ καὶ νοῦς ἄλλος
20 οὗτος, οὐ νοῦς, τολμήσας ἰδεῖν τὰ μὴ αὐτοῦ.
Ὥσπερ ὄμμα ἀποστῆσαν αὐτὸ φωτός, ἵνα ἴδῃ τὸ
σκότος καὶ μὴ ἴδῃ—τὸ καταλιπεῖν τὸ φῶς, ἵνα
ἴδῃ τὸ σκότος, μεθ' οὗ οὐκ ἦν ἰδεῖν αὐτό· οὐδ'
αὖ ἄνευ του οἷόν τε ἦν ἰδεῖν, ἀλλὰ μὴ ἰδεῖν—ἵνα
γένηται αὐτῷ ὡς οἷόν τε ἰδεῖν, οὕτως οὖν καὶ νοῦς,
εἴσω αὐτοῦ τὸ αὐτοῦ καταλιπὼν φῶς καὶ οἷον
25 ἔξω αὐτοῦ προελθὼν εἰς τὰ μὴ αὐτοῦ ἐλθών, μὴ
ἐπαγόμενος τὸ ἑαυτοῦ φῶς ἔπαθε τοὐναντίον ἢ
ἔστιν, ἵν' ἴδῃ τὸ αὐτῷ ἐναντίον.

10. Καὶ ταῦτα μὲν ταύτῃ. Ἄποιος δὲ οὖσα
πῶς κακή; Ἢ ἄποιος λέγεται τῷ μηδὲν ἔχειν
αὐτὴ ἐφ' ἑαυτῆς τούτων τῶν ποιοτήτων ἃς δέξεται
καὶ ἐν αὐτῇ ὡς ὑποκειμένῳ ἔσονται, οὐ μὴν
5 οὕτως, ὡς μηδεμίαν φύσιν ἔχειν. Εἰ δὴ ἔχει τινὰ
φύσιν, ταύτην τὴν φύσιν τί κωλύει κακὴν εἶναι,
οὐχ οὕτω δὲ κακήν, ὡς ποιόν; Ἐπειδὴ καὶ τὸ
ποιὸν τοῦτό ἐστι, καθ' ὃ ἕτερον ποιὸν λέγεται.
Συμβεβηκὸς οὖν τὸ ποιὸν καὶ ἐν ἄλλῳ· ἡ δὲ ὕλη
οὐκ ἐν ἄλλῳ, ἀλλὰ τὸ ὑποκείμενον, καὶ τὸ συμβε-
10 βηκὸς περὶ αὐτό. Τοῦ οὖν ποιοῦ τοῦ φύσιν
συμβεβηκότος ἔχοντος οὐ τυχοῦσα ἄποιος λέγεται.
Εἰ ποίνυν καὶ ἡ ποιότης αὐτὴ ἄποιος, πῶς ἡ ὕλη

ON WHAT ARE EVILS

But how do we know what has absolutely no part in form? By absolutely taking away all form, we call that in which there is no form matter; in the process of taking away all form we apprehend formlessness in ourselves, if we propose to look at matter. So this which sees matter is another intellect which is not intellect, since it presumes to see what is not its own. As an eye withdraws itself from the light so that it may see the darkness and not see it—leaving the light is so that it may see the darkness, since with the light it cannot see it; but without something it cannot see, but only not see—that it may be able to see in the way it is possible to see darkness; so intellect, leaving its own light in itself and as it were going outside itself and coming to what is not its own, by not bringing its own light with it experiences something contrary to itself, that it may see its own contrary.

10. So that is how this is. But if matter is without quality, how is it evil? It is called "without quality" because it has in its own right none of the qualities which it is going to receive and which are going to be in it as their substrate, but not in the sense that it has no nature at all. Well then, if it has a nature, what prevents this nature from being evil, but not evil in the way it would be if it had quality? Furthermore, quality is that in virtue of which something else is said to have quality. So quality occurs accidentally, and in something else, but matter is not in something else, but is the substratum on which the accident occurs. Since it has not the quality which has the nature of an accident, it is said to be without quality. Then too, if quality in itself is without quality, how could matter which

οὐ δεξαμένη ποιότητα ποιὰ ἂν λέγοιτο; Ὀρθῶς
ἄρα λέγεται καὶ ἄποιος εἶναι καὶ κακή· οὐ γὰρ
λέγεται κακὴ τῷ ποιότητα ἔχειν, ἀλλὰ μᾶλλον
15 τῷ ποιότητα μὴ ἔχειν, ἵνα μὴ ἦν ἴσως κακὴ εἶδος
οὖσα, ἀλλὰ μὴ ἐναντία τῷ εἴδει φύσις.

11. Ἀλλ' ἡ ἐναντία τῷ εἴδει παντὶ φύσις
στέρησις· στέρησις δὲ ἀεὶ ἐν ἄλλῳ καὶ ἐπ' αὐτῆς
οὐχ ὑπόστασις· ὥστε τὸ κακὸν εἰ ἐν στερήσει, ἐν
τῷ ἐστερημένῳ εἴδους τὸ κακὸν ἔσται· ὥστε καθ'
5 ἑαυτὸ οὐκ ἔσται. Εἰ οὖν ἐν τῇ ψυχῇ ἔσται κακόν,
ἡ στέρησις ἐν αὐτῇ τὸ κακὸν καὶ ἡ κακία ἔσται
καὶ οὐδὲν ἔξω. Ἐπεὶ καὶ ἄλλοι λόγοι τὴν ὕλην
ὅλως ἀναιρεῖν ἀξιοῦσιν, οἱ δὲ οὐδ' αὐτὴν κακὴν
εἶναι οὖσαν. Οὐδὲν οὖν δεῖ ἄλλοθι ζητεῖν τὸ κακόν,
ἀλλὰ θέμενον ἐν ψυχῇ οὕτω θέσθαι ἀπουσίαν
10 ἀγαθοῦ εἶναι. Ἀλλ' εἰ ἡ στέρησις ἐπιβάλλοντός
ἐστι παρεῖναι εἴδους τινός, εἰ τοῦ ἀγαθοῦ στέρησις
ἐν ψυχῇ, τὴν δὲ κακίαν ἐν αὐτῇ ποιεῖ τῷ λόγῳ τῷ
ἑαυτῆς, ἡ ψυχὴ οὐδὲν ἔχει ἀγαθόν· οὐ τοίνυν οὐδὲ
ζωὴν οὖσα ψυχή. Ἄψυχον ἄρα ἔσται ἡ ψυχή,
εἴπερ μηδὲ ζωήν· ὥστε ψυχὴ οὖσα οὐκ ἔσται
15 ψυχή. Ἔχει ἄρα τῷ ἑαυτῆς λόγῳ ζωήν· ὥστε
οὐ στέρησιν ἔχει τὴν τοῦ ἀγαθοῦ παρ' αὐτῆς.
Ἀγαθοειδὲς ἄρα ἔχουσά τι ἀγαθὸν νοῦ ἴχνος καὶ
οὐ κακὸν παρ' αὐτῆς· οὐκ ἄρα οὐδὲ πρώτως
κακὸν οὐδὲ συμβεβηκός τι αὐτῇ τὸ πρώτως κακόν,
ὅτι μηδὲ ἄπεστιν αὐτῆς πᾶν τὸ ἀγαθόν.

---

[1] This is the Aristotelian doctrine, implying the distinction
between matter and privation which forms the basis of
Aristotle's criticism of the Platonic doctrine of matter

has not received quality be said to have it? So it is rightly said to be both without quality and evil; for it is not called evil because it has, but rather because it has not quality; so that perhaps it would not have been evil if it was a form instead of a nature opposed to form.

11. But the nature which is opposed to all form is privation; but privation is always in something else and has no existence by itself.[1] So if evil consists in privation, it will exist in the thing deprived of form and have no independent existence. So if there is evil in the soul, it will be the privation in it which will be evil and vice, and nothing outside. There are some lines of argument which claim to abolish matter altogether, and others which say that though it exists it is not itself evil: so [on these assumptions] one should not look for evil elsewhere, but place it in the soul in such a way that it is simply absence of good. But if the privation is privation of a form which ought to be present, if the privation in the soul is a privation of good and produces vice in the soul corresponding to its own definition, soul then has no good in it; so then it has no life in it, though it is still soul So then soul will be soulless, if it has not even any life in it; so though it is still a soul it will not be a soul. But it has life by its own definition; so it does not have the privation of good from itself: so it is a thing of a good kind since it has some good, a trace of intellect, and it is not evil of itself. It is not then primary evil, nor is primary evil an accident of it, because the good is not altogether absent from it.

(*Physics* I. 9) and which is attacked by Plotinus in II. 4. 14 (see note there).

12. Τί οὖν, εἰ μὴ παντελῆ στέρησιν λέγοι
ἀγαθοῦ τὴν κακίαν καὶ τὸ κακὸν τὸ ἐν ψυχῇ,
ἀλλά τινα στέρησιν ἀγαθοῦ; Ἀλλ' εἰ τοῦτο, τὸ
μὲν ἔχουσα, τοῦ δὲ ἐστερημένη, μικτὴν ἕξει τὴν
5 διάθεσιν καὶ οὐκ ἄκρατον τὸ κακόν, καὶ οὔπω
εὕρηται τὸ πρῶτον καὶ ἄκρατον κακόν· καὶ τὸ
μὲν ἀγαθὸν τῇ ψυχῇ ἔσται ἐν οὐσίᾳ, συμβεβηκὸς
δέ τι τὸ κακόν.

13. Εἰ μὴ ἄρα τούτῳ τὸ κακὸν ἢ ἐμπόδιον,
ὥσπερ ὀφθαλμῷ πρὸς τὸ βλέπειν. Ἀλλ' οὕτω
ποιητικὸν κακοῦ ἔσται τὸ κακὸν αὐτοῖς, καὶ οὕτω
ποιητικόν, ὡς ἑτέρου τοῦ κακοῦ αὐτοῦ ὄντος.
Εἰ οὖν ἡ κακία ἐμπόδιον τῇ ψυχῇ, ποιητικὸν
5 κακοῦ, ἀλλ' οὐ τὸ κακὸν ἡ κακία ἔσται· καὶ ἡ
ἀρετὴ δὲ οὐ τὸ ἀγαθόν, ἀλλ' ἢ ὡς συνεργόν·
ὥστε, εἰ μὴ ἡ ἀρετὴ τὸ ἀγαθόν, οὐδ' ἡ κακία τὸ
κακόν. Εἶτα καὶ ἡ ἀρετὴ οὐκ αὐτὸ τὸ καλὸν
οὐδ' αὐτοαγαθόν· οὐ τοίνυν οὐδ' ἡ κακία αὐτὸ τὸ
αἰσχρὸν οὐδ' αὐτοκακόν. Ἔφαμεν δὲ τὴν ἀρετὴν
10 οὐκ αὐτοκαλὸν οὐδ' αὐτοαγαθόν, ὅτι πρὸ αὐτῆς
καὶ ἐπέκεινα αὐτῆς αὐτοκαλὸν καὶ αὐτοαγαθόν·
καὶ μεταλήψει πως ἀγαθὸν καὶ καλόν. Ὡς οὖν
ἀπὸ τῆς ἀρετῆς ἀναβαίνοντι τὸ καλὸν καὶ τὸ
ἀγαθόν, οὕτω καὶ ἀπὸ τῆς κακίας καταβαίνοντι τὸ
κακὸν αὐτό, ἀρξαμένῳ μὲν ἀπὸ τῆς κακίας.
15 Θεωροῦντι μὲν ἡ θεωρία ἥτις ἐστὶ τοῦ κακοῦ
αὐτοῦ, γινομένῳ δὲ ἡ μετάληψις αὐτοῦ· γίνεται
γὰρ παντάπασιν ἐν τῷ τῆς ἀνομοιότητος

---

[1] Plato speaks of the "bottomless sea of unlikeness" in
Politicus 273D6–E1. S. Augustine uses Plotinus's phrase, *in
regione dissimilitudinis*, of the state of alienation from God

12. But what is the answer if someone says that the vice and evil in the soul is not absolute privation of good, but only a [particular, limited] privation of good? In this case, if it has some good and is deprived of some, it will be in a mixed state and the evil will not be undiluted, and we have not yet found primary, undiluted evil: and the soul will have good in its very substance, but evil as some kind of accident.

13. But perhaps evil is an impediment to good, as the eye has impediments which prevent its seeing. Yes, but in this way evil will be what produces evil for the things where it occurs, and produces it in such a way that the actual evil produced is different from the evil which produces it. If then vice is an impediment to the soul, it is not evil but something which produces evil; and virtue is not the good, except in so far as it helps to produce it: so if virtue is not good, vice is not evil. Then too, virtue is not absolute beauty or absolute good; so it follows that vice is not absolute ugliness or absolute evil. We said that virtue was not absolute beauty or absolute good because absolute beauty and absolute good are prior to it and transcend it; it is good and beautiful by some kind of participation. So just as when one goes up from virtue one comes to the beautiful and the good, when one goes down from vice one comes to absolute evil, taking vice as the starting-point. One will contemplate it with the contemplation which belongs to absolute evil, and participate in it when one becomes it: one enters altogether into "the region of unlikeness"[1] when one sinks into it

in *Confessions*, VII. 10. 16. The "mud" is Orphic, taken over by Plato. Cp. *Phaedo* 69C6.

τόπῳ, ἔνθα δὺς εἰς αὐτὴν εἰς βόρβορον σκο-
τεινὸν ἔσται πεσών· ἐπεὶ καὶ εἰ παντελῶς εἴη ἡ
ψυχὴ εἰς παντελῆ κακίαν, οὐκέτι κακίαν ἔχει, ἀλλ᾽
20 ἑτέραν φύσιν τὴν χείρω ἠλλάξατο· ἔτι γὰρ
ἀνθρωπικὸν ἡ κακία μεμιγμένη τινὶ ἐναντίῳ.
Ἀποθνῄσκει οὖν, ὡς ψυχὴ ἂν θάνοι, καὶ ὁ θάνατος
αὐτῇ καὶ ἔτι ἐν τῷ σώματι βεβαπτισμένῃ ἐν ὕλῃ
ἐστὶ καταδῦναι καὶ πλησθῆναι αὐτῆς καὶ ἐξελθούσῃ
ἐκεῖ κεῖσθαι, ἕως ἀναδράμῃ καὶ ἀφέλῃ πως τὴν
25 ὄψιν ἐκ τοῦ βορβόρου· καὶ τοῦτό ἐστι τὸ ἐν
Ἅιδου ἐλθόντα ἐπικαταδαρθεῖν.

14. Εἰ δέ τις ἀσθένειαν ψυχῆς τὴν κακίαν λέγοι—
εὐπαθῆ γοῦν καὶ εὐκίνητον εἶναι τὴν κακὴν ἀπὸ
παντὸς εἰς ἅπαν κακὸν φερομένην, εὐκίνητον μὲν
εἰς ἐπιθυμίας, εὐερέθιστον δὲ εἰς ὀργάς, προπετῆ
5 δὲ εἰς συγκαταθέσεις, καὶ ταῖς ἀμυδραῖς φαντασίαις
εἴκουσαν ῥαδίως, οἷα τὰ ἀσθενέστατα τῶν τέχνῃ
ἢ φύσει πεποιημένων, ἃ ῥᾳδίαν ἔχει ὑπό τε
πνευμάτων ὑπό τε εἰλήσεων τὴν φθοράν—ἄξιον ἂν
εἴη ζητεῖν, τίς καὶ πόθεν ἡ ἀσθένεια τῇ ψυχῇ.
Οὐ γὰρ δή, ὥσπερ ἐπὶ τῶν σωμάτων, οὕτω καὶ
10 ἐπὶ τῆς ψυχῆς τὸ ἀσθενές· ἀλλ᾽ ὥσπερ ἐκεῖ ἡ
πρὸς τὸ ἔργον ἀδυναμία καὶ τὸ εὐπαθές, οὕτω καὶ
ἐνταῦθα ἀναλογίᾳ τὸ τῆς ἀσθενείας ἔσχε προσηγο-
ρίαν· εἰ μὴ ταύτῃ εἴη τὸ αὐτὸ αἴτιον ἡ ὕλη τῆς
ἀσθενείας. Ἀλλὰ προσιτέον ἐγγὺς τῷ λόγῳ, τί
τὸ αἴτιον ἐν τῷ λεγομένῳ ἀσθενεῖ τῆς ψυχῆς· οὐ
15 γὰρ δὴ πυκνότητες ἢ ἀραιότητες οὐδ᾽ αὖ ἰσχνότητες
ἢ παχύτητες ἢ νόσος, ὥσπερ τις πυρετός, ἀσθενῆ
ἐποίησε ψυχὴν εἶναι. Ἀνάγκη δὴ τὴν τοιαύτην
ἀσθένειαν ψυχῆς ἢ ἐν ταῖς χωρισταῖς παντελῶς ἢ

and has gone falling into the mud of darkness; for when the soul is fallen utterly into utter vice, it no longer *has* vice, but has changed to another nature, a worse one (for vice which is mixed with anything of its contrary is still human). So it dies, as far as the soul can die, and its death, while it is still plunged in the body, is to sink in matter and be filled with it, and, when it has gone out of the body, to lie in matter till it raises itself and somehow manages to look away from the mud; this is "going to Hades and falling asleep there."[1]

14. But if someone says that vice is a weakness of the soul—pointing out that the bad soul is easily affected and easily stirred, carried about from one evil to another, easily stirred to lust, easily roused to anger, hasty in its assents, giving way freely to confused imaginations, like the weakest of the products of art or nature, which the winds or the sun's heat so easily destroy[2]—it will be worth enquiring what this weakness is and where the soul gets it from. For weakness in the soul is not just like that in bodies; but incapacity for work and being easily affected, as in the body, so by analogy in the soul has the name of weakness: unless we are to refer weakness in the soul to the same cause as that in the body, matter. But we must get to grips with the question, what is the cause for what we call weakness in the soul; it is not density or rarity or thinness or fatness, or an illness, like fever, which makes the soul weak. This kind of weakness of the soul must be found either in those souls which are completely separate or in those which are in matter

[1] *Republic* VII. 534C7–D1.
[2] Cp. *Republic* II. 380E5.

ἐν ταῖς ἐνύλοις ἢ ἐν ἀμφοτέραις εἶναι. Εἰ δὴ μὴ
20 ἐν ταῖς χωρὶς ὕλης—καθαραὶ γὰρ πᾶσαι καὶ τὸ
λεγόμενον ἐπτερωμέναι καὶ τέλειοι καὶ τὸ
ἔργον αὐταῖς ἀνεμπόδιστον—λοιπὸν ἐν ταῖς πεσού-
σαις εἶναι τὴν ἀσθένειαν, ταῖς οὐ καθαραῖς οὐδὲ
κεκαθαρμέναις, καὶ ἡ ἀσθένεια αὐταῖς εἴη ἂν
οὐκ ἀφαίρεσις τινός, ἀλλὰ ἀλλοτρίου παρουσία,
25 ὥσπερ φλέγματος ἢ χολῆς ἐν σώματι. Τοῦ δὲ
πτώματος τὸ αἴτιον ψυχῇ σαφέστερον λαμβάνουσι
καὶ ὡς προσήκει λαβεῖν καταφανὲς ἔσται τὸ
ζητούμενον ἡ ψυχῆς ἀσθένεια. Ἔστιν ἐν τοῖς
οὖσιν ὕλη, ἔστι δὲ καὶ ψυχή, καὶ οἷον τόπος εἷς τις.
Οὐ γὰρ χωρὶς μὲν ὁ τόπος τῇ ὕλῃ, χωρὶς δὲ αὖ ὁ
30 τῆς ψυχῆς—οἷον ὁ μὲν ἐν γῇ τῇ ὕλῃ, ὁ δὲ ἐν
ἀέρι τῇ ψυχῇ—ἀλλ' ὁ τόπος τῇ ψυχῇ χωρὶς τὸ
μὴ ἐν ὕλῃ· τοῦτο δὲ τὸ μὴ ἑνωθῆναι τῇ ὕλῃ·
τοῦτο δὲ τὸ μὴ ἕν τι ἐξ αὐτῆς καὶ ὕλης γενέσθαι·
τοῦτο δὲ τὸ μὴ ἐν ὑποκειμένῳ τῇ ὕλῃ γενέσθαι·
καὶ τοῦτό ἐστι τὸ χωρὶς εἶναι. Δυνάμεις δὲ
35 ψυχῆς πολλαὶ καὶ ἀρχὴν καὶ μέσα καὶ ἔσχατα
ψυχὴ ἔχει· ὕλη δὲ παροῦσα προσαιτεῖ καὶ οἷον
καὶ ἐνοχλεῖ καὶ εἰς τὸ εἴσω παρελθεῖν θέλει· πᾶς
δὲ ὁ χῶρος ἱερὸς καὶ οὐδέν ἐστιν ὃ ἄμοιρόν ἐστι
ψυχῆς. Ἐλλάμπεται οὖν ὑποβάλλουσα ἑαυτὴν καὶ
ἀφ' οὗ μὲν ἐλλάμπεται οὐ δύναται λαβεῖν· οὐ
40 γὰρ ἀνέχεται αὐτὴν ἐκεῖνο καίτοι παροῦσαν, ὅτι

---

[1] *Phaedrus* 246B7–C1.

[2] The word προσαιτεῖ may be a reminiscence of *Symposium*
203B4, where Poverty comes begging to the feast of the gods.

[3] Sophocles *Oedipus at Colonus*, 54; cp. 16. If Plotinus
fully remembered what he was quoting, and the passion of

or in both. So if it is not in those without matter—
they are all pure, and, as Plato says, "winged and
perfect"[1] and their activity is unhindered—it remains
that the weakness must be in the souls which have
fallen, those which are not pure and have not been
purified; and their weakness will not be a taking
away of something but the presence of something
alien, like the presence of phlegm or bile in the body.
When we understand the cause of the fall of the soul
more clearly, and as it ought to be understood, what
we are looking for, the soul's weakness, will be obvious. There is matter in reality and there is soul
in reality, and one single place for both of them.
For there are not two separate places for matter and
for the soul,—on earth, for instance, for matter and
in the air for the soul: the soul's separate place is its
not being in matter; and this means not being united
to matter; and this means that not one single thing
comes into being from it and matter; and this means
that it is not in matter as a substratum; and this is
being separate. But there are many powers of
soul, and it has a beginning, a middle and an end;
and matter is there, and begs it and, we may say,
bothers it and wants to come right inside.[2] "All
the place is holy,"[3] and there is nothing which is
without a share of soul. So matter spreads itself
out under soul and is illumined, and cannot grasp
the source from which its light comes: that source
cannot endure matter though it is there, because

love for the "holy place" of Colonus with which the whole
play is charged, this must be taken as one of the strongest
affirmations of the goodness of the material world in the
Enneads. Soul is a god and the material world is holy as
being the place where it dwells; cp. Introduction, p. xxiv.

μὴ ὁρᾷ διὰ κάκην. Τὴν δὲ ἔλλαμψιν καὶ τὸ
ἐκεῖθεν φῶς ἐσκότωσε τῇ μίξει καὶ ἀσθενὲς
πεποίηκε τὴν γένεσιν αὐτὴ παρασχοῦσα καὶ τὴν
αἰτίαν τοῦ εἰς αὐτὴν ἐλθεῖν· οὐ γὰρ ἂν ἦλθε τῷ μὴ
παρόντι. Καὶ τοῦτό ἐστι πτῶμα τῆς ψυχῆς τὸ
45 οὕτως ἐλθεῖν εἰς ὕλην καὶ ἀσθενεῖν, ὅτι πᾶσαι αἱ
δυνάμεις οὐ πάρεισιν εἰς ἐνέργειαν κωλυούσης
ὕλης παρεῖναι τῷ τὸν τόπον ὃν κατέχει αὐτὴ
καταλαβεῖν καὶ οἷον συσπειραθῆναι ποιῆσαι
ἐκείνην, ὃ δ᾽ ἔλαβεν οἷον κλέψασα ποιῆσαι κακὸν
εἶναι, ἕως ἂν δυνηθῇ ἀναδραμεῖν. Ὕλη τοίνυν καὶ
50 ἀσθενείας ψυχῇ αἰτία καὶ κακίας αἰτία. Πρότερον
ἄρα κακὴ αὐτὴ καὶ πρῶτον κακόν· καὶ γὰρ εἰ
αὐτὴ ἡ ψυχὴ τὴν ὕλην ἐγέννησε παθοῦσα, καὶ εἰ
ἐκοινώνησεν αὐτῇ καὶ ἐγένετο κακή, ἡ ὕλη αἰτία
παροῦσα· οὐ γὰρ ἂν ἐγένετο εἰς αὐτὴν μὴ τῇ
παρουσίᾳ αὐτῆς τὴν γένεσιν λαβοῦσα.

15. Εἰ δέ τις τὴν ὕλην μή φησιν εἶναι, δεικτέον
αὐτῷ ἐκ τῶν περὶ ὕλης λόγων τὴν ἀνάγκην τῆς
ὑποστάσεως αὐτῆς διὰ πλειόνων ἐκεῖ περὶ τούτου
εἰρημένου. Κακὸν δὲ εἴ τις λέγοι τὸ παράπαν ἐν
5 τοῖς οὖσι μὴ εἶναι, ἀνάγκη αὐτῷ καὶ τὸ ἀγαθὸν
ἀναιρεῖν καὶ μηδὲ ὀρεκτὸν μηδὲν εἶναι· μὴ τοίνυν
μηδὲ ὄρεξιν μηδ᾽ αὖ ἔκκλισιν μηδὲ νόησιν· ἡ γὰρ
ὄρεξις ἀγαθοῦ, ἡ δὲ ἔκκλισις κακοῦ, ἡ δὲ νόησις
καὶ ἡ φρόνησις ἀγαθοῦ ἐστι καὶ κακοῦ, καὶ αὐτὴ
ἕν τι τῶν ἀγαθῶν. Εἶναι μὲν οὖν δεῖ καὶ ἀγαθὸν
10 καὶ ἄμικτον ἀγαθόν, τὸ δὲ μεμιγμένον ἤδη ἐκ
κακοῦ καὶ ἀγαθοῦ, καὶ πλείονος τοῦ κακοῦ μεταλα-

---

[1] I.e., the treatise *On the Two Kinds of Matter* II. 4.

its evil makes it unable to see. Matter darkens the illumination, the light from that source, by mixture with itself, and weakens it by itself offering it the opportunity of generation and the reason for coming to matter; for it would not have come to what was not present. This is the fall of the soul, to come in this way to matter and to become weak, because all its powers do not come into action; matter hinders them from coming by occupying the place which soul holds and producing a kind of cramped condition, and making evil what it has got hold of by a sort of theft—until soul manages to escape back to its higher state. So matter is the cause of the soul's weakness and vice: it is then itself evil before soul and is primary evil. Even if soul had produced matter, being affected in some way, and had become evil by communicating with it, matter would have been the cause by its presence: soul would not have come to it unless its presence had given soul the occasion of coming to birth.

15. If anyone says that matter does not exist, he must be shown the necessity of its existence from our discussions about matter,[1] where the subject is treated more fully. But if anyone says that there is no evil at all in the nature of things, he must also abolish the good and have no object to aim at, and, for that matter, no aiming or avoidance or intelligence; for aiming is at the good and avoidance, of the evil, and intelligence and practical wisdom deal with good and evil, and are a good in themselves. So there must be good, and unmixed good, and that which is a mixture of bad and good, when it has a larger share of evil making itself totally evil, when it has a smaller share tending, because the evil is less,

βὸν ἤδη καὶ αὐτὸ συντελέσαν ἐκείνῳ ⟨ὃ⟩ ἐν τῷ ὅλῳ
κακόν, ἐλάττονος δέ, ᾗ ἠλάττωται, τῷ ἀγαθῷ.
Ἐπεὶ ψυχῇ τί ἂν εἴη κακόν; Ἢ τίνι ἂν μὴ
ἐφαψαμένῃ τῆς φύσεως τῆς χείρονος; Ἐπεὶ οὐδ᾽
15 ἐπιθυμίαι οὐδ᾽ αὖ λῦπαι, οὐ θυμοί, οὐ φόβοι· καὶ
γὰρ φόβοι τῷ συνθέτῳ, μὴ λυθῇ, καὶ λῦπαι καὶ
ἀλγηδόνες λυομένου· ἐπιθυμίαι δὲ ἐνοχλοῦντός
τινος τῇ σνστάσει ἤ, ἵνα μὴ ἐνοχλῇ, ἴασιν προνοου-
μένου. Φαντασία δὲ πληγῇ ἀλόγου ἔξωθεν· δέχεται δὲ τὴν πληγὴν διά του οὐκ ἀμεροῦς· καὶ
20 δόξαι ψευδεῖς ἔξω γενομένῃ τοῦ ἀληθοῦς αὐτοῦ·
ἔξω δὲ γίνεται τῷ μὴ εἶναι καθαρά. Ἡ δὲ πρὸς
νοῦν ὄρεξις ἄλλο· συνεῖναι γὰρ δεῖ μόνον καὶ ἐν
αὐτῷ ἱδρυμένην, οὐ νεύσασαν εἰς τὸ χεῖρον. Τὸ δὲ
κακὸν οὐ μόνον ἐστὶ κακὸν διὰ δύναμιν ἀγαθοῦ
καὶ φύσιν· ἐπείπερ ἐφάνη ἐξ ἀνάγκης, περιληφθὲν
25 δεσμοῖς τισι καλοῖς, οἷα δεσμῶταί τινες χρυσῷ,
κρύπτεται τούτοις, ἵν᾽ ἄμουσα μὴ ὁρῷτο τοῖς θεοῖς,
καὶ ἄνθρωποι ἔχοιεν μὴ ἀεὶ τὸ κακὸν βλέπειν,
ἀλλ᾽ ὅταν καὶ βλέπωσιν, εἰδώλοις τοῦ καλοῦ εἰς
ἀνάμνησιν συνῶσιν.

to the good. What, after all, is the evil of the soul?
What soul would have it if it did not come into
contact with a lower nature? If it did not there
would be no desires or sorrows or passions or fears;
for fears are for the composite nature, dreading its
dissolution; and sorrows and pains belong to it when
it is being dissolved; desires arise when something
interferes with the composition or when one is planning a remedy to prevent its being interfered with.
Imagination is from a stroke of something irrational
from outside; and the soul is accessible to the stroke
because of what in it is not undivided. It has false
opinions because it has come to be outside absolute
truth; and it has come to be outside by not being
pure. The impulse towards intellect is a different
kind of thing; all that is necessary here is to be with
intellect and established in it, without inclination to
what is worse. But because of the power and nature
of good, evil is not only evil; since it must necessarily
appear, it is bound in a sort of beautiful fetters, as
some prisoners are in chains of gold, and hidden by
them, so that it may not appear in its charmlessness
to the gods, and men may be able not always to look at
evil, but even when they do look at it, may be in
company with images of beauty to remind them.

ENNEAD I. 9

I. 9. ON GOING OUT OF THE BODY

Introductory Note

THIS short treatise is one of the early group (No. 16 in the chronological order), written before Porphyry joined Plotinus; it cannot therefore present the arguments Plotinus used to discourage Porphyry from suicide (*Life* ch. 11). Creuzer supposed it to be an abridgement taken from the edition of Eustochius; Heinemann, a paraphrase or summary (and an inaccurate one) by Porphyry which has displaced the original text: but there seems no sufficient reason against believing, with Bréhier, Harder, Henry and Schwyzer, that it is the genuine treatise of Plotinus which held this place in Porphyry's edition.

Synopsis

If you take your soul out of your body by suicide, something evil will come with it; one must wait till the body goes from the soul by natural death; the violent emotions, too, which accompany suicide, harm the soul. One must not therefore go out of the body by suicide except in the case of desperate necessity.

Plotinus on Voluntary Death

L. G. Westerink has shown convincingly that this is not any sort of genuine quotation from Plotinus (" Elias and Plotin ", *Byzantinische Zeitschrift* 57 (1964) 26–32); the editors are agreed that it should be deleted from the works of Plotinus (*Addenda ad textum* in OCT Plotinus vol. III, p. 307). But as it is still printed in vol. I of the OCT Plotinus I have retained the text and translation. [A.H.A. 1986]

I. 9. (16) ΠΕΡΙ ΕΞΑΓΩΓΗΣ

Οὐκ ἐξάξεις, ἵνα μὴ ἐξίῃ· ἐξελεύσεται γὰρ
ἔχουσά τι, ἵνα καὶ ἐξέλθῃ, τό τε ἐξελθεῖν ἐστι
μεταβῆναι εἰς ἄλλον τόπον. Ἀλλὰ μένει τὸ σῶμα
ἀποστῆναι πᾶν αὐτῆς, ὅτε μὴ δεῖται μετελθεῖν,
5 ἀλλ' ἔστι πάντη ἔξω. Πῶς οὖν ἀφίσταται τὸ
σῶμα; Ὅταν μηδὲν ἔτι δεδεμένον ᾖ τῆς ψυχῆς,
ἀδυνατοῦντος ἔτι τοῦ σώματος συνδεῖν, τῆς ἁρμο-
νίας αὐτοῦ οὐκέτ' οὔσης, ἣν ἔχον εἶχε τὴν ψυχήν.
Τί οὖν, εἰ μηχανήσαιτό τις λυθῆναι τὸ σῶμα;
Ἢ ἐβιάσατο καὶ ἀπέστη αὐτός, οὐκ ἐκεῖνο ἀφῆκε·
10 καὶ ὅτε λύει, οὐκ ἀπαθής, ἀλλ' ἢ δυσχέρανσις ἢ
λύπη ἢ θυμός· δεῖ δὲ μηδὲν πράττειν. Εἰ οὖν
ἀρχὴν αἴσθοιτο τοῦ ληρεῖν; Ἢ τάχα μὲν οὐ περὶ
σπουδαῖον· εἰ δὲ καὶ γένοιτο, τάττοιτ' ἂν ἐν τοῖς
ἀναγκαίοις τοῦτο καὶ ἐκ περιστάσεως αἱρετοῖς,
οὐχ ἁπλῶς αἱρετοῖς. Καὶ γὰρ ἡ τῶν φαρμάκων
15 προσαγωγὴ πρὸς ἔξοδον ψυχῆς τάχα ἂν ψυχῇ οὐ
πρόσφορος. Καὶ εἰ εἱμαρμένος χρόνος ὁ δοθεὶς

---

¹ This cryptic saying is stated by the Byzantine Psellus to
have been taken by Plotinus from the *Chaldaean Oracles*
(PG122. 1125C-D): if so, it would be the only place in the

I. 9. ON GOING OUT OF THE BODY

You shall not take out your soul, so that it may not go[1]; for if it goes thus, it will go taking something with it so that it can manage to get out; and going out is moving to another place. But the soul waits for the body to depart altogether from it; then soul does not have to change its place, but is completely outside. But how does the body depart? When nothing of soul is any longer bound up with it, because the body is unable to bind it any more, since its harmony is gone; as long as it has this it holds the soul. But suppose someone contrives the dissolution of his body? He has used violence and gone away himself, not let his body go; and in dissolving it he is not without passion; there is disgust or grief or anger; one must not act like this. But suppose he is aware that he is beginning to go mad? This is not likely to happen to a really good man; but if it does happen, he will consider it as one of the inevitable things, to be accepted because of the circumstances, though not in themselves acceptable.[2] And after all, taking drugs to give the soul a way out is not likely to be good for the soul. And if each man has a destined time allotted to him, it is not

Enneads where Plotinus quotes from this sort of occultist literature; but it is by no means certain whether Plotinus is quoting the oracle or whether the oracle was later taken from Plotinus.

[2] Cp. I. 4. 7–8.

ἐκάστῳ, πρὸ τούτου οὐκ εὐτυχές, εἰ μή, ὥσπερ
φαμέν, ἀναγκαῖον. Εἰ δέ, οἷος ἕκαστος ἔξεισι,
ταύτην ἴσχει ἐκεῖ τάξιν, εἰς τὸ προκόπτειν οὔσης
ἐπιδόσεως οὐκ ἐξακτέον.

Plotinus de Voluntaria Morte
Apud Eliam

Ὁ μέντοι Πλωτῖνος περὶ εὐλόγου ἐξαγωγῆς
γράφει μονόβιβλον καὶ οὐδένα τῶν πέντε τρόπων
τούτων ἀποδέχεται· φησὶ γὰρ ὅτι ὥσπερ ὁ θεὸς οὐκ
ἀφίσταται ἡμῶν προνοούμενος, ἀλλ᾽ ἡμεῖς ἑαυτοὺς
ποιοῦμεν ἀνεπιτηδείους καὶ νομίζομεν τὸν θεὸν
πόρρω εἶναι ἀφ᾽ ἡμῶν ἀεὶ παρόντα πᾶσιν ἐπίσης,
ὡς δηλοῦσιν οἱ καθαροὶ τὸν βίον, αὐτόπται τοῦ
θείου καὶ συνομιληταὶ γινόμενοι· ὥσπερ καὶ ὁ
ἥλιος χορηγεῖ ἐπίσης τὸ φῶς, ἀλλ᾽ αἱ νυκτερίδες
ἀνεπιτήδειοι οὖσαι ἀποφεύγουσιν αὐτὸν καὶ οὐ
φωτίζονται ἐξ αὐτοῦ, ἀλλὰ σκότος αὐτὸν νομίζου-
σιν εἶναι πηγὴν φωτὸς ὑπάρχοντα· οὕτως δεῖ καὶ
τὸν φιλόσοφον μιμούμενον θεὸν καὶ ἥλιον μὴ
ἀμελεῖν πάντη τοῦ σώματος δι᾽ ἐπιμέλειαν τῆς
ψυχῆς, ἀλλὰ τὴν προσήκουσαν αὐτοῦ ποιεῖσθαι
πρόνοιαν, ἕως οὗ ἐκεῖνο ἀνεπιτήδειον γενόμενον
διαστήσοι ἑαυτὸ τῆς πρὸς τὴν ψυχὴν κοινωνίας·
ἄτοπον γὰρ τὸ πρὸ καιροῦ ἐξάγειν ἑαυτόν, πρὸ οὗ
λύσῃ ὁ δήσας.

---

[1] The "five ways of reasonable departure" are the five
good reasons for suicide according to the Stoics; cp. *Stoicorum
Veterum Fragmenta* III. 768. In I. 4. 7–8 and I. 9 Plotinus

a good thing to go out before it, unless, as we maintain, it is necessary. And if each man's rank in
the other world depends on his state when he goes
out, one must not take out the soul as long as there
is any possibility of progress.

Plotinus on Voluntary Death
(*In Elias, Prolegomena* 6. 15. 23–16. 2.)

Plotinus writes a single treatise about "reasonable
departure" and does not accept any of these five
ways:[1] he says, that just as God does not leave off
taking thought for us, but we make ourselves unfit
and think God is far from us when he is always present
equally to all, as men of pure life show, who came to
see God face to face and be his close companions; and
just as the sun dispenses his light equally, but bats,
because they are unfit for the sunlight, fly from him
and are not enlightened by him, but think that he is
darkness when he is the source of light; so the
philosopher must imitate God and the sun and not
neglect his body altogether in caring for his soul,
but take thought for it in the appropriate way till it
becomes unfit and separates itself from its community with the soul.   It is all wrong to take oneself
out before the right time, when he who bound body
and soul together looses the bond.

---

does in fact accept at least three of them, long and extremely
painfull illness, madness, and, probably, coercion to immoral
behaviour (I. 4. 7. 43–45) as reasons for suicide.